Education and Social Dynamics

Education and Social Dynamics offers a new approach to analyzing curriculum change by investigating the entanglement of education and society in markedly heterogeneous Turkey, which has recently witnessed nationwide curriculum reforms. While the new curriculum has attempted to homogenize all Turkish primary schools since 2005, Nohl and Somel, drawing on a theoretical differentiation of social entities, reveal how subsequent curricular practices have had to account for the diversity of milieus and organizations in the nation's educational sector and how inequality and competition run rampant in the standardization efforts. Using expert interviews, group discussions, and other empirical data that compare implementation within five distinct schools, the book represents a breakthrough in our understanding of developments in Turkey and their significance for extant theories of curriculum development and reform worldwide. By linking specific case study material from Turkey to intensifying international concerns, it provides an important and relevant global commentary.

Arnd-Michael Nohl is Professor of Education at Helmut-Schmidt-Universität, Germany.

R. Nazlı Somel is a PhD student at Helmut-Schmidt-Universität, Germany.

T0346789

Studies in Curriculum Theory
William F. Pinar, Series Editor

Education and Social Dynamics
A Multilevel Analysis of Curriculum Change in Turkey
Nohl/Somel

Provoking Curriculum Studies
Strong Poetry and the Arts of the Possible in Education
Ng-A-Fook/Ibrahim/Reis (Eds.)

Trajectories in the Development of Modern School Systems
Between the National and the Global
Tröhler/Lenz (Eds.)

The "Reason" of Schooling
Historicizing Curriculum Studies, Pedagogy, and Teacher Education
Popkewitz (Ed.)

Reconceptualizing Curriculum Development
Inspiring and Informing Action
Henderson (Ed.)

Social Efficiency and Instrumentalism in Education
Critical Essays in Ontology, Phenomenology, and Philosophical Hermeneutics
Magrini

Nonviolence and Education
Cross–Cultural Pathways
Wang

Contemplating Curriculum
Genealogies/Times/Places
Hurren/Hasebe-Ludt (Eds.)

International Handbook of Curriculum Research, Second Edition
Pinar (Ed.)

Teaching as a Reflective Practice
The German Didaktic Tradition
Westbury/Hopmann/Riquarts (Eds.)

Curriculum as Institution and Practice
Essays in the Deliberative Tradition
Reid

Queer Theory in Education
Pinar (Ed.)

The Lure of the Transcendent
Collected Essays by Dwayne E. Huebner. Edited by Vikki Hillis.
Collected and Introduced by William F. Pinar
Huebner

For additional information on titles in the Studies in Curriculum Theory series, visit www.routledge.com/education.

Education and Social Dynamics

A Multilevel Analysis of Curriculum
Change in Turkey

**Arnd-Michael Nohl
and R. Nazlı Somel**

Routledge
Taylor & Francis Group

LONDON AND NEW YORK

First published 2016
by Routledge

2 Park Square, Milton Park, Abingdon, Oxfordshire OX14 4RN
52 Vanderbilt Avenue, New York, NY 10017

Routledge is an imprint of the Taylor & Francis Group, an informa business

First issued in paperback 2019

Library of Congress Cataloging-in-Publication Data
Nohl, Arnd-Michael.
  Education and social dynamics : a multilevel analysis of curriculum
change in Turkey / Arnd-Michael Nohl & R. Nazli Somel.
    pages cm.—(Studies in curriculum theory)
  Includes bibliographical references and index.
  1. Curriculum change—Turkey. 2. Social change—Turkey.
I. Somel, R. Nazli. II. Title.
  LB1564.T9N64 2015
  375′.00109561—dc23
  2015012692

ISBN: 978-1-138-90349-4 (hbk)
ISBN: 978-1-138-35014-4 (pbk)

Typeset in Bembo
by Apex CoVantage, LLC

Contents

Preface

The personal experience and academic concerns that incited the inquiry presented in this volume are multifold. In general terms, we both perceive issues of education as social matters, deeply embedded in society and its history, and are inclined to study such matters by combining theoretical reflection with qualitative empirical research. Besides, for us, Turkey is not only a society in which the social dynamics shaping education are intriguing and thought provoking but also one in which we are existentially involved.

When we started to think about the relation between education and social change, it felt natural to focus our inquiry on the introduction of a new curriculum in Turkish primary schools, which started in 2005. R. Nazlı Somel had worked as a primary school teacher in Turkish villages two years before the introduction of the new curriculum; Arnd-Michael Nohl had been a short-term international consultant for the Support to Basic Education Programme of the European Commission between 2003 and 2006, a program that became the principal supporter of the curriculum change. Based on one author's experience with qualitative field research in an Istanbulian school in 2006 (Nazlı), and on the other's background in theoretical inquiry into how education is organized and how the organization of education is connected to the collective experience of those involved (Arnd), we came to realize that we could pursue our shared academic concern for the relation between education and society by inquiring into the curriculum change that took place in Turkey in the beginning of the millennium.

Our subsequent research was funded by the Deutsche Forschungsgemeinschaft (German Research Association), to which we are indebted for the confidence given by its referees and members of the board of education science to our initial research proposal. This research would not have been possible without so many people active in the field of education in Turkey having been willing to share their experiences in expert interviews or group discussions. Therefore, we acknowledge the contributions of a broad range of people, from the former minister of education, the president of the curriculum authority, to bureaucrats, to all those who were involved in curriculum practice: the teachers, pupils, and their parents at schools in a rural village and town and at schools both in poor and well-to-do urban areas.

The interviews and group discussions, conducted between 2011 and 2013, were transcribed by Muzaffer Kaya, Perihan Büşra Aldındağ, and Emre Özütemiz. Özgür Balkılıç has translated all transcripts for the present volume. Sara Vock and James Morrison have edited the book draft.

Although this book was cooperatively composed by its two authors, we had the opportunity to discuss its content with many colleagues. We debated preliminary interpretations of our empirical data in several research workshops with Annegreth Warth and Gökçe Güvercin. Müge Ayan Ceyhan commented on several of our papers. In a workshop at Bilgi University, Istanbul, Müge Ayan Ceyhan and Kenan Çayır (who also organized the workshop), together with Hülya Altınyelken, Işıl Ünal, Fatma Gök, Ali Alper Akyüz, and Cenk Saraçoğlu, shared with us their criticism on the project report. Christoph Schroeder, Gregor Lang-Wojtasik, Ralf Bohnsack, Sabine Hornberg, and Steffen Amling reviewed a draft version of the book manuscript. The anonymous reviewers of Routledge, as well as William Pinar (Studies in Curriculum Theory Series Editor) and Naomi Silverman (our editor at Routledge), made important suggestions for the content and style of this book. To all those who contributed to this book, mentioned by name or remaining in necessary anonymity, we are deeply grateful, for without their cooperation, this book would not have been written.

1   Introduction

> Modern education from its inception is a living struggle, a replica, on a small scale of the conflicting purposes and tendencies which rage in society at large.
>
> Karl Mannheim (1968, p. 138)

Education is often conceived of as a motor of social change. Numerous public opinion leaders have requested educationalists to make an effort to overcome social evils, or to pursue the happiness of future generations. Since the introduction of obligatory primary schooling, itself an effort taken to foster the establishment of modern national societies (see Boli et al., 1985; Meyer et al., 1992), education has been seen as a motor for the advancement of society; even critical scholars of education have underpinned its capacity to transform social structures to achieve a more just order (Apple, 2004; Freire, 2000; Giroux, 1983).

Conversely, education may also be seen as driven by social change. Of late, international actors of educational policy (OECD, 2012), including private foundations (e.g., Jorman & Murray, 2012), have demanded educational reform to stay current with the pace of social change. Based on the results of large-scale research on student performance, modifications for teaching were proposed to enable learning to meet the assumed expectations of society (see, e.g., OECD, 2013; Schleicher, 2014; see critically Meyer & Benavot, 2013).

There are scholars who focus on the complex relation between education and society which, concerning both inertia and change, influence each other; educational change, then, may be seen both as driven by and as influencing social change (Bourdieu & Passeron, 1990; Dale, 1999; Verger et al., 2012, p. 9). This last position already alludes to the complicated character of the subject matter in question: Education is a part of, and not opposed to, society.

The complicated relation between education and social change is also reflected in the discourse regarding the Turkish curriculum change of 2005, the subject matter of this book. On one hand, the leading curriculum developer of the time, in an interview with the authors justified the introduction of the new curriculum by stating that the current "education system now comes very narrow to Turkey"; that is, that education needed to keep up with social change. On the other hand, the Turkish minister of national education, maintaining that education is "one of the most important instruments" within the "struggle for democratization and modernization" and the "formation of a prosperous society,"[1] claimed that education should change society. Both, however, assumed society to be a largely homogeneous unit that can be juxtaposed to education as a similarly uniform entity. As we show in this book, neither education nor society are homogeneous. Moreover, they are intermingled with each other.

1.1 Curriculum and Change in Society

The entanglement of education and society becomes most evident in school curricula. The very introduction of mandatory curricula in schooling is a reaction to social change and itself a major transformation of education (Kliebard, 2002, p. 20). At the same time, mandatory curricula were not simultaneously introduced in all parts of society—urban and middle-class education facilities might see it first; poverty-ridden rural schools last—pointing to the asynchronicity of social change.

Social change varies not only with regard to pace but also in terms of direction, as the sociological analysis of schooling has shown. Vis-à-vis the mandatory curriculum, it becomes evident that social milieus may be reproduced or transformed in different directions. For example, while the offspring of certain social milieus are better equipped by their background to meet the "arbitrary" expectations of the curriculum, other children have difficulties in mastering the curricular activities (Bourdieu & Passeron, 1990, p. 22); this, again, points to the heterogeneity of society.

In contrast to society's heterogeneity, the curriculum, as a set of formal rules, is an attempt to homogenize education (especially where schooling is compulsory). Indeed, the curriculum is a core feature of organizing education: Without a mandatory curriculum in a given area, neither graded education (according to age groups and achievement levels) nor "ensemble instruction" (Kliebard, 2002, p. 20), that is, teaching many children at a time, would be possible. The curriculum provides the school with formal rules that define a subject matter and teaching goals, which are to be equally delivered by any teacher. In this sense the curriculum, as a core formal rule of the school organization, is always connected to a certain degree of standardization and generalization of education.

Curricula "spell out what the schools they address should be doing" (Westbury, 2008, p. 46). The debates and discussions on the curriculum, ideally, illustrate "what the public expects from education" (Hopmann, 1999, p. 95). Such expectations always consist of a specific mixture of references to the past and wishes for the future. "Through the curriculum . . . we choose what to remember about the past, what to believe about the present, what to hope for and fear about the future" (Pinar, 2008, p. 493). As education is a means of both "social continuity" and the "renewal of life" (Dewey,

1985, p. 5), the curriculum combines knowledge handed down by previous generations and visions of what might become necessary in the future. As such, the curriculum is built both on previous social change and expected developments.

However, the "educational political common sense" (Hopmann, 1999, p. 95) about the curriculum may not necessarily reflect the expectations of the whole society. As many scholars have pointed out, the curriculum reflects "socially organized knowledge" (Young, 2000, p. 14). Through a vast range of analyses, it has been convincingly shown that curricula are not at all neutral; rather, they are strongly influenced by certain strata of society. Apparently, certain social groups (for example, the educated middle classes) have succeeded in turning their own milieu-specific expectations into a general standard for teaching (Apple, 2004; Bourdieu & Passeron, 1990; Whitty, 1985). The curriculum "is always part of a selective tradition, someone's selection, some group's vision of legitimate knowledge" (Apple, 1993, p. 223). This selection also applies to the ways in which such knowledge is taught; however, all this does not exclude the possibility that the curriculum is useful for all children.[2]

From the viewpoint of social change, this implies that as far as a curriculum reflects the educational expectations and legitimate knowledge of certain social milieus, previously partial and particular instructional expectations are rendered general and official; that is, what have previously been the particular educational expectations and legitimate knowledge of certain social milieus become the standard for all children, irrespective of social background after these milieus have successfully introduced their concerns into the curriculum. In this sense, in a society undergoing change in different paces and directions, the curriculum (with its—at times tacit—messages on everyday life practices, taste, political order, etc.) may be assumed to serve as an instrument for mainstreaming and homogenizing society.

These features may easily suffice to clarify why the change of a curriculum—as it is investigated in this volume—constitutes an ideal focal point to study the intermingled relation between education and social change. However, there is evidence that the curriculum is not solely a device for generalizing previously particular educational expectations and thus bringing society on the line of a specific social milieu. During its practicing—which, by over-simplification is often called "implementation"—a curriculum undergoes change again. We are warned that "almost any blueprint for basic [curriculum; the authors] reform will be altered during implementation." As Tyack and Tobin (1994) further stated, "over and over again teachers have selectively implemented and altered reforms" (p. 478). As we empirically show in this book, not only the "organizational routines" (Spillane et al., 2011, p. 586) of teachers, but also the educational orientations prevalent in social milieus of pupils and their parents may influence practical instruction in schools. Thus, although the curriculum, particularly in times of change, is a device for mainstreaming and homogenizing society, the varieties in pace and direction of social change become part of the picture once the curriculum is put into practice in the classroom. It is in this sense—by taking into account both curriculum making and curriculum practicing—that we study the intermingled relation of education and society herein.

1.2 The Rationale of Studying Primary Education

The subject matter of our research—the 2005 curriculum change for primary schools in Turkey—was particularly useful for our inquiry: With its centralized educational sector, for which all curricular (and most other) decisions are taken by the Ministry of Education, the subject matter at hand offers a unique opportunity to analyze the emergence of a new consistent curriculum with a very broad, and indeed a country-wide, official validity. At the same time, Turkish society is all but homogeneous: Characterized by a rapid population growth and migration from the countryside to the cities, as well as by an enormous inequality of income and wealth, these social dynamics converge toward the appearance of a broad variety of social milieus for whose children primary schools must cater.

In contrast to secondary and tertiary education, the focus on primary education enables us to analyze a segment of the educational sector in which almost all members of society are or have been included. Only here can we scrutinize education in the frame of social dynamics in their full breadth, including both very poor social milieus and rural contexts, where enrolment in secondary and tertiary education is low. Moreover, only primary education is based on a unitary national curriculum, whereas on higher levels of education the curriculum also has to take into account specific elements of the diversified branches (for example, different foci of vocational education programs).[3]

We hope that readers who are not interested in Turkey as such can appreciate the opportunities that this national context offers, and are able to relate and transfer to other countries the parts of our analysis whose validity extends over the Turkish borders. We also hope that those readers who are more interested in our account of Turkey and its educational sector find our methodological approach and basic theoretical frame as inspiring for further research as we did. It has been our goal to pay enough attention to peculiarities of Turkey without viewing the country as a specific case of an "Oriental," "Eastern," or "Islamic" country, for example. In this sense, we subject the curriculum change in Turkey to close scrutiny within a general approach of curriculum inquiry, and adapted or extended our methodological and basic theoretical frame where needed.

1.3 Inquiring Curriculum Change

While the debates on curriculum change have "been dominated for a long time by concepts of rationally planned organizational development, these have been called into question by observations that real changes very often do not conform to the neat designs of organizational planners, but are contested and resemble political struggles" (Altrichter, 2000, p. 3). Altrichter draws our attention to the "relationship between intentionality and unintended consequences" and to the coincidence of "contingency, necessity and chance" (p. 3). We need to analyze curriculum change "under the perspective of coordination of action between various social actors in complex multilevel systems" (Altrichter, 2010, p. 148), wherein the "logic of action" (p. 150) may differ from one level to the other. For an empirical analysis including many levels, we have to develop a basic conceptualization of the respective social levels (Helsper et al., 2010, p. 119); that is, in a multilevel analysis such as the one undertaken in this book, the different social entities have to be denoted with distinct basic concepts (such as organization or milieu, for example) related to each other (Nohl, 2013, pp. 103–105).

In our analysis we firstly differentiate between the "intended" and the "taught" curriculum; the former referring to what is composed in the form of written documents by the authorities, and the latter constituted by the practice in school instruction (Cuban, 1992, p. 222). This distinction motivated us to inquire into both the making of the new curriculum and its practice in schools: Because curriculum analysts warn that what the schools publicly declare and praise as their curriculum may not conform to the more implicit and tacit practices within the classroom (Cuban, 1992; Popkewitz, 1988; Tyack & Tobin, 1994), we did not confine our analysis to official statements only, but also attempted to reconstruct the more tacit orientations of those involved in school instruction. The school instruction then may be additionally influenced by what Cuban (1992) called the "historical curriculum"; that is, "the accumulated weight of previous innovations and mandates embedded in a district's or school's standard offerings of subject matter and activities" (p. 223).

Along with distinguishing between the "intended," the "taught," and the "historical curriculum," it is important to specify the levels of curriculum change. Especially for "large-scale reforms" (Fullan, 2000, p. 23) such as the Turkish curriculum change, it is decisive to consider on which level the respective actors (from the curriculum makers to its practitioners) are involved. This certainly applies to top-down processes; in other words, for curriculum changes such as the one in Turkey, started by the ministry rather than in single schools (McLaughlin & Mitra, 2001). Such changes must always be scrutinized within the context of social change, as they are always related to social crisis and transitions (cf. Cuban, 1990) and therefore should be examined by taking the "ideological dilemmas" (Cuban, 1999, p. 83) into consideration. In this sense, we have to analyze the curriculum change by considering both the different (organizational) levels within the educational sector and the context of society and its social milieus.

Previous research on curriculum reform has differentiated between the teaching programs and the "school culture" (Gordon & Patterson, 2008, p. 26), between "external change forces" and actors within the educational sector (Goodson, 2001, p. 47), or between the nation, the federal states, districts, school, and class (Bredo, 1989), which are only loosely coupled with each other. Whether the level of school administration is even decoupled from classroom instruction, as Cuban (1990, p. 11), likewise referring to New Institutionalism (Meyer & Rowan, 1977; Weick, 1976), argued, is certainly a question of empirical analysis that we also pursue in our research.

Because the levels and units of a society—from societal sectors to single organizations and milieus—are not independent from each other, the various changes in society may be interrelated. Thus, education is not only involved with social change but also entangled in social dynamics; that is, in the social dynamics evolving between social units and levels that are in flux and, during these changes, rub against each other, reciprocally reinforce or retard, or even obstruct each other. Therefore, this volume is concerned with how education is embedded in the dynamics of society rather than with the change of single social units. For the empirical research we took into account the following factors which structure curriculum change:

- the way the "intended" curriculum was developed within the Ministry of Education, including the conflicts, problems, and solutions that emerged during its making;
- regarding the "taught" curriculum, differences concerning the size and geographic situatedness of respective school organizations: We compared small schools in the countryside with large, urban schools;
- differences concerning the generational affiliation of teachers: Most importantly, we compare the organizational milieus of those teachers who had been professionally socialized before the curriculum change with those who have started their service thereafter;
- differences between social milieus that participate in school education: We take into account rural and urban social milieus; regarding the latter, we compare between poor and middle-class backgrounds; and
- differences between the educational discourse institutionalized in society and the educational sector ("historical curriculum"), the formal rules of the new curriculum ("intended curriculum"), and the curricular practices in the respective schools ("taught curriculum").

Regarding these factors, the curriculum change is an intricate formation insofar as it may lead to very diverse practices; as such, its levels and entities (institution, organization, milieu) must be taken into account.

1.4   The New Primary School Curriculum

After a 2-year development process and a 1-year pilot phase, the new curriculum for Turkish primary schools was introduced in 2005/2006, in grades 1–5, whereas the curricula for grades 6–8 were changed successively, so that in 2008 the new curriculum was operative in the whole of primary school.

In principle, the new curriculum followed a constructivist approach that was supposed to be student-centered (İnal et al., 2014). Through activities that "aim at posing questions, solving problems and at the science-like elaboration and evaluation of knowledge" the pupils are supposed to develop their "own cognitive structure" (Aşkar et al., 2005, p. 40). Overall, the new curriculum underpins the teaching of basic skills (problem solving, creative thinking, communication skills, an attitude of inquiring, and entrepreneurialism). Concerning the changing roles of teachers and pupils, Altinyelken (2013) writes:

> The new educational programmes recommend that the majority of the lesson time should be spent on classroom activities. The role of teachers has been modified in the sense that rather than directly providing information, they are expected to facilitate, guide and supervise pupils' learning processes. Pupils' roles and responsibilities are also redefined as they are expected to assume more responsibility for their own learning, and participate in learning and teaching activities by raising questions, handling materials, developing projects, doing research, and cooperating and discussing with their classmates and teachers. The new curriculum also advocates increased use of learning and teaching materials and aims to stimulate the use of information and communications technology.
>
> (p. 113)

According to Avenstrup (2007), who assisted in the change of the Turkish curriculum on behalf of the European Commission, this reform is part of a worldwide "change of paradigm in education" (p. 1). The European Commission itself underpinned that the new curriculum takes into account the "EU educational standards" (DGEC, 2008, p. 97). Indeed, within international curriculum research, Rosenmund (2006), comparing 100 countries, revealed that national curricula are increasingly moving from a content-oriented to a student-centered approach. At time, this is interpreted as the global convergence of national curricula (Bromley et al., 2011; Karseth & Sivesind, 2010) or as a phenomenon of "educational borrowing and lending" (Steiner-Khamsi, 2004); that is, the partial adoption of foreign curricula. While the discourse on borrowing and lending underpins the importance of "re-contextualizing" global ideas in local practices (Steiner-Khamsi, 2012), Bromley et al. (2011) assumed "much loose coupling in practice" (p. 564), and Dale (1999) asserted that "the effects of globalization are mediated, in both directions and in complex ways, by existing national patterns and structures," that is, by "the societal effect and the cultural effect" (p. 3).

1.5 Research Methodology

The study of curriculum is, obviously, a complex endeavor that has to take into account a vast range of phenomena in different social entities and on more than one level of society. In our inquiry we have combined a historical analysis of continuity and change within the evolving Turkish educational sector and Turkish society in general, with an empirical reconstruction of curriculum making and practicing. The historical analysis, based on the relevant literature, helped us to better understand the significance and origins of the curriculum change, along with peculiarities of curriculum practices. To inquire into the making of the 2005 curriculum, we collected documents and conducted expert interviews (Meuser & Nagel, 2009) with the minister of education of the time, curriculum designers, bureaucrats, and educational activists. Expert interviews, conducted with school principals, and group discussions (Bohnsack, 2010) with teachers and their pupils' parents in five different schools provided us with deep insight into curricular practices across a wide range of socio-geographic and socioeconomic circumstances.

The qualitative methodology of the Documentary Method (Bohnsack, 2014; Nohl, 2010) helped us to interpret the data material and to make sure that we do not remain at its surface meaning, also capturing its "tacit dimension" (Polanyi, 1966). Comparing the different cases, we took care to relate our findings to the respective social level and social entity to which they belonged. Such a multilevel analysis (Nohl, 2013; Weiß & Nohl, 2012) is especially important in the field of curriculum change, which is contested not only by many different actors, but rather importantly, by actors who are located on distinguishable levels of society.

This empirical analysis would not be possible without a firm theoretical basis. Indeed, we ground our investigation in basic theoretical concepts derived from different streams of discussion in the social sciences. To mention a few: New Institutionalism, the sociology of knowledge by Karl Mannheim and Ralf Bohnsack, as well as the sociology of culture by Pierre Bourdieu; these are only some of the many important reference points of this study. By combining their basic theoretical concepts and by challenging them with our empirical analyses, we also venture to say we further elaborate the theoretical frame in which curriculum analyses may be accomplished.

The relation of empirical and theoretical inquiry also involves the temporality of research. To our experience, theoretical reflection is not an endeavor carried out and finished prior to empirical analysis. While there certainly are basic, fixed concepts that structure subsequent empirical investigation, other theoretical arguments and concepts are only developed during or after the empirical reconstructions. We conceive of this relation of basic concepts and empirical research as reciprocally reflective: Basic concepts enable the researchers to perceive empirical phenomena, while empirical results may challenge existing basic concepts and constitute a basis for the search of alternative concepts. We try to express this reciprocally reflexive relation in the structure of the book as well; for this reason, instead of preceding the whole empirical analysis with a theory chapter, we elaborate on our basic theoretical concepts where and as far as needed for empirical research. This implies that some concepts are only explained in the second half of the book because we only needed them then. Other concepts, however, are dealt with shortly in early chapters, and then further elaborated in later ones. This enables us to show the ways in which we had to expand our theoretical frame during empirical research. We followed the same strategy for the research methodology, which is only reflected upon when and as far as needed. However, to facilitate reading, we briefly summarize previous methodological and theoretical considerations at the outset of each chapter, before indulging into further elaborations. Hence, it is also possible to read each chapter separately.

1.6 Overview of Chapters

At the outset of chapter 2 we start our inquiries by asking "how to conceive of change" (section 2.1). While following Norbert Elias, who defined social change as the consequence of the interplay between several actors, we see the need to differentiate the ensuing process structures according to their intensity and to the social levels and entities in which they evolve. Concerning intensity, a distinction proposed by Paul Watzlawick and colleagues seemed useful: There are first-order changes within a given entity which itself is left untouched in its core elements, and there are second-order changes of the respective entity itself, the very structure, core elements and goals of which are altered. Both forms of change can be studied on different social levels (from the individual level to society at large) and in specific social entities (for example, in milieus, organizations, or social sectors). The frictions, intermingling, and mutual amplification between these entities and social levels account for the social dynamics in which education is embedded.

With this basic distinction within the concept of change and its importance for social dynamics in mind, we venture into a historical analysis of education between the decline of the Ottoman Empire and the turn to the 21st century. In a first step (section 2.2), we scrutinize how the first modern schools (that is, secular) in the 19th century and on the primary, secondary and tertiary levels were established in the Ottoman Empire. When these organizations and institutions were linked to each other an educational sector emerged, which existed parallel to traditional religious education until the foundation of the Turkish Republic. In the early republican era, the religious educational institutions were abolished and the secular educational sector enlarged to progressively include all children of the new state. Similar to other societal sectors, the educational sector was constituted by a multiplicity of organizations, which shared a main function (that is, education) and were related to each other. This educational sector was then expanded and differentiated as regards the range of school types (vocational schools, private high schools, etc.) until 1980, a process we scrutinize in section 2.3.

On the background of this education history we then broaden our perspective and take into account the social dynamics of the Turkish society since the turning point marked by the military coup of 1980 (section 2.4). We follow the major events and structures in the political and economic sector, the demographic development of the country, and its educational sector. Education saw a massive expansion regarding grades 6–12. At the same time, secondary education was significantly diversified in quality, including a growing importance of instruction in prestigious private schools. The qualification of employees played an ever-increasing role for the economy, which underwent a sweeping privatization and—with varying success—was integrated into the global market, between 1980 and 2000. However, because not all social milieus profited from economic liberalization, it also led to increasing income gaps and to the emergence of a new bourgeois middle class. Three years after the coup, the military regime was replaced by a single-party government, followed by often changing coalition governments in the 1990s. Political instability, the continuing influence of the military, and economic turmoil then constituted the foundation on which, in November 2002, a new Islamic party achieved a landslide victory and opened a short-lived window of opportunity for political reforms that included education.

One of these reforms was the development of a new primary school curriculum, which is the focus of chapter 3. Before we empirically analyze how the new syllabus, supposed to replace a behavioristic teaching approach by a constructivist one, was organized, we need to consider some important basic theoretical concepts and the methodology of the empirical investigation (section 3.1). Reviewing the academic discussion on curriculum reform (Tyack, Cuban, etc.), we focus on its theoretical approach, which is predominantly based on New Institutionalism. "Institution" here refers to informally typified and stabilized expectations in society; for example, toward "good education," while in organizations the behavior of members is defined by formal rules that are enforced by sanctions. Such formal rules are rendered manageable by informal and practical regularities, which, if shared by groups of organization members, constitute what we propose to call an "organizational milieu". The analysis of curriculum change, accordingly, has to take into account various social entities (educational sector, institutions, organizations, organizational milieus) that may be nested in each other. Thus, we anticipated a multiplicity of—possibly antagonistic—individual and corporative actors involved in the curriculum development who are situated on different levels of the educational sector. We conclude the section by briefly describing the methods of data gathering of this multilevel analysis (mainly documents and expert interviews) as well as our interpretative approach (Documentary Method).

The development of a new curriculum in Turkey can indeed be described as a peculiar process in which different actors were involved (section 3.2). The appointment of a new minister of education in Turkey opened the way for a group of academics to turn their own scientific convictions into educational policy. Within education science, the previous behavioristic approach had already been criticized, and new teaching methods, based on constructivism and the idea of 'multiple intelligence,' had been developed. In spite of bureaucratic resistance and on the basis of this discussion, these academics, backed by the government and the European Commission, entered the ministry as an organizational milieu in 2003, led by Professor Ziya Selçuk, the newly appointed president of the supreme curriculum authority, the Board of Education. They then succeeded to organize a relatively homogenous curriculum for grades 1–5 within 1 year's time. This curriculum is briefly described in its key features in section 3.3.

Difficult as it is, the organization of a curriculum does not lead to a single form of curricular practice. As we discovered during our fieldwork in different schools around the country, curricular practices, first of all, significantly varied according to the dominant organizational milieus of teachers, which is the main subject matter of chapter 4. Our sampling strategy allowed us to compare and typify two different teachers' organizational milieus, which are characterized by their generational location. Along with a discussion on this basic concept, rooted in the sociology of knowledge (Mannheim, Bohnsack), we introduce the reader to the method of group discussion with which we elucidated the teachers' curricular experiences. The documentary interpretation of the teacher discussions allowed us to reconstruct the implicit orientations that underlie teachers' instructional practices (section 4.1).

The general assumption was that the generation of teachers who had been trained and socialized in the old, behaviorist curriculum would have difficulties in adopting the constructivist teaching approach of the new syllabus, while a more recent generation of teachers, who were trained after 2000, would internalize constructivist teaching more easily. To our surprise, this assumption turned out to be sketchy and insufficient. Irrespective of their generational ties, there were teachers who explicitly approved of the new curriculum, and teachers who refused it. However, their rather tacit instructional practices were oriented according to a combination of generational and professional experience. Older teachers, generationally distant to the new curricular approach, drew on their long-standing professional experience to creatively handle the requirements of the new curriculum (section 4.2), while young teachers closely stuck to the new curriculum but also tried to prepare their pupils for the standardized exams that regulate the entrance to high school (section 4.3). There were also organizational milieus of teachers who were positioned between these two teacher generations and who mixed their teaching orientations (section 4.4). These contrasts of three organizational milieus, structured by their respective ties to professional generations, significantly influence school instruction because the respective teachers are not equally distributed throughout the schools in the country. Due to the staffing policy of the ministry and its formal regulations, but also because of the varying prestige of schools, some of the latter are able to attract experienced teachers, while other schools are solely staffed with young teachers (section 4.5). The fact that schools are dominated by specific organizational teacher milieus in an unbalanced way, dependent on their varying prestige, alluded to the significance of social inequality in curricular practices, a point that needed further scrutiny.

Therefore, in chapter 5 we explored inequality among schools and its connection to curricular practices. This also included the social milieus of pupils who were as unequally distributed among schools as were teachers' organizational milieus. While teachers' organizational milieus are a direct part of school organizations (insofar as they are constituted within schools and dependent on their existence), social milieus also exist outside of educational organizations, albeit not fully independent from them. They are, as we make clear, based on homologous experiences in various dimensions (such as gender, generation, life course, education, socioeconomic location). These social milieus may—similar to organizational milieus—be empirically investigated with the method of group discussion. With regard to education, socioeconomic and geographic location, our group discussions with pupils' parents turned out to be very beneficial for the analysis. To theoretically grasp social inequality among both schools and social milieus we then introduce the concept of economic, social, cultural and symbolic capital as outlined by Pierre Bourdieu (section 5.1).

In this analysis, we first consider the curricular practices in schools of middle-class districts in Istanbul and a central Anatolian province capital (section 5.2). These schools are dominated by an organizational milieu of teachers who are professionally experienced and belong to the older generation. As mentioned earlier, these teachers, based on their experience, freely and creatively follow the new curriculum. Only in passing they mention the preparation for the centralized entrance tests, which pupils have to successfully pass if they wish to enroll in a "good" high school. Teachers' focus on the curriculum and indifference toward these exams are vouched for by the pupils' parents. In the middle-class milieu that dominates these schools, parents appreciate the general education provided to their children and make use of private services to prepare them for the entrance tests. In terms of capital, these findings point to the use parents make of their endowment with economic and cultural resources to safeguard their children's success in education and their subsequent social positioning.

Parents' expectations toward the school are quite different in a poor district of Istanbul (section 5.3). There, parents want their children to succeed in the standardized entrance tests, but cannot afford private instruction. Endowed with only little economic and cultural resources, they demand test preparation by the school. The school itself is ill-equipped and only staffed by young teachers, who have experienced the importance of standardized tests in their own lives. Without being able to creatively use the curriculum in their instruction, teachers in this organizational milieu devote themselves to prepare pupils for the entrance exams. In the final analysis these instructional practices, in which the curriculum is only superficially practiced, serve to close the gap between the high importance given to educational success in social positioning and the poor endowment with economic, symbolic, and cultural resources on part of the pupils' social milieus and the school organization.

Educational performance, measured by success in the centralized entrance tests, is significantly less important in the schools of a village and a small town of a central Anatolian province (section 5.4). As the group discussions with parents reveal, in the social milieus dominating these schools, education has only a small value for social positioning. Although they are not able to send their children to private tutoring services for test preparation, these parents do not expect teachers to help their pupils with the centralized exams. In these schools we found a mixture of experienced and young teachers who only have limited resources to practice the new curriculum. Similar to their pupils' parents, they do not assign much importance to entrance exam preparation. The contrast between these rural schools and those in the middle-class districts once again draws our attention to the unequal endowment with resources on part of the educational organizations. While the middle-class schools are able to attract both experienced teachers (cultural resource) and private donations (economic resource), on which they capitalize in the instructional practices, the rural schools lack these endowments, and thus cannot secure instructional practices in full accordance with the curriculum's stipulations; however, they are also not expected to do so by the pupils' parents.

Evidently, instructional practices are at times only "loosely coupled" (as New Institutionalists would put it) to the new curriculum, while being heavily influenced by the resources of the school organization, its organizational teacher milieus, and the social milieus of pupils and parents. Apart from the new curriculum there are also other educational expectations, manifested in the standardized entrance exams, to which in specific cases instruction is rather tightly coupled. In chapter 6 we focus on this undeclared competition between different sets of expectations with which educational organizations are confronted in varying ways. First, we inquire into how the curriculum itself was communicated, substantialized, and hence institutionalized. While the new curriculum had originally been prepared by a small, albeit homogeneous organizational milieu, it subsequently had to be related to the general public and the teaching staff. The curriculum developers, in their public communication campaign attempting to convince the public, underscored the new curriculum's continuity to the old one and marginalized its new teaching approach, that is, constructivism. Within the ministry, the instructional material (such as textbooks) could only be developed with the assistance of a broad range of previously uninvolved bureaucrats whom the curriculum developers had approached with distrust. Conversely, the core curriculum developers were eager to directly and personally train the teachers throughout the country to guarantee that the new curriculum was accurately conveyed to them. Doing so, they relied on ex-cathedra teaching that was both insufficient to train teachers and unable to take into account their practical experience. All in all, the new teaching approach risked to be diluted during this substantialization process; thus, the curriculum was institutionalized in a partial and mutated manner (section 6.1).

In contrast, the standardized entrance exams, though not a formal rule of primary schools, were very well institutionalized in society and in the educational sector. Not only did these exams define the career of pupils (in other words, their access to more or less prestigious high schools), they were also a major point of public attention: The media reported on the success of individual pupils, schools, districts, and private instruction centers in the exams. The latter also used these exams for their advertisement. Within and between the schools, as well as between districts and provinces of Turkey, there was an informal yet fierce competition concerning success in the entrance exams, which have emerged as an important criterion for their—informal—evaluation (section 6.2).

Regarding the schools investigated in our research, we have found different patterns of how they are loosely or tightly coupled to these institutionalized expectations. Whereas instruction in middle-class schools was only loosely coupled to the entrance exams and tightly coupled to the new curriculum, the inverse situation was found in the urban lower-class school. In the rural schools, again, loose coupling prevailed with respect to both institutions (section 6.3).

The yield of our inquiries is then summarized in chapter 7. We discuss our empirical results and basis theoretical concepts with regard to ongoing debates in comparative education, policy and inequality research, organization theory, and curriculum reform. In particular, we use our empirical findings to tackle the general problem of education and change. On the background of phenomena such as a curriculum, which are meant to mainstream society, we here underpin the need to analytically differentiate between distinct social levels on which change occurs in a heterogeneous way, at different directions and paces.

Notes

1 Hüseyin Çelik, cited from Ergüder: Her yönüyle yeni müfredat (1). Radikal, 26.8.04. http://www.radikal.com.tr/haber.php?haberno=126079 (retrieved June 1, 2015).
2 As Young (2008) has pointed out in a critical revision of the "new sociology of education," irrespective of its origins, there is "powerful knowledge" that "provides more reliable explanations and new ways of thinking about the world" (p. 14).
3 For an overview on the most important school types of the Turkish educational sector, see the appendix to this volume.

References

Altinyelken, H. K. (2013). Teachers' principled resistance to curriculum change: A compelling case from Turkey. In A. Verger, H. K. Altinyelken, & M. D. Konik (Eds.), *Global education reforms and teachers: Emerging policies, controversies and issues* (pp. 109–127). Brussels: Education International.

Altrichter, H. (2000). Introduction. In H. Altrichter & J. Elliott (Eds.), *Images of change* (pp. 1–10). Buckingham: Open University Press.

Altrichter, H. (2010). Theory and evidence on governance: Conceptual and empirical strategies of research on governance in education. *European Educational Research Journal, 9*(2), 147–158.

Apple, M. (1993). The politics of official knowledge: Does a national curriculum make sense? *Teachers College Record, 95*, 221–241.

Apple, M. (2004). *Ideology and curriculum.* London: Routledge.

Aşkar, P., Paykoç, F., Korkut, F., Olkun, S., Yangın, B., & Çakıroğlu, J. (2005). *Yeni Eğitim Programları İnceleme ve Değerlendirme Raporu.* Istanbul: Eğitim Reformu Girişimi.

Avenstrup, R. (2007). *The challenge of curriculum reform and implementation: Some implications of a constructivist approach.* Retrieved April 14, 2010, from http://tedp.meb.gov.tr/doc/Pubs/4a2%20SBEP%20website%20content%20download%20implementing%20the%20New%20Curriculum.pdf

Bohnsack, R. (2010). Documentary method and group discussions. In R. Bohnsack, N. Pfaff, & W. Weller (Eds.), *Qualitative analysis and documentary method in international educational research* (pp. 99–124). Opladen: Barbra Budrich.

Bohnsack, R. (2014). Documentary method. In U. Flick (Ed.), *Sage handbook of analyzing qualitative data* (pp. 217–223). Thousand Oaks, CA: Sage.

Boli, J., Ramirez, F. O., & Meyer, J. W. (1985). Explaining the origins and expansion of mass education. *Comparative Education Review, 29*, 145–170.

Bourdieu, P., & Passeron, J.-C. (1990). *Reproduction in education, society and culture.* London: Sage.

Bredo, E. (1989). Ideological dichotomies and practical realities in educational reform. *The Urban Review, 21*, 127–144.

Bromley, P., Meyer, J. W., & Ramirez, F. O. (2011). Student-centeredness in social science textbooks, 1970–2008: A cross-national study. *Social Forces, 90*, 547–570.

Cuban, L. (1990). Reforming again, again, and again. *Educational Researcher, 19*, 3–13.

Cuban, L. (1992). Curriculum stability and change. In P. W. Jackson (Ed.), *Handbook of research on curriculum* (pp. 216–247). New York: Macmillan.

Cuban, L. (1999). The integration of modern sciences into the American secondary school, 1890–1990s. *Studies in Philosophy and Education, 18*, 67–87.

Dale, R. (1999). Specifying globalization effects on national policy: A focus on the mechanisms. *Journal of Education Policy, 14*, 1–17.

Dewey, J. (1985). Democracy and education. In J. A. Boydston (Ed.), *John Dewey—The middle works, 1899–1924* (Vol. 9, pp. 1–370). Carbondale: Southern Illinois University Press.

DGEC (Directorate General for Education and Culture of the European Commission). (2008). *The Educational System in Turkey 2006/2007.* Brussels: Author.

Freire, P. (2000). *Pedagogy of the oppressed.* New York: Continuum.

Fullan, M. (2000). The return of large-scale reform. *Journal of Educational Change, 1*, 5–28.

Giroux, H. (1983). Theories of reproduction and resistance in the new sociology of education: A critical analysis. *Harvard Educational Review, 53*, 261–293.

Goodson, I. F. (2001). Social Histories of Educational Change. *Journal of Educational Change, 2*, 45–63.

Gordon, J., & Patterson, J. A. (2008). "It's what we've always been doing": Exploring tensions between school culture and change. *Journal of Educational Change, 9*, 17–35.

Helsper, W., Hummrich, M., & Kramer, R.-T. (2010). Qualitative Mehrebenenanalyse. In B. Friebertshäuser & A. Prengel (Eds.), *Handbuch Qualitative Forschungsmethoden in der Erziehungswissenschaft* (pp. 119–135). Beltz: Weinheim & München.

Hopmann, S. (1999). The curriculum as a standard of public education. *Studies in Philosophy and Education, 18*, 89–105.

İnal, K., Akkaymak, G., & Yıldırım, D. (2014). The constructivist curriculum reform in Turkey in 2004—In fact what is constructed? *Journal for Critical Education Policy Studies, 12*, 350–373.

Jorman, R., & Murray, H. (2012). *Education justice in the Middle East and North Africa: A scoping study of education contexts in Egypt, Jordan, Lebanon, Palestine, and Syria*. New York: Open Society Foundations.

Karseth, B., & Sivesind, K. (2010). Conceptualising curriculum knowledge within and beyond the national context. *European Journal of Education, 45*, 103–120.

Kliebard, H. M. (2002). *Changing course: American curriculum reform in the 20th century*. New York: Teachers College Press.

Mannheim, K. (1968). *Ideology and utopia*. London: Routledge.

McLaughlin, M. W., & Mitra, D. (2001). Theory-based change and change-based theory: Going deeper, going broader. *Journal of Educational Change, 2*, 301–323.

Meuser, M., & Nagel, U. (2009). The expert interview and changes in knowledge production. In A. Bogner, B. Littig, & W. Menz (Eds.), *Interviewing experts* (pp. 17–42). London: Palgrave.

Meyer, H.-D., & Benavot, A. (Eds.). (2013). *PISA, power, and policy: The emergence of global educational governance*. Oxford: Symposium Books.

Meyer, J. W., Ramirez, F. O., & Soysal, Y. N. (1992). World expansion of mass education, 1870–1980. *Sociology of Education, 65*, 128–149.

Meyer, J. W., & Rowan, B. (1977). Institutionalized organizations: Formal structure as myth and ceremony. *American Journal of Sociology, 83*, 340–363.

Nohl, A.-M. (2010). The documentary interpretation of narrative interviews. In R. Bohnsack, N. Pfaff, & W. Weller (Eds.), *Qualitative analysis and documentary method in international education research* (pp. 195–218). Opladen: Barbara Budrich.

Nohl, A.-M. (2013). *Relationale Typenbildung und Mehrebenenvergleich: Neue Wege der dokumentarischen Methode*. Wiesbaden: VS.

OECD. (2012). *Education today 2013—The OECD perspective*. Paris: Author.

OECD. (2013): *Lessons from PISA 2012 for the United States, strong performers and successful reformers in education*. Paris: Author. Retrieved June 1, 2015, from http://dx.doi.org/10.1787/9789264207585-en

Pinar, W. F. (2008). Curriculum theory since 1950: Crisis, reconceptualization, internationalization. In M. Conellli, M. He, & J. Phillion (Eds.), *The Sage handbook of curriculum and instruction* (pp. 491–513). Los Angeles, CA: Sage.

Polanyi, M. (1966). *The tacit dimension*. New York: Doubleday.

Popkewitz, T. S. (1988). Educational reform: Rhetoric, ritual, and social interest. *Educational Theory, 38*, 77–93.

Rosenmund, M. (2006). The current discourse on curriculum change. In A. Benavot & C. Braslavsky (Eds.), *School knowledge in comparative and historical perspective* (pp. 173–195). Hong Kong: Comparative Education Research Centre.

Schleicher, A. (2014). *Strong performers and successful reformers in education: Lessons from PISA 2012 for Turkey* [PowerPoint]. Retrieved September 18, 2014, from http://www.tusiad.org/__rsc/shared/file/AndreasSchleicher-15022014.pdf

Spillane, J. P., Parise, L. M., & Sherer, J. Z. (2011). Organizational routines as coupling mechanisms. *American Educational Research Journal, 48*, 586–619.

Steiner-Khamsi, G. (Ed.). (2004). *The global politics of educational borrowing and lending*. New York: Teachers College Press.

Steiner-Khamsi, G. (2012). Measuring and interpreting re-contextualization: A commentary. In A. Verger, M. Novelli, & H. K. Altinyelken (Eds.), *Global education policy and international development* (pp. 269–278). London: Bloomsbury.

Tyack, D., & Tobin, W. (1994). The "grammar" of schooling: Why has it been so hard to change? *American Educational Research Journal, 31*, 453–479.

Verger, A., Novelli, M., & Altinyelken, H. K. (2012). Global education policy and international development: An introductory framework. In A. Verger, M. Novelli, & H. K. Altinyelken (Eds.), *Global education policy and international development* (pp. 3–31). London: Bloomsbury.

Weick, K. E. (1976). Educational organizations as loosely coupled systems. *Administrative Science Quarterly, 21*, 1–19.

Weiß, A., & Nohl, A.-M. (2012). Overcoming methodological nationalism in migration research: Cases and contexts in multi-level comparisons. In A. Amelina, D. D. Nergiz, T. Faist, & N. Glick Schiller (Eds.), *Beyond methodological nationalism* (pp. 65–87). London: Routledge.

Westbury, I. (2008). Making curricula: Why do states make curricula, and how? In F. M. Connelly, M. Fang He, & J. Phillion (Eds.), *The Sage handbook of curriculum and instruction* (pp. 45–65). London: Sage.

Whitty, G. (1985). *Sociology and school knowledge.* London: Methuen.

Young, M. (2000). *The curriculum of the future.* London: Routledge.

Young, M. (2008). From constructivism to realism in the sociology of the curriculum. *Review of Research in Education, 32*, 1–28.

2 Education and Social Change in Turkish History

Change is an intriguing issue, both in society in general and in education, particularly. Many questions entwine around this subject matter, starting with the entities that undergo change, its manifestations, and up to different forms and degrees of change. The present chapter serves both as a first step into this complex subject matter and as an introduction to Turkish history. By combining our theoretical concern with historical analysis, we hope to sharpen the concepts we use to inquire into processes of change and to display our understanding of Turkish (educational) history. The latter is important to understand the background on which we later analyze the 2005 change of curriculum, in chapters 3–6.

First, we briefly discuss preliminary concepts and theoretical differentiations that are useful for the study of change (section 2.1), before venturing into the history of the late Ottoman Empire and the Turkish Republic until 1980. While our focus lies on the emergence (section 2.2) and expansion (section 2.3) of the educational sector, other historical dynamics connected to education are also touched upon. In the course of this analysis, we introduce further theoretical concepts. A broader perspective on the history of Turkish society between 1980 and 2003, which includes the political, economic, demographic, and cultural realm (section 2.4) then helps us to understand the dynamics to which the new curricula was supposed to respond—as well as those aspects to which it did not give an answer—when it was initiated 3 years after the turn of the century. Finally (section 2.5) we again engage in our theoretical discussion on change and, on the background of our historical inquiry, justify why change in education and society is best studied at the primary school level.

2.1 What Is Social and Educational Change?

Numerous scholars have been concerned with change in society, including change in the educational sector. While for historians social change is often a central subject matter of empirical inquiries, sociologists have tried to explain such processes in theories of modernization (see, e.g., Eisenstadt,

1968), differentiation (Alexander, 1990) or social conflict (Bourdieu & Passeron, 1990). In our analysis, we do not wish to discuss these theories or to adopt them; nevertheless, we acknowledge the need to reflect on social change and to theoretically define concepts that are pivotal for its empirical analysis.

This need is already evident if one takes into regard the thoughts of Norbert Elias, one of the most prominent scholars of social change. According to Elias (1978), change is "a question of the consequences flowing from the intermeshing of the actions of numerous people" (p. 146); it is an "order of interweaving human impulses and strivings, this social order, which determines the course of historical change" (Elias, 2010, p. 366). We agree with Elias (1978) that this "immanent order of change" (p. 149) has to be analyzed to understand how the change of a curriculum is embedded in the educational sector and the society at large. His own work, however, is a good example of the need for theoretical differentiation: While for Elias (2010), who assumes a "structured sequence of continuous change" (p. 457), change is a normalcy of society, our empirical analyses made it necessary to differentiate between various degrees and intensities of change. Moreover, if we want to identify the "structure of processes" (Elias, 1978, p. 164) of social change, we have to draw a distinction between different levels and social entities in which these process structures evolve.

Limited to the educational sector, Waks (2007, p. 281) has proposed to differentiate between various levels to which change may refer, such as "individuals, groups, organizations, systems." In our own inquiry, we differentiate the levels and social entities by drawing a distinction between *societal sectors, institutions, organizations*, and *organizational and social milieus*. These concepts will be elucidated and further discussed throughout this and the following chapters. Although our research is focused on the educational sector, we use also these concepts in reference to social entities in other societal sectors, such as in the political or economic realm. Some entities even pertain to more than one societal sector or—in the case of social milieus—lie on a social level below the functional differentiation of society into sectors.

In addition to differentiating levels on which change occurs, Waks (2007) suggested defining two degrees or intensities of change in education: "first-order" and "second-order change" (2007, pp. 282–283). With this, he draws on a seminal proposition by Watzlawick et al. (1974, p. 10), who spoke of "two different types of change: one that occurs within a given system which itself remains unchanged, and one whose occurrence changes the system itself." While the former is called "first-order change," the authors denote the latter as "second-order change" (pp. 10–11).

This distinction is certainly very abstract and has to be substantiated according to the social entity undergoing change. Cuban (1992, p. 218), for example, referred to organizations when he wrote that "first-order . . .

changes are intentional efforts to enhance the existing system by correcting deficiencies in policies and practices. Such changes try to make what exists more efficient and effective without disturbing basic organizational features." Changes in the organizational features, then, would be considered to be of a second-order nature. Similarly, Waks (2007, p. 294) defined second-order changes on the institutional level as pertaining to the "primary principles, norms, or laws that serve as the basis of a system, whether a pattern of actions or operative ideas."

In the light of this definition we can—for the time being—conceive of first-order change as a *reproductive variation*, that is, as a change which reproduces the given social entity by varying its procedures and practices. Second-order change then refers to *transformative change* which alters the direction and goals of the social entity itself. We will have to reconsider this distinction throughout this book, both due to its possible theoretical flaws and to the challenges of empirical inquiry.

The analysis of change in the educational sectors and other parts of society has to take into account the grades of change, the different levels and entities on which change occurs, as well as interdependencies between these social entities and levels. Table 2.1 displays the complexity of this endeavor, applying the binary differentiation of "change" on the different social entities relevant for our analysis:

Table 2.1 Forms of change in different social entities

	Society	Societal sectors	Institutions	Organizations	Organizational milieus	Social milieus that extend into organizations
Reproductive (first-order) change	?	?	?	?	?	?
Transformative (second-order) change	?	?	?	?	?	?

As all these different social entities may have their own direction and pace of change, and as these entities are often interlinked, the one entity's change may coincide with another entity's change into a different direction, or with the inertness of another entity. This implies that not only two different kinds of change in society exist, but that this heterogeneity of change may lead to unforeseen social dynamics. Therefore, the study of education and social change has to consider both the social entities and the social dynamics between them. Such dynamics may be overseen if one only studies processes from a bird's-eye view, as we do in the following section. However, as soon as we draw these processes closer, starting with the historical analysis of Turkey between 1980 and 2003 (section 2.4), the dynamics between different societal sectors, organizations, and social milieus catch our eyes.

2.2   The Formation of the Educational Sector in the Ottoman Empire

Until the 19th century and similar to the preceding development in central Europe (Zymek, 2008, p. 208), education in the Ottoman Empire was predominantly bound to religion insofar as new generations were educated for and through Islam. Here we have to differentiate between the predominantly non-formal education in the countryside and a small range of educational facilities organized by the state: State-organized education had the primary purpose of educating personnel for the state. Broadly speaking, there existed the following types of schools: *Sibyan, Madrasahs,* and *Enderun* schools. In *Sibyan* schools, "religious and moral knowledge" was taught and the children were trained in "memorizing the Qur'an" (Okçabol, 2005, pp. 23–24), and boys and girls were instructed by imams. This was followed by *Madrasahs*, where in addition to religious knowledge, scientific knowledge was taught. Graduates of the *Madrasahs* went on to work as civil servants, imams, or teachers. Another important recruiting agency for state servants was the *Enderun* school, where children who had been snatched from their non-Muslim families in conquered territories were educated to be Muslims and prepared for state service (Okçabol, 2005, p. 24). While the rural population did not benefit from these schools, they did have places to teach children, such as "dervish lodges" and "religious orders" (İnal, 2008, p. 28) where predominantly religious knowledge was taught (Somel, 2001, p. 192).

In the background of the chasm between the state-organized education of power elites and the non-formal education in the countryside, we find a state which related to its own population primarily through tax payments and military service. Even the formal character of *Sibyan* schools (and sometimes also the *Madrasah*) should not be overestimated. These schools and their teachers were financed by local foundations and parents, and there were no signs of centralized control (Somel, 2001, pp. 18–19). A stronger integration of state and society—as it can be made possible by an educational sector, and as it can be observed in nation states—was not necessary because the imperial apparatus of rule of the Ottoman Empire had been financed since its foundation, in 1299, until its largest expansion in the 16th and 17th centuries, by conquering ever-new areas and by the subsequent payment of tribute.

For these times, thus, we cannot speak of an education system or an educational sector in the narrower sense; rather, it was a "Bildungswesen" (that is, an area of education). With this term Müller and Zymek (1987, p. 18) denoted "those yet unsystematized types of school and educational opportunities" which lack a comprehensive order. As shown, the different types of school (*Madrasah, Enderun*), while preparing people for a specific career, were not related to each other. For this reason, no dynamics could evolve within the educational area, which would have led to systematization.

Buildup of New Educational Organizations in the 19th Century

With the first military defeats in the 18th and 19th centuries (in the war of 1768–74 against Russia large areas in the east were lost; in the beginning of the 19th-century uprisings and independence movements rose in Southeast Europe; Egypt defected) the Ottoman Empire not only lost its core basis of finance (that is, the payment of tributes); it also became evident that the hitherto victorious armies lacked the equipment and training which made the European armies so superior. On the background of these problems, Sultan Mahmut II (1808–39) started creating new facilities which were to raise the new cadres of a modern army (Zürcher, 2005, p. 44). A military school for medicine and a military academy were founded (in 1827 and 1834, respectively), and their alumni were to play an important role in the following years.

These new educational facilities can, first of all, be conceived of as simple *organizations* (see Luhmann, 1964): They are characterized by explicit rules that, as formalized expectations toward behavior, define roles within the organization (for example, that of an officer cadet), but may not yet have an established meaning for society at large. Anybody who wishes to become or remain a member of the organization must obey these organizational rules (which, for example, regulate the time of education), otherwise he or she would risk exclusion (see also section 3.1). The successful graduation from the teaching program established by the organization then gave the graduates the opportunity to enter the new army that was developed in the following years.

Parallel to the buildup of a new army, the state bureaucracy was expanded. Its cadres were, for the time being, only educated informally; that is, they were not trained in organizations which aimed directly at education: Many of the future high-ranking bureaucrats started their career in the foreign office and its embassies, whose number in Europe constantly grew. Here these bureaucrats were able to learn foreign languages and engage with Western literature and science (Matuz, 1985, pp. 223–224). It was only later, starting from 1839, that professional schools for the education of bureaucrats were established (Somel, 2001, p. 15).

In spite of the differences between the informal education of bureaucrats and the organized military education, both systems shared the feature that education remained exclusively as a means to an end: the modernization of the state apparatus and of the army (Somel, 2001, p. 15). Other expectations toward an education that was independent from these ends had not yet developed.

An edict, however, with which Mahmut II introduced compulsory basic education for boys in 1824, was a first impulse to turn education into an issue of independent expectations. Other indicators for the growing importance of modern education in society were the compulsory enrollment in quadrennial boys' schools (*sibyan mektebi*) since 1846 (Okçabol, 2005, p. 27) and the decree of 1847, which stipulated the teaching of writing in these schools (previously, boys had been taught to memorize the Quran) (Akyüz, 1993, p. 140). However, we should not assume that compulsory primary education was indeed enforced by these organizations, or that all graduates of boys' schools were alphabetized. Compulsory primary education could not be enforced in Turkey until far into the 20th century (Akyüz, 1993, p. 131). Nevertheless, this formal rule of 1824 may be conceived of as a precursor of the first modern educational institutions.

We here conceive of institutions in the "sense of a social order which provides anticipatory reliability" (Kuper & Thiel, 2009, p. 484) for the actions of persons; they orient action on a societal level. By doing so, institutions both enable and restrict action (Ortmann, 2004, pp. 24–26). In contrast to compulsory primary education, as it was introduced in 1824 with a formal rule, institutions pertain to expectations toward behavior that has become self-evident, that is, a matter of fact. The *Sibyan* school as a general form (as opposed to as a single school), for example, may be denoted as such an institution, as a "reciprocal typification of habitualized actions by types of actors" had been constituted for this school form (Berger & Luckmann, 1991, p. 72). In other words, there existed "normative expectations" (Bohn-sack, 2014, p. 42), stabilized in society, toward the customary instruction process in boys' schools, as well as toward the qualifications of teachers and the knowledge to be conveyed to the children.

Beginning of Sector Formation Through Reciprocal Organization

The origins of an educational sector in the Ottoman Empire are certainly not to be found on the primary school level, but—similar to the development in central Europe (Zymek, 2008)—in the area of secondary and tertiary education. Furthermore, the development of a societal sector had less to do with *institutions* (that is, with socially based expectations toward habitualized practices), than with the emergence of new educational *organizations* on the tertiary level.

Before we attend to the constitution of an educational sector in the Ottoman Empire, we have to further clarify the relation of institution and organization: Institutions "restrict and enable" actions but cannot be held responsible for them; in contrast, organizations are "directly attributed actions and their consequences, they are classified as accountable, responsible" (Ortmann, 2004, p. 25). For example, the *Madrasah* as such, in its generalized form, was an institution, whereas a specific *Madrasah*, such as the Yakutiye *Madrasah* in Erzurum, was an organization to which, as a corporative actor, practices could be attributed. The new educational organizations that were founded in the Ottoman Empire only gradually began to become established as institutions. The professional school for bureaucrats, founded in 1859 as the "mülkiye mektebi," was hence (and first of all) an organization that could be made responsible for the success and failure of its actions.

Only later could action practices (for example, the knowledge conveyed to each class) be established as reciprocally typified and thus institutionalized.

A core problem of the newly established educational organizations at the end of the 18th century (military academies and professional schools) was related to their novices: Some were so badly educated that they could not even read or write (Somel, 2001, p. 21). Quadrennial schools for adolescents (*Rüşdiye*) were established after 1839, partly to satisfy the need of the military academies and professional schools for modern-educated pupils (Akyüz, 1993, p. 142). In these, both religious and secular knowledge was taught. In 1852 there were 12 *Rüşdiye* in Istanbul, and in 1869 a decree ordered that every town with more than 500 households should have a *Rüşdiye* (Akyüz, 1993, p. 143). Because a gap to the tertiary level still existed, schools of the upper secondary level (*İdadi mektebi*) were introduced (Akyüz, 1993, p. 144). Later, these *İdadi* schools systematically built on the *Rüşdiye* and instruction lasted 3 years. In the second half of the 19th century the *İdadi* schools were able to establish themselves, whereas the *Rüşdiye* failed.

The professional schools of the tertiary level were still related to the army and the bureaucracy to which their graduates were sent. However, with the buildup of *Rüşdiye* and *İdadi* schools, there emerged educational organizations whose core reference in their environment again were educational organizations (that is, the professional schools). Besides, at least the *İdadi* schools were able to institutionalize; in other words, expectations toward the qualifications generally conferred by these schools were established in society. Later, education started to be organized exceeding the establishment of schools: In 1857 the ministry for public education was founded; since 1869, with the decree for public education (*Maarif-i Umumiyye Nizamnamesi*) it also developed a provincial administration (Somel, 2001, pp. 90–108). Whereas the staff of the modern secondary schools had previously been recruited exclusively among graduates of the religious *Madrasah*, since 1848, the year when teacher-training centers were established and expanded, *Madrasah* graduates were more and more excluded from the teaching profession.

We may conceive of these developments as the beginning of an educational sector, in the sense of a "societal sector." This denotes a structure of different organizations and institutions that relate to each other and whose core functions (which focus on education) are discernible from the functions of the environment. Without adopting their focus on organization, we here follow Scott and Meyer (1991), who underpinned that such societal sectors

> are likely to stretch from local to national or even international actors. The boundaries of societal sectors are defined in functional, not geographical terms: sectors are comprised of units that are functionally interrelated even though they may be geographically remote.
>
> (pp. 117–118)

Organizations within one societal sector (for example, the *İdadi* schools) tend to institutionalize, especially if they have similar "services, products or functions" (p. 118); that is, they are associated with expectations toward behavior that are established in society and reciprocally typified. Therefore, institutions which emanated from organizations should play an important role for societal sectors as well.

Strong Islamic elements certainly still existed in the Ottoman educational sector, both concerning teaching staff and the instruction contents (Fortna, 2002; Somel, 2001). But the function of this sector had turned from the advancement of religiousness to the qualification of new generations. As Fortna (2002, pp. 123–124) showed in an analysis of the correspondence between the Sublime Porte and the regional directors of education and of their annual reports, education became the focus not only in instruction itself but also in the communication between the organizations of the educational sector. Here, one can speak of a societal sector that gradually unfolded an independent existence and distinguished itself from its environment (see also Müller & Zymek, 1987, p. 18).

The formation of a secular sector of education went so far as to replace the religious boys' schools (*Sibyan*) by primary schools, which were founded in 1872 under them name of *İbtidai mektebi* (Somel, 2001, pp. 27–28). Before, the secular and modern schools of the secondary (*Rüşdiye* and *İdadî*) and tertiary levels could be perceived as complementary to the Islamic educational area of Sibyan schools and *Madrasahs*, because they prepared children for different careers. However, from then on the commitment of the Ottoman reforms to secularize education and withdraw it from the grip of the religious class (*Ulema*) was expressed in the new primary schools (*İbtidai*) (Somel, 2001, p. 15).

The Establishment of the Educational Sector in the Early 20th Century

The beginnings of a sector of secular education which, as shown, can be found on the tertiary and secondary levels, affected the life-course expectations of educated young men in the Ottoman Empire. Until far into the 19th century it was self-evident that one's life course was embossed by religious education. Graduates of the *Sibyan* school and the *Madrasah* were expected to have specific skills and habits, and were aware of such social expectations toward them. These institutions—the *Sibyan* school and *Madrasah*—were snatched away from their matter-of-course character and the lack of alternatives when the first graduates of the new professional schools gained ground in the bureaucracy and in the army. With the new, secular educational organizations, a new life course began to be institutionalized (see Kohli, 2007), one that referred to the secular education of bureaucratic and military elites and competed with the ruling class of the Ulema, who was religiously educated in the *Madrasah* (İnal, 2008, p. 37). When these elites—of whom the majority had lived in Western Europe for a certain time—came to power in the beginning of the 20th century, the secular educational sector began to prevail over the *Ulema*.

This development had begun in the second half of the 19th century, when a group of well-educated bureaucrats and intellectuals was formed, pursuing liberal and, at the same time, Islamic thinking, along with promoting the idea of a nation-state. These "Young Ottomans," with some representatives in France and later called "Jeune Turcs" (Young Turks), were not even impressed by the adoption of a constitution in 1876, particularly as it was annulled shortly after. The "new generations being trained in schools like the Mülkiye and Harbiye (War Academy) continued to be attracted by the liberal and constitutional ideas, as well as the Ottoman patriotism, of the Young Ottomans, whose books they read and discussed clandestinely" (Zürcher, 2005, p. 86). Toward the end of the century, a resistance group was formed; the group was called "İttihat ve Terakki Cemiyeti" (Committee of Union and Progress, CUP), and largely consisted of expatriates in and from France. In 1908 the CUP successfully enforced the reinstatement of the constitution that had been suspended in the meantime. The time of the Young Turks (Matuz, 1985, p. 251) had begun, in which individuals with a secular life course came into power.

Whereas the bureaucrats of the sultan had been eager to design the reforms in such a way that they would not overly risk losing the support of the Ulema, the reforms of the Young Turks did not stop at the religious branch of secondary education. The *Madrasah* was tied to the ministry of education, its curriculum modernized, and Western languages were introduced as obligatory subjects (Zürcher, 2005, p. 122). In particular, girls and women benefited from the extension of schools and from the introduction of compulsory primary education for girls in 1913. Additionally, academic education for women was created (Zürcher, 2005, p. 123).

While no *new* educational institutions were created during the rule of the Young Turks, educational issues continued to gain in significance within the social debate. "Educational issues were for the first time discussed extensively in teachers' magazines and other press, new viewpoints were expressed. Some of these were the seed from which the educational practices during the time of the Republic grew" (Akyüz, 1993, p. 230). Among these new viewpoints there was also the mindset of the political leaders of the CUP, whose attitudes were influenced by "nationalism, a positivist belief in the value of objective scientific truth, a great (and somewhat naive) faith in the power of education to spread this truth and elevate the people" (Zürcher, 2005, p. 132).

It was only 10 years later that a convenient occasion for definitively establishing the secular educational sector emerged, with the foundation of the modern Turkish Republic. After the devastating defeat of the Ottomans in World War I, the followers of Mustafa Kemal had been victorious in a war against the allied powers (among them Brits, Italians, and Greeks). This victory allowed a population which had become increasingly Muslim and

Turkish in constitution to live in an own country, located about the border of today's Turkey. The new power elites of Turkey tried to distinguish themselves from the Young Turks of the Ottoman Empire; yet, however much Mustafa Kemal (the founder of the Turkish Republic) underpinned the difference vis-à-vis the regime of the Young Turks, he tied in with some of their ideas and political concepts (Kafadar, 1997, p. 125).

On one hand, Mustafa Kemal's concepts for the educational sector were based on the state of institutionalization and formation of a sector achieved in the late Ottoman Empire; on the other hand, however, he could radicalize the reforms after the Ulema had lost an important stronghold with the end of the sultanate (1922) and the caliphate (1924). For a start, the law on the unification of education ("Tevhid-i Tedrisat Kanunu") was adopted on March 3, 1924. According to this law, all educational and scientific institutions were attached to the Ministry of National Education. This included all schools previously organized by the Ministry of Endowments and Islamic Affairs; even the education of imams was to be organized by the Ministry of National Education (Akyüz, 1993, p. 285). Only few days after the adoption of this law, the minister of education issued a decree that led to the closure of the (religiously embossed) *Madrasah* (Kafadar, 2002, p. 352).

With this (temporary) end of the *Madrasah*, that is, of "the thousand year old educational institution of Islamic civilization and culture" (Kafadar, 2002, p. 353), a Turkish national(ist) and occidentalist mindset was also established. This Westernization of the educational sector also crystallized in the beginning of co-education, which was introduced in urban primary schools in 1924 and later in secondary schools as well (Okçabol, 2005, p. 39). All these innovations in education cannot—according to Kafadar (1997, p. 138)—be denoted as simple reforms; rather, they need to be called a revolution "characterized by a radical and at times harsh trait which was directed at realizing a complete social change."

Although the secular educational sector had originated in the Ottoman Empire, the radical character of the educational sector's change in the Turkish Republic was at least founded in the fact that it was not only secular (that is, oriented toward education *beyond* a religious conduct of life), but that it also served to subordinate religion to the state and religiousness to all other conducts of life. In this respect, it may be called a *laicist* educational sector.

With the change from secularism to laicism in the 1920s, the educational sector was finally established: Apart from the schools of the military, which were able to preserve their independence, all educational organizations were arranged in such a way that a) they reciprocally referred to each other, b) transitions from one school to the other were established and c) a central organization (the ministry) coordinated them. In 1937–38, around the time of Mustafa Kemal's death, the Turkish educational sector had the following shape and size (Table 2.2).

The function for which the educational organizations catered henceforth was focused on a common idea, that of laicist education. The educational sector of Turkey had found its own point of reference.

Table 2.2 Numbers of schools and pupils, 1937–38

	Number of facilities	Number of pupils
Preschool	47	1555
Primary school	6700	764,691
Middle school	214	74,107
General high school	68	20,916
Vocational high school	78	10,358
University	19	9384

Source: Okçabol (2005, p. 46).

Conclusions

If one attempts to divide the history of Turkish education until this point in time into different phases, then for the early 19th century (1) we cannot speak of an educational sector, but rather of an educational area in which the institutions and organizations were scarcely related to each other and rather bound to the military, bureaucracy, and religion. Then, in the time before the foundation of the republic (2) there was a gradual systematization (Müller & Zymek, 1987, p. 13) within which the arrangement of educational institutions and organizations was still unclear and being tested (as evident in the gradual replacement of the *Rüşdiye* by the *İdadi* or the continuity of the *Madrasah,* for example). This can be considered a reproductive change ("first-order change"; Watzlawick et al., 1974, pp. 10–11) in the area of education, whose basic aims and functions were not touched upon. In contrast, the Kemalists, in the early Turkish Republic (3) succeeded to constitute a single secular and even laicist educational sector according to their ideas, with which "hardly abolishable principles of organizing and structuring were pushed through and functional assignments and delimitations were established" (Müller & Zymek, 1987, p. 13). The transition from an area of education, which partly served the education of power elites but most dominantly catered for the religious education of the poor, to an educational sector in which different organizations of primary, secondary, and tertiary education were related to each other was certainly a "second-order change," in the sense employed by Watzlawick et al. (1974, pp. 10–11), that is, a transformative change. Interestingly, the respective individual organizations and institutions (for example, the *Madrasah*), apart from abolishment, did not undergo such a transformative change but—if at all—a reproductive variation instead. The transformative change on the level of society was in fact made possible by the emergence of *new* institutions and organizations, and the subsequent *removal* of the old ones.

2.3 The Expansion and Differentiation of Laicist Education in Modern Turkey

The constitution of an educational sector with a laicist orientation was only possible due to the authority of a government that was extraordinarily popular after the victorious war. As concerns the early days of the Turkish Republic, in many social milieus (including those represented in the parliament and therefore influential in the formation of the new republic), however, the idea of secular education—let alone with a laicist orientation—had yet to find any support. While a phase of secular education had already become institutionalized in the life course of civil servants and merchants in the urban milieus, all rural milieus (from the peasant to the great landowner) as well as large milieus of the small and middle-sized towns were still largely bound to the traditions of religious education (Zürcher, 2005, pp. 186–187).

Different from the concept of institution, pertaining to those expectations toward behaviors that are established on the *societal* level (see earlier), by milieu we refer to those collective forms of practical conduct of life which lie *beneath* the level of the society at large. Milieus are based on practical commonalities of experience; in other words, based on a collective "'stratification' of experience (Erlebnisschichtung)" (Mannheim, 1972, p. 112). These collective experiences do not need to have been made together, that is, within face-to-face relations (as in Tönnies's, 2011, concept of "community"), but can also be only identical in structure; in other words, homologous (see also sections 3.1, 4.1, and 5.1).

Given the religious affiliations of many social milieus in the early Turkish Republic, it was important for the Kemalists to advance the secularization of society beyond the educational sector. Therefore, a series of reforms took place in the 1920s and 1930s which influenced everyday life and were—directly or indirectly—of great importance for education. Thus, in 1926 the European calendar was adopted and a series of laws were passed by the parliament, by which the people's dressing habits and religious practices were to be Westernized or rendered more Turkish. The most extensive reforms, however, were the paradigm shifts in language and in the alphabet. In 1928, the parliament decided that the Turkish language should be based on the Latin alphabet instead of on the Arab-Persian alphabet. While this law facilitated communication with Western states, it made communication with Oriental countries more difficult (Zürcher, 2005, p. 188) and cut off the Turkish society from its Ottoman heritage.

Mustafa Kemal himself toured the country in 1928 to explain the significance of the Latin alphabet to the people, as the introduction of the Latin alphabet was linked to the idea of bringing literacy to as many people as possible (Akyüz, 1993, p. 299). In 1927, only 10.7% of the population were literate (Okçabol, 1999, p. 252), and with the introduction of the Latin alphabet, the whole population became analphabet in a sense. For this reason, in 1928, people's schools ("millet mektepleri") were founded. On one hand, they were to alphabetize adults, and on the other hand aimed to give them civil and cultural instruction (Okçabol, 1999). While in its first years a huge number of citizens took part in this campaign (485,632 were counted in 1928–29; Okçabol, 1999, p. 252), the number declined to 53,330 in 1934–35.

This makes evident that only part of the milieus of Turkish society was reached by the educational reforms. The percentage of literate people had— if one can trust the figures—only grown up to 22.4% in 1939–40 (Sakaoğlu, 1992, pp. 46–51). In some social milieus, apparently one was not eager to learn the Latin (and therefore Western) alphabet if one could write (in Arabic letters) at all. This also had to do with the fact that reading and writing were not part of everyday life in the countryside and in the lower classes of society, therefore lacking in functionality. Furthermore, we have to assume alphabetization courses were not offered in remote villages.

The conflict between state organizations of education and social milieus, however, went beyond learning simple qualifications, and also pertained to the ideological legitimation of the state. While in the Ottoman Empire religious education directly served the legitimation of the sultanate, the republican educational sector, orientated toward laicism, was pervaded by civil education. The (obligatory) school was not only committed to developing a national consciousness, but—secured by a one-party regime—also to the creation of a modern state citizen in general (Üstel, 2004; Taşçı Günlü, 2008). As Gök (1999) exposed, the educational policy of the one-party era "resonated in the slogan 'for the people and where necessary in spite of the people'" (p. 6).

As it became clear after the death of Mustafa Kemal (on November 10, 1938) and during the presidency of Ismet İnönü, the secularization of society was not nearly as successful as the laicization of the educational sector.[1] Toward the end of World War II, dissatisfaction with the regime and the ruling Republican People's Party grew. In rural areas, the Kemalist regime at the time stood more for police and tax control than for modernization. Due to the sheer number of villages, the extension of schools had been hardly noticeable up to that point. Besides, the Kemalists found it difficult to ensure the ideological loyalty of the rural population, who maintained their traditional ways of life and their religious orientation. The bourgeoisie, too, (in the country as well as in the city) increasingly distanced themselves from the Kemalists when they were hit by expropriations and property taxes. Originally a stronghold of Kemalism, the bureaucrats suffered as a result of inflation (Zürcher, 2005, pp. 206–208). All this soon also had consequences for the reform of educational organizations.

To understand these consequences, one must also take into account the political changes within and around Turkey: Following World War II, in which Turkey sided neither with Germany nor with the Allies, an association with Western NATO countries was now pushed ahead as a consequence of the 'Cold War,' among other things (Koçak, 2003, p. 178). This repositioning of Turkey in the international arena, as well as the social unrest within the country, increased the political pressure toward the introduction of a multi-party system.

Even before the first free elections in 1950, the Kemalist Republican People's Party (RPP) prepared for the expected competitive situation that lay ahead by attempting to take into account the population's religious expectations to a greater extent. The government permitted courses for the training of imams and preachers. This process continued in 1950, when the "Democratic Party" (DP) won the elections. In 1951, the new government established the first "imam and preacher schools"; in the school year of 1953, religious studies became an optional subject in primary school (Okçabol, 2005, p. 59); in the school year of 1956/1957, religious studies were reinstated as an optional subject in middle schools, to be followed by secondary schools in 1967/1968 (Kafadar, 2002, p. 354). Such measures were also viewed as an important device against Soviet communism. Even if the DP did not generally challenge the laicist constitution of the state, the first years of the multi-party system can be regarded as a sort of "culture struggle," the subject of which, among other things, was the question of how Turkey was to be further modernized.

Even when the military seized power and issued a new and laicist constitution in 1960, its cultural and educational policy can certainly be regarded as a balancing act, on one hand, between the innovations of the Kemalist republic, and on the other hand, as the (religious) sensibilities of parts of the population which had not entirely benefited from these innovations. As much as the military leaders felt committed to Westernization and to the legacy of Mustafa Kemal, the civilian governments succeeding their regime—in particular those led by the conservative parties—tried to accommodate Islam.

For the laicist educational sector, the reintroduction of religion at the time implied only an interior differentiation of the sector (Müller & Zymek, 1987, p. 14): Without putting the web of the educational sector's central organizations into question, a branch was instituted with the schools for imams and preachers, one that referred to a discrete (religious) career track. In contrast to the *Madrasah*, whose graduates had been able to find jobs in various higher professions, these new schools (as the name implies) only served for the education of imams and preachers. However, this changed when the number of imam and preacher schools was significantly increased during the 1960s and 1970s, as well as when they were opened to women. According to Okçabol, this challenged the very foundation of the laicist education sector—and particularly its unity—since the imam and preacher schools "developed into an alternative to the laicist education system" (Okçabol, 2005, p. 71). The careers of its graduates signaled that the imam and preacher schools did not solely signify another pillar of the laicist educational sector with a specific career path; both female graduates (who were not eligible to become imams whatsoever) and men who were not employed as imam or preachers piled into non-religious vocations and study programs (Gökaçtı, 2005).

Extension and Interior Differentiation of the Educational
Sector vis-à-vis Economic, Political, and Demographic Developments

Apart from their function as a device in the Cold War against communism, the opening of imam and preacher secondary schools and the introduction of religious education in general schools during the 1950s and 1960s had also met the desires of those social milieus who could not identify with the early republican Kemalism and continued their religiously embossed conduct of life (Gökaçtı, 2005, pp. 178–189). However, the educational sector was also heavily challenged by other aspects of social change, especially by the demographic and socio-economic shifts in society.

The number of industrial companies rose from 2600 in the year 1950 to 8700 in 1980, and the number of industrial workers went from 162,000 to 786,000 (TÜİK, 2007, p. 303). Internal migration increased due to industrialization and because of the Westernization process, including the increasing adoption of Western lifestyles (which not everybody could afford to pursue, but which were nevertheless increasingly seen as an ideal). Movement from the countryside to the cities was enormous. In 1927, 3.3 million people lived in the city and 10.3 million in the countryside; by 1950 the absolute numbers had increased—due to population growth—but the ratio had not changed: 5.2 million city dwellers now had 15.7 million rural counterparts. However, in 1980 the cities had as many as 19.6 million inhabitants, with 25 million people living in the countryside, indicating a massive internal migration (TÜİK, 2007, p. 9). This did not mean, however, that all internal migrants found industry work; rather, most of them had to rely on casual labor.

The economic development of the country, the population growth, and interior migration did not leave educational sector expectations untouched. Kepenek and Yentürk (2007) outlined the connection of social change and education between 1945 and 1960, which constitutes the background of these changes, with the following words:

> As a consequence of the fact that the rural regions opened to the market and of the opportunity to influence the government by means of the general right to vote, the demand of large masses for education increased or became more apparent. Education, traditionally a means of finding employment in the public sector, now was also necessary to grasp the job opportunities that developed when the economic dynamic assumed new proportions. . . . Furthermore, the economic development and urbanization had increased the economic and social necessity of education.
>
> (p. 134)

The educational sector, which had been ill-equipped even at the time of the establishment of the republic in providing basic education to the population, did not stand a chance in the face of this rapid population growth. While the population had increased from 13.6 million to 20.9 million between 1927 and 1950, it had doubled by 1975, and was at 44.7 million in 1980 (TÜİK, 2007, p. 9). Such population growth implied—in combination with the low average age of the Turkish population—high demands on the educational sector. In 1950, there were just over 4.8 million children aged 5 to 14; in 1980, there were 11 million.

The quantitative development of the Turkish educational sector during that period cannot be directly compared to the figures mentioned previously. Nevertheless, it becomes clear that the schools, while subjected to massive expansion, could neither remedy the deficits dating back to the founding of the republic nor keep up with the population growth (Table 2.3).

This expansion of the educational sector, tripling the number of primary schools and increasing more than tenfold that of middle schools and secondary schools, had consequences for teacher training and employment policies. After 1960, to meet the demand, conscripts that had completed secondary education were allowed to teach instead of going into military service; later, they were employed on a permanent basis. Likewise, women could become provisional teachers after finishing secondary education and a short traineeship (Okçabol, 2005, pp. 68–69). At the same time (and even then), a certain scientification of the teaching profession was noticeable. In the mid-1960s, for instance, the first educational university department was established in Ankara.

The concurrence of success and failure becomes particularly clear when one looks at the number of illiterates. While at a census in 1950 only 4.1 million people above the age of 15 claimed to be literate (as opposed to 8.7 million illiterates), the number of literates increased to 17.9 million in 1980. In spite of this success, the number of illiterates also increased, amounting to 9.3 million (TÜİK, 2007, p. 16). This overall situation shows that the educational sector in Turkey had become well established, with a rising number of

Table 2.3 Quantitative figures of education, 1950–80

Educational institution	1950–51			1979–80		
	Schools	Students	Teachers	Schools	Students	Teachers
Preschool	52	1760	71	122	4909	277
Primary school	17,428	1,616,626	35,871	44,296	5,622,407	199,245
Middle school (imam and preacher schools)	406 (7)	68,187 (876)	4528	4103 (339)	1,180,233 (130,072)	30,930 (685)
Secondary schools	88	22,169	1954	1108	531,760	36198
Vocational/technical secondary school (imam and preacher schools)	326 (–)	53,289 (–)	4488 (–)	1719 (249)	514,923 (47,941)	28,599 (5397)
Lyceum	34	24,815	1950	347	270,278	20,699

Source: Okçabol (2005, pp. 63, 80), from the State Statistical Institute.

alumni of higher education institutions. However, the number of illiterates remained high, meaning that while the educational sector itself expanded and became more differentiated, there were still social groups such as ethnic minorities (Kurds, for example), women, and people in rural areas who were not sufficiently included (Gök, 2007).

Besides the enlargement of the educational sector, the interior differentiation was an important dimension of its development. Given the growing number of jobs in the industry, the extension of vocational education was one part of it. As Günlü (2008) explained,

> Turkey was entering into a new stage of capital based development in the 1960s and 1970s. . . . Technical schools educating manpower for modern capital based enterprises were turned into technical high schools, trade institutes into industrial vocational high schools, and institutes for girls into vocational high schools for girls in the 1973–1974 education year.
>
> (pp. 118–119)

As a consequence, a broad range of different vocational schools was established (Okçabol, 2005, p. 72). As Table 2.3 shows, between 1950 and 1979 enrollment at vocational high schools grew by nearly ten times. This interior differentiation led to the development of independent educational paths. Apart from the problem of imam and preacher schools discussed previously, the degrees of vocational high schools made graduates only eligible for study programs specific for their vocation, whereas other study programs remained closed for them. In contrast to the educational path embossed by imam and preacher schools, these vocational education paths, however, did not ideologically differ from general education.

Whereas Turkish politics during the 1950s and 1960s had been dominated by the antagonism between the party of the Kemalists and a more conservative party, the political landscape of Turkey became more diversified toward the end of the 1960s. Left- and right-wing political parties emerged and students became radicalized. There were politically motivated acts of violence, which the government—hardly able to function in other political areas—was incapable of controlling. On March 12, 1971, the army leaders forced the formation of a new government that was to restrict civil rights and the autonomy of the media. Under martial law, the army now persecuted leftists, about 5000 of whom were arrested (Zürcher, 2005, pp. 253–258).

The union rights of civil servants were abolished during this time; subsequently, the teachers' union was banned. The universities, which were being expanded at the time, had to surrender their administrative autonomy. The expansion of vocational schools and secondary schools continued; additionally, within the Ministry of National Education, organizational units for apprenticeship and for adult education were instituted (Okçabol, 2005, pp. 76–79). The imam and preacher schools, originally intended for vocational education, were turned into secondary schools in 1970, providing their graduates with a university entrance qualification (Kafadar, 2002, p. 354), thus completely turning into a parallel course of education.

Following the 1973 elections, civilian-elected politicians were again coming to power, with governments such as that led by conservative and economically liberal Süleyman Demirel taking turns with those like Bülent Ecevit's, the new leader of the social democrat RPP. Both were forced to form coalitions with other parties, including the Islamist party, led by Necmettin Erbakan, and their ability to act was thereby limited. Toward the end of the 1970s, politically motivated violence heavily increased. In 1979, between 1200 and 1500 people were victims of political assassinations by left- or right-wing supporters (the latter being more dominant, if nothing else, due to their collaborators among the police). Above all, this situation affected the educational sector, insofar as numerous acts of violence occurred in secondary schools and universities (Okçabol, 2005, p. 80).

Political violence, however, was not the decisive motive behind the military coup that followed on September 12, 1980, although it was often used as a justification. An important reason for the coup was the economic crisis toward the end of the 1970s, which ended in 90% inflation in 1979 and left Turkey completely dependent on foreign loans. The civilian government had not been able to obtain a credit agreement with the most important international sponsors (including the IMF and the World Bank), coupled with major reforms, because of the resistance of the people (in the form of political and labor organizations) (Zürcher, 2005, pp. 260–277).

Conclusion: Social Consequences of the Expansion of the Educational Sector

Whereas the establishment of a laicist educational sector in the early era of the Turkish Republic can be described as transformative change (second-order change), its extension between 1950 and 1980 in fact constituted of a series of changes that only served the consolidation and differentiation of the educational sector and that can only be referred to as reproductive (first-order) change. Solely the fact that the imam and preacher schools did not serve only the education of religious staff anymore, but increasingly— though still small in numbers—functioned as an alternative and general educational path alludes to tendencies which altered the laicist character of the educational sector and its core goals and functions.

Apart from the different degrees of change in the area of education, other noteworthy changes took place—albeit in mutual reaction with the educational sector—in different societal sectors and social milieus. With the extension and interior differentiation of the educational sector (especially after 1950), social expectations and practices changed. Social resources in the form of time, space, and capital were rearranged, especially where education— most importantly primary education—was no longer at the discretion of the individual, being now an institutionalized part of every life course. Money spent for school uniforms could not be invested in seeds; the school time of adolescents could not be used for the rural family's harvest. In this way, the arrangement of societal sectors was altered; in other words, education received a different position vis-à-vis politics, the economy, and the military.[2]

At the same time, the allocation of education time became an institutionalized expectation toward the individual: Children were accorded a childhood which was marked by school attendance, and with the extension of secondary and tertiary education, a previously unknown phase of youth was institutionalized (Warth, 2011). Conversely, the institutionalization of childhood and youth was also related to socially based expectations toward the skills that graduates of primary—and possibly secondary—education should have: Car drivers needed to have a primary school diploma, and in some occupational fields one was expected to know foreign languages. The improving qualification of workers rendered possible both more complex work processes and economic and administrative innovation.

Finally, education—and the development of an educational sector—is an important factor in the change of the society at large. When, in the 19th century, Ottoman bureaucrats started being recruited according to success (rather than by descent), there began a gradual (and partly still continuing) change from a feudal and corporative society to a functionally differentiated and capitalist society, which orientated itself (even if not totally) along meritocratic principles, at least in the sense that social positions (e.g., jobs) were legitimized by meritocracy. The position a person obtained in the Ottoman Empire was largely predetermined by his or her ties to an ethnic group and—for males—a professional order handed down from father to son. In 1980, however, positions in Turkish society were legitimated by the qualifications one had obtained in the educational sector. This should not imply that many positions—such as in the bureaucracy—were not assigned according to the party membership. But the fact that this was a frequent matter of complaint indicated that there existed an institutionalized expectation to legitimize such assignments by qualification.

In this regard, we can maintain that the extension of the educational sector—of course, in connection to economic and political developments—led to a transformative change of society. While education (secular or laicist) was previously limited to a few social milieus, and was important for only some parts of other societal sectors (economy, politics), organizations of these sectors increasingly oriented recruitment processes toward a candidate's success in the educational sector. In this way, formal education became an institutionalized expectation toward every member of society, whose life course was, consequently and among others, embossed by success in the educational sector.

2.4   Society and Education from 1980 to 2003

The year 1980 marks far-reaching shifts in the political and economic sectors of Turkey that transformed society in the long run (Ahmad, 2003, pp. 181–212; Tanör, 2004; Zürcher, 2005, pp. 278–298). In this section, we investigate the changes and continuities of Turkish society by applying a broad perspective that, along with debating educational issues, also considers the dynamics in other aspects of society: politics and economics (most importantly), and demographics.

Military Reign and Motherland Party Governments Between 1980 and 1991

When the military seized power in Turkey, on September 12, 1980, it not only brought to an abrupt end a period of political instability, unrest, and violence, but also annihilated the democratic system and enforced economic measures with considerable short- and medium-term effects on society. The military seized power all the way down to the level of the municipalities. Military commanders "were put in charge of education, the press, chambers of commerce and trade unions, and they did not hesitate to use their powers" (Zürcher, 2005, p. 279). At the Ministry of National Education, retired officers were assigned to the decision-making positions (Okçabol, 2005, p. 86). The generals relentlessly persecuted everyone who they suspected of engaging in political activities. Between 1980 and 1983, 650,000 people from both left and right of the political spectrum were arrested; 171 people died under torture and 300 under obscure circumstances. Universities were under strict control; 120 professors and 3854 teachers were fired (Tanör, 2004, pp. 95–96).

Then, in 1982, the people were asked to give their consent to a constitution which would change and restrict the political system on a sustained basis (Tanör, 2004, pp. 43–54). Only three parties were admitted for the first elections, to be held in 1983. The Motherland Party won the elections, led by Turgut Özal, an economic consultant and influential bureaucrat in the pre-1980 period; Özal had been active before 1980 and had cooperated with the military regime. Based on a sophisticated system of patronage (Ahmad, 2003, p. 190), the Motherland Party managed to stay in power until 1991 (Tanör, 2004, pp. 62–85). The party recruited its voters from economic-liberalist and Islamic circles, and was influenced by a peculiar synthesis of Turkicist and Islamic thinking. During the rule of the Motherland Party, the country saw a political liberalization, albeit dilatory and very limited. "By the beginning of 1986 the party structure created by the military rulers had virtually disintegrated and the most prominent of the banned leaders had emerged behind proxy parties" (Ahmad, 2003, p. 194). These and other parties prepared for overtaking power from Turgut Özel, but only succeeded in the 1990s (see later).

Major Economic Consequences of the Coup d'État

The coup d'état had aimed at changing the economy, in addition to the political order. The military government had appointed Turgut Özal to implement a package of economic measures inspired by the IMF and put together (but not implemented) already on January 24, 1980. The economic policy of the Motherland Party under Turgut Özal and ruling since 1983 was then much in accordance with the will of the generals. Hence, in the 1980s an open-market economic policy replaced the state-controlled import-substituted industrialization strategy. As Gülalp (2001) pointed out, import-substituted industrialization (ISI) was

> a model of state-led development. It consisted of an attempt to utilize a nationalist ideology by combining the basic principles of the welfare state with an emphasis on rapid industrialization. In practice, ISI was a process in which technology, capital goods, and inputs were imported, and the final product was locally manufactured to cater to the state-protected domestic market.
>
> (p. 436)

With the turn to an open-market policy, prices were left to the conditions of the market, which was also open to foreign products. At the same time, the price of labor (and hence wages) was reduced to stimulate investment, to reduce production costs and to bring down domestic demand. However, attempts to attract foreign capital remained largely unsuccessful. In 1989 the financial market, including foreign currency, was also liberalized (Kepenek & Yentürk, 2007, pp. 200–213).

Between 1979 and 1988, the inflation-adjusted income of workers, civil servants, and farmers declined by around 50% (Kepenek & Yentürk, 2007, p. 506; Boratav, 2005, pp. 49, 56). Given the heavy restrictions imposed on trade unions, the workers' bargaining position was considerably weak vis-à-vis the private sector employers, who were able to increase their corporate profits from 26.5% in the 1970s to 35.6% between 1984 and 1988 (Boratav, 2005, p. 43). The inflation dropped from 107.6% in 1980 to rates between 20% and 50% in the years leading to 1987, only to rise again to well over 70% afterwards (Kepenek & Yentürk, 2007, p. 574). Contrary to their intention, the Motherland Party governments were not very successful in the privatization of state enterprises (Kepenek & Yentürk, 2007, p. 422).

As Buğra (2002, p. 117) argued, "only a few SEEs [state-owned enterprises; the authors] had been privatized by 1990." The state itself had "not gotten smaller in the 1980s," as the "share of public investment in total investment continued to increase until 1988 because of the massive infrastructure projects." Nevertheless, Buğra asserted that the military and the successive Motherland Party governments

> were successful in generating an undeniable economic vitality. By the end of the decade, the Turkish economy had gone a long way toward integration with the world economy through trade and foreign investment. These developments had served the enrichment of new groups of

businessmen, which significantly included smaller Anatolian ones but by no means only them, and contributed to the emergence of a new group of professionals now able to find highly lucrative employment opportunities especially in the service sector.

(p. 120)

These economic dynamics, however, lead to "ever-widening income disparities" (Buğra, 2002, p. 120), one of the reasons for the growing discontent with the Motherland Party toward the late 1980s.

Population Growth, Wealth Disparities, and Internal Migration Between 1980 and 2000

Parallel to the economic developments after 1980, the quest for a better life, which since the 1950s had already carried millions of Turkish citizens into the cities, in addition to a state of war in the Kurdish region, brought an ever-increasing number of people to the metropolises (Hacettepe, 2006). While in 1980 only 43.91% of the population had lived in the cities, numbers rose to 59.01% in 1990 and 64.9% in 2000 (State Institute of Statistics, n.d., p. 46). This led to a considerable growth of the cities, 10 of which had more than 1 million citizens in 1990. Istanbul, the biggest Turkish city since its foundation, grew from 4.74 million inhabitants, in 1980, to an official number of 10.02 million citizens in 2000 (Kocaman, 2008, p. 8). The growth of the cities was not only a result of interior migration, but also a result of the population growth, from 44.737 million (1980) to 56.473 million in 1990 and 67.804 million in 2000 (State Institute of Statistics, n.d., p. 45).

This growing and urbanizing population participated in economic wealth on unequal terms. As noted earlier, the open-market policies of the 1980s had led to a growing income gap in the country. In 1994, the poorest 20% of the population earned 4.9% of the nation's income, while the richest 20% of the population earned 54.9% of the country's income (Kepenek & Yentürk, 2007, p. 543). This led to a relatively high Gini-Index of 0.49, as compared to 0.366 in the U.S., and 0.268 in Germany.[3]

The proportion of persons officially employed in the economy changed considerably between 1980 and 2000, reflecting shifts in the structure of the Turkish economy. In Table 2.4 we capture the most important indicators of this development. While employment in services almost doubled, the absolute figures for agriculture mostly remained stable and hence faced a drop in the proportion within total employment.

Developments in the Educational Sector

The stable number of agricultural workers who usually did not need any formal education, and the growth of services with higher expectations toward

Table 2.4 Structure of Turkish economy, 1980–2000

Census year	Total employed	Agriculture		Industry		Construction		Services		Activities not adequately defined	
		Number	%	Number	%	Number	%	Number	%	Number	%
1980	18,522,322	11,104,501	60	2,140,887	11.6	765,072	4.1	4,335,230	23.4	176,632	1
1990	23,381,893	12,547,796	53.7	2,992,864	12.8	1,184,242	5.1	6,515,508	27.9	141,483	0.6
2000	25,997,141	12,576,827	48.4	3,470,360	13.3	1,196,246	4.6	8,719,693	33.5	34,015	0.1

Source: State Institute of Statistics (n.d., p. 55).

Table 2.5 Literacy and educational level of adult population, 1980–2000, in percentage

Census year	Illiterate	Literate but no school completed	Completed school			
			Primary school	Junior high school or comparable vocational school	High school or comparable vocational school	Higher education
Total						
1980	43.77	8.15	35.65	3.79	5.03	3.60
1990	26.72	5.66	48.29	5.78	8.47	5.08
2000	17.25	6.40	47.77	8.23	12.55	7.80
Male						
1980	24.84	10.74	46.75	5.39	6.61	5.68
1990	13.21	5.69	55.00	7.94	10.83	7.32
2000	7.02	5.26	50.29	11.19	16.01	10.23
Female						
1980	62.41	5.59	24.73	2.22	3.48	1.56
1990	40.21	5.63	41.59	3.63	6.11	2.83
2000	27.39	7.52	45.27	5.31	9.12	5.39

Source: State Institute of Statistics (n.d., p. 51).

educational degrees were also reflected in the population's literacy rates and education levels. Table 2.5 provides information on the changes among the population aged 25 and above between 1980 and 2000.

Although the proportion of illiterates in society was considerably reduced, there remained a considerable number of people who did not know how to read or write. At the same time, the education level of an increasing proportion of the population grew; however, it is behind this relatively slow growth that lay the quantitative problems of the Turkish educational sector: Schooling had to be provided for an ever-growing population. Disparities between men and women, but also—as we see later—between regions and social classes had to be tackled.

In spite of the migration from rural to urban areas and the enormous population growth, the educational sector succeeded in catering for an ever-increasing portion of children. Whereas in 1980/1981 7.9 million pupils were enrolled, 11.2 million pupils were educated in 1994/1995, with numbers rising to 13.4 million in 2002/2003 (MoNE, 2006, pp. 4–7; MoNE, 2010, pp. 11–12; our own calculations). While the gross enrollment rates for primary education had been high since 1970, secondary and high school enrollment considerably grew

Table 2.6 Gross enrollment rates (percentage of the respective age group), 1980–2000

Type of school	1980/1981	1990/1991	2000/2001
Primary school	97.7	102.0	100.7
Secondary school	40.6	60.3	
High school	28.4	38.5	64.0
Higher education	6.4	15.7	28.0

Source: DTP (2013).

only since 1980. In 1997, primary and lower secondary schools were merged, and instruction from grade 1 through 8 became compulsory. Table 2.6 shows the growth in gross enrollment rates between 1980 and 2000.

The massive expansion of the educational sector was accompanied by increasing expectations of employers toward employees' educational attainments, manifested in the sectoral distribution of educational degrees: Between 1980 and 2000, for instance, the rate of illiterates in agriculture declined from 46.5% to 23.1%. In the productive sector, the illiterate rate fell from 9.3% to 1.5%, while between 1980 and 2000 the rate of high school graduates rose from 7.6% to 21.3%. In the financial sector, during the same period, the rate of high school graduates rose from 35.6% to 39.5%, and the number of university graduates went from 25.5% to 42.1% (Kepenek & Yentürk, 2007, pp. 492–493). On one hand, these figures show that the qualification of the workforce in Turkey has continually and—in some sectors—considerably improved since 1980; on the other hand, these figures also imply that the respective educational degrees became a necessary qualification for obtaining job positions in these sectors.

The growing demand for qualified staff, and the deteriorating income of blue-collar workers, low-rank employees, and civil servants became an important background for the widespread conviction that education was an important means of maintaining or fostering one's social position. As inquiries into the return to education in Turkey reveal, educational degrees had a significant effect on wages, "monetary returns to a year of university education" being "higher than that at other levels of education by a large margin" (Tansel & Bircan, 2008, p. 8). For example, in 1994, a male employee with a middle school degree earned 8.28% (females: 14.38%) more than a primary school graduate; a male high school graduate earned 18.83% (females: 42.94%) more than a middle school graduate, and a male with a 4-year university degree earned 16.6% (females: 41.17%) more than a high school graduate (Tansel, 2010, pp. 21–22).

The institutionalized features of education, hence, were changed after 1980. While before this period members of society were expected to have

basic (primary) education (and had expected this expectation), this reciprocally typified expectation then constantly increased. As an institution, education became synonymous with secondary or even tertiary education.

Since 1980, the state answered the growing importance of education for
social positioning by diversifying and part-privatizing the educational sector as
well as by channeling passages between educational organizations on the basis
of standardized central exams. This becomes particularly evident if one looks at
the transition from secondary to tertiary education: With the rising number of
high school graduates, an increasing number of people tried to attend university.
While in "the 1960s the acceptance rate to higher education was around 75%,
it deteriorated to below 15% in the beginning of the 1980s" (Özoğlu, 2011,
p. 5). In 1990, only 20% of all applicants were able to find a place in higher
education (including applied universities and open education facilities), a ratio
that grew to 27.9% in 1995 and 31.2% in 2000 (MEB, 2012, pp. 65–75).

Access to one of the growing but chronically insufficient number of universities was subjected to a centralized exam, for which many—albeit not all—
students prepared through private tutoring or instructional courses. The
number of course participants grew from 101,703 in 1980 to 188,407 in
1990 and 556,282 in 2000 (Tansel & Bircan, 2008, p. 29). As a survey study
conducted in 2002 revealed, participation in university preparatory courses
varied considerably among different income groups (Table 2.7).

As Table 2.7 shows, while far less than half of the students whose parents
earned less than 500 million Turkish Liras (TL) were enrolled in preparatory
courses, enrollment for those with a family income of more than 750 million TL
reached around 70% and more. Still, it is important to note that the majority of
all private tutoring students came from poor households, indicating the hopes
and importance accorded to success in education, even in these families. The

Table 2.7 Percentages of students who receive private instruction by income levels of the
households

Income level (Turkish liras)	Number of observations	No private tutoring %	Private tutoring %
<250 million	46,533	68.54	31.46
250–500 million	47,314	53.10	46.90
500–750 million	14,333	38.37	61.63
750 million–1 billion	5671	30.56	69.44
1–1.5 billion	2175	28.46	71.54
1.5–2 billion	967	28.65	71.35
>2 billion	1114	24.33	75.67
Missing	1893	70.95	29.05
Total in numbers	120,000		

Source: Tansel and Bircan (2005, p. 18).

reason for 24–28% of middle class and rich students not participating in private tutoring remains unclear, but may be related to the discrepant quality of high school education.

After 1980, an informal hierarchy of public high schools had emerged (Ercan, 1999, p. 33). These schools significantly varied in their focus (including a large variety of vocational high schools), in their equipment and teaching staff, as well as in their prestige. This informal hierarchy was also based on geographical location: Prestigious high schools were located in urban middle-class districts, whereas high schools which offered only few educational opportunities were to be found in poor quarters and in the countryside. This is because the liberal politics, set-up in interior migration and the economy increased socio-economic gentrification in the big cities, which at the same time resulted in a differentiation of the quality of education according to space.[4] Together with the social differences, which existed even prior to 1980, the discrepancies in opportunities between state schools (Ünal et al., 2010) grew when, as a result of neoliberal politics, the financing of state schools was partly transferred to parents and local resources (Karapehlivan, 2010). The national entrance exams, as well as international performance tests, give evidence for these discrepancies (EARGED, 2010). The informal hierarchy was predominantly manifested in the respective high school graduate's average success rate in the university entrance exams. For instance, in 1990, 89.9% of those finishing a "science high school" and 70.2% from the "Anatolian" high schools won the right to enter university, against only 21.9% from "ordinary high schools" and 16.6% from vocational high schools (MEB, 2012, 65). In 2000, the ratio of those from ordinary and vocational high schools fell to 14.1% and 16.4%, respectively, while those from Anatolian and science high schools remained high, at 66.7% and 78.5%, respectively. At the same time, one must keep in mind that in the year 2000, science high schools catered for far less than 1% of all high school students, and Anatolian high schools for less than 5% of the total high school population (MEB, 2012, p. 75).

In addition to public high schools, private high schools were opened in the 1980s, catering to 4.2–4.4% of all students in general high schools (nonvocational) between 1995 and 2001 (MoNE, 2008, pp. 6–7). There are, however, indications to high variations between provinces, with high rates in Istanbul and other metropolises, and very low rates or no private high schools in more rural provinces (ERG 2011, pp. 11–34). Private high schools offered a considerably higher chance of successfully passing the university entrance exam: In 1990, 66.2% of all private high school new graduates entered university study programs. The informal hierarchy of high schools then also captured the private facilities; subsequently, the success rate of students graduating from private general high schools fell to around 35% in the 1990s, only to rise again to 48.8% in 2000. Private science high schools, however, kept a high success rate of above 65% in the 1990s, increasing to 79.5% in 2000 (MEB, 2012, pp. 65–75).

The discrepancies in the success of students from the various high schools; that is, the disparities in their access to university study programs may be explained by the quality of education received in their respective high schools. However, attention should also be drawn to the fact that these high schools recruit their students very selectively. Since the 1990s, centralized exams were organized regulating access to the great variety of available high schools; this enabled the most prestigious high schools, most importantly the science high schools and Anatolian high schools, to attract the best students. In 2003, for instance, 48.23% of students who were ranked among the first percentile in the high school entrance exams chose to attend a science high school, and 47.28% enrolled in an Anatolian high school (MEB, 2012, p. 12). Thus, the competition that had started with university entrance exams also affected—slowly but surely—lower levels of education. The informal hierarchy of high schools inevitably motivated pupils (and their parents) to enhance their entrance exam preparation. As a result, private tutoring courses in which students were also prepared for high school entrance exams emerged in the late 1990s. As we show in chapters 5 and 6, this also affected primary education and the introduction of a new curriculum.

The expansion of public education and the integration of ever-wider social groups were only scarcely accompanied by discussions regarding equality in education. If one compares this to central Europe and the U.S., issues like equality of opportunities and positive discrimination were only raised by small circles, while in the ministry and in successive governments education was rather discussed under the headings of ideological formation and economic development.

Another feature of inequality that has to be discussed separately is the boom of imam and preacher middle and high schools, which gradually evolved as an alternative educational path, at least since girls were allowed to enroll (from 1976) and graduates could pursue education in all academic disciplines (after 1980) (Gökaçtı 2005, pp. 178–250). Therefore, if not an entire educational sector, they constituted an educational institution that was separate from the laicist institutions which, since the foundation of the republic, had made up the entire educational sector (Table 2.8).

Table 2.8 Number of students in imam and preacher schools (middle and high school)

School year	Number of students	
	Middle school	*High school*
1981/1982	147,071	69,793
1990/1991	209,377	100,176
1996/1997	318,775	192,727
2000/2001	–	91,620

Source: Çakır et al. (2004, pp. 67–68).

With the growing number of high school students, the imam and preacher schools were able to increase their share of all high school students up to 13% in 1997 (Akşit & Çoşkun, 2004). These schools, however, were also seen as the "backyard" of the Islamic party (Akşin, 2004, p. 172), an accusation that in 1997 was part of a major political upheaval in the Turkish society, which included a military intervention and subsequently led to constraints for this type of schools, causing a significant drop in enrollment numbers (Çakır et al., 2004, pp. 11–12).

With regard to school syllabi, the ideological mission of the military coup of 1980 had its effects on education. Conservative ideologies were used to foster social cohesion (İnal, 2004), and the eclectic "Turkish-Islamic Synthesis" was turned into a semi-official ideology, entering school instruction and school books (Copeaux, 2000). A concrete example of the ideological changes was a report by the State Planning Organization, issued in 1983, in which religion was regarded as an element ensuring national security (DPT, 1983). Accordingly, all subjects in schools were to be taught in harmony with religious views. One of the most obvious effects of the growing conservative outlook on education was manifested in science subjects, such as, in the teaching of the evolution theory, for instance (Öztürkler, 2005). Moreover, religious education in primary and lower secondary schools was made compulsory (Gökaçtı, 2005).

Political Instability in the 1990s

In spite of the military-inspired ideological climate (and the restrictive constitution) toward the end of the 1980s, most of the pre-coup politicians and their parties had been able to enter the political arena again. "Given Özal's failure to curb inflation or to ameliorate the country's ailing economy as he had promised" (Ahmad, 2003, p. 198), his Motherland Party rapidly lost the confidence of voters, and, in the 1991 early elections, its majority of seats in parliament. The elections brought into the parliament two conservative, two left-of-center, and one Islamist party, as well as some members of a radical right party and Kurdish politicians. Although no party had a majority on its own, the "True Path Party" (TPP), led by Süleyman Demirel, was the biggest. From 1991 until the next elections, in December 1995, several successive coalition governments were formed between conservative and social democrat parties. With varying decisiveness and success, these governments took steps in the democratization of the political system, including steps regarding human rights issues (Tanör, 2004, pp. 90–107; Zürcher, 2005, pp. 292–298).

The coalition governments were not successful in pacifying the violent conflict with the Kurdish movement, which had already started in 1984 but gained momentum in the 1990s. Oppression by the state, including military warfare as well as illegal killings, on one hand, and terrorist acts by the Kurdish Workers' Party (PKK), conversely, reciprocally intensified. Successive

Kurdish parties were closed down; some of their members in parliament lost immunity and were convicted to long prison sentences.

The economic policy of the coalition governments did not significantly deviate from the path taken by the military regime and the Motherland Party governments of the 1980s. In spite of its vows to liberalize markets, it had difficulties in privatizing state-owned industries and in attracting foreign capital (Tanör, 2004, pp. 90–107; Zürcher, 2005, pp. 292–298). In the long run, this failure in interior and economic policy delegitimized both conservative and social democrat parties, pushing voters to the Islamist "Welfare Party" of Necmettin Erbakan. The latter "successfully united around a politics of identity both those who lost and those who gained from globalization and from the 'neo-liberal' restructuring of the economy in the post-1980 period" (Gülalp, 2001, pp. 440–441). The party was able to rely on "Islamic networks" (Buğra, 2002, p. 127) and promoted "private initiative," but also a so-called just order for the economy (Gülalp, 1999, pp. 27–28).

In the local elections of March 1994, the Welfare Party turned out as the third biggest party. Moreover, it succeeded in taking over the mayor's office from the social democrats in Ankara as well as in Istanbul, where Recep Tayyip Erdoğan was elected mayor. In the general elections of 1995, the Welfare Party received the most votes, leaving two conservative and two left-of-center parties behind. After long coalition negotiations, a government under Prime Minister Erbakan was formed with the TPP (Akşin, 2004, pp. 167–169). "In its first months, however, the new cabinet (in which sensitive posts such as internal affairs, foreign affairs and economy were manned by people from the 'secular' TPP) went out of its way to avoid confrontation and acquire respectability" (Zürcher, 2005, p. 299). After the coalition stabilized and the Welfare Party received a high 30% in the midterm elections, the Islamists responded to the pressure of more radical supporters and started to display a more radical attitude (Gülalp, 1999, pp. 38–39).

On more symbolic level, some developments then gave rise to worries about the laicist nature of the state, such as the attempt to improve diplomatic relations with Islamic countries and the growing number of imam and preacher schools (see earlier). The military used these worries as an authorization to once again severely interfere with politics. During a Security Council meeting on February 28, 1997, the military forced the civilian government to adopt a package of measures that was clearly directed against the interests of the Welfare Party. This was primarily an attempt to remove members of the Islamic movement from the state apparatus (as with most governments, Erbakan's coalition, too, had been very proficient at giving out ministerial positions to as many followers as possible) or to prevent them from entering it. To this end, the number of imam and preacher schools was to be reduced and, most importantly, they were to be limited to the upper secondary school level. These events of 1997 brought down the Erbakan government; in 1998 his Welfare Party was banned, and Erbakan was excluded from political activity for 5 years.

Economy in the 1990s

The gradual turn from an ISI policy to an open-market policy started in the 1980s and affected the economy in very different ways, with variations in time and economic criteria. Export growth, supported by export promotion, was quite successful in the 1980s but "did not last in the 1990s" (Eder, 2001, p. 192). At the same time, the attractiveness of Turkey for foreign financial investment did not grow in the 1990s, due to competition from other countries which had opened their markets in the meantime. The already high Turkish trade deficit "grew extraordinarily" in 1996, in spite of measures taken in 1994 (Kepenek & Yentürk, 2007, p. 585). All in all, Turkey had followed a very peculiar liberalization policy:

> In essence, Turkey's liberalization did not transform the behavior of economic groups that have long relied on import substitution policies. Instead, a new export elite began to prosper largely because of export subsidies and export promotion schemes. Side payments to various interest groups, such as subsidies for the agricultural elite and industrial incentives for various industrial groups, as well as the lowering of import tariffs on certain goods, were all crucial for building various large electoral coalitions for successive governments in the 1980s and 1990s.
>
> (Eder, 2001, p. 203)

Along with the new export elites—and in some cases as an overlapping phenomenon—the liberalization of markets created new opportunities for small- and middle-sized businesses. As Buğra (2002, p. 113) summarized, the "new logic of 'flexible production'" led to a "decreasing role" of the "nation-state" and "interest associations" such as trade unions. Furthermore, it led to "trends toward descaling, downsizing and decentralization of business firms and increasing significance of small and medium enterprises" as well as to an "increasing significance of international forces of competition implying the emphasis of export production and opening up to the world market" (Buğra, 2002, p. 113). The growth was significant between 1992 and 2002, especially in enterprises with between 10 and 250 employees.

While the employment figures of large businesses did not even double in this decade, the same figures for smaller businesses nearly tripled (TÜİK, 2006, p. 4). In contrast to big businesses, which were predominantly organized through the Turkish Industrialists' and Businessmen's Association (TÜSİAD), many of the newly emerging small- and middle-sized enterprises became members of the Independent Industrialists and Businessmen's Association (MÜSİAD) founded in 1990 (Gülalp, 2001, pp. 439–440). This association of pious businessmen gained importance not only in the economy, but also in the political realm (see later).

In contrast to the export elites and small- and middle-sized businesses, employed persons faced huge financial instability during the 1990s. Changing from year to year, income showed significant gains, at 109.5%, as well as losses, at 57.4%. Moreover, the wages of civil servants and workers sometimes were quite disparate: In 1991, for instance, workers' wages grew by about 100%, whereas civil servants only received an additional 18.3% (Kepenek & Yentürk, 2007, p. 511). Membership in trade unions and number of strikes continued at the same low level as they were after the military coup (pp. 520–521).

The financial situation of the state was increasingly deteriorating. The sale of state industries was supposed to support the increasingly indebted—due to, among other things, a reduction of corporate taxes—government. Nevertheless, Turkey's foreign debt continued to increase. The IMF made further loans, contingent upon political and economic conditions. In 1999 a stability program, according to the terms of the IMF, was agreed upon, aimed at reducing the galloping inflation (Boratav, 2004, p. 198), making it "clearly evident that the proposed reforms and the measures to end the imbalances were based on orthodox stability policies and the classic IMF recipes" (Kepenek & Yentürk, 2007, p. 587). The structural provisions foreseen in this program (especially those concerning the banking sector) were not implemented in the following 11 months and led the IMF and private investors to suspect that the government did not back them. This caused a liquidity crisis of both the state and the banks in the winter of 2000/2001, with devastating effects on the real economy and causing a huge devaluation of the Turkish Lira (Kepenek & Yentürk, 2007, pp. 592–594). After the crisis, Kemal Derviş, a former vice president of the World Bank, was appointed minister of economy and subsequently oriented his policy according to the IMF (Boratav, 2004, pp. 230–231).

The Rise of the Justice and Development Party

After the coalition government, under Islamist Necmettin Erbakan, was brought down in 1997 by the military (in what has been called a "post-modern coup d'état" in Turkey), a coalition of a left-of-center and a conservative party ruled the country. This government predominantly occupied itself with implementing the measures imposed by the military and with rescuing the troubled economy. Only the party on the left, led by political veteran Bülent Ecevit, profited from these policies—and the surprising arrest of the Kurdish separatist movement PKK leader, Abdullah Öcalan, in 1999—emerging as the biggest party in the general elections of 1999. Together with an extreme-right party (with whom Ecevit shared a rather nationalist outlook) and the Motherland Party, a government was formed. In addition to its weak performance in economic policy before the financial crisis of 2001, this government was renowned for its failure to organize help during a devastating earthquake in 1999 and for the open rows between the prime minister and the president of the republic. In 2002, with Ecevit's health deteriorating, elections were scheduled for November of the same year (Zürcher, 2005, pp. 300–305).

Meanwhile, there was an attempt to reorganize the Islamist spectrum of the political realm, which had been under heavy pressure by the military and the judiciary. MPs of the outlawed Welfare Party formed the Virtue Party in 1998, a party that could only gain 15.4% of the votes in the elections of 1999. In 2001, the Virtue Party (VP) was accused of being the direct successor of the Welfare Party, and was subsequently closed by the courts. As Zürcher (2005) wrote,

> This brought to head the debates within the VP between the conservatives, who were in favour of a strict Islamist line, and the modernists who wanted to turn the party into a broad right of centre movement and jettison the Islamist rhetoric. When the modernists lost out, they broke away under the leadership of Abdullah Gül and Tayyip Erdoğan to form the Justice and Development Party (Adalet ve Kalkınma Partisi or AK Parti) on 14 August 2001. The Islamists went under a new name yet again, this time that of Party of Happiness (Saadet Partisi).
>
> (p. 304)

Even before its official foundation, the Justice and Development Party's proponents were supported by the MÜSİAD, the Islam–affine association of businessmen (see earlier), which had turned away from the more radical Islamists as it did not want to get into conflict with the state (Doğan, 2010, p. 296). These "small- and midrange enterprisers who live mostly in midsize cities," as well as "young executives" with "university education, especially in technical fields," built the "nucleus" (Insel, 2003, pp. 297–298) of a "new Islamic bourgeoisie" (Yankaya, 2013; see also White, 2002).

Propagating a center-right policy and promising to strive for economic stability, the JDP won 34.28% of the votes in the general elections and, due to a 10% barrier, obtained an absolute majority in the parliament. The only other party to get over this barrier, the RPP, received 19.38% of the votes. The citizens of Turkey, in this way, punished the parties and politicians that had been in government in the previous years. Already fragmented, the other parties on the center-right and center-left fell well below 10%. Ziya Öniş (2007) provided the following reasons for the JDP's landslide victory:

> First, the party has been extremely successful in constituting a cross-class electoral alliance, incorporating into its orbit both winners and losers from the neoliberal globalization process. Business support, notably from small- and medium-sized business units falling under the umbrella of a major nationwide business association [MÜSİAD; the authors], constitutes a crucial element of the JDP's electoral support. Second the strong track record of the JDP's predecessors, the Welfare and the Virtue Parties . . . at the level of the municipal governments is another element of key importance. Third, the failures of the conventional or established parties of either the center-right or the center-left in achieving sustained

and equitable growth, avoiding costly financial crises, and tackling the problem of pervasive corruption have also paved the way for the party's unprecedented electoral success in the recent era.

(p. 207)

Supported by a majority of the parliament, a new government under Prime Minister Abdullah Gül was formed on November 18, 2002. The leader of the JDP, Recep Tayyip Erdoğan, who had been confined to a short prison sentence and to a lifelong ban from politics in 1998, had not been eligible to run for a seat in parliament. Only after a constitutional amendment and a by-election, in an electoral district in which Erdoğan won a seat in parliament, could he become prime minister on March 14, 2003. In the meantime, the initial activities for developing a new primary school curriculum were already under way.

2.5   Change and Primary Education

History is a sequence of social changes, some of which are rather reproductive (that is, first-order changes), and some of which are transformative (that is, second-order changes) (Waks, 2007). Turkish history, and doubtlessly the history of Turkish education, is in no way different. Both in the historical course of education between the late Ottoman Empire and Turkey of 1980 and in the years thereafter we find several significant instances of change on various social levels, from "societal sectors" (Scott & Meyer, 1991) to institutions, organizations, and social milieus. On the background of this complex history of education, what is the rationale to inquire into a curriculum change in primary education that happened to start in the beginning of the new millennium? Before we answer this question, and as a preparation for our answer, we would like to first summarize the major findings of this chapter.

A Selective Summary

It is important to note that the very beginning of a modern, secular educational sector had been incited by the need of the army and the bureaucracy for educated personnel, rather than by the productive sector; in other words,, it was a development incited by the state or state institutions. While religious organizations and institutions of education continued to exist for a while, parallel educational pathways gradually developed, constituting an educational sector on its own and coexisting with the Islamic institutions. The old educational institutions (*Madrasah* and boys' school) were not reformed or transformed; rather, new ones emerged, replacing the old schools only after the foundation of the republic. This transformative change hence evolved as an overlapping of the old and the new, rather than as a blunt rupture (section 2.2).

The end of the old Islamic institutions and the establishment of a single (laicist) educational sector were rendered possible first and foremost by the beginning reign of the Kemalists in the early Turkish Republic (that is, by political forces). However, this completion of the transformative change was not based on discussions within education, and in the following years it became clear that the laicization of the educational sector had been enforced in spite of some social milieus keeping distance from it. Thus, the transformative change in education was not paralleled by a similar change of all parts of society. Since the 1950s, educational policy had to meet the concerns of these milieus, and schools for the education of religious personnel were opened, later even seeming to assume the character of *Madrasah*s; in other words, they began to constitute a distinct educational path.

This, however, is only to be conceived of as one of several differentiations within the educational sector, which also accommodated for the growing demand (on the part of the industry) for vocational education (reproductive variation). While secondary education, on the whole, remained small until 1980, enrollment in primary education (grades 1 to 5) in the same year was nearly total. This implied that by 1980, primary education had become an institutionalized expectation in everyone's life course. The expansion of the educational sector had, at least on the primary level, started to cover entire new generations in Turkey (section 2.3).

Our brief history of the formation and development of an educational sector—from the Ottoman Empire until Turkey in 1980—already revealed that it is impossible to inquire into education without also taking into account other social dynamics. To prepare the argumentative background for the following chapters, in which we will analyze curriculum change in the context of different social dynamics, we therefore broadened our focus when scrutinizing the years between 1980 and 2002 (section 2.4). The interplay between the different societal sectors as well as with social milieus reveals the heterogeneity of social change during that period.

The political and economic dynamics initiated or accelerated by the 1980 coup d'état took their course in different ways, leading to social changes that varied among different sectors of society and its milieus. This already makes clear that even if political rulers aim at social change, it should not be conceived of as only an intentional, linear process. While none of these changes alone were transformative, we can speak of an overall society transformation after 1980, with respective effects on the educational sector. It is, however, difficult to subsume this transformative change under one heading; rather, we should underpin some of its most important results, differentiated according to the respective sector or milieu:

1. While remnants of the military regime endured, the country saw an important political pluralization after 1990. The established parties, however, failed to form stable governments.
2. The liberalization of the economy, though reluctant in the first years, brought the ISI to an end and cleared the way for the emergence of new companies which competed in a globalized market.

3. With the rising demand of the economy for qualified staff, and the economy's growing expectations toward educational degrees, the importance of education for the reproduction of social positions grew.
4. Secondary education was considerably expanded and at the same time differentiated, both within public education and in the slowly growing private education. Whereas previous processes of interior differentiation had catered for various vocational expectations, this time the quality of schooling was differentiated. Subsequently, competition in the educational sector (between pupils and between educational organizations) grew.
5. Population growth, rural exodus, and the guerilla war in the Kurdish region led to an unexampled growth of the cities, most importantly Istanbul. While many interior migrants strived to climb the social ladder, new districts with very poor populations emerged. The gentrification of the cities was paralleled by a correspondent spatial differentiation of school quality.
6. Along with poor milieus of interior migrants, new rich milieus also evolved, which were economically based on the opportunities of the open-market economy. These bourgeois milieus fostered an Islamic outlook and, in the 2000s, supported the Justice and Development Party that formed a new government in 2002.

These trajectories, in sum, resulted in a transformative change of the Turkish society, with consequences for the educational sector, too; the educational sector, most importantly, became more expanded (in secondary education), more differentiated, and more competitive during what can be called a reproductive variation.[5]

Why Inquire Into Primary Education?

Vis-à-vis the massive expansion of secondary and tertiary education, and the expansion of the internal differentiation they experienced during the republican era, primary education at first glance appears to have been nearly unaffected by social and educational change. Indeed, as we pointed out previously, enrollment in primary education has become nearly total since 1980, at the latest, and the only important change on this level of education seems to be its extension from 5 to 8 years in 1997 (see section 2.4). In contrast to a far-from-all-inclusive enrollment in secondary and tertiary education, this (nearly) full coverage of primary education implies that every Turkish citizen, regardless of his or her success in education (or lack thereof), is confronted once in his or her life with the expectations stipulated in the primary school curriculum. Moreover, as for nearly all young citizens primary school is the first educational step provided by state institutions—and even the first state institution with which a child is effectively confronted—primary education is one of the most important devices for introducing children to society and for delivering social messages, tacitly or overtly, to them. What a child has learned and become acquainted to in primary school will most probably carry weight throughout his or her whole educational career. It is in this sense that the primary school curriculum, basic as it is, closely relates education to society and its dynamics.

The introduction of a new curriculum instead of the evolvement or expansion of new educational facilities is a matter of change that involves the broadest range of actors possible, from the minister of education to a parent who helps his or her daughter during homework. Curriculum change allows us to inquire into the dynamics between different levels of society, from the ministry of education to regional education administrations, individual schools, and the milieus connected to them; it is the practices in and between these social entities which influence how the curriculum structures instruction. Inquiring into curriculum change, therefore, allows us to shed light on the inner life of educational organizations without abstracting them from their environment.

Institutions of secondary and tertiary education in Turkey are both externally (into vocational and general schools) and internally differentiated.[6] With these differentiations, institutions appeal to differential social groups and milieus, and hence tend to be more socially segmented. In contrast, primary education includes children from all social milieus, who are—at least ideally—taught according to the same curriculum. Therefore, the contexts in which the primary school curriculum is put into practice vary significantly. As we show in section 2.4, the Turkish society has undergone a transformative change since 1980. However, the various social milieus of Turkey were affected by this change in different ways and directions. If the introduction of a new curriculum, then, is meant to reflect (and promote) social transformation—as we will see in the next chapter—this implies that the pace and direction of change that come with the curriculum may chafe against the various social contexts (differential in their pace and direction of change) in which it is practiced.

For these reasons, our research focuses on the change of the primary school curriculum in Turkey. In the following chapters we inquire into the relation of education and social dynamics by focusing on the curriculum change that started after the new government took power. This curriculum change in primary education will give us the opportunity to study the effects of social change on educational reform and the role of different social and organizational milieus within such processes. Doing so, we seek insight into the "intermeshing of the actions of numerous people" (Elias, 1978, p. 146), albeit divided up into different social entities (institutions, organizations, milieus), and thus carving out the "immanent order" of change (Elias, 1978, p. 149).

Notes

1 Different from secularism in many Western countries, Turkish laicism followed the model of French laicism in highlighting the importance of a strict separation of state and religion. In Turkey, this separation—in contrast to France—was understood as a subordination of religion to the control of the state. In this sense, society (as differentiated

from the state) cannot be laicist; it can only be secularized, that is, withdrawn from the primacy of religion in the conduct of life.

2   The problems faced in enforcing compulsory school education, especially in rural areas and areas which were embossed by corporative and feudal relations (rather than by functional differentiation), allude to the continuity of this alteration in the arrangement of different societal sectors even in 1980. We have to take into regard that the state (due to a lack of infrastructure) had problems in providing access to education for all social groups.

3   From http://stats.oecd.org/Index.aspx?DataSetCode=IDD (retrieved June 24, 2014).

4   As we show in chapter 5, this also influenced the practicing of the new curriculum.

5   For an overview on the institutions of primary, secondary, and tertiary education in Turkey, see the appendix to this volume.

6   This internal differentiation, albeit nearly unstudied in the Turkish context, bears similarities with what in the U.S. context is called "tracking" (Oakes, 2005).

References

Ahmad, F. (2003). *The making of modern Turkey*. London: Routledge.

Akşin, S. (2004). Siyasal Tarih (1995–2003). In S. Akşin et al. (Eds.), *Yakınçağ Türkiye Tarihi 1980–2003* (pp. 163–186). Istanbul: Milliyet.

Akşit, B., & Coşkun, M. K. (2004). Türkiye'nin Modernleşmesi Bağlamında İmam-Hatip Okulları. In Y. Aktay (Ed.), *Modern Türkiye'de Siyasi Düşünce: İslamcılık* (pp. 394–410). Istanbul: İletişim.

Akyüz, Y. (1993). *Türk Eğitim Tarihi*. Ankara: Kolej.

Alexander, J. C. (1990). Differentiation theory: Problems and prospects. In J. C. Alexander & P. Colomy (Eds.), *Differentiation theory and social change* (pp. 1–15). New York: Columbia University Press.

Berger, P. L., & Luckmann, T. (1991). *The social construction of reality*. London: Penguin.

Bohnsack, R. (2014). Habitus, Norm und Identität. In W. Helsper et al. (Eds.), *Schülerhabitus* (pp. 33–55). Wiesbaden: Springer.

Boratav, K. (2004). İktisat Tarihi (1980–2003). In S. Akşin et al. (Eds.), *Yakınçağ Türkiye Tarihi 1980–2003* (pp. 187–245). Istanbul: Milliyet.

Boratav, K. (2005). *1980'li Yıllarda Türkiye'de Sosyal Sınıflar ve Bölüşüm*. Ankara: İmge.

Bourdieu, P., & Passeron, J.-C. (1990). *Reproduction in education, society and culture*. London: Sage.

Buğra, A. (2002). Political Islam in Turkey in historical context: Strengths and weaknesses. In N. Balkan & S. Savran (Eds.), *The politics of permanent crisis* (pp. 107–144). New York: Nova Science.

Çakır, R., Bozan, İ., & Talu, B. (2004). *İmam Hatip Liseleri: Efsaneler ve Gerçekler*. Istanbul: TESEV.

Copeaux, E. (2000). *Tarih Ders Kitaplarında (1931–1993) Türk Tarih Tezinden Türk-İslam Sentezine*. Istanbul: Tarih Vakfı Yurt Yayınları.

Cuban, L. (1992). Curriculum stability and change. In P. W. Jackson (Ed.), *Handbook of research on curriculum* (pp. 216–247). New York: Macmillan.

Doğan, A. E. (2010). İslamcı Sermayenin Gelişme Dinamikleri ve 28 Şubat Süreci. In İ. Uzgel & B. Duru (Eds.), *AKP Kitabı* (pp. 283–306). Ankara: Phoenix.

DPT. (1983). *Milli Kültür Özel İhtisas Komisyonu Raporu*. Ankara: DTP.

DTP. (2013). *DPT Ekonomik ve Sosyal Göstergeler (1950–2001)*. Retrieved January 20, 2013, from http://www.dpt.gov.tr/PortalDesign/PortalControls/WebIcerikGosterim. aspx? 1Enc=83D5A6FF03C7B4FC036A27D8D4D6C986

EARGED (T. C. Milli Eğitim Bakanlığı Eğitimi Araştırma ve Geliştirme Dairesi Başkanlığı). (2010). *PISA 2009 Projesi Ulusal Ön Raporu.* Ankara: MoNE.

Eder, M. (2001). The Challenge of Globalization and Turkey's Changing Political Economy. In B. Rubin & K. Kirişci (Eds.), *Turkey in world politics* (pp. 189–215). Boulder, CO: Lynne Rienner.

Eisenstadt, S. (1968). Transformation of social, political, and cultural orders in modernization. In *Social change* (pp. 256–276). Boston: Little, Brown.

Elias, N. (1978). *What is sociology.* London: Hutchinson.

Elias, N. (2010). *The civilizing process.* London: Blackwell.

Ercan, F. (1999). 1980'lerde Eğitim sisteminin yeniden yapılanması: Küreselleşme ve neoliberal eğitim politikaları. In F. Gök (Ed.), *75 Yılda Eğitim* (pp. 23–38). Istanbul: Tarih Vakfı Yayınları.

ERG (Eğitim Reformu Girişimi). (2011). *Eğitim İzleme Raporu 2010.* Istanbul: Author.

Fortna, B. (2002). *The imperial classroom: Islam, the state, and education in the late Ottoman Empire.* Oxford: Oxford University Press.

Gök, F. (1999). 75 Yılda insan yetiştirme eğitim ve devlet. In F. Gök (Eds.), *75 Yılda Eğitim* (pp. 1–8). Istanbul: Tarih Vakfı Yayınları.

Gök, F. (2007). The History and Development of Turkish Education. In M. Carlson, A. Rabo, & F. Gök (Eds.), *Transactions: Vol. 18. Education in "Multicultural" Societies* (pp. 247–255). Istanbul: Swedish Research Institute in Istanbul.

Gökaçtı, M. A. (2005). *Türkiye'de Din Eğitimi ve İmam Hatipler.* Istanbul: İletişim.

Gülalp, H. (1999). Political Islam in Turkey: The rise and fall of the Refah Party. *The Muslim World, 89,* 22–41.

Gülalp, H. (2001). Globalization and political Islam: The social bases of Turkey's Welfare Party. *International Journal of Middle East Studies, 33,* 433–448.

Günlü, R. (2008). Vocational education and labor market integration in Turkey. In A.-M. Nohl, A. Akkoyunlu-Wigley, & S. Wigley (Eds.), *Education in Turkey* (pp. 107–130). New York: Waxmann.

Hacettepe (Hacettepe Universitesi Nüfus Etütleri Enstitüsü). (2006). *Türkiye Göç ve Yerinden Olmuş Nüfus Araştırması.* Ankara: İsmat.

İnal, K. (2004). *Eğitim ve İktidar. Türkiye'de Ders Kitaplarında Demokratik ve Milliyetçi Değerler.* Ankara: Ütopya.

İnal, K. (2008). *Eğitim ve İdeoloji.* Istanbul: Kalkedon.

Insel, A. (2003). The AKP and normalizing democracy in Turkey. *South Atlantic Quarterly, 102*(2–3), 293–308.

Kafadar, O. (1997). *Türk Eğitim Düşüncesinde Batılılaşma.* Ankara: Vadi.

Kafadar, O. (2002). Cumhuriyet Dönemi Eğitim Tartışmaları. In T. Bora & M. Gültekingil (Eds.), *Modernleşme ve Batıcılık* (pp. 351–381). Istanbul: İletişim.

Karapehlivan, F. (2010). *Restructuring state-education relationship and its implications on the right to education* (Unpublished doctoral thesis). University of Essex.

Kepenek, Y., & Yentürk, N. (2007). *Türkiye Ekonomisi.* Istanbul: Remzi.

Koçak, C. (2003). Siyasal Tarih (1923–1950). In S. Akşin et al. (Eds.), *Yakınçağ Türkiye Tarihi 1908–1980* (pp. 127–213). Istanbul: Milliyet.

Kocaman, T. (2008). *Türkiye'de İç Göçler ve Göç Edenlerin Nitelikleri (1965–2000).* Ankara.

Kohli, M. (2007). The institutionalization of the life course: Looking back to look ahead. *Research in Human Development, 4,* 253–271.

Kuper, H., & Thiel, F. (2009). Erziehungswissenschaftliche Institutionen und Organisationsforschung. In R. Tippelt & B. Schmidt (Eds.), *Handbuch Bildungsforschung* (2nd ed., pp. 483–498). Wiesbaden: VS.

Luhmann, N. (1964). *Funktionen und Folgen formaler Organisation*. Berlin: de Gruyter.

Mannheim, K. (1972). The problem of generations. In P. Altbach & R. Laufer (Eds.), *The New Pilgrims* (pp. 101–138). New York: McKay.

Matuz, J. (1985). *Das Osmanische Reich—Grundlinien seiner Geschichte*. Darmstadt: Wissenschaftliche Buchgesellschaft.

MEB (Milli Eğitim Bakanlığı). (2012). *İlköğretimden Ortaöğretime Ortaöğretimden Yükseköğretime Geçiş Analizi*. Ankara: MoNE.

MoNE (Ministry of National Education). (2006). *Türkiye Eğitim İstatistikleri 2005–2006– Education Statistics of Turkey*. Ankara: MoNE.

MoNE (Ministry of National Education). (2008). *National Education Statistic: Formal Education 2007–2008*. Ankara: MoNE.

MoNE (Ministry of National Education). (2010). *National Education Statistics: Formal Education 2009–2010*. Ankara: Author.

Müller, D. K., & Zymek, B. (1987). *Datenhandbuch zur deutschen Bildungsgeschichte: Vol. 2. 1. Teil: Sozialgeschichte und Statistik des Schulsystems in den Staaten des Deutschen Reiches, 1800–1945*. Göttingen: Vandenhoeck & Ruprecht.

Oakes, J. (2005). *Keeping track*. New Haven, CT: Yale University Press.

Okçabol, R. (1999). Cumhuriyet döneminde yetişkin eğitimi. In F. Gök (Ed.), *75 Yılda Eğitim* (pp. 249–262). Istanbul: Tarih Vafkı Yayınları.

Okçabol, R. (2005). *Türkiye Eğitim Sistemi*. Ankara: Ütopya.

Öniş, Z. (2007). The political economy of Turkey's justice and development party. In H. Yavuz (Ed.), *The emergence of a new Turkey* (pp. 207–234). Salt Lake City: Utah University Press.

Ortmann, G. (2004). *Als Ob. Fiktionen und Organisationen*. Wiesbaden: VS.

Özoğlu, M. (2011). *Özel Dershaneler: Gölge Eğitim Sistemiyle Yüzleşmek*. Ankara: SETA.

Öztürkler, R. N. (2005). *Türkiye'de Biyolojik Evrim Eğitiminin Sosyolojik Bir Değerlendirmesi* (Unpublished master's thesis). Ankara Üniversitesi Eğitim Bilimleri Enstitüsü.

Sakaoğlu, N. (1992). *Cumhuriyet Dönemi Eğitim Tarihi*. Istanbul: İletişim.

Scott, W. R., & Meyer, J. W. (1991). The organization of societal sectors: Propositions and early evidence. In W. W. Powell & P. J. DiMaggio (Eds.), *The new institutionalism in organizational analysis* (pp. 108–140). Chicago: University of Chicago Press.

Somel, S. A. (2001). *The modernization of public education in the Ottoman Empire 1839– 1908—Islamization, autocracy and discipline*. Leiden: Brill.

State Institute of Statistics. (n.d.). *2000 Census of Population—Social and economic characteristics of population*. Ankara: Author.

Tanör, B. (2004). Siyasal Tarih (1980–1995). In S. Akşin et al. (Eds.), *Yakınçağ Türkiye Tarihi 1980–2003* (pp. 27–162). Istanbul: Milliyet.

Tansel, A., & Bircan, F. (2005). *Effect of private tutoring on university entrance examination performance in Turkey* (Discussion Paper No. 1609). Bonn: IZA.

Tansel, A., & Bircan, F. (2008). *Private supplementary tutoring in Turkey—Recent evidence on its recent aspects* (Working Paper in Economics No. 08/02). Ankara: ERC.

Tansel, A. (2010). *Changing returns to education for men and women in a developing country: Turkey, 1994–2005*. Unpublished manuscript.

Taşçı Günlü, S. (2008). Adult literacy campaigns and nation building. In A.-M. Nohl, A. Akkoyunlu-Wigley, & S. Wigley (Eds.), *Education in Turkey* (pp. 175–194). New York: Waxmann.

Tönnies, F. (2011). *Community and society*. Mineola, NY: Dover.

TÜİK (Türkiye İstatistik Kurumu). (2006). *2002 Genel Sanayi ve İşyerleri Sayımı General Census of Industry and Business Establishments 2002*. Ankara: Author.

TÜİK (Türkiye İstatistik Kurumu). (2007). *İstatistik Göstergeler—Istatistical Indicators 1923–2006.* Ankara: Author.

Ünal, I., Özsoy, S., Yıldız, A., Güngör, S., Aylar, E., & Çankaya, D. (2010). *Eğitimde Toplumsal Ayrışma.* Ankara: Ankara Üniversitesi.

Üstel, F. (2004). *"Makbul Vatandaş" ın Peşinde—II. Meşrutiyet'ten Bugüne Vatandaşlık Eğitimi.* Istanbul: İletişim.

Waks, L. J. (2007). The concept of fundamental educational change. *Educational Theory, 57,* 277–295.

Warth, A. (2011). Freiwilliges Engagement in der Jugendarbeit- Zur Entwicklung eines neuen Sozialisationskontextes in der Türkei. In A.-M. Nohl & B. Pusch (Eds.), *Bildung und gesellschaftlicher Wandel in der Türkei* (pp. 121–146). Würzburg: Ergon.

Watzlawick, P., Weakland, J., & Fisch, R. (1974). *Change: Principles of problem formation and problem resolution.* New York: Norton.

White, J. B. (2002). *Islamist mobilization in Turkey: A study in vernacular politics.* Seattle: University of Washington Press.

Yankaya, D. (2013). *La nouvelle bourgeoisie islamique: le modèle turc.* Paris: Presses Universitaires de France.

Zürcher, J. E. (2005). *Turkey—A modern history* (3rd ed.). London: I. B. Tauris.

Zymek, B. (2008). Geschichte des Schulwesens und des Lehrerberufs. In W. Helsper & J. Böhme (Eds.), *Handbuch der Schulforschung* (pp. 203–237). Wiesbaden: VS.

3   Curriculum Making

With the new curriculum we have moved from a strictly behavioristic curriculum to a cognitive, constructivist approach. [. . .] The standards of the European Union have been taken into account. Eight skills deficient among our children have been identified. Those are critical thinking, problem solving, scientific inquiry, creative thinking, entrepreneurialism, communication, use of information technologies, and the skill to nicely use the Turkish language.[1]

With these words the Turkish minister of national education, Hüseyin Çelik, announced on August 11, 2004, that a new primary school curriculum had been developed and that after a year of piloting it was due to be implemented in the entire country, starting from 2005/2006. Along with references to the content and approach of the new curriculum, the minister of education's press statement implied that the curriculum development was a technical matter accomplished without any problems and according to the initial plans. As we reveal in this chapter, this statement blurs the complicated process of the curriculum change, which encountered numerous obstacles and at times even risked failing.

   The complicated character of curriculum development is certainly not unique to the Turkish case. As numerous inquiries have convincingly shown, writing a new curriculum and transferring it to practical instruction are polymorphic issues that are difficult to accomplish (by the actors involved) and also challenging to understand (by their scientific observers). Following up our general discussion of *change* in section 2.1, in section 3.1 we discuss different approaches to understanding curriculum change, taking into consideration both basic theoretical concepts and methodologies. This also gives us the opportunity to introduce the reader to our own approach, which we use in this and the following chapters. Drawing on a broad range of documents and on expert interviews conducted with a variety of actors, we then scrutinize the curriculum development process in Turkey in section 3.2. Our focus here will be on the organization of the curriculum, that is, on the question of how the new curriculum was actually brought into being until its adoption as a formal rule by the ministry of education. After a short look at the content and approach of the new curriculum (section 3.3), we finally summarize the theoretical output and identify questions that remain open (section 3.4).

3.1 Studying Curriculum Change: Theoretical and Methodological Considerations

When the minister for national education stated that the "standards of the European Union have been taken into account," he indicated that the Turkish curriculum reform needs to be analyzed in a wider, European or even global frame of curriculum development (Altinyelken, 2010, p. 19). In Comparative Education, such processes are discussed under the headword "educational transfer," a concept that "can be defined as the movement of educational ideas, institutions or practices across international borders" (Beech, 2006, p. 1). "Educational transfer" is a broad concept which many scholars conceive of as a continuum (Phillips & Ochs, 2004; Johnson, 2006), extending from the coercive mechanism of "imposition" to the "diffusion of a generic global educational culture" (Perry & Tor, 2008, pp. 519–520, 510).

While imposition implies that the entity that takes over educational ideas, institutions, or practices is not sovereign, being under the rule of another entity instead (such as in colonialism, for instance; cf. Johnson, 2006), educational borrowing refers to the "conscious adoption in one context of policy observed in another" (Phillips & Ochs, 2004, p. 774), thus perceiving the receiving entity as an actor engaged in a "deliberate and unidirectional process" (Perry & Tor, 2008, p. 510). During this process, the borrowed policy does not remain unchanged, as "borrowing always implies a decontextualization process in which a model, practice, or discourse is transplanted from its original context and applied to a new one" (Steiner-Khamsi & Quist, 2000, p. 275). During this "application," the "borrowed ideas or practices are resisted, modified or indigenized as they are implemented in the recipient country" (Beech, 2006, p. 9). Therefore, "the process of recontextualization, 'indigenization' or local adaptation, will become key for understanding the educational transfer process" (Steiner-Khamsi & Quist, 2000, p. 275).

Contrary to what one would assume, borrowing "rarely has much to do with the success, however defined, of the institutional realization of particular policies in their countries of origin" (Halpin & Troyna, 1995, p. 304), but often may only function as its legitimization. Refining an old notion in comparative education, Schriewer (2003, p. 276) spoke of an "externalization" in which the fact that the newly introduced policy comes from abroad is used "to provide justification and legitimization." Such a "justificatory performance" (Schriewer, 1988, p. 68) can be observed where countries refer to policies which have gained plausibility throughout the world, and one may ask if the Turkish minister of education predominantly used the "standards of the European Union" for *legitimizing* the curriculum change.

Although there are educational transfers between specific countries (see, e.g., Halpin & Troyna, 1995; Johnson, 2006; Phillips & Ochs, 2004), borrowing is, in many cases, intermingled with the diffusion of educational ideas, institutions, and practices throughout the globe. In Comparative Education, such processes of diffusion are prominently discussed by Meyer and colleagues, who maintained that a world culture of education has been established; this culture, they argued, originated in Western nation-states and became attractive for newly evolving nation-states in other parts of the world. Based on extensive statistical data, they stated that

> Mass schooling made sense in so many contexts because it became a central feature of the Western, and subsequently the world, model of the nation-state and its development. Nation-states expand schooling because they adhere to world models of the organization of sovereignty (the modern state) and the organization of society as composed of individuals (the modern nation).
>
> (Meyer et al., 1992, p. 129)

Thus, this world educational culture does not only pertain to the school, but also includes a general concept of the "modern individual" as a member of the rationally organized society (Boli et al., 1985, p. 158). This whole phenomenon of homogenizing educational ideals and policies has been termed "isomorphism" (Meyer et al., 1997, p. 152); in other words, the emergence of "similar structural patterns worldwide despite divergent social, economic, and political situations" (Hornberg, 2009, p. 246).

However, the works of Meyer and colleagues have come under criticism for several reasons. First, scholars "criticized the disregard of economic and political processes and balances of power" (Hornberg, 2009, p. 247), a point used by Dale (2000, p. 447) to speak of an "educational agenda" driven by "political-economic factors" rather than a fairly innocent "educational culture." Secondly, Meyer and colleagues have confined their research to official statements, curricula, and education policies. As Dale (1999) asserted, "their focus is 'curriculum categories,' rather than 'what is taught'" (p. 13). Referring to the proponents of the world education culture approach, he added: "Indeed they willingly concede that what is taught may well vary across countries" (p. 13).

Although we are not able to fully cover the international dimension of the process, in our own analyses we seek to take into account political and economic factors that influenced the introduction of the new curriculum in Turkey. Even more importantly, we do not confine our analyses to the intended curriculum, manifested in official documents, but focus on the "taught curriculum" as seen through the eyes of teachers and parents. This brings us back to considering the analysis of the curriculum change itself.

Researching Curriculum Change

The distinction between intended and taught curriculum can be traced back to seminal papers by Cuban (1992, pp. 222–223; Cuban, 1995), who differentiated between "intended," "taught," "learned," "tested," and "historical" curriculum. The *intended* curriculum is composed of the written documents with which the authorities (the state, a district, a single school, etc.) determine the contents and skills to be conferred to children. The *taught* curriculum is "what teachers do (lecture, ask questions, listen, organize classes into groups, etc.) and use (chalk, texts, worksheets, machines, etc.) to present contents, ideas, skills, and attitudes" (Cuban, 1992, p. 222), thus referring to the— sometimes informal—practices in the classroom.[2] The *learned* curriculum usually deviates from what pupils are expected to learn from teachers; for instance, pupils also learn to get along with the teacher and to quickly finish work (irrespective of understanding it). The learned curriculum, hence, must also be differentiated from the *"tested* curriculum" (Cuban, 1995, p. 5; italics added), in which pupils' knowledge and skills are measured—this distinction will become important throughout chapters 5 and 6 of this volume. While the first four types of curriculum originate in the present time of instructional practice, the "historical curriculum" consists of the "formal purposes, official content, buried assumptions about knowledge, the organization and relationships within classrooms, schools, and districts that are inherited." As Cuban (1992) detailed, it "contains the accumulated weight of previous innovations and mandates embedded in a district's or school's standard offerings of subject matter and activities" (p. 223).

These differentiations within the term *curriculum*, which have also been adopted by other scholars (see, among others, Waks, 2003, 2007), give us a useful concept to capture phenomena recurrent in our own empirical analyses.[3] However, they stem from empirical observations only, and have yet to be embedded in a basic theoretical frame. Therefore, in what follows, we revisit Cuban's distinction between different types of the curriculum and reformulate them by drawing on concepts of both institution and organization.

Cuban's consideration of curriculum *change* has been as path-breaking as his distinction of curriculum *types*. To this regard, he drew on the proposition by Watzlawick et al. (1974), which we already discussed in chapter 2, and suggested that there are two types of planned change "First-order . . . changes are intentional efforts to enhance the existing system by correcting deficiencies in policies and practices. Such changes try to make what exists more efficient and effective without disturbing basic organizational features" (Cuban, 1992, p. 218).

While Cuban clearly referred to the organization as the entity which undergoes change, Watzlawick et al. (1974, p. 10) had given a broader definition, stating that this type of—reproductive—change "occurs within a *given system* which itself remains unchanged." "Second-order change," then, "changes the *system* itself" (Watzlawick et al., 1974, p. 10; italics by the authors), it is transformative (see section 2.1), or, as Cuban (1992) put it:

> Second-order, or fundamental, changes seek to alter the essential ways that organizations are put together because of major dissatisfaction with present arrangements. Fundamental changes introduce new goals, structures, and roles that transform familiar ways of performing duties into novel solutions to persistent problems.
>
> (p. 218)

Cuban's definitions are not only limited to the organizational level (for this criticism, see Waks, 2007); he also sees the intended curriculum—for example, "new goals"—as the self-evident starting point of change which then extends to the taught curriculum (that is, "novel solutions").

These limitations, however, give Cuban the chance to offer a coherent explanation for his observation (based upon numerous studies of the American schooling system): While the intended curriculum has recurrently been responsive to societal impulses, and hence has undergone processes of second-order (transformative) change, the taught curriculum has remained remarkably untouched by such pressure and—if at all—only displayed first-order (reproductive) change (Cuban, 1992, p. 232). Schools in a decentralized educational sector like that of the USA are, as he underpinned, "highly vulnerable to" their "environment and must come to terms with it in a series of accommodations and compromises" (p. 239). This implies that schools have to pay utmost attention to their environment's changing expectations and "to satisfy what their constituencies believe is proper for schools" (p. 240).

Although this has been formulated for the case of decentralized schooling, it is also possible to apply the same argument for more centralized school systems (such as that of Turkey), as the overall important point in Cuban's argument is that second-order change in school occurs when there is a respective expectation on the part of the public—be it a district's or a country's constituency. However, as Cuban (1992) observed, this change is limited to the "administration and policy making" (p. 241), while, conversely, the "nature of teaching" is "complex: it is highly personal and seemingly invulnerable to prescriptions imposed from outside the classroom" (p. 239). In other words, as such, transformative (second-order) change accomplished on the part of the administration by adding new goals to the curriculum or totally transforming it, does not necessarily result in a subsequent transformation of instructional practices. This observation by Cuban is confirmed by Tyack and Tobin (1994), who identified *collective* features which resist the pressure for transformative change: The "grammar of schooling" (for instance, the class system), despite a series of reforms, has remained stable for a long time. Popkewitz (1988, p. 82) went as far as seeing the changes made in the official part of schooling as a "social practice of ritual and rhetoric" which "functions to legitimate the ongoing power relations of schools" rather than to change instruction itself.

The authors mentioned earlier explained their empirical observations by referring to the neo-institutionalist arguments offered by John W. Meyer and colleagues, whose work on world educational culture we have already discussed. As Cuban (1992) put it, the "tight coupling" observed between public expectations and changes in the intended curriculum "loosens considerably when it comes to the central core of the system's work: classroom instruction" (p. 240). In New Institutionalism, this "loose coupling" of the official organization from its practices is not seen as a failure of the organization, but as a mechanism by which the organization guarantees operativeness—the organization gains legitimization towards its environment while allowing continuity and autonomy in organizational practices; as Cuban put it: "The decoupling of instruction from administration and policy making achieves an autonomy and isolation that teachers find satisfying" (p. 241).

Although Cuban here draws on a theoretical approach—New Institutionalism—which focuses on the differentiation of institution and organization, he does not systematically take these concepts into account. Accordingly, his paper is rightly criticized because "it runs together the *entities* undergoing change" (Waks, 2007, p. 283; italics in original). According to Waks (2007, pp. 281–289), only a clear distinction of the different levels of education will help to precisely identify processes of change. This criticism gives us the opportunity to further discuss these concepts—which we already touched upon in chapter 2—and to show how we relate our own approach to that of New Institutionalism. Only later will we again attend to Waks's propositions as to how to conceptualize change in education.

Isomorphism With Institutional Environments

Almost parallel to their inquiries into a world educational culture (see earlier), a group of authors in the 1970s began to question theories that view the organization solely as a "rational formal structure" assumed to be "the most effective way to coordinate and control the complex relational networks involved in modern technical or work activities" (Meyer & Rowan, 1977, p. 343). In addition to—and sometimes instead of—technical rationality and efficiency accorded to organizations, these authors pointed to the institutionalized environments in which organizations flourish:

> Organizations are driven to incorporate the practices and procedures defined by prevailing rationalized concepts of organizational work and institutionalized in society. Organizations that do so increase their legitimacy and their survival prospects, independent of the immediate efficacy of the acquired practices and procedures.
>
> (Meyer & Rowan, 1977, p. 340)

Accordingly, this group of authors extended their attention to the role of institutionalization in society, generally (Zucker, 1977), and in education, particularly (Rowan, 1982): Organizations which adopt institutionalized expectations of their environment increase their legitimacy (DiMaggio & Powell, 1983; Meyer & Rowan, 1977)—an argument adopted by the students of curriculum change, whose work we discussed previously. Although one might assume that this is especially the case for organizations in societal sectors such as education, in which the technical output of the organizations' core activities (that is, teaching) is more difficult to assess, Meyer and Rowan (1977) asserted that, in general, the "technical properties of outputs" are not only technical but are themselves "socially defined" (p. 354) and hence subject to institutionalization. In chapters 5 and 6 we attend to mechanisms of output control which, by pretending to be technical in nature, have successfully been socially institutionalized.

Insofar as the institutional environment is relevant for all organizations acting in the same societal sector, an "isomorphism with environmental institutions" can be observed. Organizations

> (a) . . . incorporate elements which are legitimated externally, rather than in terms of efficiency; (b) they employ external or ceremonial assessment criteria to define the value of structural elements; and (c) dependence on externally fixed institutions reduces turbulence and maintains stability.
> (Meyer & Rowan, 1977, pp. 348–349)

However, different mechanisms of isomorphism exist with institutional environments: Along with "mimetic isomorphism," within which organizations observe each other as to how they react towards environmental expectations, and "normative isomorphism," in which standards of an occupation are increasingly defined by its members, "coercive isomorphism results from both formal and informal pressures exerted on organizations by other organizations upon which they are dependent and by cultural expectations in the society within which organizations function" (DiMaggio & Powell, 1983, p. 150). If—as we see in section 3.2—a new curriculum is developed and made compulsory for all schools in the country, this is a 'formal pressure,' thus leading to "coercive isomorphism" (p. 150). At the same time, instructional practices may—as we see in chapters 4 to 6—also be influenced by 'cultural expectations' that are prevalent in society.

Loose and Tight Coupling

Isomorphism with institutional environments does not imply that the organization's practices necessarily change according to formal rules that have been newly developed to answer environmental expectations. As Meyer and Rowan (1977) have observed, "to maintain ceremonial conformity, organizations that reflect institutional rules tend to buffer their formal structures from the uncertainties of technical activities by becoming loosely coupled, building gaps between their formal structures and actual work activities" (pp. 340–341).

This is the mechanism with which Cuban (1992) and other scholars have explained that the intended curriculum changes, while the taught and learned curricula may remain stable. Here, the formal rules of an organization may become "powerful myths" (Meyer & Rowan, 1977, p. 340) to the extent that although they do not effectively alter organizational practices, they still remain unquestioned.

The concept of "loose coupling" goes back to the works of Glassman (1973) and Weick (1976), who underpinned that "coupled events are responsive, but that each event also preserves its own identity and some evidence of its physical or logical separateness" (Weick, 1976, p. 3). Both authors, however, argued that loose coupling is usually accompanied by "tight coupling" (Glassman, 1973, p. 91), leading to a "distribution of tight and loosely coupled systems within any organization" (Weick, 1976, p. 11). Tight coupling, again, implies that there is coherence between environmental expectations and organizational activities, the latter being under effective control of the environment. While Weick (1976) and Glassman (1973) tended to conceive of loose and tight coupling as mutually reinforcing mechanisms, Meyer and Rowan (1977), as well as DiMaggio and Powell (1983), neglecting the importance of tight coupling, have solely concentrated on loosely coupled systems. However, as we see throughout this volume, "the institutional rules governing social action [. . .] have been found to vary in the degree to which they lead either to ceremonial conformity and loose coupling or to real conformity and tight coupling" (Rowan, 2006a, p. 24), especially as far as the educational sector is concerned.

Institution and Organization

Despite their import for research, the concepts of organization and institution are only weakly defined in New Institutionalism. Early works by Meyer and Rowan (1977) and Zucker (1977) referred to Berger and Luckmann's definition, writing that "institutionalized rules are classifications built into society as reciprocated typifications or interpretations" and "may be simply taken for granted or may be supported by public opinion or the force of law" (Meyer & Rowan, 1977, p. 341). While the authors indicated that institutions might be characterized by implicit *or* explicit typifications, Berger and Luckmann (1991) in their original definition, underpinned that these typifications themselves refer to the habitualization of action:

> Institutionalization occurs whenever there is a reciprocal typification of habitualized actions by types of actors. Put differently, any such typification is an institution. What must be stressed is the reciprocity of institutional typifications and the typicality of not only the actions but also

the actors in institutions. The typifications of habitualized actions that constitute institutions are always shared ones. They are available to all members of the particular social group in question, and the institution itself typifies individual actors as well as individual actions. The institution posits that actions of type X will be performed by actors of type X.

(p. 72)

Whereas this definition does not rule out that institutional rules are defined by law or other explicit regulations, it makes clear that the explication of institutional rules (the typification) is only secondary, as it refers to patterned (habitualized) actions that are primordial. In this sense, a law—or a curriculum—newly agreed upon by a parliament or any other authority is not yet an institution; we may speak of it as an institution only if this regulation either typifies already existing habitualized actions or if this explicit regulation *leads* to such a habitualization of action. The reference to existing patterned or habitualized action is also stressed by DiMaggio and Powell (1991), who argued against conventionalist approaches that see institutions as the "outcomes of purposive actions by instrumentally oriented individuals" (p. 8). In this sense, institutions, rather than a matter of choice, are the very basis upon which actors make their choices (see also Zucker, 1977). This is especially the case where the respective typifications are only implicit.

Regarding the quote by Berger and Luckmann, it should be noted that habitualization here does not refer to the milieu-specific "habitus" (Bourdieu, 2010) of the actors, but to more general routines and patterns of action which are located on a level "above" milieus and specific habitus, that is, on a societal level. Furthermore, typification always implies that the respective institutionalized expectations are idealized and do not totally coincide with the action and actors to which they refer; in fact, from case to case they may even be counterfactual (Bohnsack, 2014a).

If we take this definition of institutionalization seriously, then the mechanisms of loose and tight coupling, so aptly reconstructed by New Institutionalists, do not only pertain to phenomena where organizations have taken *institutionalized* rules of their environment into their organizational formal structure, leaving their organizational activities untouched. There may be also other environmental expectations which are not yet institutionalized (but that are formulated as laws and other explicit rules) and which are adopted by the organization, being only loosely coupled with the latter's activities. In particular, those cases in which "formal pressures" are "exerted on organizations by other organizations upon which they are dependent" (DiMaggio & Powell, 1983, p. 150) may not involve institutionalized expectations based on habitualized action. These cases, such as, when a ministry of education imposes a new curriculum on the country's schools, may nevertheless lead to loose coupling. We will have to take this into consideration when examining the relation of the Turkish ministry of education to individual schools.

Although institutions are in many ways connected to *organizations*, it is important to clearly differentiate these concepts (see also section 2.2). While institutions only "restrict and enable" action but cannot be seen as the originator responsible for it, to organizations the "actions and the consequences of action are directly attributed, they are classified as accountable, as responsible" (Ortmann, 2004, p. 25). Thus, organizations can be seen as "corporate" or "collective actors" (Kussau & Brüsemeister, 2007, p. 26; see also Mayntz & Scharpf, 1995, pp. 49–50).

Organizations are characterized by explicit formal rules that define expectations towards the behavior of their members. Such rules must be paid attention to by all those who want to become and remain members of the organization, and turn unspecified actions into those which are attributable to the organization. The "obligations, expectations, rights and resources stated" in the rules,

> pertain neither to concrete contents and situations (but to generalizable 'cases') nor to specific persons, but to positions ('posts'), divisions, departments etc., and finally the corporation itself (e.g. as a legal person) and hence constitute formal relations between positions/organizational units/organizations.
>
> (Ortmann et al., 1997, p. 319)

Actions in the organization become accountable due to the membership role. Membership is a prescinded rule of the organization which renders formalization possible. An expectation toward action, established by a rule, may be "described as formalized if it is covered in a social system by this membership rule, i.e., if there is a clear consensus that the disregard or nonobservance of this expectation contradicts the continuance of the membership" (Luhmann, 1964, p. 38). The membership role detaches those activities in the organization that are defined by formal rules from the erratic motivations of individuals. As long as one wants to remain a member, one will perform the requested actions regardless of whether one is directly motivated to do so. Moreover, the expectation for a specific action is not perceived as a personal imposition on the part of another person, but as "mediated by a system on which the people involved depend on" (Luhmann, 1964, p. 36). In this way, the membership role differentiates between expected behavior that is critical because it is indispensable and other behavior expectations which are not connected to the membership role.

Thus, the formalization of rules made possible by the membership role distinguishes organization from institution. While in institutions expectations are based on the reciprocal typification of action, and actors and may be contravened without any reaction on part of the institution (which is not an actor itself), in organizations nonconformity with rules may be sanctioned by the organization and may be answered by expulsion of the member. The membership to an organization, therefore, is controllable by the actors; both the organization and the individual decide when someone becomes a member. Significantly contrary to other social entities (like milieus)—to which we attend further on—the membership in an organization is obvious, as the limits of the organization (that is, the limit between those who are members and those who are not) can be easily recognized (Luhmann, 1964, p. 35).

Informal Regularities and Organizational Milieus

As formal rules may be only loosely coupled to the organization's practices, it is important to understand how these practices (such as instruction by teachers, for instance) are structured by other elements of the organization, that is, to study "the nature and location of whatever processes control teachers' work" (Bidwell et al., 1997, p. 285). Moreover, irrespective of loose or tight coupling, formal rules and behavioral expectations connected to membership are not identical to concrete actions (Luhmann, 1964, p. 59; Ortmann, 2003); that is, the intended curriculum is never identical to the taught curriculum. If following a rule implies applying a generalizable procedure of practice to a specific situation, then both the situation and the rule remain unclear: "Is situation S a case in which it is appropriate to apply rule R and if so, then how?" (Ortmann, 2003, p. 34). This double ambiguity of formal rules (as concerns their own meaning and the situation in which they should be applied) cannot be compensated by another formal rule, for if one would define the application of a formal rule by using another rule, this second formal rule would need a third formal rule for its application, and so forth (Ortmann, 2003, p. 46). Thus, formal rules are not self-evident, and cannot be finally defined by meta-rules (in other words, by formal rules that regulate their application). Therefore, an endless regress would take place if one were to structure organizational practices by formal rules only.

There are several mechanisms by which organizational practices relate to formal rules (see also sections 4.1 and 5.1). One of these is important for the present chapter and has to do with what sometimes is called "organizational routines" (Zucker, 1987, p. 456), "work cultures" (Rowan, 2006b, p. 211) or, in education, "local cultures of teaching practice" (Bidwell & Yasumoto, 1999, p. 237). Such routines and work cultures begin to be constituted when formal rules are tentatively put into practice from situation to situation. As Ortmann (2003) suggested, "in organizations a double or even triple game is played in which formal rules are substituted/complemented, filled/fulfilled, avoided/undermined by informal rules" (p. 104). Informal rules are practical and—in contrast to their formal counterparts—do not need any explication. They are constituted when members of the organization (teachers, for instance), who are not able to draw on previous routines and common practices that have emerged outside the organization, have to put a formal rule into practice (a new curriculum, for example). As far as the subsequent new practices following the respective formal rule are based on a reciprocal attunement of the organization's members, collectively shared informal rules emerge, along which the formal rule is put into practice (Nohl, 2014, pp. 191–192). These informal rules, which are practical in nature, need not to be explicit. Routinized as they are, they have to be conceived of as habitualized regularities rather than as "normative expectations" (Bohnsack, 2014a, p. 39).

Collectively shared informal rules, if routinized, form the nucleus of a "conjunctive space of experience" (Mannheim, 1982, p. 204) which ties together those members of the organization who follow these regularities. Where a whole set of informal rules is shared by a group of organization members (for example, by a collegium of teachers; see Bidwell & Yasumoto, 1999), we speak of an "organizational milieu" (Nohl, 2014, p. 193). The organizational milieu of a group of organization members comprises all those implicit stocks of knowledge, informal rules, and habitualized practices that have emerged in the organization. When those tied together in an organizational milieu are confronted with new formal rules, they may tend to intuitively understand and put them into practice according to the perspective of their organizational milieu which is self-evident to them.

Informal rules and regularities, as well as the organizational milieus based on them, guarantee the swift functioning of the organization vis-à-vis formal rules that are not self-explicative. Whether they are tightly or loosely coupled to the practices of the organization, formal rules are made sense of in organizational milieus. However, this does not imply that putting formal rules into practice is a simple process; in more complex organizations several and even contradicting (sets of) informal rules—and, accordingly, various organizational milieus—may exist, leading to practical conflicts or verbal controversies as to how formal rules have to be put into practice. Our inquiries into the curriculum development and practices provide an abundance of empirical examples for this.

Types and Changes of Curriculum Revisited

The concepts discussed up to this point do not only refer to different social levels that must be taken into account when analyzing curriculum change; they also allow us to revisit Cuban's distinction of five types of curriculum and to connect them to the concepts of "institution," "formal organizational rules," "organizational milieu," and even further concepts to be discussed in the following chapters.

The curriculum, to the extent that it is defined in the formal rules of an organization (a school) or of a set of organizations (for instance, all primary schools under the control of the ministry of education), is the intended one. When these formal rules of the curriculum are put into practice, we then speak of the "taught curriculum" (Cuban, 1992, p. 222). If there are shared informal rules of instructional practice among groups of teachers, this taught curriculum is based on the respective organizational milieus. At this point one must assume a variety of taught curricula that are certainly also influenced by the (collective) attitudes and practical routines of the pupils with whom the teachers interact. The "learned curriculum" (Cuban, 1992, p. 222), again, refers to the pupils and their shared stock of knowledge and skills that may be embedded in a "conjunctive space of experience" (Mannheim, 1982, p. 204), that is, also a milieu—we attend to this point in chapter 5. The "tested curriculum" (Cuban, 1995, p. 5) may have various points of reference, as the respective tests may be based on teachers' informal rules and organizational milieu-specific routines, on the formal rules of the curriculum itself, or even on a set of formal rules decoupled from the curriculum. Additionally, all these types of curriculum are influenced by those components which have become reciprocally typified in society over the time and have, thus, been institutionalized. This "historical curriculum" (Cuban, 1992, p. 223) is composed of the remains of previous intended, taught, learned, and tested curricula that have not only endured but also gained an orientating power for education.

Curriculum change, then, may occur on all social levels and in all entities described. Here we adopt Waks's (2007) suggestion that reproductive and transformative change may not only take place on the level of single organizations but also on the institutional level. Moreover, he maintained that more comprehensive change occurs in institutions where new "primary principles, norms or laws that serve as the basis of a system" (p. 294) emerge and become reciprocally typified. Transformative "*organizational* change," then, may only refer to the "readjustment of an existing organization to new institutional ideas and norms" (p. 294; italics original). While Waks's suggestion on the hierarchies of institutional and organizational change may be true for specific empirical cases, we would like to underpin that changes on the organizational level are, in one way or another, linked to the institutional aspect of the curriculum. Moreover, we have to differentiate between at least two aspects of the organization, as reproductive and transformative changes of the curriculum may occur both in the formal rules and in the informal regularities that pertain to organizational milieus. Only after one has scrutinized the forms change has assumed in these different social entities and the social dynamics between them can one assess if change is very limited or rather comprehensive in scope.

Multilevel Analysis

The different types of curriculum, which are each connected to one or more levels of school instruction—from institution to organizational milieu—are not only important as basic theoretical concepts, but also have implications for empirical research that has to consider the interplay of the practices evolving on each level (that is, the social dynamics). Accordingly, we do not limit our research to a "unitary 'subject of steering'" (Mayntz & Scharpf, 1995, p. 32), because change in the educational sector cannot be "appropriately conceived of as the purposeful implementation of the intentions of single, powerful and visible actors as, e.g., ministries of education, inspectorates, school administrations etc." (Rürup & Bormann, 2013, p. 11). Therefore, it is important to view the implementation of new policies as well as policy development itself as the result of "interactional constellations between discrete governmental and non-governmental actors who are subject to different normative demands, who differ as regards their own interests and identities and who act upon different interpretations of the situation" (Mayntz & Scharpf, 1995, p. 32).

These actors, who may be an organization, a group of people, or individual persons, are interdependent insofar as none of them are able to develop and implement any policy on its/his/her own. Given that each actor has its/his/her own intentions and goals for acting but is also dependent on other actors whose intentions may deviate from its/his/her own, policy development should not be understood as a simple matter of intentional planning. As Altrichter and Maag Merki (2011) pointed out, in addition to various actors' disparate intentions there are also unreflected—habitualized or spontaneous—aspects of action incorporated in this process. Therefore, the results of policy development may be "trans-intentional" (p. 20). Moreover, even intentional actions should not be abstracted from the structures (for example, financial resources, professional experience, situational opportunities) under which actors perform their practices. Already in this sense the term "intended curriculum" seems to be oversimplified, as the phenomenon it depicts is certainly not the product of a single or unified intention, but rather—as we see in section 3.2—the result of a multitude of actors with their respective—and sometimes disparate—goals. This, by the way, reminds us of Elias' characterization of social change as the "consequences flowing from the intermeshing of the actions of numerous people" (Elias, 1978, p. 146), to which we attended in chapter 2.

The fact that educational policy is a process in which intentional, trans-intentional, and also structural aspects of action play an important role (Altrichter & Maag Merki, 2011, p. 29) calls for a methodology that is able to differentiate between the conscious intentions of specific actors and those "trans-intentional" results, which may emanate from the interplay of different actors as well as from structural constraints. As the latter may not be reflected by the actors involved—and therefore may not be explicated by them—empirical research must be able to also take into account aspects of policy development beyond the consciousness of the actors. With the Documentary Method, further described in the following, we use an approach that meets this criterion (Asbrand, 2014).

The individual and corporate (organizational) actors, in whose interplay educational policy is formed and practiced, act on different levels. Therefore, we are interested in the "mutual interweavement and dependence of different actors and levels of the education system" (Rürup & Bormann, 2013, p. 11), and try to analyze how "the coordination of action in a multi-level system with numerous actors takes place" (Kussau & Brüsemeister, 2007, p. 16).[4] As discussed, we differentiate between the levels of the institution, of the organization with its formal rules, and of organizational milieus. In addition, we use the concept of "educational sector," introduced in chapter 2. To take into account those structural constraints evident in the educational practices of students and their parents from different social backgrounds, we additionally discuss a concept of "social milieu" in chapter 5.

On each of these levels and by each of these social entities, the new curriculum is "recontextualized"; that is, it is "reinterpreted and practically transformed within the frame of level-specific circumstances and resources for practice" (Fend, 2009, p. 181). This recontextualization, as a practical accomplishment in multilevel processes, has to be scrutinized in a multilevel analysis (see Helsper et al., 2010; Nohl, 2013; Weiß & Nohl, 2012). Accordingly, an analysis of curriculum change should not be confined to the process of development. If policy is the result of actions on the part of various actors—including those who practice new formal rules—research needs to cover both curriculum policy development and practice. In this sense, research has to take into account all types of the curriculum—from the "intended" to the "historical" (Cuban, 1992, 1995). Therefore, in the following sections of the present chapter we focus on the development aspect of curriculum change, while in chapters 4–6 we analyze how the new curriculum is practiced in various Turkish schools.

Curriculum Development in Historical Analysis

The development of a curriculum should not be conceived of as a sequence of historical facts but as a sequential process in which different events, actions, intentions, and goals of various actors, embedded in social structures, are involved over a specific period in time (see Dehnavi, 2013, pp. 46–48; Groppe, 2009, p. 101). Instead of assuming the existence of objective historical facts and separating them from actors' perspectives, orientations, and practices perceived as subjective reactions to these facts, we adopt a methodological approach that takes all the empirical sources of our analysis as manifestations of the perspectives and orientations of the actors who have authored these sources—whether they are organizations, organizational milieus, or individuals. Therefore, every empirical source to be investigated in this chapter and the ones to follow is taken as embedded in a certain perspective with its own limits (Mannheim, 1952a). However, these sources, with their respective perspectivities, are not left unrelated. As much as possible, we compare our empirical sources and considered where they coincide or disagree; this comparison then has enabled us to understand the formation of the new curriculum as a sequence of the relations between various actors, their orientations, and practices (Elias, 1978, p. 146).

Expert Interviews and Documents

It is important to note that the perspective of actors is influential not only in the interviews which we conducted, but also in the documents collected during our investigation. Some documents—popular-scientific articles and statements of organizations, for example—are easily related to specific actors, but one still has to keep in mind that they usually do not reflect an individual (organization)'s standpoint only, being often based on collectively shared convictions that are the result of the intellectual work of numerous people. The perspectives behind other documents—newspaper articles and other reports, for example—are more amorphous, and more often than not it is impossible to identify whose perspectives have influenced them.

Almost all documents used in this volume have been retrieved on the Internet. With the exception of the scientific publications and newspaper articles, many of these documents—albeit available online—have a semi-public character. Rhetorically and even grammatically imprecise, they address specific segments of the public or even an in-house readership only. The range of such documents available online was so rich that it did not seem necessary to search for more in the archives of the ministry, an endeavor with many anticipated bureaucratic obstacles.

Instead of archival materials—which might or might not have given us deeper insight—we conducted expert interviews with 11 actors involved in the development of the new curriculum in Turkey, ranging from the minister of education to those academics and bureaucrats who actually wrote the curriculum, and to activists of NGOs in the field of education (see appendix). While expert interviews in qualitative and quantitative research are commonly used to gather information on a subject matter to be later empirically investigated with other methods, they were for us—and on their own—an important instrument of data gathering. Accordingly, we conducted the expert interviews so that they convey the "operational knowledge" (Meuser & Nagel, 2009, p. 30) of the actors, that is, their insider's knowledge of the curriculum development process. Rather than focusing on the experts' person and individual biography, we approached them as representatives of their respective organizations, posing questions that "allow a reconstruction of the logic and procedure of the decision-making process" (p. 34).[5]

Following Meuser and Nagel's (2009, p. 31) seminal elaboration of this method, we used open guidelines for the interview and posed questions that motivated the actors to freely and extensively narrate their own experiences. Predominantly, the questions referred to the "institutional-organizational context" (p. 35) in which the actors worked. They motivated the interviewees to give their own account of the curriculum process, to describe specific situations, and to provide us with information we had not anticipated. The "narrative passages" (Meuser & Nagel, 2009, p. 32) of the interviews, in particular, in which the respondents reported the sequence of their actions and of the events they experienced, were most important for our analysis.

Documentary Interpretation

The diverse documents as well as the expert interviews were interpreted with the Documentary Method, an approach developed by Ralf Bohnsack (2010a,

2014b) on the basis of Karl Mannheim's (1952a, 1982) sociology of knowledge (see also Bohnsack et al., 2010). The Documentary Method shares with other advanced methods of qualitative data interpretation the conviction that what is communicated verbally and explicitly in interview texts and other documents is not the only element of significance to the empirical analysis, and that, above all, it is necessary to reconstruct the meaning that underlies and is implied with these utterances. While the actor or author may be consciously aware of what he or she is doing—for instance, expressing a political standpoint or educational creed—this action or text also has a second level of meaning, to which the actor or author does not necessarily have access.

The Documentary Method distinguishes between these two levels of meaning by referring to the first level as that of the "intentional expressive meaning" and "objective meaning," and to the second level as that of the "documentary meaning." The intentional expressive meaning designates what "was meant by the subject just as it appeared to him when his consciousness was focused upon it" (Mannheim, 1952a, p. 46). The objective meaning does not refer to the intentions of the actors, but rather to the "objective social configuration" (p. 46) that exists beyond the intentions and specific characteristics of the actors. When we classify a conclusion as a political statement or as an educational creed, we are resorting to general and, as it were, objective knowledge; we are filing facts according to their topic. In other words, we are working out what a text or an action is about.

The "documentary" meaning then gauges the action or text according to the process by which it surfaced; that is, by its "modus operandi" (Bohnsack, 2010b, p. 101). By drawing on other actions or texts by the same actor or author, documentary interpretation sees the modus operandi "as proof" of a "synoptical appraisal" undertaken by the researcher, which "may take his global orientation [in original: "habitus"; the authors] as a whole into its purview" (Mannheim, 1952a, p. 52). The important point here is the way in which a text or action is constructed, or the limits within which its topic is faced, that is, the "framework of orientation" (Bohnsack, 2010b, p. 107) within which a problem is handled. While in everyday life one intuitively resorts to the practical level and simply demonstrates how to, for example, tie a knot, scientific researchers must rely on finding ways of verbally explicating the process by which texts and actions come about, or their frameworks of orientation. This is done by falling back on practice. In this practice, a "tacit" (Polanyi, 1966) or "atheoretical" knowledge (Mannheim, 1982, p. 67) exists, but we are not required to pinpoint or explicate it in terms of common-sense theory.

For this reason, our interpretation of the data material focuses on their practical aspect: The expert interviews are not only analyzed as to what practices are narrated by the curriculum developers; the interviews themselves are conceived of as a practice within which interviewees make sense of their world and tackle problems (for instance, that of curriculum development) within their respective orientation frame (Nohl, 2010). The written documents, again, are not only interpreted according to the objective meaning articulated. In addition, we have paid careful attention to the orientation frames within which the documents were composed by their authors. Thus, the practical accomplishments during the development of a new curriculum were always analyzed by regarding the perspectives and orientation frameworks of the actors involved. Our analysis, however, did not focus on these orientation frames only, but aimed at also elucidating the historical process of curriculum development as seen through their orientations.

3.2   Organizing a New Curriculum

By the turn of the century, the content and approach of primary education in Turkey had come under ever-growing criticism, not only by scholars of education but also in the political realm. In the run-up to the general elections of 2002, both the Justice and Development Party (JDP) and its most important rival, the Republican People's Party (RPP),[6] promised reforms in education, advocating to leave the existing "approach based on memorizing" in favor of a "democratic and contemporary approach which takes the human being into its center" (JDP, 2002, p. 31) or—as the RPP wrote in its party program—to "redetermine principles and methods" of education in order "to raise a generation who is investigative, interrogative and self-confident" (RPP, 1997, pp. 155–156). This political quest for change in education, though bereft of any specific ideas as to how the school and its curriculum should be designed, turned into political commitment when the JDP won a landslide victory on November 3, 2002, and was able to form a single-party government. After the new prime minister had repeated the pledge for a "reform of national education"[7] in his government policy statement, an "Urgent Action Plan," issued on January 3, 2003, allotted to "renew the curricula" to get rid of "memorizing" and "prejudiced attitudes," as well as to prepare a "contemporary curriculum which teaches pupils learning" (T.C., 2003, p. 93). While universities and the "State Planning Institution" were mentioned as cooperation partners, the ministry of education itself was held responsible for the curriculum renewal.

The cabinet member representing the ministry of education at the time was Erkan Mumcu, a member of the JDP who, as a young politician, did not have an Islamist past like so many of his colleagues. As Mr. Mumcu later recalled, his appointment as minister of national education did not reflect the original intentions of the party. But when the president of the republic, who had the right to veto the appointment of ministers, "didn't find him [the first candidate; the authors] appropriate," Erkan Mumcu became the person on whom the ruling party and the president could "agree."[8] Mr. Mumcu had been one of several well-known liberal and conservative figures that the JDP had succeeded in adding to its ranks before the elections.

Being most concerned with a fundamental reform of the university system, Mr. Mumcu searched for staff that would be able to take care of the school system and design a "strong and comprehensive change in the curriculum."

Looking for a person with a "scientific, more progressive" attitude who would "behave more radically" in matters of a curriculum change, he met with a range of "education scientists and bureaucrats," only to understand that most of them were "rather mechanical and reformist"-minded, defining the problems of the ministry and the education system as matters of "number of schools and teachers." Only very few of them were—according to Erkan Mumcu—inclined to discuss issues "at the foundation of the business, i.e. what is learning, how does the human being learn, what is teaching." Among them was Ziya Selçuk, a professor of the Ankara-based Gazi University. As Erkan Mumcu underpinned, he wanted to appoint this professor as the president of the Board of Education because he had a "vision" for change. He then struggled and finally succeeded in convincing the JDP's leader, Erdoğan, who had proposed to appoint his own long-time advisor, to accept this decision. In fact, Mr. Mumcu had intended to later promote Ziya Selçuk to the post of "undersecretary," responsible for the whole education system, after he had successfully reorganized the Board. As we will see, this plan was ultimately not realized.

The Board of Education (BoE) is the organizational unit within the Ministry of National Education (MoNE) responsible for developing and accrediting curricula and schoolbooks. The Board responds directly to the minister and consists of around 10 members (from education science, education bureaucracy, and political parties) with decision-making authority and a bureaucratic administration of approximately 600 personnel. Since 1980, the Board had had 14 presidents before Ziya Selçuk was appointed on March 21, 2003.

Like Erkan Mumcu, Ziya Selçuk gave his own account of the curriculum process. Upon our request, Mr. Selçuk narrated how—according to his perspective—the curriculum development started:[9]

> I (1) had things as an academic [. . .] I wanted to do something about these issues in Turkey. During his period in the Ministry of Education, Erkan Mumcu proposed to work together and he asked me what my aim was I mean what my project was and what I intended to do. (2) I said that the curriculum was being used as a tool of the existing order and state regime to shape society and educate good citizens in their own terms. When education was used like this, the tradition of an authoritarian state is being maintained. But Turkey is a different country than in the years when it had been founded, the world is different, after Mr. Özal, mmm, the systematic of Turkey that we used to call established order was cracked, shaken and the gap between what was written and what was lived enlarged. The education system (1) is now too narrow for Turkey and no comprehensive change has been carried out in terms of the design of the curriculum since 1968, much has changed since '68 what I term as a comprehensive change was that for the first five classes in [the curriculum of; the authors] '68. This change does not

have a holistic structure, a design, does not include higher education at all. I indicated the requirement of relating education with economy and democracy and said that if education was not related to democratic processes and economic processes it cannot become a subject in real life. It only appears to you as a repertoire of procedures.

We have quoted from Selçuk's interview so extensively because the lines cited have an abundance of overt and tacit meaning that require further interpretation. Firstly, Mr. Selçuk implicates that the "things" he had in mind concerning a new curriculum were his personal and individual ideas (he only uses the first-person singular), that they were deeply connected to his role as an "academic," and that they had not yet been implemented (as he said he "wanted to do" them). As we further discuss later, all three implications of these first lines of the interview may be legitimately challenged.

Secondly, it is only after he draws the interviewer's attention to these "things" in his mind that Mr. Selçuk mentions the proposal by the minister of education at the time, Erkan Mumcu, to "work together." The temporal sequence in which Mr. Selçuk here puts his proposal implies that the idea of a new curriculum had not been generated upon the minister's initiative and request, but had been, rather, the professor's own concern long before then. This is further confirmed by the way in which Mr. Selçuk quotes the minister, who—according to his wording—expected him to already have a "project" and "aim" in mind.

Thirdly, by narrating the conversation he had with the minister of education, Mr. Selçuk is able to introduce his ideas to the interviewer as much as he had presumably conveyed them to Erkan Mumcu. Rather than a didactical and philosophical justification, the professor here gives a political and a sociological explanation for a new curriculum: By saying that the alleged social engineering attitude of the existing curriculum was the product and reproductive factor of an "authoritarian state," Ziya Selçuk ably relates his own ideas to political slogans of the ruling JDP. He contests the social engineering attitude in education by drawing attention to the change Turkey has undergone since its foundation, to the crackling and shaking of the "established order," and then comes to the conclusion that there is a growing "gap" between "what was lived" and "what was written," that is, between the written rules of the state and social practice, including the political debate and the economy. It is in this sense that the "education system" is "too narrow for Turkey." Mr. Selçuk hereby implies to shift the rationale of the curriculum from a device which forms society to a device which is formed according to society. It is not the society that is in question anymore (and needs to be educated to specific goals set by the existing regime); it is the curriculum that must be shaped so that it serves the existing social practice itself. This shift of rationale is introduced as a contrast to the Kemalist early republic, that is, to the "years" when Turkey was "founded." By doing so, Mr. Selçuk again uses a typical—though in the beginning of the 2000s not always outspoken—discourse fragment of the JDP, which was supported by social groups critical of the dominant Kemalist ideology during the early republic and thereafter (see section 2.2).

Fourthly, Ziya Selçuk explicates some coordinates of the "project" the minister had asked him for: Education should become "related" to economy and democracy to turn into a "subject of real life" rather than a "repertoire of procedures." Here, again, Mr. Selçuk draws on pivotal concerns of the new governmental party, which claimed to not only promote democracy at the start of their reign but also advocated a liberal frame for the economy.

While we show that Mr. Selçuk was by no means the only advocator of a new curriculum in Turkey (although he could rely on important preliminary work, both theoretical and practical, including his own), the way in which he presented his thoughts indicates his outstanding ability to relate his educational ideas to a wider public and to the political discourse. The election victory of the JDP then gave Mr. Selçuk the opportunity to convey his ideas to political circles that were interested in change in education as well as bereft of specific ideas regarding the direction of this change.

As our analysis reveals, this window of opportunity was opened on the basis of a specific—though not contingent—course of political decisions and dodges: Had the republic's president not refused the JDP's original candidate; had the JDP not attached liberals to its ranks, and had Mr. Mumcu not resisted the appointment of the JDP leader's advisor, this window would have remained shut. The window of opportunity, however, opened in a time when the old curriculum had already been heavily criticized within the educational sector and the search for a new one had already started. Around the turn of the century, several books and articles on constructivist teaching and learning theory had been published, as well as on the "multiple intelligence" thesis, which later became another major column of the new curriculum (among others, Altan, 1999; Köseoğlu & Kavak, 2001; Saban, 2001; Talu, 1999; Yaşar, 1998). In addition to these theoretical antecedents to the new curriculum, there was also considerable practical experience that preceded it. In fact, it was Ziya Selçuk himself who had founded the "Private Gazi Elementary School which was organized and structured around MI [multiple intelligence; the authors] theoretical frameworks in 1998" (Chen et al., 2009, p. 18). This is confirmed by the school's self-representation, in which it prides itself of being the "first in Ankara" to "implement the multiple intelligence theory" a well as being the "place where the changing curriculum has taken shape" (Gazi, n.d., p. 19). Indeed, in 2002, just 1 year before the beginning of the change in curriculum, a book called "Practices of Multiple Intelligence" was published by Ziya Selçuk and two coauthors, in which they—along with an extensive and easy-to-read introduction to the multiple intelligence theory—presented daily teaching plans and worksheets for all core subjects from grade 1 to 5, resulting from their practical experience in the Gazi Private Primary School in the school years 1998/1999 and 2000/2001 (Selçuk et al., 2002, p. 3). Neither the Gazi Private Primary

School experience nor the second practical source for the new curriculum, the "Maya college"—a private school founded by Ziya Selçuk in 2002— were mentioned by Mr. Selçuk during his interview. This latter college, in which Mr. Selçuk and his friends continued their activities after they had left the Gazi School, claims that its founder "has used the experience of Maya in the constructivist curriculum works he conducted with his friends in the National Ministry of Education."

All of the preceding is evidence that these measures were not only "things . . . I wanted to do" (as Mr. Selçuk supposed in the beginning of his interview); rather, there were many things that had already been done. The new curriculum was not developed from scratch; it had significant preceding layers, both in theory and in school practice. Moreover, though Ziya Selçuk was a pivotal and critical actor in the whole process, he was certainly not alone. The multiple intelligence approach and the constructivist teaching philosophy had been adopted and further developed by a range of academics, mostly originating from the Gazi University, before Ziya Selçuk was offered the presidency of the Board of Education in 2003. Several of our interview partners from the academia confirmed that they had "known constructivism anyway," that they had criticized the central "role of the teacher" and "education based on memorizing" prevalent in the old curriculum even before they became involved with the curriculum reform.

Naturally, both constructivism and the multiple intelligence approach, which later became so important for the new curriculum, were not developed in Turkey. Originating from a long-lasting philosophical debate among European and US-American scholars, constructivism had been diffused around the world and became a widely spread background for teaching approaches with the works of Vigotzky, Piaget, and Dewey (Altinyelken, 2011, pp. 138–141; Gough, 2008; Moll, 1990; Murray, 1979; Phillips, 2000). The multiple intelligence approach, developed by Gardner (1983) and discussed throughout the world (Chen et al., 2009), though less well known, was also not directly borrowed for developing a new curriculum in Turkey, but discussed and practically used before. When Ziya Selçuk came into the position to build a bridge between the scientific and the political realm, he thus proposed an approach that had already become popular among Turkish scholars of education due to a certain "isomorphism" (in the sense of New Institutionalism; see section 3.1) of constructivism and multiple intelligence around the globe.

Resistance and Assistance

If Ziya Selçuk was successful in relating new curricular ideas to the political project of the JDP, he was less fortunate when it came to bureaucracy. In March 2003 Erkan Mumcu was transferred to the ministry of culture; he was succeeded by Hüseyin Çelik, a strong figure in the JDP. While the new minister continued to support Ziya Selçuk—and actually was the one who effectively appointed him as the president of the BoE—he expressed his "concern" about his plans, as Mr. Selçuk reported:

> There was such a concern in that era, education was one of the main instruments to control the system of Turkey if we touched on this we would touch on the state. There was such a feeling in those days like 'let's do not touch such things' (.) in the structure of the state apparatus for now. //mmh// It was said that there would emerge such an impression that if you touched on this mmm look, the Justice and Development Party immediately after its election, mmm, is trying to convert one of the tools of the system, that their intentions are different.

The significance of the reform proposed by Mr. Selçuk was—according to this warning voice—not confined to the educational sector, extending to the "state" as such. Here, an important difference between the ruling JDP and the "state" or "state apparatus," that is, the bureaucratic tradition ruling Turkish institutions, is implicated. Even the ruling party had—as Ziya Selçuk was warned—to obey specific aspects if it did not want to be regarded as "converting one of the tools of the system"; the resistance Ziya Selçuk was to face from within the "state" was already reflected in such words. Against this warning, however, the professor later underpinned the comprehensive character of the "transformation" he had planned, which amounted to a "change of mindset": Along with the curriculum, changes in the "financing" of schools and the "teacher training" would be necessary if this endeavor was to make sense at all. When Ziya Selçuk here purposefully used the concept of "transformation," it served not only to describe the comprehensive character of his plans, but also to make everybody aware of the fundamental character of the envisaged change. As one of Selçuk's colleagues (a later curriculum commission leader) put it: "We said that everybody will change his mind, everybody will perceive the novelty really as a novelty." This made the radical terminology necessary, because "if we would have said we revise the old (2) that would not have been different from what has been done in the past."

Ziya Selçuk would soon discover that the warnings of the new minister were justified. As he admitted, the bureaucracy was very disturbed and upset that a very different perspective had paved its way into it; that is, that a perspective outside the bureaucratic tradition had entered it. As Mr. Selçuk added, this also had to do with his person: an outsider who was regarded as an "aberrant" and "ephemeral" phenomenon. Other people, who were later involved in the curriculum process, attributed the bureaucracy's reservations to the fact that "the old patterns have been turned upside down" with the reform. This led to—as different interview partners have univocally called it—"passive resistance" by the bureaucracy, which resorted to "delaying" procedures and "putting letters under the desk pad."

When the newly appointed president of the BoE started to assemble the team that would actually develop the new curriculum, he faced tacit resistance not only from within the ministry, but also from other bureaucracies:

> We had great difficulty because, the experts we needed were working at the universities but YÖK's [Higher Education Council; the authors] permission is required to work with experts from universities we wrote an official letter to YÖK but the permission was not given. That is they wrote back a short letter telling that it was not approved. In fact, it was not given in order not to support an activity that the JDP intended to do, this was orally communicated to me. When I failed in this, I met with the presidents whom I knew in person one by one. Most of them said no, they did not accept.

The appointment, by Ziya Selçuk, of "experts" from the "universities" was "not approved" by the Higher Education Council ("YÖK"), which allegedly did not want to "support" a project by the new ruling party. A similar passive resistance was then displayed by the university presidents approached by the professor.[10]

In theoretical terms, Mr. Selçuk was confronted with a collective way of practicing formal rules to the disadvantage of curriculum change. While on the surface the bureaucracy of the council, of the ministry of education, and of the universities act in line with the written law and administrative regulations, their passive resistance—though based on presumably various motivations—reveals that the people in these positions share a common stance toward Selçuk's plea for a new curriculum. This shared outlook is rather implicit and pertains to the way one interprets the law and to the tacit modus operandi in which one perceives the political realm; for example, instances such as the change of government and the subsequent projects. Although we do not assume that these shared informal rules of practicing the law have constituted a complete organizational milieu, this phenomenon reveals how important the informal side of organizations may be (see section 3.1).

When the president of the Board of Education understood that he would not be able to assign experts to his project on the organizational and, as we see later, traditional way, he approached "academics individually." We delve deeper into this selection process in the following pages, but already at this point it is documented in Selçuk's wording that he did not have any problems in finding the right academics:

> This time I met academics individually. mmm then it was necessary to do this job by creating another budget other than that of universities or [the ministry of; the authors] national education, without using what we call revolving funds. This time we applied to the European Union we wanted to benefit from a grant project of theirs. I got a lot of support in this issue and we recruited people under individual contracts.

The usual channels of paying these experts (the "revolving budgets" of the universities and the budget of the ministry) being blocked, Mr. Selçuk approached the European Union to finance his endeavor by using a "grant project." The experts were then hired on an "individual" basis, by-passing the blocked channels of both the Higher Education Council and of the "universities."

While this narration implies that Mr. Selçuk had already been informed about the "grant project" and the availability of its budget, this was not quite the case. When the interviewer clarified that, to his knowledge, the respective project was not scheduled to finance a new curriculum, Mr. Selçuk admitted that they "indirectly," and with "pressure," profited from the project. Further inquiries into the matter, including online interviews with project executives, revealed that the support of the respective project to the curriculum development was the result of a highly peculiar process: Initially, the president of the BoE had informed the "Delegation of the European Union to Turkey" and its representative, Prof. Dr. Mustafa Balcı, about the curriculum plans, rather than asking for financial assistance. Mr. Balcı then mentioned the "Support to Basic Education Programme" (SBEP), in which—as Mr. Selçuk saw it—"a lot of money" was being expended without significant and palpable output. At this point, the idea to use the SBEP as a financial source for curriculum development must have been born.

The "Support to Basic Education Program" had been procured by the European Commission in the beginning of the century to provide "direct support of the Ministry of National Education's (MoNE) Basic Education Reform Programme" (SBEP, 2003, vol. 1, p. IV). With a budget of €100 million, this grant assigned €70 million for infrastructure (e.g., school buildings) and €22 million for "technical assistance" (vol. 1, p. IV), that is, for example, for consultancy.

During the inception phase (starting in September 2002), "national level project plans" (vol. 1, p. IV) were developed in consultation with the MoNE. One plan concerned the quality of teaching and learning, and suggested to elaborate the "conceptual framework" of the existing curriculum as well as a scientifically valid "assessment and examination system," activities for which 177 (2.33% of the whole budget) working days were allocated (SBEP, 2003, app. E6.13, p. 1, and app. E.19, p. 18). This plan reveals that even after the inception phase (that is, by mid-April 2003) the SBEP did not emphasize activities concerning the primary education curriculum in general. In particular, the activities agreed upon after an intensive consultation process with various stakeholders were limited to *improving* the *existing* primary school curriculum. Apparently, the stakeholders involved in the consultation process (many of them bureaucrats of the MoNE) did not know about, or ignored, Selçuk's plea for a new curriculum. Even when the European Commission and the Ministry of National Education finally approved the inception report in July 2003 (3 months after Selçuk was appointed president of the Board of Education), nobody mentioned the plans for a new curriculum. That means that the ministry approved a report which foresaw to improve the existing curriculum, while its own BoE was about to develop a new one.

However, in the period that followed the approval of the inception report, a major change took place in the SBEP, shifting its focus from other activities in the national level component to the support for comprehensively developing a new curriculum. The team leader of the SBEP, Anders Lönnqvist, newly appointed in the summer of 2003, gave a comprehensive account of the sequence of events:[11]

> As I had not been involved in developing and pushing through the Inception report, I maybe had 'less passion' for trying to follow it to the last point. Therefore, when I was approached by the then president of the Board of Education . . . about trying to find some ways to support the development of the new curriculum, I wasn't in any way against it. I just told him it might be difficult to convince the EC Delegation and the partners in the consortium. He made me understand that the curriculum was of highest priority for the country and that SBEP was the only solution for that. [. . .] We had a huge incidental budget of €15 million and we were quite sure we were not going to be able to use all that money. So, I proposed first to Mustafa Balci, the task manager in the ECD, and later to the consortium, that we could transfer some funds from the incidentals to the fees. [. . .] In the end we got approval through an amendment to shift budget to cover several thousand national person days by shifting funds from the incidentals budget. We also got days to develop textbooks in line with the new curricula, and that required us to rent a whole floor in the 'Teachers' House' (a hotel for teachers), and to engage 100+ experts for all subject areas to work there. [. . .] At the end of the project we had €30,000 left in the incidental budget.

Although Mr. Lönnqvist's account differs in certain points from that of Prof. Selçuk, these differences can be interpreted as a result of their respective positions. In addition to Mr. Lönnqvist's information, the SBEP's website provides details on the support given to the curriculum development process. While this online text from early summer, 2006, generally speaks of "providing support" and makes clear that the "Board of Education" was the main actor in authoring new curricula,[12] only 1 year later, at the end of the SBEP, the "Project Coordination Center"—a MoNE unit for administrating international projects—published a report in which it tended to disguise the pivotal role of the Board of Education during the curriculum development process. The report also generally spoke of a "cooperation of the Board of Education, General Directorate of Primary Education and the Department of Educational Research and Development" (T.C., 2007, p. 17); this reveals that the SBEP not only adapted to the plans of developing a new curriculum, but also turned out to identify itself with the project. Moreover, by describing the SBEP and the two MoNE units as cooperation partners within the curriculum development process, it is implicated that the new curriculum, originally opposed by the ministerial bureaucracy, was eventually identified with by all relevant ministerial units. However, there was still a long way to go until the curriculum process was welcomed by the ministry, and even by the BoE. When Ziya Selçuk took office, in 2003, and subsequently tried to appoint academics for writing the new curricula, he could not yet rely on the assistance of the ministerial bureaucracy, but had to bypass it by recurring to the funds from the European Commission.

Insertion of a New Organizational Milieu

Ziya Selçuk started the curriculum development even before he was equipped with the funds from the Support to Basic Education Program. According to a semi-official paper of the BoE, the ensuing process was "participatory" and open to discussion:

> A participatory approach has been taken as a basis during the preparation of the curricula. Within this frame, the preparation worked as follows:
>
> 1. First of all a meeting of the 'Curriculum Council' was held in which academics from various universities took part and discussed what kind of human beings we aim to bring up [. . .] In this meeting it was discussed what kind of a curriculum we need in order to raise qualified individuals and which way we should follow in the preparation of curricula.
> 2. After the Curriculum Council meeting, four different meetings in the fields of Turkish, mathematics, science and social sciences were organized in which the field experts and educationalists for each course participated.
>
> (TTK, 2004, p. 24)

This report implied that the general outlook of the new curricula—their teaching philosophy—had still been undefined until these meetings, and that the suggestions of the academics might have been decisive for the curriculum development process. The interviews conducted with people involved in the process, most importantly the conversation with Ziya Selçuk, revealed that these meetings also had other functions: Whereas the BoE's semi-official paper presents these meetings as focused on the discussion of the curriculum and its approach, the meetings offered an important opportunity for Mr. Selçuk to identify those with whom he could expect an unproblematic cooperation. Recalling the way he invited academics to these meetings, the then president of the BoE declared:

> Those, mmm, the academics those I had visited, mmm, I invited and said, what do you think, that is I did not say that I'd like to work with them, I said what do you think, afterwards, mmm with groups of academics which consisted of approximately ten people from physics, chemistry,

mathematic, Turkish, I conducted meetings with groups consisting of ten people //mmh// somehow informal meetings. Then mmm I called those people (.) whose perspective was close to mine one by one (2) I told that I'd like to do something, let's form a team, you take the lead, we would provide whatever you need, then they formed their teams // mmh// this was fully name after name, I mean, this, this, and this person.

Only the academics that Mr. Selçuk could personally approach were invited to the meetings. The meetings in which the curriculum was freely discussed, then, did not serve to make a decision on its central teaching philosophy; rather, the free discussion enabled Mr. Selçuk to filter and identify those with whom "our perspective corresponded to the highest degree." On the background of this experience he then proposed to these people to cooperate with him. While he himself chose the leaders for the curriculum commissions on Turkish, Mathematics, Social Studies, History, and Life Studies, these leaders then were asked to appoint—to some extent—"their own teams" (see later). This twofold strategy ensured more than a maximum homogeneity among curriculum commissions leaders: By delegating the appointment of commission members to their respective leaders, Ziya Selçuk was also able to ensure like-mindedness within the commissions without having to know and to appoint every single member.

At least two of the commission leaders were chosen because they had been close colleagues of Ziya Selçuk and their work and teaching philosophy had been well known to him, rather than for the opinions and suggestions they raised during the meetings, One of them, Prof. Kaya, even suggested that the president of the BoE had discussed the very idea of developing a new curriculum with him in advance:

> Ziya Selçuk is our colleague, he was the one we used to work together for years. //mmh// Therefore, when he became the president of the Board of Education mmm when we met in person what can we do how can we act, what kind of function shall the president of the Board of Education undertake.

Professor Kaya here underpinned his long acquaintance with Ziya Selçuk, which is the basis for their mutual discussions on what Mr. Selçuk should regard as his tasks as the president of the BoE. Mr. Kaya here implied that the curriculum initiative was not Prof. Selçuk's decision, but rather a decision made by the two of them. However, his way of legitimizing the curriculum reform does not refer to social change (the main reference point of Ziya Selçuk) but to the alleged failure of the Turkish education sector as mirrored in the "PISA" research:

> When you look at the results of the PISA exams, the necessity of making a fundamental reform in education in Turkey became most obvious

in that exam (1) students are no longer as they were in the past mmm students I mean the existence of students in the school is different than that in the old times (1) schools are different, expectations in schools are different //mmh// although expectations from teachers are *different*, *persons* (1) who will make this difference need to become different, a lot of things have to be changed, the text books (1) as a system are not in the shape that might appeal to a student mmm or a student might benefit from (2).

It is not necessarily a contradiction that Prof. Kaya referred to the education sector's own problems and failures ("PISA") while Prof. Selçuk took social change as a legitimizing factor. While the latter's argumentation may have served to convince Turkish politicians and the general public (for whom the PISA research was virtually unknown), Prof. Kaya, who had not been involved in political discussions, was able to confine himself to internal discussions concerning the educational sector. These discussions pertained not only to the PISA results, but also to the changes undergone by "schools," "teachers," and "pupils."

It is implied in Mr. Kaya's account that he was not chosen for a curriculum commission after the first two official meetings had taken place (see earlier), but that his appointment had been a matter of course. Another commission leader, Prof. Aydın, did not even attend the initial meetings, as he had been abroad during the entire academic year of 2002/2003. Yet, his appointment was based on a long-standing friendship with Ziya Selçuk anyway. As Prof. Aydın recalled,

> our acquaintance with Ziya Selçuk goes well back to the past //mmh// he had graduated one term before me in the department and there is a one-term difference between us, he is a friend with whom we frequently mmm were together (1).

This friendship was certainly not the only reason for Prof. Aydın's appointment, but it ensured that Ziya Selçuk was aware of his works and the approach underlying them. Mr. Aydın underpinned that he had previously developed "curricula which aimed at competencies." As he stated,

> these works became more of a reference, that is in terms of teaching life skills //mmh// for children, and surely he was trying to form a team in which everybody would work in harmony mm would work as a *team* (1).

His works—and their long-existing acquaintance—thus became "credentials" which facilitated his appointment as a commission leader. Prof. Aydın here explained what had already been implied in the interviews by Selçuk and Kaya: As he alleges, the president of the BoE sought for "creating a team" with whom he could "work in harmony."

The same is true for the formation of the commissions, a task Ziya Selçuk had largely delegated to their leaders. Prof. Kaya described how his commission was formed:

> We selected some of the academics by their work only mmm I mean teachers applied who had had overseas experience, knew foreign countries //mmh// mmm a big thing was opened, from these teachers, those were chosen who were in their master's and doctorate programs and who had worked in this field, I mean they were selected //mmh// // mmh// the selection was decided upon, I mean, by the ministry, by us mmm I mean the groups were formed like this.

The commissions, each of which was composed of around 25 experts, comprised both academics and teachers. Although Mr. Selçuk had implied that they were totally formed by the commission leaders, Prof. Kaya indicated that they were only able to nominate their academic members, while the MoNE decided on those with a teacher's background.

In more theoretical terms, we may say that by selecting like-minded colleagues, the majority of whom he had known for a long time, Prof. Selçuk formed a group of people who shared a specific outlook on the curriculum, who had a constructivist attitude, and who were also willing to work for the new government. These homologous orientations made it likely that they would handle the task of developing a new curriculum in a similar way and that they would assign a shared meaning to the formal rules and regulations within the BoE. In this sense, the curriculum commissions—at least to the extent that their members had been chosen by Mr. Selçuk and his colleagues—constituted the nucleus of an "organizational milieu" (see section 3.1) inserted into the BoE.

After the commissions had been formed, the president of the BoE continued to foster the homogeneity in their day-to-day practices. When we asked him how the commissions worked, Prof. Selçuk didn't touch on this topic, but elaborated on his communication with the commission leaders:

> We specified our philosophy (1) theoretical foundations (1) value system (1) principles (1) //mmh// methods (1) which techniques we underlined in terms of the constructive approach, in the meantime we, of course, also proposed a model (1) we always debated this with the core team //mmh// we intensely debated so to speak what does this mean, what do we understand from this, the international conjuncture is like this (1) this is being done in this way in the world, this is our perspective (1) what do you say //mmh// debating this with people in this way we formed a common language, primarily with the core of the commissions //mmh// afterwards those, as specific to their courses, brought forward proposals within this philosophic and theoretical frame.

At the outset of the commissions' work, the pivots of the new curriculum were already clear, according to Ziya Selçuk's account, When he highlighted that "we have put forward" the most important points of the new curriculum, including a "model," he was apparently referring to himself alone, excluding the colleagues he had chosen as leaders of the curriculum commissions. This is evident from the next sentence, in which he added that he discussed the general frame of the new curriculum with this "core group" of commission leaders. In his account of this discussion, however, the ideas of his colleagues do not gain any value on their own (they are not even mentioned). Rather, the discussion first of all serves to sharpen the profile of Mr. Selçuk's own "perspective" ("bizim bakış açımız şu") on the curriculum. It was during these asymmetric discussions that the core team, already selected from like-minded people, created a "common language."

Ziya Selçuk is absolutely convinced that his commission leaders, together with their teams, then developed "proposals" for the respective curricula in accordance to "this philosophy and theoretical frame of perspective." This again indicates the existence of a common organizational milieu that he had inserted into the bureaucracy of the Board of Education. Within this organizational milieu (whose core members were the commission leaders and Ziya Selçuk), it went without question that during the curriculum development everybody adhered to the pivots set forth by Mr. Selçuk.

In spite of the existence of this organizational milieu, Prof. Selçuk himself underpinned the heterogeneity of the curriculum developers. In the following section of the interview he contrasted his practice to the "tradition" of curriculum development:

> But the tradition was like this, write a letter to universities //mmh// mmm, there will be curriculum work on the subject mathematics and assign those who are convenient, this was the tradition in Turkey, contrary to this tradition we followed a way that //mmh// nominated a particular *person*, afterwards they formed their own teams within those there was a certain balance between academics and teachers (1) // mmh// and inspectors were invited, people from civil society associations were called, people from unions I mean it was transformed into a trans-disciplinary place //mmh// I mean it was not a place where merely teachers sat and did something, only academicians worked.

In the usual way of developing a new curriculum, of which Mr. Selçuk here reminded the interviewer, the identification of "suitable" colleagues is delegated to the "universities"; such a way would have led to a randomly chosen team of very diverse curriculum developers. Although he had first tried to follow this structure (see earlier), the professor here passed the impression that he had purposefully decided to "do the opposite of the tradition," and hence to form teams of like-minded curriculum developers. In light of his previous account, it is evident that this was not quite the case; rather,

Mr. Selçuk was compelled to search for new ways of developing a curriculum when he discovered that the usual channels were blocked. This means that the resistance displayed by the ministry, the Council of Higher Education, and the university rectors unintentionally allowed for the selection of like-minded curriculum developers and the subsequent "trans-intentional" (Altrichter, 2010, p. 150) formation of a new organizational milieu in the Board of Education. Hereby a new organizational strategy for curriculum development was established.

However, within the homologous orientations rendered possible by the cooptation procedure, the commissions were made up of—as Mr. Selçuk highlighted—people with "different perspectives." These perspectives did not pertain to the basic (constructivist) approach toward teaching and learning; as is documented in Mr. Selçuk's words, the difference of *professional* perspectives is valued instead: Along with a "balanced" quantity of "teachers" and "academics," other insiders, and outsiders to the educational sector took part in the curriculum development, going as far as persons from "civil society."

This openness to outsiders was confirmed by respective NGOs. In an interview conducted with a representative of an influential civil society organization, its education expert Nuray Pars highlighted that the BoE, to her experience, had previously been a "black box," but that had changed under the presidency of Ziya Selçuk. The interviewee recalled how the organization's initiative to revise the history and social knowledge lesson was taken into consideration by the Board:

> (2) during (.) this curriculum reform mmm we did such a work mmm how is a history or a history and social science course being taught now, whereas *how would it be useful to teach it* mmm such a work was accomplished, an academic presented this, it was presented in a close-circuit meeting but we had also invited Mr. Selçuk to this close-circuit meeting (1) alongside with Mr. Selçuk a professor mm who was the head of the commission that was in charge of preparing the social sciences curriculum mm came to that meeting and listened (1) and they invited that academic and some other people to this mmm (2) they directly mm in-invited them to the commission where the curriculum work, the curriculum work on social sciences mm was being held, I, too, participated alongside with our academic (1) and the *presentation* was, in essence, held for our colleague and his opinions and criticisms //mmh// mm were taken, I was about to be dumbfounded.

As this account shows, the NGO succeeded in attracting the Board's attention to its work. Moreover, to the surprise of our interviewee, the NGO was invited to meet with the respective curriculum commission and freely express their "critique."[13]

In addition to criticism, the commissions also received proposals concerning the content of the curricula. The following account shows Prof. Kaya's assertion that a lot more than 25 people (the number of commission members) have contributed to the curriculum:

> Hundreds of people contributed, nameless people (1) for example a letter reached us from (2) //mmh// while preparing the curriculum a retired police officer, okay, wrote a letter //mmh// . . . he said that I, //mmh// he said, I had worked in police stations for 35 years, he said, the most interesting thing I saw, he said, was students, he said, did not know that harming public property is punished, //mmh// he said they didn't know that breaking a glass is penalized, //mmh// we said Allah Allah and inspired by the letter of this guy we included a gain in there //mmh// and we wrote as an annotation that this gain was stipulated as the result of a warning by a retired police officer to the commission, maybe if you have read it it might have caught your attention, well we used to give this as an example in our conferences or somewhere like this I mean //mmh// I mean we gave the message that we were open to contributions or something like that the civil society associations used to write letters (1), some minority groups, sub-culture groups, you see the Alevite communities, I don't know what communities sent letters, do it like this and do it like that (1) I mean we did something about every opinion from everyone, we overhauled them whether they were worthless or not, but how do they say I mean we took on the serious ones as something.

Among the "anonymous" contributors was a policeman whose proposal the commission later took as an example of its openness to outside advice. It is important to note, however, that this policeman's suggestion (regardless of whether it is justifiable to include criminal law in school instruction) only referred to new content, without challenging the general approach of the curriculum. Similarly, the suggestions by "civil society organizations"—among them the religious minority of "Alevites"—were not at all perceived as a possible criticism towards the constructivist approach of the curriculum. In these cases, the commission evaluated suggestions only in terms of their content and their quality of being "mentionable." Thus, homogeneity and heterogeneity accompanied each other during the curriculum development: The former pertained to the nucleus of an organizational milieu with a shared outlook on the constructivist character of the curriculum and the cooperation with the new government, and the latter fed from internal and—more importantly—external advice concerning the curricula's contents.

Concerted Working Process of Curriculum Commissions

The commissions did not work solely on the basis of a general philosophy agreed upon by their leaders and the president of the Board of Education. As we have already shown, there were other sources from which the commissions drew ideas for the respective curriculum. In general, we can differentiate between two principal sources used in the curriculum development. On one hand, the BoE took into account "around 120 theses" on didactical issues in Turkey, as well as some relevant analyses of a specialized unit of the MoNE, accomplished long before the curriculum development was launched; in addition, the Board had all provincial directorates of education throughout the country organize working groups that prepared evaluation reports on the existing curriculum, to be finalized by November 14, 2003, and subsequently forwarded to the curriculum commissions; moreover, it was around the same time that civil society organizations were asked to report their evaluation of the existing curriculum to the curriculum commissions (TTK, 2004, p. 25). On the other hand, the BoE provided the commissions with literature and curriculum examples "from around the world." As Prof. Selçuk explained, the BoE also requested expertise from the European Union:

> We provided foreign support for this //mmh// mmm we kindly requested from the European Union, we gave the names of foreign experts as we needed //mmh// those experts //mmh// they came from different countries //mmh// hm I mean how a textbook is designed etc., etc., //mmh// we provided intense education to everyone on these.

Given the complicated selection process for consultants to be hired in the name of the European Commission—which involves the SBEP, the MoNE, the European Commission, and the consultancy company that actually contracts the consultant—it is striking that Ziya Selçuk highlighted that these consultants were nominated by the curriculum commissions and by himself, without mentioning any power of decision from other bodies. We do not have to know how this procedure took place "in reality" to be able to conclude that, in Mr. Selçuk's perspective, even the international guidance was solely chosen by his team and worked on its behalf. This is especially evident in the final sentence, in which he claimed that "we provided intense education to everyone." Again, we see that according to Selçuk's perspective—which was confirmed by other Turkish interviewees—the European organizations (most possibly the "Support to Basic Education Program"; see earlier) only had a *supportive*, and not *decisive* role in the curriculum development process. Furthermore, this European advice was focused on the design of textbooks, an issue tackled only after the curricula had been developed (see "Test Results and Competition Among Public Schools" in chapter 6).

Within the commissions, the design of curricula followed a specific sequence which we here present in an ideal-typical way, that is, abstracting this sequential order from the many specific circumstances and peculiarities these processes encountered in practice. As Prof. Aydın conveyed,

> for one thing, when we commenced this curriculum development process, we had to start by deciding needs //mmh// hm which knowledge and skill and qualifications we will provide for the children of that age group.

For this "analysis of need," the commissions took into account the Turkish legislation, reports from MoNE inspectors, international reports on desirable "skills" of "children in this age group" as well as the curricula of private schools in Turkey (presumably including the ones founded by Mr. Selçuk) which, according to Mr. Aydın, "may be in advance of the practices of National Education"; in other words, in advance of the practices of public schools. Mr. Aydın then concluded by saying:

> that is by accessing every kind of data source and information source as much as possible and by brainstorming over them we sought for an answer for our question, which skills and knowledge do we have to teach to our children, //mmh// //mmh// I mean that is this was our approach about ıhm the content of the program (1).

The preceding account, first of all, implies that the "skills and knowledge" introduced into the curriculum as learning goals had not derived from the old curriculum; instead, they were newly defined in a rather open and even unstructured ("brainstorming") process. As another commission leader, Prof. Kaya, reported, this radical openness was then turned into a thorough filtering process in which, first of all, the connection between goals to be taught to children were discussed:

> That is to say (.) we used to write the gain (2), discussed it among 15 people (1) what could be the second step of this gain, the third, the fourth, the fifth and let's say we wrote something. This took nearly a week or something like that. //mmh// We used to write and afterwards there were teachers we used to tell teachers you can use this, how would you deliver it, would the student achieve this gain after you delivered it //mmh// it happened in such a way that that we would completely change the gain we had noted and agreed upon after five or six days //mmh// I mean there was a good deal of debate (1).

The "gains" were not only systematized during the discussion ("second step," etc.), but also exposed to the criticism from "teachers" within the commission, who evaluated their feasibility. Prof. Kaya, later, even maintained that he had been asking school children he encountered in trains and busses for their feedback on specific goals of whose feasibility he was unsure. From time to time, this evaluation process led to a "full" change of goals.

Another control mechanism was the adaptation of goals between the different curricula. Prof. Aydın elaborated on this issue:

> We developed the curriculum of the life science course but mmm on the level of primary education these curricula are a whole, (1) therefore the courses of Turkish, mathematic, social sciences, science and technology had to be appropriate to the skills that they would want to be gained by the students (1) mmm that is to say this course mmm had to be in

harmony with the school curriculum, the curriculum on the school level rather than mmm with its own curriculum (1) consequently while composing the program of the life science course, we had to take care of the school curriculum in addition to those that I named, as a matter of fact we did so.

Here, Prof. Aydın stressed the importance of the curricula being "in harmony" with each other to secure the unity of the overall school curriculum. Again, he here takes the constructivist approach of the curricula as a self-evident matter of fact that does not need to be mentioned at all. Instead, he focused his concerns on the adequacy of each branch's goals towards those of the others. As Prof. Kaya reported, the adequacy of gains was also a matter of timing, which made the respective curriculum commissions ask their counterparts for revisions and additions of their own gains to ensure a "coordinated" curriculum.

After the first proposal of the curricula had been completed it was discussed by academics, groups of teachers, and school inspectors (in meetings that took place between February 23 and April 28, 2004) as well as by "civil society organizations" and partners from the "private" and "public sector," as Ziya Selçuk confirmed in his interview. Although 39 NGOs had been invited to a meeting on May 4, 2004, only 14 took part. Teachers' unions, albeit invited, did not attend whatsoever. Mrs. Pars, the representative of a NGO that took part in the meeting, expressed her astonishment over the reluctant participation of NGOs in the meeting and gave reasons for it:

> What I saw especially at the *Board of Education (1)* very openly mmm the civil society associations were called again and again to give their opinions (1) mmm some of them written and some others as being invited, and I recalled to be irritated by this, the Board of Education (1) wanted support, as like this mmm the Civil Society Associations remained // mmh// very distant. surely, there is this doubt, something accumulated over years (1) and mmm well furthermore due to the mmm political line mmm of this government, there is a further doubt like whether they use us, will we really be asked, //mmh// okay we said, but what then, (1) they do this not because they wish to themselves but through pressure of the European Union etc., all these might be possible and *true* (1) but they remained very distant (1).

As Mrs. Pars underpinned, the reluctant participation of NGOs in the meeting organized by the MoNE may have resulted from "suspicions" that had grown "over the years" against a state that did not really take the opinions of NGOs into account.[14] Furthermore, Mrs. Pars mentioned the NGOs general unease about the new government, whose true intentions they still did not know. In this way, she alluded to a similar passive resistance as that experienced by Ziya Selçuk within the bureaucracy at the time he wanted to launch the new curriculum.

According to an unpublished summary of the meeting, the general teaching and learning approach of the curricula was not at all discussed or criticized. There was, however, some criticism towards the contents of the curricula, which supposedly neglected this or that topic or overemphasized others. As Prof. Aydın narrated, these discussions were then taken as a background for the revision of the curricula by the respective commissions:

> *For three days* these draft programs were opened up for debate (1) I guess, one mmm something like this happened in the sixth month of the curriculum work (1) after these drafts were ready, those debates were pursued (1) the feedback was received from those debates (1) we as commission worked on these again (1).

Whereas the suggestions of academics, teachers, and of representatives of NGOs were being taken into regard for the revisions that took place after the meetings, the meetings per se were altogether perceived as a general expression of acceptance. As Ziya Selçuk summarized their results, "a basis had been formed."

At this point, it is worth commenting on the dynamic and committed character of the curriculum commissions. As several interviewees maintained, in unison, there were experts in the commissions "who were really excited and really wanted to do something"; on that account, the curriculum commissions worked "night and day." Ziya Selçuk explained this high motivation through a conviction that there was, without a partisan view, "really something done for this country" and for its "children." Without questioning this view, we might add that the dynamism and commitment of the curriculum development process may also have gained from the likemindedness of its core actors, that is, from their belonging to a single organizational milieu, as far as teaching and learning were concerned. In a way, Mr. Selçuk himself pointed to the shared orientations of the curriculum teams by drawing the interviewer's attention to the "naivety" and "transparency" governing their work.

The dominance of the homologous orientations within this organizational milieu went so far as to make commission members feel that no hierarchical and bureaucratic structure existed in the Board of Education. The account of Önder Kaplan, a rank and file member of a curriculum commission, is evidence for this:

> Well (1) we were not confronted with any hierarchy //mmh// this surprised us too at the time, this most probably I always attributed this to the thing but if it resulted from the personality of Professor Selçuk (2), we came and left the Board of Education extremely easily at any time we wanted (1) our fellow teachers worked there overtime (1) then

there is something like the Department of Curriculum Development, it is affiliated with one council member in each curriculum (1) but let me confess something to you (1) I for example did not know our social sciences curriculum (2) was attached to what was the name of this guy, whatever, I mean, I mean a council member (1) we learned this years after we had left (2) I mean we were doing work under his supervision so-called supervision yet we never saw him.

For Önder Kaplan, the working process within the curriculum commission—dominated by shared challenges and duties and structured by the homologous orientations of the organizational milieu inserted in the BoE—was so central that hierarchical relations within the Board considerably lost importance. Although he acknowledged that such hierarchies existed ("so-called supervision"), he highlighted that they did not structure their working process.

In the end, however, the curriculum had to be evaluated and approved by the BoE itself. While all other interviewees, including Ziya Selçuk, did not even mention the evaluation process, Dr. Küre, a member of the decision-making body of the BoE and later a high-ranking ministerial bureaucrat, underpinned its importance. Before mentioning this evaluation, he drew the interviewer's attention to the practice-oriented feedback of teachers and academics, which he apparently saw as an important criterion for approving the curricula; in the following text, this feedback is mentioned as "such an effort": "After such an effort mmm it was brought to the council (1) the council then approves it then this curriculum was applied in the whole of Turkey."

Although Mr. Küre underpinned the importance of the criticism raised by practitioners and academics, in his account it seems to be self-evident that the subsequent decision process led to an approval of the curriculum. On July 12, 2004, the new curricula for Mathematics and Turkish (grades 1–5), Life Knowledge (grades 1–3), Science and Technology as well as Social Knowledge (grades 4–5) were approved and promulgated by the Turkish Board of Education. Contrary to what the bureaucrat indicated, they were not "implemented throughout Turkey" but first piloted in several provinces for 1 year. Only in the 2005/2006 school year did the ministry introduce the new curriculum in all Turkish primary schools, starting with grade 1 and then expanding its scope year by year.

3.3   The New Curriculum's Approach

Although the new curriculum's contents and pedagogical approach are not themselves a subject matter to be extensively analyzed in this volume, a brief description of the new curriculum's approach is appropriate at this point. Instead of an analysis of the new curriculum in its own right, we here draw on material used by the ministry as well as on analyses published by NGOs and education scientists.

In its information campaign for teachers (see also chapter 6), the MoNE emphasized the radical character of the curriculum change, presenting teachers with slides that stipulated that "the rigid behaviorist curriculum was exchanged for a cognitive and constructive approach;

- education—not just teaching—was emphasized;
- common skills that are to be passed on to our children were identified;
- sports, health, environment, guide and counseling, career, entrepreneurism, and natural disaster awareness were incorporated into the curriculum's backbone through an inter-disciplinary approach;
- 'knowledge,' 'skill,' 'understanding,' and 'attitudes' were used instead of the abstract term 'behavior';
- instead of the dominant linear way of thinking, the principle of reciprocal causality was highlighted;
- the curricula were enriched by activities;
- sensibility towards the Turkish language became the core skill of each course." (TTK, 2005)

These slides, first of all, underpin that the "cognitive and constructivist approach" was not the only novelty of the new curriculum, which also focused "education" (as opposed to "teaching"), used new concepts such as "knowledge" and "attitude," and put an emphasis on "activities." As Altinyelken (2013) highlighted,

> The new educational programmes recommend that the majority of the lesson time should be spent on classroom activities. The role of teachers has been modified in the sense that rather than directly providing information, they are expected to facilitate, guide and supervise pupils' learning processes. Pupils' roles and responsibilities are also redefined as they are expected to assume more responsibility for their own learning, and participate in learning and teaching activities by raising questions, handling materials, developing projects, doing research, and cooperating and discussing with their classmates and teachers.
>
> (p. 113)

This student-centered approach fits in with the constructivist epistemology on which the new curriculum is based. Accordingly, in its information material, the MoNE wrote that

- "an individual who has an active role and is actively involved in learning *physically* constructs knowledge,
- an individual who interprets events according to himself/herself *symbolically* constructs the knowledge,

- an individual who expresses the meaning that is his/her own construct to others *socially* constructs knowledge,
- an individual who tries to explain knowledge that he/she does not completely conceive *theoretically* constructs knowledge." (TTK, 2005)

It is made clear, through these words, that knowledge is not a product of construction only; what is constructed, it is implied, also depends on the learner. In addition to this information on the curriculum's approach, the teachers were also informed about a broad range of new contents to be conveyed with the new curriculum. Similar explanations could be found in the teacher manuals that were later developed for introducing teachers to the new curriculum through writing.

A critical assessment of the new curriculum, published by the Education Reform Initiative, confirmed the new teaching and learning approach and emphasized that the curriculum developers had made a considerable effort to make this approach clear:

> In the new curricula, the learning and teaching processes and the teacher's role are considered in more detail than they had been elaborated on in the previous curricula. Proposals were made on the implementation process concerning acquiring knowledge and skills, and "Activity Examples" were provided. Nonetheless, it was highlighted that these activities are examples and that the practices have to be flexible by taking individual differences and environmental conditions into account. In the previous curricula, there had been no explanation regarding the learning and teaching process, and very few examples of activities were included.
>
> (Aşkar et al., 2005, p. 24)

In the preceding quote, one can sense a generally deprecating attitude toward the old behaviorist curriculum, which presumably explains why the authors of this report praised the new curriculum even though they also list a broad range of criticism, ranging from the implementation of the constructivist approach to the coherence of the curriculum contents. All in all, however, the authors were confident that the curriculum was indeed bringing novelty into education by introducing constructivism to schools and by basing student activities "upon the Theory of Multiple Intelligences" (Aşkar et al., 2005, p. 24).

Whereas the Education Reform Initiative confined its criticism to pedagogical matters, there were other NGOs and educational activists who also pointed to the broader meaning of the curriculum change and its ideological background (Sağdiç, 2006; Eğitim Sen, 2007). İnal et al. (2014), among others, argued that the new curriculum's contents promoted a neoliberal outlook and aimed at turning children into market participants. Additionally, as Ünder (2012, p. 43) argued, the constructivist approach of the new curriculum was attractive for the ruling JDP because it undermined the "hegemony and the privileged position of science and positivism, which have buttressed modernist discourse and policies opposed by Islamism." As a matter of course, in the early years after the introduction of the new curriculum, this criticism was confined to the "intended curriculum" (Cuban, 1992). Problems of curriculum practice, although anticipated, were not yet criticized.

3.4   Preliminary Conclusions

The empirical analyses of this chapter have focused on the emergence of a new curriculum in Turkish education. As we have made clear from the outset, such analyses need both a framework of basic theoretical concepts and a research methodology comprehensive enough to grasp the large variety of actions, events, and dynamics evolving on different levels of society and in different social entities (see section 3.1). The main research question for this chapter was how the new curriculum was developed as a formal rule for all school organizations of the country after the Justice and Development Party's coming to power in November 2002.

The comprehensive analysis of the different and sometimes even antagonistic practical dynamics taking place between November 2002 and the promulgation of the new curriculum in July 2004 reveals a complex interplay of various points. If we solely look at the factors that existed before the minister of education assigned the president of the BoE with developing a new curriculum, we can identify the following:

1. There existed a widespread discontent with the old curriculum, its contents, and most importantly, its teaching approach, which alludes to a "misalignment" (Waks, 2007, p. 289).
2. This discontent was also translated into parties' election programs, which univocally promised to change the curriculum but remained rather abstract.
3. A landslide victory gave one party the power and legitimacy to start reforms in different areas.
4. This victory was also made possible by the integration of non-partisan (more liberal) public figures, one of whom, due to political power games, was appointed minister of education.

While these factors lie on the level of society and in the political realm, when the minister of education appointed Prof. Dr. Ziya Selçuk as president of the BoE and thus assigned him with curriculum development, the societal factors were connected to the following factors, which are situated in a specific academic organizational milieu:

5. The first theoretical inquiries into new curricular approaches were made in the country.

6. On the basis of pioneering school experiments, practical experience with new curriculum approaches was gained.
7. The minister found in Ziya Selçuk a protagonist of these new curriculum approaches (constructivism and multiple-intelligence).
8. This protagonist was well-connected to other colleagues, with whom he shared important orientations concerning both the curricular approach and cooperation with the new ruling party.

What then followed were various actions with at times different or even antagonist intentions within the educational sector:

9. Ziya Selçuk used the window of opportunity[15] opened after the 2002 election and the appointment of Erkan Mumcu as minister of education.
10. Prof. Selçuk faced passive resistance in his own ministry, from the Higher Education Council ("YÖK"), and from universities, which can be interpreted as a shared—albeit informal—orientation according to which the law and other legal procedures were put into practice. Had this informal resistance not existed, Ziya Selçuk would have had to develop the curriculum with a variety of academics chosen by their respective universities rather than with those chosen by him.
11. Alternative ways of financing the curriculum change through using European Commission funds were created.
12. This enabled Mr. Selçuk to assemble a team of academics with homologous orientations, who were then introduced into the Board of Education as an independent organizational milieu.
13. The commission leaders, chosen by the president of the BoE, then again tended to co-opt like-minded academics into their commissions, hence enlarging the organizational milieu.
14. The members of this organizational milieu authored the new curricula in strong cooperation with and under the guidance of Ziya Selçuk.
15. Although during the curriculum development process various suggestions from outside of this organizational milieu had been taken into account, they were limited to the contents of the curricula. In contrast, the teaching approach of the new curriculum, based on constructivism and the multiple intelligence theory, was fiercely endorsed by the organizational milieu and was never allowed to be questioned.

In more abstract ways, one may say that the development of this new curriculum was dependent on three pillars: a general—and rather abstract—urge for change on the societal level (which was not confined to the old curriculum but referred to different social matters); the existence of a group of academics who had previously experimented with a new curricular approach, were acquainted with each other and able to later constitute a homogenous organizational milieu within the BoE; and on the strong leadership of an individual who was, in spite of various obstacles, able to translate the societal urge for change into organizing a new curriculum by turning a group of like-minded academics into an efficient organizational milieu. Although so far we have only inquired into the curriculum change as far as the constitution of new formal rules is concerned, the dynamics of this process, with its numerous and sometimes antagonistic actors, reveal that the resulting curriculum was certainly "trans-intentional" (Altrichter, 2010, p. 150) and could be anticipated neither by the minister of education nor by the president of the BoE or any other actor.

The global and local dimensions of the curriculum development were as follows:

16. While the principal approach of the new curriculum was based on theories that had been dispersed throughout the world and led to a certain isomorphism, it was certainly not directly borrowed with the aim of developing this new curriculum.
17. Rather, we identify theoretical work and—even more importantly—practical experience with constructivism and the multiple intelligence approach created in the Turkish education sector that became inspiring for the new curriculum.
18. During the curriculum development, different commissions took fragments of curricula from abroad, which were then integrated in the already existing frame of the new Turkish curriculum.

In this sense, the new curriculum was influenced by a "world culture" (Meyer et al., 1992) of education—promoting constructivist and multiple intelligence learning theories—rather than by the "borrowing" (Halpin & Troyna, 1995; Steiner-Khamsi & Quist, 2000) of specific curricula.

All in all, this change from a behavioristic to a constructivist curriculum can be termed *transformative* (Cuban, 1992; Watzlawick et al., 1974), as far as the formal rules imposed on school organizations are concerned. As we see in the following chapters, this transformative change may not extend to the level of instructional practice in schools, as the characteristics of the intended curriculum may become overlapped by different issues as soon as the "taught curriculum" (Cuban, 1992) comes into play.

Notes

1 Unfortunately, Çelik's press communiqué could not be found on the Internet. However, this quote is confirmed by articles in Hürriyet (http://arama.hurriyet.com.tr/arsivnews.aspx?id=248657) and Radikal (see http://www.radikal.com.tr/haber.php?haberno=124730) newspapers on August 12 and 11, 2004, and by a press bulletin of the ministry issued on August 12, 2004 (see http://www.meb.gov.tr/haberler/haberayrinti.asp?ID=5821) (retrieved June 1, 2015).
2 Most of the research on the new curriculum in Turkey has been confined to the intended curriculum (see Altınay, 2009; Argün et al., 2010; Aşkar et al., 2005; Bora, 2009; Çayır, 2009; Demirel, 2009; Öztürk, 2011; Ubuz et al., 2010; Zembat, 2010).

In contrast, analyses of teachers' experience with the new curriculum in Turkey (see Bulut, 2007; Çelik-Şen & Şahin-Taşkın, 2010; Gelen & Beyazit, 2007; Kırmızı & Akkaya, 2009) come close to the 'taught' curriculum.

3 The only analysis of the new curriculum in Turkey that is theoretically elaborated is Altinyelken's (2010), which compares the implementation of constructivist curricula in Uganda and Turkey. She places her study in the frame of "educational transfer" between countries and global institutions (such as the OECD), including the questions of how and why "countries borrow or lend educational policies" (p. 19). Here she referred to the research by Dale, Steiner-Khamsi, Phillips, and Ochs (see earlier). Constructivist curricula, as Altinyelken maintained, are borrowed by poorer countries from the West. Her main research question, however, concerned the implementation of these curricula. In this regard, drawing on the work of Cuban (1992), she differentiated between the "intended," the "taught," and the "learned curriculum" (Altinyelken, 2010, p. 29). While the latter was not part of her study, the collection of documents, participant observation in the classroom, and numerous interviews with ministerial bureaucrats, education scientists, school administrators, and teachers in the capitals of both countries served Altinyelken (2010, pp. 33–45) to illuminate the taught curriculum.

4 The German-language literature cited in this and the previous paragraphs has unfortunately been published under the catchword "educational governance," a term that—in the English-language literature—usually refers to a new form of bureaucratic organization which is controversially discussed in education science (see Ball, 2007; Ball & Junemann, 2012). In our research we use the cited literature solely in its methodological aspect, that is, as an "analytic tool" (Altrichter, 2010, p. 147), which, however, in the literature is not always thoroughly separated from the mentioned form of bureaucratic organization.

5 Expert interviews, as we used them, have some similarities with the oral history approach, in which these narratives are seen as the "intersection of historical processes and personal experience" (Cándida Smith, 2002, p. 715). However, while oral history has been mainly concerned with analyzing 'history from below' (Perks & Thomson, 2003), that is, the experience of people who did not have decisive roles in the course of history, our research focuses on those who were able to shape a—albeit small—part of Turkish education history themselves.

6 While the JDP, newly founded in 2001 by reformist powers within the Islamic movement, propagated economically liberal and politically center-right policies in their election campaign (see section 2.3), the RPP saw itself as the heir of Mustafa Kemal's (the state founder) laicist and center-left policy (see section 2.2).

7 *Resmi Gazete*, November 29, 2002, http://www.resmigazete.gov.tr/eskiler/2002/11/20021129.htm (retrieved August 1, 2013).

8 This and the following quotes without references are taken from the oral accounts of our respective interviewees. For details, see the appendix to this volume.

9 For the rules of transcription, see the appendix to this volume. The Turkish original of all transcripts reproduced in this volume can be retrieved on the following website: http://www.hsu-hh.de/systpaed/index.php?brick_id=4ez2NjBre8SpiU3J (retrieved June 1, 2015).

10 Ziya Selçuk's narration was confirmed by someone he wished to appoint as an expert for curriculum development. As Ahmet Aydın told us, when the BoE made the application for him, "my university first didn't give the permission for this assignment to go to me." As he assumed, the "university at that time did not favor a change in curriculum," or at least not "by this team."

11 Email communication with Anders Lönnqvist dating September 30, 2012.
12 http://tedp.meb.gov.tr/main.php?ID=01–05–01 (retrieved November 7, 2012).
13 According to the interview with Mrs. Pars, this NGO's initiative was presumably so warmly welcomed because its approach, though rather abstract, had a lot in common with that of Ziya Selçuk.
14 Conversely, most NGOs specialized in education had only been recently founded.
15 Steiner-Khamsi (2006, p. 670) drew attention to the importance of such a window of opportunity, which "points to the temporal dimension of policy formation, and concerns identifying the catalytic moment for policy change."

References

Altan, M. Z. (1999). Çoklu Zeka Kuramı. *Kuram ve Uygulamada Eğitim Yönetimi, 1*, 105–117.

Altınay, A. (2009). "Can veririm, kan dökerim": Ders kitaplarında militarizm. In G. Tüzün (Ed.), *Ders kitaplarında insan hakları tarama sonuçları II* (pp. 143–165). Istanbul: Tarih Vakfı Yayınları.

Altinyelken, H. K. (2010). *Changing pedagogy—A comparative analysis of reform efforts in Uganda and Turkey* (Unpubished doctoral thesis). University of Amsterdam.

Altinyelken, H. K. (2011). Student-centred pedagogy in Turkey: Conceptualisations, interpretations and practices. *Journal of Education Policy, 26*, 137–160.

Altinyelken, H. K. (2013). Teachers' principled resistance to curriculum change: A compelling case from Turkey. In A. Verger, H. K. Altinyelken, & M. D. Konik (Eds.), *Global education reforms and teachers* (pp. 109–127). Brussels: Education International.

Altrichter, H. (2010). Theory and evidence on governance: Conceptual and empirical strategies of research on governance in education. *European Educational Research Journal, 9*, 147–158.

Altrichter, H., & Maag Merki, K. (2011). Steuerung der Entwicklung des Schulwesens. In H. Altrichter & K. Maag Merki (Eds.), *Handbuch Neue Steuerung im Schulsystem* (pp. 15–39). Wiesbaden: Springer.

Argün, Z., Arıkan, A., Bulut, S., & Sriraman, B. (2010). A brief history of mathematics education in Turkey: K–12 mathematics curricula. *ZDM Mathematics Education, 42*, 429–441.

Asbrand, B. (2014). Die dokumentarische Methode in der Governance-Forschung. In K. Maag Merki et al. (Eds.), *Educational Governance als Forschungsperspektive* (pp. 177–198). Wiesbaden: Springer/VS.

Aşkar, P., Paykoç, F., Korkut, F., Olkun, S., Yangın, B., & Çakıroğlu, J. (2005). *Yeni Eğitim Programları İnceleme ve Değerlendirme Raporu*. Istanbul: Eğitim Reformu Girişimi.

Ball, S. J. (2007). *Education PLC: Understanding private sector participation in public sector education*. London: Routledge.

Ball, S. J., & Junemann, C. (2012). *Networks, new governance and education*. Bristol, England: Policy Press.

Beech, J. (2006). The theme of educational transfer in comparative education: A view over time. *Research in Comparative and International Education, 1*, 2–13

Berger, P. L., & Luckmann, T. (1991). *The social construction of reality*. London: Penguin.

Bidwell, C. E., Frank, K. A., & Quiroz, P. A. (1997). Teacher types, workplace controls, and the organization of schools. *Sociology of Education, 70*, 285–307.

Bidwell, C. E., & Yasumoto, J. Y. (1999). The collegial focus: Teaching fields, collegial relationships, and instructional practice in American high schools. *Sociology of Education, 72*, 234–256.

Bohnsack, R. (2010a). *Rekonstruktive Sozialforschung.* Opladen: Budrich.

Bohnsack, R. (2010b). Documentary Method and Group Discussions. In R. Bohnsack, N. Pfaff, & W. Weller (Eds.), *Qualitative analysis and documentary method in international educational research* (pp. 99–124). Opladen: Barbra Budrich.

Bohnsack, R. (2014a). Habitus, Norm und Identität. In W. Helsper et al. (Eds.), *Schülerhabitus* (pp. 33–55). Wiesbaden: Springer.

Bohnsack, R. (2014b). Documentary method. In U. Flick (Ed.), *SAGE handbook of analyzing qualitative data* (pp. 217–223). Thousand Oakes, CA: Sage.

Bohnsack, R., Pfaff, N., & Weller, W. (Eds.). (2010). *Qualitative analysis and documentary method in international educational research.* Opladen: Barbara Budrich.

Boli, J., Ramirez, F.O., & Meyer, J. W. (1985). Explaining the origins and expansion of mass education. *Comparative Education Review, 29,* 145–170.

Bora, T. (2009). Ders kitaplarında milliyetçilik. In G. Tüzün (Ed.), *Ders kitaplarında insan hakları tarama sonuçları II* (pp. 115–141). İstanbul: Tarih Vakfı Yayınları.

Bourdieu, P. (2010). *The logic of practice.* Cambridge: Polity Press.

Bulut, M. (2007). Curriculum reform in Turkey: A case of primary school mathematics curriculum. *Eurasia Journal of Mathematics, Science & Technology Education, 3,* 203–212.

Cándida Smith, R. (2002). Analytic strategies for oral history interviews. In J. F. Gubrium & J. A. Holstein (Eds.), *Handbook of interview research* (pp. 711–731). Thousand Oaks, CA: Sage.

Çayır, K. (2009). "Avrupalı olmadan önce biz olmalıyız": Yeni öğretim programları ve ders kitapları ışığında Türkiye modernleşmesine dair bir okuma. *Kuram ve Uygulamada Eğitim Bilimleri, 9,* 1659–1690.

Çelik-Şen, Y., & Şahin-Taşkın, Ç. (2010). Yeni ilköğretim programının getirdiği değişiklikler: Sınıf Öğretmenlerinin Düşünceleri. *Yüzüncü Yıl Üniversitesi, Eğitim Fakültesi Dergisi, VII,* 26–51.

Chen, J.-Q., Moran, S., & Gardner, H. (Eds.). (2009). *Multiple intelligences around the world.* San Francisco: Jossey-Bass.

Cuban, L. (1992). Curriculum stability and change. In P. W. Jackson (Ed.), *Handbook of research on curriculum* (pp. 216–247). New York: Macmillan.

Cuban, L. (1995). The hidden variable: How organizations influence teacher responses to secondary science curriculum reform. *Theory Into Practice, 34,* 4–11.

Dale, R. (1999). Specifying globalization effects on national policy: A focus on the mechanisms. *Journal of Education Policy, 14,* 1–17.

Dale, R. (2000). Globalization and education: Demonstrating a "common world educational culture" or locating a "globally structured educational agenda"? *Educational Theory, 50,* 427–448.

Dehnavi, M. (2013). *Das politisierte Geschlecht: Biographische Wege zum Studentinnenprotest von ,1968 'und zur Neuen Frauenbewegung.* Bielefeld: Transcript.

Demirel, M. (2009). A review of elementary education curricula in Turkey: Values and values education. *World Applied Science Journal, 7,* 670–678.

DiMaggio, P. J., & Powell, W. W. (1983). The iron cage revisited: Institutional isomorphism and collective rationality in organizational fields. *American Sociological Review, 48,* 147–160.

DiMaggio, P. J., & Powell, W. W. (1991). Introduction. In W. W. Powell & P. J. DiMaggio (Eds.), *The new institutionalism in organizational analysis* (pp. 1–38). Chicago: University of Chicago Press.

Eğitim Sen. (2007). *Milli Eğitim Bakanlığı'nda AKP'nin 4 Yılı.* Ankara: Eğitim Sen Yayınları.

Elias, N. (1978). *What is sociology.* London: Hutchinson.

Fend, H. (2009). *Neue Theorie der Schule.* Wiesbaden: VS.

Gardner, H. (1983). *Frames of mind: The theory of multiple intelligences.* New York: Basic Books.

Gazi (Gazi Üniversitesi Vakfı Özel Okulları). (n.d.). *Gazi Üniversitesi Vakfı Özel Okulları.* Ankara: GÜ.

Gelen, İ., & Beyazıt, N. (2007). Eski ve Yeni İlköğretim Programları İle İlgili Çeşitli Görüşlerin Karşılaştırılması. *Kuram ve Uygulamada Eğitim Yönetimi, 51,* 457–476.

Glassman, R. B. (1973). Persistence and loose coupling in living systems. *Behavioral Science, 18,* 83–98.

Gough, N. (2008). All around the world science education, constructivism, and globalisation. In B. Atweh et al. (Eds.), *Internationalisation and Globalisation in Mathematics and Science Education* (pp. 39–55). Dordrecht: Springer.

Groppe, C. (2009). Theoretische und methodologische Voraussetzungen und Probleme einer bildungshistorischen Familienbiographie. In J. Ecarius, C. Groppe, & H. Malmede (Eds.), *Familie und öffentliche Erziehung* (pp. 93–116). Wiesbaden: VS.

Halpin, D., & Troyna, B. (1995). The politics of education policy borrowing. *Comparative Education, 31,* 303–310.

Helsper, W., Hummrich, M. & Kramer, R.-T. (2010). Qualitative Mehrebenenanalyse. In B. Friebertshäuser & A. Prengel (Eds.), *Handbuch Qualitative Forschungsmethoden in der Erziehungswissenschaft* (pp. 119–135). Weinheim: Beltz.

Hornberg, S. (2009). Potential of the world polity approach and the concept "transnational educational spaces" for the analysis of new developments in education. *Journal for Educational Research Online, 1,* 241–253.

İnal, K., Akkaymak, G., & Yıldırım, D. (2014). The constructivist curriculum reform in Turkey in 2004—In fact what is constructed? *Journal for Critical Education Policy Studies, 12,* 350–373.

JDP (Justice and Development Party). (2002). *Herşey Türkiye İçin. AKP Seçim Beyannamesi.* Ankara: Author.

Johnson, D. (2006). Comparing the trajectories of educational change and policy transfer in developing countries. *Oxford Review of Education, 32,* 679–696.

Kırmızı, F. S., & Akkaya, N. (2009). Türkçe Öğretimi Programında Yaşanan Sorunlara İlişkin Öğretmen Görüşleri. *Pamukkale Üniversitesi Eğitim Fakültesi Dergisi, 25,* 42–54.

Köseoğlu, F., & Kavak, N. (2001). Fen Öğretiminde Yapılandırıcı Yaklaşım. *Gazi Eğitim Fakültesi Dergisi, 21,* 139–148.

Kussau, J., & Brüsemeister, T. (2007). Educational Governance: Zur Analyse der Handlungskoordination im Mehrebenensystem der Schule. In H. Altrichter, T. Brüsemeister, & J. Wissinger (Eds.), *Educational Governance* (pp. 15–54). Wiesbaden: VS.

Luhmann, N. (1964). *Funktionen und Folgen formaler Organisation.* Berlin: de Gruyter.

Mannheim, K. (1952). On the interpretation of Weltanschauung. In *Essays on the sociology of knowledge* (pp. 33–83). New York: Oxford University Press.

Mannheim, K. (1982). *Structures of thinking.* London: Routledge.

Mayntz, R., & Scharpf, F. W. (1995). Steuerung und Selbstorganisation in staatsnahen Sektoren. In R. Mayntz & F. W. Scharpf (Eds.), *Gesellschaftliche Selbstregelung und politische Steuerung* (pp. 9–38). Frankfurt: Campus.

Meuser, M., & Nagel, U. (2009). The expert interview and changes in knowledge production. In A. Bogner, B. Littig, & W. Menz (Eds.), *Interviewing experts* (pp. 17–42). London: Palgrave.

Meyer, J. W., Boli, J., Thomas, G. M., & Ramirez, F. O. (1997). World society and the nation-state. *American Journal of Sociology, 103*(1), 144–181.

Meyer, J. W., Ramirez, F. O., & Soysal, Y. N. (1992). World expansion of mass education, 1870–1980. *Sociology of Education, 65*, 128–149.

Meyer, J. W., & Rowan, B. (1977). Institutionalized organizations: Formal structure as myth and ceremony. *American Journal of Sociology, 83*, 340–363.

Moll, L. C. (Ed.). (1990). *Vygotsky and education*. Cambridge: Cambridge University Press.

Murray, F. B. (Ed.). (1979). *The impact of Piagetian theory*. Baltimore: University Park Press.

Nohl, A.-M. (2010). The documentary interpretation of narrative interviews. In R. Bohnsack, N. Pfaff, & W. Weller (Eds.), *Qualitative analysis and documentary method in international education research* (pp. 195–218). Opladen: Barbara Budrich Publishers.

Nohl, A.-M. (2013). *Relationale Typenbildung und Mehrebenenvergleich: Neue Wege der dokumentarischen Methode*. Wiesbaden: VS.

Nohl, A.-M. (2014). *Konzepte interkultureller Pädagogik* (3rd ed.). Bad Heilbrunn: Klinkhardt.

Ortmann, G. (2003). *Regel und Ausnahme*. Frankfurt: Suhrkamp.

Ortmann, G. (2004). *Als Ob: Fiktionen und Organisationen*. Wiesbaden: VS.

Ortmann, G., Sydow, J., & Windeler, A. (1997). Organisation als reflexive Strukturation. In G. Ortmann, J. Sydow, & K. Türk (Eds.), *Theorien der Organisation* (pp. 315–354). Opladen: Westdeutscher.

Öztürk, I. H. (2011). Curriculum reform and teacher autonomy in Turkey: The case of history teaching. *International Journal of Instruction, 4*, 113–128.

Perks, R., & Thomson, A. (Eds.). (2003). *The oral history reader*. London: Routledge.

Perry, L. B., & Tor, G. (2008). Understanding educational transfer: Theoretical perspectives and conceptual frameworks. *Prospects, 38*, 509–526.

Phillips, D. C. (Ed.). (2000). *Constructivism in education: Opinions and second opinions on controversial issues*. Chicago: University of Chicago Press.

Phillips, D., & Ochs, K. (2004). Researching policy borrowing: Some methodological challenges in comparative education. *British Educational Research Journal, 30*(6), 773–784.

Polanyi, M. (1966). *The tacit dimension*. New York: Doubleday.

Popkewitz, T. S. (1988). Educational reform: Rhetoric, ritual, and social interest. *Educational Theory, 38*, 77–93.

Rowan, B. (1982). Organizational structure and the institutional environment: The case of public schools. *Administrative Science Quarterly, 27*, 259–279.

Rowan, B. (2006a). The new institutionalism and the study of educational organizations: Changing ideas for changing times. In H.-D. Meyer & B. Rowan (Eds.), *The new institutionalism in education* (pp. 15–32). Albany: SUNY.

Rowan, B. (2006b). Lessons learned and future directions. In H.-D. Meyer & B. Rowan (Eds.), *The new institutionalism in education* (pp. 203–215). Albany: SUNY.

RPP (Republican People's Party). (1997). *CHP Parti Programı*. Ankara: Author.

Rürup, M., & Bormann, I. (2013). Innovation als Thema und Theoriebaustein der Educational Governance Forschung. In M. Rürup & I. Bormann (Eds.), *Innovationen im Bildungswesen* (pp. 12–41). Wiesbaden: Springer.

Saban, A. (2001). *Çoklu Zekâ Kuramı ve Türk Eğitim Sistemine Yansıması*. Ankara: Nobel Yayın.

Sağdiç, İ. (2006). *Yeni Eğitim Programı (Müfredatı) Üzerine*. Ankara: Eğitim Sen.

SBEP (Support to Basic Education Project). (2003). *Inception report* (2 Vols.). Ankara: MoNE.

Schriewer, J. (1988). The method of comparison and the need for externalization: Methodological criteria and sociological concepts. In J. Schriewer & B. Holmes (Eds.), *Theories and methods in comparative education* (pp. 25–83). Frankfurt: Lang.

Schriewer, J. (2003). Globalisation in education: Process and discourse. *Policy Futures in Education, 1*, 271–283.

Selçuk, Z., Kayılı, H., & Okut, L. (Eds.). (2002). *Çoklu Zeka Uygulamaları.* Ankara: Nobel.

Steiner-Khamsi, G. (2006). The economics of policy borrowing and lending: A study of late adopters. *Oxford Review of Education, 32,* 665–678.

Steiner-Khamsi, G., & Quist, H. O. (2000). The politics of educational borrowing: Reopening the case of Achimota in British Ghana. *Comparative Education Review, 44,* 272–299.

T.C. 2003=T.C. 58. Hükümet (2003). *Acil Eylem Planı.* Ankara: Author.

T.C. 2007=T.C. Ministry of National Education Projects Coordination Center (2007). *Support to Basic Education Programme: Project outcomes.* Ankara: MoNE.

Talu, N. (1999). Çoklu Zeka Kuramı ve Eğitime Yansımaları. *Hacettepe Üniversitesi Eğitim Fakültesi Dergisi, 5,* 64–72.

TTK (Talim Terbiye Kurulu Başkanlığı). (2004). *Talim Terbiye Kurulu Program Geliştirme Çalışmaları.* Unpublished manuscript.

TTK (Talim Terbiye Kurulu Başkanlığı). (2005). *Yeni İlköğretim Programları ve Yeni Yaklaşımlar* [PowerPoint]. Ankara: Author.

Tyack, D., & Tobin, W. (1994). The "grammar" of schooling: Why has it been so hard to change? *American Educational Research Journal, 31,* 453–479.

Ubuz, B., Erbaş, A. K., Çetinkaya, B., & Özgeldi, M. (2010). Exploring the quality of the mathematical tasks in the new Turkish elementary school mathematics curriculum guidebook: The case of algebra. *ZDM Mathematics Education, 42,* 483–491.

Ünder, H. (2012). Constructivism and the curriculum reform of the AKP. In K. İnal & G. Akkaymak (Eds.), *Neoliberal transformation of education in Turkey* (pp. 33–45). New York: Palgrave.

Waks, L. J. (2003). How globalization can cause fundamental curriculum change. *Journal of Educational Change, 4,* 383–418.

Waks, L. J. (2007). The concept of fundamental educational change. *Educational Theory, 57,* 277–295.

Watzlawick, P., Weakland, J., & Fisch, R. (1974). *Change: Principles of problem formation and problem resolution.* New York: Norton.

Weick, K. E. (1976). Educational organizations as loosely coupled systems. *Administrative Science Quarterly, 21,* 1–19.

Weiß, A., & Nohl, A.-M. (2012). Overcoming methodological nationalism in migration research. Cases and contexts in multi-level comparisons. In A. Amelina, D. D. Nergiz, T. Faist, & N. Glick Schiller (Eds.), *Beyond methodological nationalism* (pp. 65–87). London: Routledge.

Yaşar, Ş. (1998). Yapısalcı Kuram ve Öğrenme-Öğretme Süreci. *Anadolu Üniversitesi Eğitim Fakültesi Dergisi, 8,* 68–75.

Zembat, I. Ö. (2010). A micro-curricular analysis of unified mathematics curricula in Turkey. *ZDM Mathematics Education, 42,* 443–455.

Zucker, L. G. (1977). The role of institutionalization in cultural persistence. *American Sociological Review, 42,* 726–743.

Zucker, L. G. (1987). Institutional theories of organization. *Annual Review of Sociology, 13,* 443–464.

4 Divergent Curricular Practices of Organizational Milieus

Teachers' Professional Generations

The new curriculum was imposed on all primary schools in Turkey as a formal rule starting on the 2005/2006 school year. This "coercive isomorphism" (DiMaggio & Powell, 1983, p. 150), initiated by the Ministry of National Education (MoNE), was accompanied by efforts to substantiate the new curriculum by the means of textbook production, the development of teacher manuals, and teacher training. We may regard these activities as attempts to institutionalize the new curriculum and hence to complement the formal pressure on schools and teaching staff through more practice-oriented and habitualizable components. These institutionalization attempts related and attuned the curriculum—originally developed by a rather homogeneous organizational milieu (see section 3.2)—to the expectations of bureaucrats, school inspectors, and textbook developers, and thus rendered it more heterogeneous than when it was firstly developed (see "Test Results and Competition Among Public Schools" in chapter 6).

Following arguments from New Institutionalism we may assume that the new curriculum, as a formal rule imposed on each and every school organization throughout the country, was then not "applied" or "implemented" in a one-to-one manner in the classroom. As curriculum research scholars convincingly maintain, the "intended" curriculum has to be differentiated from the "taught" curriculum (Cuban, 1992). The latter—that is, instructional *practice*—may only be "loosely coupled" (Weick, 1976, p. 11) with the formal rules of the school organizations, or may be even "decoupled" (Meyer & Rowan, 1977, p. 357) from them.

While New Institutionalism has been very inspiring for curricular research, the concepts of loose coupling and decoupling, although theoretically and empirically valid, only assert that classroom practices may considerably differ from the official curriculum. Because these practices themselves are not systematically analyzed by the New Institutionalists, it is not possible for the latter to give any further insight into classroom activities. As Bidwell et al. (1997) pointed out, "left unsettled by the loose-coupling analysis are the nature and location of whatever processes control teachers' work" (p. 285). Therefore, drawing on the research perspective of the praxeological sociology of knowledge and the Documentary Method (Bohnsack, 2010a; Mannheim,

1982), we wish to go a step beyond the claims of New Institutionalism and systematically inquire into the orientations which underlie and structure the classroom practice of the new curriculum.

This and the following chapters are devoted to an analysis of practical orientations guiding instruction in Turkish primary schools. While in the present chapter we scrutinize teacher's orientations toward the new curriculum, in chapter 5 we also include the influence of the school organization as well as the orientations of pupils' parents regarding instruction. Such empirical analysis of curriculum practice is a demanding and challenging endeavor, which needs to be explicated in its basic theoretical and methodological aspects. Thus, before we delve into the empirical analysis, we discuss the basic theoretical concepts, the methods of data collection and interpretation, and the sampling strategy used for studying curricular practices (section 4.1). We then focus on the orientations of the teaching staff and compare two organizational milieus, which we typify with regard to teachers' affiliation to professional generations. On one hand, there are teachers who were professionally socialized in and attached to the practices of the old—behavioristic—curriculum, but who could also draw on a huge amount of professional experience (section 4.2); on the other hand, we reconstruct the orientations of novices who started their professional career around the time the new—constructivist—curriculum was introduced (section 4.3). There are, to be sure, also organizational milieus of teachers who occupy an intermediary, between-generations position (section 4.4). Although we had expected such generational differences, the peculiar way each generationally embossed organizational milieu practiced instruction did indeed surprise us. Moreover, as we finally discover, these organizational milieus were not equally distributed throughout the country, but were allocated in schools in an unbalanced way. Concluding the chapter, we scrutinize the formal and informal mechanisms that render these organizational milieus' influence on curricular practices so powerful (section 4.5).

4.1   Analyzing Curricular Practices

Instructional practices, even if referring to the same curriculum, are widely acknowledged as manifold (see, among others, Altinyelken, 2011; Edwards, 2011; Supowitz & Weinbaum, 2008). Curriculum researchers who are not content with pointing to the mere diversity of curriculum practices have analyzed how they are influenced by, for example, social geographies (Hargreaves, 2002), globalization (Yates & Young, 2010), and social inequality (Lewis, 2007). The identification of such social contexts that influence curricular practice renders necessary a purposive and selective sampling strategy that is based on preliminary theoretical assumptions (Schittenhelm, 2009). These theoretical assumptions only guide the preliminary sampling strategy, but should not anticipate the empirical results of research. As will become evident in this volume, empirical inquiry may elicit surprising phenomena, which the researchers should take into account during further data sampling and interpretation (Glaser & Strauss, 1969).

Among the wide range of possible differences that may be reasons for (possible) differentiations in practices of the new Turkish curriculum, we have chosen to structure our sampling along two major dividing lines: the socioeconomic and geographic situation of the school and the teachers' "generation location" (Mannheim, 1972, p. 113). Whereas the socioeconomic and geographic situation refers to the social milieus from which a school predominantly recruits its pupils, the generation location pertains to the organizational milieu of teachers. Both dimensions, however, are deeply enshrined into the school organization: Organizational and social milieus may decisively influence the way formal rules (such as the curricula) are practiced. Moreover, as we see throughout this and the following chapter, both dimensions influence the school organization not only from outside, but also become factors within the school; that is, they become part of the organization.

The *generation location* of teachers (in other words, the generational dimension of their organizational milieus) was chosen because of the anticipated significance of this dimension for curricular practices. While gender, ethnicity, and employment modes (Güvercin, 2014) may gain importance for teachers in other regards, the generation location can be directly related to the introduction of the new curriculum. In Turkey, in spite of minor changes in the content of the syllabi, the curriculum had not been changed since 1968 (see Erdoğan, 2011). This implies that until the curriculum reform, which came into effect in 2005, all Turkish primary school teachers had become acquainted with the 1968 curriculum as pupils, later going through teacher training according to the same curriculum and then gaining teaching experience accordingly. In contrast, all these teachers trained around the time when the old curriculum began to receive heavy criticism, and acquired expertise and practical experience according to the new curriculum when it was introduced throughout the country in 2005. In this sense, we assume that the teaching staff of Turkish schools is divided—as regards their teaching experience—between those who by 2005 had only started their career and the older generation, who experienced the new curriculum as a change. This division, we anticipate, may be the basis of specific generational experiences, that is, of the formation of teacher generations.

While the generation location of teachers in Turkey, until now, has not received any attention by scholars, the *socioeconomic and geographic situation* of the school (its involvement with the social milieus of pupils) has been highlighted by several surveys on schools' performance (EARGED, 2010; Tansel, 2010) as well as in-depth inquiries regarding social inequality and education (Bakış et al., 2009; Somel, 2015; Ünal et al., 2010). Along with the gender issue and regional discrepancies (Alacacı & Erbaş, 2010), these analyses draw attention to the significance of differences between rural and urban contexts as well as between poor and middle-class social locations. While most of this research conceives of pupils' social milieus as a separate factor from the school, in our inquiry we focus on the interwovenness of social milieus and school organization in curricular practices.

Despite our focus on variations of curricular practices that are based on teachers' generations and the pupils'/parents' social milieus of pupils (as part of the schools), we do not regard these as objective conditions that directly influence—subjective—practices. Instead, drawing on the praxeological sociology of knowledge (Bohnsack, 2010a; Mannheim, 1982) we conceptualize the "generation location" (Mannheim, 1972, p. 113) of teachers as well as the socioeconomic and geographic situatedness of the school, with its social milieus as aspects of the "collective experience" (Mannheim, 1968, p. 241) with which the instruction practice is interwoven. It is in this collective experience that we make sense of the new curriculum as a formal rule of the educational organization (see Nohl, 2014, pp. 190–196, and section 3.1).

Generation and—in a certain sense (see chapter 5)—the social milieus of the school are structures rooted in commonalities of the "stratification of experience" (Mannheim, 1972, p. 112). This affiliation to a "conjunctive experiential space" (Mannheim, 1982, p. 194) connects even individuals who are not personally acquainted. To be enrolled in primary school in a certain time and under similar social circumstances (for instance, in the 21st century under a combination of poverty and educational aspiration) may constitute such an experiential commonality, which then may become the basis for a shared milieu affiliation. In this sense, "conjunctive experience" and milieus bear similarities with Tönnies's (2011) concept of "community" ("Gemeinschaft"). A community, however, as Tönnies conceived of it, is based on the tradition of the group and its face-to-face relations. In contrast, the social or organizational milieu as a conjunctive experiential space may be constituted by people whose experience is structurally identical but not based on cooperative practice. For example, teachers' classroom experience is usually not created together or in a group, but may still be a homologous and hence conjunctive experience.[1]

Mannheim suggested that the collective orientations based on these commonalities exist predominantly in the form of habitualized and incorporated stocks of pre-reflective or "atheoretical" knowledge (Mannheim, 1952a, p. 38). At the same time, these orientations reach out "beyond their actualization in individual psyches" and "by their very nature cannot be realized by an individual" (Mannheim, 1982, p. 209). Therefore, this collective orientation "is not primarily something to be thought, but rather something to be given effect through the interplay of various individuals" (p. 209). The unfolding of these collective orientations—for they are not primarily products or objects of reflection—is only possible in the practical interplay of those actors who belong to the same "conjunctive experiential space" (p. 206), that is, to the same social or organizational milieu.

Group Discussions and Their Documentary Interpretation

The group discussion, a method developed by Ralf Bohnsack (2010b), is an ideal instrument to analyze practical orientations and their embeddedness in a conjunctive space of experience. During such discussions, collective orientations and experiences are cooperatively articulated by members of the group. At the discussions Nazlı Somel conducted with teachers and their pupils' parents, a natural discourse usually evolved among participants, one that was neither moderated nor interfered with by the researcher. Only when the group's discourse stopped did the researcher pose a new open question to initiate further narrations by the group.

Along with stocks of knowledge "made explicit by the participants themselves," the group members draw on knowledge "which is so much taken for granted by the participants that it must not and often cannot be made explicit by themselves" (Bohnsack, 2010b, p. 103); hence, this knowledge is "atheoretical" (Mannheim, 1952a, p. 38). While the explicit knowledge of participants is rather theoretical (though mostly in the form of everyday theories) and abstracted from practical experience, the atheoretical knowledge is embedded in and orientates practice. As the participants themselves may not be able to explain their practical knowledge, the task of the researchers, "thus, is the theoretical explication of the mutual implicit or intuitive understanding of the participants" (Bohnsack, 2010b, p. 104).[2]

Similar to the documentary interpretation of expert interviews (see section 3.1), group discussions are—in a first step—interpreted according to their "objective meaning" (Mannheim, 1952a, p. 46), that is, according to "what has been said, depicted, or discussed, what has become the topic" (Bohnsack, 2010b, p. 110). This has "to be separated from how—that means: in which framework—the topic is dealt with." This "framework of orientation" is the focus of the second step of interpretation. To reconstruct the framework of orientation with which a topic (such as instructional practices) is dealt, we do not only take into regard the participants' accounts of their practical experience. The group discourse itself—for example, the mutual reference to each other as well as points of high metaphorical density or commitment—is interpreted as a practice in which orientations are embedded (Bohnsack, 2010b). Such an orientation is easier to detect if one contrasts it to other orientations of different groups; in other words, if one compares contrasting cases. In fact, comparative analysis not only facilitated the documentary interpretation of single cases but also helped to identify typical patterns of orientation (see later).

Sampling Strategies

As mentioned earlier, our analysis of curricular practices aimed at reconstructing both the generational dimension and the socioeconomic and geographical situatedness of the school. We assumed that we would find teachers of both the older and the younger generation in all primary schools. To include schools dominated by different social milieus—that is, to analyze the different situatedness of schools and facilitate the construction of typologies toward the situatedness of the schools—we had to take into consideration schools that differed with regard to their sociogeographic situation and the socioeconomic background of pupils and their parents. In Turkey, such a vast contrast would be easily achieved by comparing an upper-middle-class private school from a Western metropolis (Izmir, Ankara, or Istanbul) to a small village school in a Kurdish province at the Iranian or Iraqi border. However, we decided to exclude dimensions that we anticipated to render school education problematic, if not impossible, from the outset. Thus, we refrained from including schools and whole provinces that are well known for facing significant problems due to the (Kurdish) mother tongue of pupils, as well as schools and provinces with a high proportion of children from seasonal migrant worker families, and those with a lack of teachers.[3] Due to similar considerations we did not take into account private schools whose teacher–pupil ratio is twice as good as in the average state school (ERG, 2012, p. 83) and in which constructivist teaching had started even before 2003 (Ayan Ceyhan, 2009; Selçuk et al., 2002). We finally chose to carry out our empirical investigation in state schools of two Western provinces in Turkey that still offered the maximal contrasts for which we had sought. The first, Istanbul, as the biggest (though not only) metropolis of Turkey, is a highly urbanized province that offers all the components of urban life but also accommodates both (very) poor and middle-class milieus; the second is a province which we call "Dalen" to disguise the identity of research participants.[4] Dalen is situated in the Western part of central Anatolia, which is significantly characterized by agriculture even though its capital also has components of urban life that include a university and a variety of other educational and cultural organizations. Table 4.1 provides the reader with the most important statistical data, which already alludes to the tremendous differences between these provinces.

Although Dalen is almost 3000 km^2 larger than Istanbul, its population amounts to only 2% of Istanbul's. Dalen, a province where around 18% of the soil is used for agriculture and more than 60% is forests, has a significant rural population (against a near non-existent one in Istanbul), well above the Turkish average. The educational degrees obtained by the population in Istanbul are slightly higher than the Turkish average, and slightly lower in Dalen. While these educational degrees in the total population refer to the significance of education over longer periods in time, the current enrolment in schools is reflected in Table 4.2.

With the enrolment rates for primary education in both provinces being similar (with an advantage for Dalen as concerns secondary education), those ratios which give an—albeit vague—indication for the quality of education are discrepant, with Dalen showing a far lower rate of pupils per class and per teacher than Istanbul. As we see further in the following, all these statistical data only reflect the average of each province. But along with the contrasts

Table 4.1 Characteristics of provinces included in research

Provinces	Population	Population density (population/ km²)[1]	Population living in villages (%)	Population above age 15 with maximum 8 years school degree (%)	Population above age 15 with technical college degree or above	GNP per capita	Share of agricultural workforce (%)	Share of industrial workforce (including construction work) (%)	Share of workforce in services (%)
Istanbul	13,255,685	2666	1.02	51.86	11.8	14,591[2]	0.4	39.9	59.6
Dalen	271,208	34	37.3	61.19	8.83	13,265[3]	19.9[4]	34.1[5]	46.1[6]
Total of Turkey	73,722,988	98	23.74	59.25	9.23	9384	25.2	26.2	48.6

Source: Publications of the Turkish Statistics Institution; own calculations.
All data, if not otherwise suggested, from 2010.

[1] Numbers for year 2012.
[2] In 2008.
[3] Figure for the statisticial region which includes three more industrialized provinces, a rural province, and Dalen.
[4] Percentage for the statisticial region which includes three more industrialized provinces, a rural province, and Dalen. If one takes into account that 37.3% of the population of Dalen lives in villages, we can assume that the share of agricultural workforce in Dalen is far higher than 19.9%.
[5] Percentage for the statisticial region which includes three more industrialized provinces, a rural province, and Dalen.
[6] Percentage for the statisticial region which includes three more industrialized provinces, a rural province, and Dalen.

Table 4.2 Educational figures of provinces included in research

Provinces	Number of primary school pupils	Enrolment in primary education (in %)	Number of pupils per class	Number of pupils per teacher	Enrolment in secondary education (in %)
Istanbul	1.9 million	99.38	35.4	28.2	70.73
Dalen	31,600	98.46	23.7	16.2	90.28

Source: MoNE (2012, p. 6); author's own calculations.

between provinces, their interior heterogeneity was also very important for our research. Both Istanbul and Dalen are provinces that provided us with the opportunity to include five primary schools that reflect the differences—and at times discrepancies—of social contexts. Following theoretical considerations in Dalen, we include the school of a small village we called "Demirli," to which additional pupils are transported from neighboring villages; a school in the small town of "Tuzlu," and a school in the province's capital, called "Safran." Within Istanbul we chose a middle-class school in the district of "Tahsin" and a school situated in a squatter area in the district of "Enver." With this choice of schools we intended to include both different educational conditions and a variety of social groups to which the Turkish educational sector caters.[5] The five schools included in our research had the following characteristics (Table 4.3).

These data show that the differences in the educational context, already vast between Dalen and Istanbul, are even more significant if one compares individual schools. While in Dalen the schools in the village and the small town have a ratio of pupils per teacher and per class that is below the province's average and even confronts the village with a possible closure of the school, in the ratio in Safran is above the province's average. In the middle-class school of Tahsin, Istanbul, we have a ratio that is slightly below the province's average, whereas in the squatter area school the ratio is far higher. Furthermore, in the latter school of Enver, which faces an increase in enrolment due to interior migration, pupils are educated in shifts: two classes use one classroom; one in the morning and one in the afternoon.[6]

Field Research

Field research started after the necessary permissions from the MoNE were obtained, first in Dalen province (as of October 2011) and six months later in Istanbul (as of April 2012). Nazlı Somel conducted the field research; in Dalen, she was at times assisted by Muzaffer Kaya. Each research period lasted three months. During the first days of field research at each school, informal interviews with the teacher responsible for guidance and psychological counseling were conducted; general insights into the profile of pupils,

Table 4.3 Schools of the sample

Province	Schools included in research	Form of education	Number of pupils	Number of pupils per class	Number of teachers	Number of pupils per teacher	Change of pupil population	Estimated characteristics of parents
Dalen	"Lale" school in Demirli village	Full-day primary education, pupils transported from neighboring villages	148 (131 from neighboring villages)	13–24	16	9.25	Decreasing	Small farmers
	"Sardunya" school in Tuzlu town	Full-day primary education, pupils partly transported from neighboring villages	446 (71 from neighboring villages)	21–22	30	14.87	Decreasing	Workers, small farmers and low-rank civil servants
	"Zambak" school in small city of Safran	Full-day primary education	2000	25–35	Approx. 80	25	Stable	Middle-class (medium-level civil servants and small- and middle-size entrepreneurs)
Istanbul	"Papatya" school in middle-class district of Tahsin	Full-day primary education	1248	35–36	55	22.69	Stable	Middle-class (medium-level civil servants and small- and middle-size entrepreneurs)
	"Karanfil" school in squatter house area of Enver	Primary education in morning and afternoon shifts	4300	50–55	106–110[1]	40.57	Increasing	Workers and small entrepreneurs

Source: Data from 2011/2012, collected by the second author.

[1] Because in this school ca. 40% of the teachers are only employed on a fee basis, there is a high circulation of teachers, causing different staff sizes throughout the year.

their parents, and teachers were gained from this person. For the group discussions with *teachers*, we attempted to include teachers with short- and long-term professional experience, thus including those who gained the majority of their professional experience with the old curriculum as well as those only acquainted with the new one. The discussions then were conducted with groups of teachers who seemed to be relatively homogeneous regarding their professional experience. The *pupils* were recruited for discussions by approaching various real groups (that is, friendship circles) within classes. Although the pupils' discourses turned out to be very interesting, and also generally confirmed the theses developed in this volume, we decided to save their interpretation for later publications. A high variety of *parents* were also included in the research. However, because we focused on the organizational aspect of the school, only the group discussions with parents who seemed to be the dominant parent milieu at each school—especially those with members of the "school-family-union," a council elected by parents to facilitate the school's affairs—were analyzed. These latter group discussions were especially fruitful for our comparisons, as the respective parents were dedicated to the school's educational matters. Only in the school of Demirli village did we approach parents in the villages where they lived (pupils were transported to Demirli from several neighboring villages), but did not interview the parents' council members separately.[7] Table 4.4 provides an overview of the group discussions carried out in the five schools.

The group discussions lasted between 25 and 150 minutes. The participation of group members, the liveliness of discussions as well as the degree to which the group found a self-organizing momentum, paying less attention to the researcher than to its own internal discussion, varied considerably. However, all discussions were successful and provided us with important data that reflected the collective experience of the participants. The discussions were audio-recorded and then selectively transcribed.

Table 4.4 Overview of group discussions

Schools	Pupils from 8th grade	Parents	Teachers	Total
Lale school in Demirli village	5 (including pupils from 7th grade)	6	2	13
Sardunya school in Tuzlu town	4	2	2	8
Zambak school in Safran small city	4	3	3	10
Papatya school in Tahsin	2	2	3	7
Karanfil school in Enver	3	2	3	8
Total	18	15	13	46

Note: Although the majority of these discussions were conducted in two sessions, we only provide the group numbers.

Comparative Analysis and the Construction of Sociogenetic Typologies

The sampling strategies described previously were necessary to render the construction of typologies possible. Typifying implies identifying those orientations which are not only documented in a singular case but that can also be detected across several cases, that is, in a number of group discussions. In the sense of Weber's (1949) "ideal types," such a typification abstracts from the peculiarities and specificity of the cases and focuses on the common features of the respective types of collective orientation. Once typical orientations (for example, typical ways of handling the new curriculum) were identified, we inquired into the existential background of these orientations, that is, into their social genesis (Mannheim, 1968, pp. 237–256). The construction of such "socio-genetic" typologies (Bohnsack, 2014, p. 229) is possible if one can relate the respective orientation to a certain "social location" (Mannheim, 1972, p. 102); for example, to the "generation location" (Mannheim, 1972, p. 113) of teachers. However, showing that a specific orientation can be found only among persons of a certain—quasi 'objective'—social location is not enough; or in other words, it would be insufficient to show a specific way of practicing the new curriculum among teachers who have a job experience of over 20 years. A "socio-genetic investigation" (Mannheim, 1982, p. 81) requires the revealing of how the respective orientation is embedded in a certain "experiential contexture" (p. 84) by "trying to penetrate into the existential background of an experiential space" (p. 248); for example, into the experience of the older teachers with the previous curriculum. In other words, the inquiry has to go beyond the objectivist identification of a certain social location and needs to reveal the experiences connected to it.

As Bohnsack (2010b) cautions us, the reconstruction of one typification is "only valid" if this "space of experience can be worked out in its relation to other spaces of experience," that is, "to other typifications" (p. 111); therefore, the construction of sociogenetic typologies has to be *multidimensional*. Our sampling strategies rendered possible the reconstruction and typification of several dimensions, all connected with each other: In the present chapter we focus on the generational dimension of curricular practices, and will discover that this dimension is connected not only to the "generation location" (Mannheim, 1972, p. 113) of the teachers, but also to their professional expertise. In chapter 5 we explore how classroom practices are influenced by school-dominant social milieus as well as by its resources. Here, we typify both the socioeconomic background of pupils' parents (comparing lower- and middle-class milieus) as a sociogenetic background of instructional practices and the sociogeographic location of the school (comparing rural and urban contexts), which is deeply interwoven with the meaning of school education for pupils.

Such a multidimensional typology not only renders possible a comprehensive understanding of the subject-matter—that is, curriculum practices—but also helps us to assess the validity of our empirical results: "The degree of validity and generalizability of a single typification . . . depends on how manifold, i.e., how multidimensional the single case may be located within an entire typology, how often it can be related to other typifications" (Bohnsack, 2010b, p. 112). Thus, as a result of our multidimensional inquiry we understand that practicing the new curriculum is not only sociogenetically based on the generational experiences of teachers but also on the socio-economic aspects of the milieus dominating the respective school and its geographical situation. Furthermore, these dimensions are not separate from but—to a certain extent—interwoven with each other.

The Generational Dimension of Organizational Milieus

As we argued in the outset of this chapter, the new Turkish curriculum formed a set of formal rules imposed on school organization; these rules were accompanied by textbooks, teacher manuals, and teacher training which substantiated the curriculum and with which its developers tried to institutionalize the new curriculum. Throughout Turkey, teachers then had to come to grips with these formal rules imposed on their teaching. However, formal rules are not self-explicative: they have to be put into practice somehow. In section 3.1 we draw the reader's attention to one specific mechanism by which formal rules are related to organizational practices: When formal rules are tentatively put into practice from situation to situation, informal rules evolve; where they are collectively shared, they form the nucleus of an *organizational milieu*.

In contrast to social milieus which also exist beyond the organization (see chapter 5), organizational milieus depend on the organizational membership of those who are affiliated to it. In addition to the organizational milieu being constituted on the basis of informal rules and routines which emerged within the organization, the validity of these habitualized practices is also dependent on the inclusion of each actor in the respective organization. Teaching habits (for instance, those through which a curriculum is put into practice) have been both developed and are valid in the school organization. In fact, teachers (with their teaching habits) can be assumed to constitute the most important organizational milieus—albeit not the only ones—of the school.

The generational dimension within these organizational milieus needs further theoretical consideration. Having started one's career in a specific time (when teacher candidates in Turkey were still trained in non-academic teacher schools, and when the behavioristic curriculum of 1968 was still valid) has allowed for "a specific range of potential experience, predisposing" these teachers "to a certain characteristic mode of thought and experience, and a characteristic type of historically relevant action" (Mannheim, 1972, p. 106). Unlike societal generations, this *professional* generation is predominantly based on professional experience, although, as we shall see in the following sections, general social experience may reinforce a specific "tendency 'inherent in'" (p. 106) a certain professional generation. With regard to teachers, their early professional experiences "coalesce into a natural view" of the educational world (p. 113) and form the basis of a specific "'stratification' of experience" (p. 112). "All later experiences then tend to receive their meaning from this original set, whether they appear as that set's verification and fulfillment or as its negation and antithesis" (p. 112). In this sense the natural world, acquired at the beginning of one's career, also orientates subsequent teaching practices.

Because early experience not only grounds the affiliation to a specific generation but also constitutes the primordial perspective within which later experience is made, the introduction of a new curriculum must be assumed as an important event which divides teachers into generations, most importantly into a generation formed in the times of the old curriculum and a later generation whose constitution is characterized by a "'fresh contact'" (Mannheim, 1972, p. 108) with the new curriculum, that is, a generation for whom the new curriculum was the first professional experience. In this sense, the professional generation location can be assumed to constitute a significant dimension of teachers' organizational milieus with homologous orientations toward school instruction and classroom activities; it is within this dimension the teachers give sense to the formal rules of the new curriculum and put them into practice. In the following sections we empirically inquire into this dimension. Although our assumptions concerning the importance of the generation location turned out to be fruitful, the empirical results will also reveal unanticipated aspects of this experiential dimension that will oblige us to revise this experiential dimension of teachers' organizational milieus and define it more precisely.

One of these unanticipated aspects was that assuming the existence of only two generations turned out to be superficial. As our empirical results indicated, between the generation of teachers strongly attached to the practices of the old curriculum and the generation that is only acquainted with the new one, there were also groups of teachers who were no longer attached to the old curriculum, even though they had been trained in it. The generational dimension of curricular practices, hence, was not merely connected to the binary difference between the times before and after the new curriculum was introduced. The experience in some teacher groups alluded to an intermediary generation that combined elements of the old and the new generation. Table 4.5 provides an overview of the teacher groups and their affiliation to one of the three generations.

Next, we first inquire into the orientations of those organizational milieus of teachers that are characterized by their affiliation to the old generation (section 4.2) and then contrast them to the organizational milieu whose teachers are only acquainted with the new curriculum (section 4.3). Finally, we briefly attend to the instructional experience in the intermediary position between generations (section 4.4).

Table 4.5 Overview of teacher groups according to generation location

Teacher groups with an average professional experience of more than 20 years/ "old generation"		Teacher groups with an average professional experience of 5 to 15 years/ "intermediary generation"		Teacher groups with an average professional experience of less than 7 years/ "new generation"	
Group names	Gender (m-f)/ min. and max. professional experience (y)	Group names	Gender (m-f)/min. and max. professional experience (y)	Group names	Gender (m-f)/ min. and max. professional experience (y)
Pink	2m-2f/16–37y	Black	1m-2f/5–16y	Orange	2m-2f/4–11y
Red	2m/27–33y	Green	1m-3f/5–11y	Yellow	2m-4f/2–5y
Brown	2m/25–41y	Violet	1m-1f/10–14y	Gray	2f/3–7y
Blue	4m/20–34y			Turquoise	1m-2f/4–8y
White	1m-2f/11–27y			Khaki	1m-2f/4–7y

4.2 The Generation of Experienced Teachers

Practicing the old curriculum constitutes the core professional background of the generation of teachers who have—in their overwhelming majority—started service before 1991, as they have only worked with the new curriculum for around 6 years. Many of them had not even been trained at universities (teacher training was only transferred to universities by 1981), but rather in teacher high schools or teacher colleges. We typified this peculiar generational dimension of teachers' organizational milieus by interpreting five group discussions: four of them with class teachers, one with branch teachers. After reconstructing the instructional experience of these five groups, we summarize their typical approach to the new curriculum.

Group Brown: Principled Resistance

The two teachers who participated in this discussion were members of the left-wing teacher union "Eğitim Sen" and had worked together, in the same school, for a long time. On the background of this shared experience their discourse is parallelizing; that is, their contributions are rather complementing of each other instead of being antithetical. These participants emphasized their union membership during the discussion and presented themselves as teachers who oppose and do not implement the new curriculum. As described during the group discussion, they combine some elements of the 1968 curriculum with practices they developed over time and with some skills acquired in training through the union (for example, drama education organized by the "Eğitim Sen") instead of following the new formal rules.

Similar to many other groups, these teachers criticize the new curriculum for technical mistakes and practical dysfunctions. However, they go beyond such immanent criticism and display a "principled resistance" toward the new curriculum, as Altinyelken (2013, p. 109) called it, referring to "overt or covert acts that reject instructional practices." According to their point of view, the new curriculum—in contrast those of 1968 and the one introduced with the foundation of the republic—does not follow goals which cater for the needs of the country. Allegedly, the lack of such goals leads to—as these teachers put it, using wording also expressed by their union—a "chaotic" situation and ultimately serves the intention of raising "ignorant," "religious," and "individualist" people who adore the free market. Mentioning the introduction of a new form of alphabetization (in "adjacent cursive writing") the teachers delved into a highly metaphorical discussion in which they complained about the lack of an evaluation of curricular practices as well as a lack of curricular aims:[8]

Im: regarding children (.) for example mm we commenced with cursive writing, we took over at the first class (1) where did it come from now, whom did you ask to, how did it happen, why did it happen, etc.,

Am: └no, there was just one motive, you see, Ziya Selçuk told so, well, my grandpa, what was that (.) used to write very neat

Im: └Where is Ziya Selçuk now,

Am: └(moreo-) Ziya Selçuk ran and left the baby in the mosque courtyard

Im: └ me:an (.) without seeing its results

Am   └@(2)@ ┘

Im: there is also something like this ever-changing, you know staff who make the curriculum they do not exist now //mmh// you know we will call them to account for or we will say what happened? You know where did you achieve and where did you not (.) what was your goal, there is nothing no one to be questioned about the curricula that he brought on the table; neither is anyone asking us, have you applied and then what happened?

Am: └neither-┘

        └nor the process of giving account too

Im: └there is no process of accounting (.) what kind of changes have occurred in children I mean what had happened with the previous children and what happened with those, we had nothing, eee no data, also, to compare them //mmh//

The group conceives of education—and also the newly introduced curriculum—as a process in the end of which one should expect pupils to have undergone measurable changes in a certain direction. These teachers concurred in that it remained unclear out of which need and according to whose opinion the new curriculum was designed. To their view, the curriculum was developed by a very limited cadre (or, indeed, one person) that shaped it according to its own subjective aims. The fact that this person—they here referred to Professor Selçuk—had resigned (see "Test Results and Competition Among Public Schools" in chapter 6) is interpreted as a lack of leadership (here criticized as leaving the "baby" in the yard of the "mosque," a metaphorical expression for abandoning one's infant). After Ziya Selçuk stepped down, the curriculum allegedly became an aimless practice without a leader.

In this passage, which summarizes the perspective on the new curriculum entertained by the *Brown* group, it is—in its more tacit components—documented that these teachers see education as a planned process with general outputs. They assume that this plan and its goals have to be defined in a centralized way and that they, later, need to be discussed with the practitioners (that is, the teachers) in a relationship of reciprocally giving "account." However, the new curriculum is first of all—in contrast to its predecessor—seen as deficient in this regard, and secondly, it is seen as the product of the subjective expectations of a person who had once been in charge (for example, the handwriting according to Selçuk's grandfather) rather than as the output of the ministry and of Turkey's needs.

This taunting account of the curriculum change reveals that this group, on one hand, does not see the transformative character of the change; on the other hand, however, it indicates that the change was abrupt and affected teachers' classroom activities. In a certain way, group *Brown* both downplays the causes of the change and demands a serious evaluation of its practical consequences. By doing so, this group discourse combines justifications for practicing and for rejecting the curriculum. Further adding to this apparently contradictory attitude, *Brown* criticized the fact that the new curriculum does not allow teachers to freely design instruction:

Am: (.) now, this new curriculum nullified the teacher's efficacy, the teacher's creativity from the beginning (.) in this sense it demonstrates that it does not trust the teacher at the preparation and application steps we, in the past (.) taught- it (.) the general perspective of the 68 curriculum (.) and mmm (.) it provided a general framework that the teacher would fill with his/her local content the 68 curriculum had the principle to go from near to distance and the principle of teaching by making and living (1)

Here, the teacher contrasted the new curriculum—the detailed propositions of which he perceives as obligatory and as a manifestation of a lack of "trust" in the individual teacher—to the syllabus of 1968, which only defined a "general frame work" and left ample space for substantiation from teachers and according to "local" needs. Indeed, group *Brown* criticized not only the detailed character of the new curriculum, which limits teachers' discretion, but also the proposed classroom activities, which according to them are not productive. In the following passage the old curriculum is again, albeit tacitly, the reference point of the group's discourse:

Im: you know, about the issue of education that we used to define it as expected behaviors and skills of using knowledge (.) a child is indeed in

such a situation that eee his/her word within this planning, (.) it is supposed to make him/her active but I think there is definitely (.) not such
a concern. *I observe* this too anyway. Fellow teachers who are aware of
this may produce their own activities through their own special efforts
to improve the child //mmh// this is something different but (1) mmm
I think that this does certainly not work. The teacher used to make an
annual planning one way or another in the past and this annual planning used to track a course of line, for example, you cannot teach division without multiplication without teaching summation and deduction;
now (.) some steps are being passed, in this new curriculum when it is
readily put in front of us the teacher cannot read the whole of it and
rearrange again according to his/her own thinking //mmh// s/he does
not do this, (.) maybe this is easier for him/her, but when the child (.) has
finished that year (.) it seems to have acquired nothing that is desired to
be reached. She/he cannot formulate a sentence, she/he cannot express
herself/himself. [. . .] at the end (.) when the year comes to an end and
you take the child it is not a student at the fourth year (.) at the level of
the fourth year, //mmh// but at the level of the second year, maybe

The group here voiced its own educational expectations, which are
determined by the old curriculum in four ways: Firstly, the teacher spoke
of "expected behaviors and skills of using knowledge" as the goal of educational activities, thus using the codes of the behaviorist paradigm. The
teacher described these expectations as old, but then used his underlying
code to also criticize the new curriculum. Secondly, the teacher claimed
that the new curriculum, due to prescriptions which are both rigid and
deficient ("some steps are being passed"), that it does not work, and that it
leads "fourth year" children to a level which would only correspond to the
"second year," tacitly taking the levels of the old curriculum as a basis for
his assessment. Thirdly, it is documented in this discourse that these teachers,
based on their professional experience, have their own convictions regarding the learning needs and sequences of pupils ("you cannot teach division
without multiplication"). And, fourthly, they again compared the rigid and
detailed prescriptions of the new curriculum to the times when teachers
were encouraged to make their own "annual" plans. On the background of
this principled criticism, the *Brown* group gave an account of its daily teaching practices, carrying on its commitment to the curriculum of 1968:

Im: └ eh (.),°now° how I am doing this, for once there is the book which is
put in front of me, the one that we call annual plan in the beginning of
the term, I have discarded the things that I did not approve of //mmh//
unnecessary or I've changed their place; (.) after that, using my experience accumulated over years, you see, this course in that day used to
make children become active too, from my perspective we can roughly

estimate to what extend we can make them active in a class composed of 38 pupils (.) I am forming my questions *myself* //mmh// action and activity for children, you see, if I would use drama I can use drama on this subject and material what materials I am supposed to use, I go to a shop and buy a pack of dried nuts and fruits and then with these dried nuts and fruits mmm as handing them over to their hands I try to exercise that subject; you see, I find a stick, I find a tree branch, I find a thing, it, related with it, what is it, putting it in front of them, making a story from it, why it is here I improve their imagination through estimation-about every issue I say this from my own perspective. Mm since I took drama lessons, I use it and these lessons were not provided by the State or something, let's admit it I learned from here or there with my own efforts, //mmh// those I improved with the courses that the union opened, mm I try to use technology as (1) few (1) as possible, just to reinforce, since children, we see, spend enough time in front of the screen at home, we know it; I also see that distraction becomes more common; this (.) is one of the causes. I do my own planning in my courses. Surely, you take the core of the curriculum (1) but as I said I change their places, I change the order,

In this account of a teacher—which is followed by a parallel contribution by his colleague—the practical approach of group *Brown*, as an alternative to the intended curriculum, becomes more apparent. These teachers organize activities that render pupils "active"; this is done, for example, by refusing to assign homework that consists of ready-made computer printouts and by obliging pupils to prepare essays in their own words in school. They use ordinary materials (rather than intelligent technology) that are easily obtained and that foster the imagination of pupils. Additionally, this teacher uses drama education techniques taught by the teacher union.

By doing so, this group—similar to other groups analyzed in the following—takes the curriculum as a defining frame for the teaching process, even though these teachers in particular oppose the new curriculum in principle. Alternatively, they change the sequence of topics, "discard" some of them, and introduce self-designed activities. In other words, while using "the core of the curriculum," the *Brown* group structures its instructional practice according to the teaching habits developed during its long time experience with the old syllabus, which allowed—and obliged—teachers to design their own plans.

Group Pink: Creative Mixtures

Group *Pink* is formed by four class teachers, three of whom have worked for more than 30 years. In contrast to *Brown*, the teachers in group *Pink* agree with the new curriculum and its constructivist approach in principle, although they criticize some of its practical aspects. At the same time, they characterize the old curriculum as based on memorization, a criticism that was also often used by the curriculum developers:

?m: now the new curriculum (.) in its substance I mean in essence demands the constructivist approach, says construct take what the child knows the child achieve a result by constructing; I mean let's raise a generation who is not based on memorizing and accepting, but a generation who thinks, questions, produces, produces ideas (.) that is the aim (1) mm a curriculum according to this.

   As this group made clear from the outset, they approve of the "constructivist" goals of the new curriculum, and think that the curriculum was designed according to these goals. However, the group added a caveat to this approval after their initial statement:

?m: (1) but, there is that, in the first classes to my mind, mm it says, you see, do not give information for memorizing (.) let them be researchers, let them find, but I am a class teacher, to what degree does a child in the first grade do this, I am primarily asking this question (.) according to me, she/he cannot do it, cannot do it generally (.) whether a child in the second, third grade can do it, that is very difficult (2) According to me the basic knowledge, I mean, instead of the child searching, finding, learning and then reconstructing it, the basic knowledge must be communicated, provided to the child (.) //mmh// that is to say, it needs to be given ready-made, it needs to be taught (.) I think it would be more useful if this curriculum approach is followed after certain grades (.) there would be a sort of accumulation, knowledge accumulation in the child (.) eh, she/he would learn some techniques, afterwards there should be a slow transition (1) we are already doing this in this way in practice that is not quite the practice that the curriculum demands, it goes on as the mixture of old and new //mmh//

   In the preceding passage, group *Pink* argued that pupils can only learn according to the constructivist curriculum (becoming "inquirers") after they have acquired specific skills and a certain amount of knowledge. Thus, these teachers criticize the new curriculum, of which they approve in principle, by drawing on their own experience with children in the first grades. Moreover, they leave the new curriculum aside in these classes and teach according to their own experience—formed under the old curriculum—only to then, in higher grades, have a "slow transition" to the new curriculum. By doing so they create a "mixture of the old and the new." Although group *Pink*, in contrast to group *Brown*, approves of the new curriculum, both groups share the way of putting it into practice by heavily drawing on their own professional experience.

Group Red: Fractured Evaluation of the New Curriculum

Similar to group *Brown*, the following group (*Red*) is constituted by two class teachers who are affiliated to the left-wing teacher union "Eğitim Sen." However, these teachers do not totally disagree with the new curriculum, but defend it in an eclectic way, voicing both praise and criticism, as the following passage exemplifies:

Am: after the 1968 curriculum, they persistently told us that letters will absolutely be not taught, first sentence (.) word: (.) after word syllable: letter is the last. This was persistently em- emphasized. From night to morning, the system has changed as a result of a (.) I mean (.), one decision change, you see, within a year, it has been transferred to the system of letter or the system of letter based on voice

Mm: I guess examples from the European countries have been taken (.) I mean they tried to get closer to the curricula (1) there I mean the mathematics curriculum etc. over there was much simpler (1) //mmh// in ours there were really difficult questions to be solved //mmh// (2)

Am: ⌊There still is⌋

Mm: this, maybe, well there might be in different sources but, well, the essence of the curriculum has become simpler

In this discourse on the changes within the curriculum (for example, from a "sentence"-based alphabetization to a "letter"-based one) it is documented that group *Red* observes the curricular provisions for their instructional practice from a certain distance, and allows itself to approve or disapprove of this or that detail. At the same time, it is evident that this group—in contrast to *Pink*—does not welcome the new approach, rather assuming a position that could be characterized as a fractured evaluation. This standpoint provides the group with two advantages: Firstly, they do not have to develop a philosophical or political discussion (like the one entertained by *Brown*); rather, they see parts of the curriculum as developed over night, whereas other parts appear to have been taken from tried and tested practices in Europe. Secondly, they are able to insert their own—non-constructivist—practices, developed during the times of the old curriculum, into the new curriculum without the need to justify it philosophically. In fact, they do not even conceive of these self-designed practices as a contradiction to the curriculum.

The following passage reflects an example of said fractured evaluation, in which the group disapproves of some provisions of the curriculum without fully opposing it. The teachers, similar to groups *Pink* and *Brown*, discussed how they use the new curriculum only as a frame within which they define the learning processes according to their "own methods":

Am: we tried to (.) teach with our own methods rather than in the way it suggested us to (.) I mean we have a gain, it is obvious, (.) how shall we

teach this gain, we used to try to give it through one-to-one implementa-
tions but we saw that it took too much time (.) or (1) we found a better
method of our own, we taught gains in such a way, //mmh// that is the
feature of one-to-one application, what it said in here in the Turkish class,
it said so, okay, we would do it like this, what the guidebook said, it is
in our hands or we previously read but the guidebook stands necessarily
here (1) the textbooks are in front of children, step by step, here, I mean
we look at now, anymore but mmm (.) we understood after one or two
years we understood what has to be done and how much has to be given
and that it might also be like this according to our own methods. (.) in
mathematics while persistently teaching the natural numbers (1) to children, here it said something as handing over one card each to every one
of them and do something with the cards, eee we used different methods
for this //mmh// (2)

The group explicitly referred to the teacher "guidebook," whose suggestions they at times disregard in favor of using "different methods" they have
developed on their own. As is documented in this discourse, these departures
from the guidebook (and, hence, sometimes also from the curriculum) are
not the consequence of a total opposition against the new approach, but
an attempt to improve instructional practice where the guidebook or the
curriculum proved to be ineffective with regard to meeting teachers' own
expectations of an educated pupil.

It is characteristic of *Red*, as well as for all other groups of this organizational milieu, that these teachers both obey the general frame of the
curriculum and plan their own (order of) classroom activities. This instructional orientation is based on the generational dimension of this organizational milieu in two ways: Firstly, these teachers use the curriculum in the
same way as they had used the old one, that is, by perceiving it as a general
framework to be substantiated by the teachers themselves. Secondly, and in
connection with the first point, they are able to draw on their long time
experience of creating teaching methods and classroom activities according
to the needs of the respective class and within a general curricular frame.
We theoretically reflect on this combination of generation and professional
experience once we have empirically analyzed the last two groups of the
old generation.

Group White: Taking Into Account Pupils' Feedback

In contrast to the previous groups, all of which were constituted by class
teachers, *White* was composed of three branch teachers with a variation
of political opinions and union affiliations. They fully accept the teaching approach of the new curriculum (that is, constructivism) without reservations. Conversely, they criticized the teaching material (textbooks)

developed according to the new curriculum, as can be seen in the following passage:

Tf:	└that is, we do not follow the guide books one by one (.) I mean, we follow *but* (.) we skip and then we, yes, go back,
Sf:	└skip and go back┘
Dm:	└(°hıhı°)┘
Tf:	we sometimes teach one by one as our own, yes (.) we do not follow one by one
Dm:	└there is anyway not such an obligation, that is, this is just
Sf:	as choosing which of those are appropriate for the class and student, then to //mmh// it
Dm:	└as example (do something)
Tf:	we perform according to it
Dm:	└that is, I am not very content with texts concerning Turkish, the texts are so ordinary that there are no texts which might attract the child's attention,
Tf:	└I am not content at all either (1), exactly┘ └yes┘
Dm:	either too difficult: for example, at seventh grade, there are such texts indeed
Tf:	└ yeah ┘
Dm:	there are on the university level, I mean, how (hea-) by materials
Tf:	└ yeah (2) exactly the same ┘
Dm:	it strangles: there, the convention on the rights of the children, for example, you cannot already teach such things to children, their mind is already very confused, there are too many foreign words //mmh// the text is absolutely at the university level (1)
Tf:	└ yeah, ┘ └exactly

Similar to the other groups of the old teacher generation, group *White* follows the new curriculum as a general frame but changes the order and content of classroom activities. Moreover, these teachers also fall back on methods and contents they had previously developed themselves. The criteria for deciding whether to use the proposed material or one's own are derived from two sources: On one hand, they have developed their own expectations toward the adequacy of activities for different levels on the basis of their past experience; on the other hand, they take their interaction with children and the children's feedback into account.

Group Blue: Differences in the Teaching Staff

The four class teachers forming group *Blue* are all members of the teacher union "Eğitim Sen," and criticized the new curriculum for omitting specific national values, reducing knowledge transfer, aiming at the nurture of a religious generation, and more. However, they do not completely oppose the new curriculum; instead, they follow and modify it, as is documented in the following passage from their group discussion:

Am:	here, (.) there are guide books, the guide books (.) are overlapped with those text books // mmh// (1) then, (.) mmm but, it can happen that the them(.)es (2) in some periods of days and weeks (1) are not suitable (.) you arrange it according to that, //mmh// it is different, beyond it (2) the guide books (2) the text books (.) after that (.) of course, it does not, you

support it (1) it's not enough, let's say a Turkish (1), there is one text in Turkish for one week, that, in a week on that text, you do not wander around (2) stand on it that is to say, that text, let's say, takes two days, takes three days //mmh// (2) beyond that you further develop it (.) enrich it by sources (.) (3) I work on it for a week; for example, I present it as a week but (.) since (.) it does not work to revise it //mmh// I indicate it in that way, I fill in the gaps (1)

Bm: we are doing photocopy (.), photocopy ( )
Cm: └ that is, we do not plan it very much (.) it ( )
Dm: └ now (.) colleagues of ours mmm (.) to tell the truth, it was not different before 2005 (.) it is neither different after 2005 (.) there is no change, in essence: (.) there is a nonvisible curriculum of ours (.); everyone has the curriculum in their heads, okay there is a frame curriculum (.) here previously the '68 curriculum; afterwards, lasting, after the '68 program, transforming after the change of two governments; @(.)@ a permanent government policy in education, since there is no permanent government policy in education (.) of governments, with each government the education policy has been changed in this country

As voiced by Am, these teachers follow the curriculum on the basis of the teacher manual, but also add their own teaching material to it (such as a text in Turkish class) or revise the sequence of activities according to specific occasions (such as nation-wide "days and weeks" organized for specific topics). These modifications, however, are not reflected in the official documents; in other words, the teachers write their weekly plan according to the teacher manual ("I present it as a week"), although they have modified their instructional practice. The other teachers then implicitly agreed with Am's statement and finally maintained that planning instruction is not a point on which they reflect a lot. In fact, they spoke of a "nonvisible curriculum" which is in everybody's "head." As Dm concluded, in spite of ever-changing educational policies, this tacit program—based on the "68 curriculum"—was not changed with the introduction of the new curriculum, which rather serves as a frame for teaching. Here, again, we understand that these teachers of the older generation perceive the new curriculum—similarly to the old one—as a framework within which they fall back on their own planning and instructional experience, built up over a long period of time.

In their group discussion, *Blue* focused on education policy and general social questions rather than discussing their own teaching practices. Only when the researcher asked about the homework they assigned to the children did another discourse on instructional practice evolve:

Cm: I mean homewo:rk, actually:, is fo- forbidden (1) //mmh// so-called forbidden (1)
Am: └ so-called ┘
Cm: but, (.) we give homework mmm on this subject I give it like this (.), I give something that (.) reinforces the topic I tackle (.) mmm (.) I prepare and give things which I believe will reinforce the learning (1) you prepare it yourself, or from the web (.) you get a work that you are fond of (.) that you like, and you revise and multiply it and hand it over. Mostly rather than writing, doing on the

> notebook, 90 percent is photocopy. As Am told (.) just now (1) you hand over photocopied
>
> Dm: ⌐you see, in theory, Cm ⌐
>
> Cm: homework (.) they do it and hand them back to you
>
> Dm: ⌐there is a new curriculum in theory, isn't it, (1) but in practice, what percentage of Turkey's (.) teachers, 80 or 90 percent (.) we still follow the old curriculum (1) well, I do not say anything for those who are graduated without experiencing this curriculum (1) I mean their formation, I do not know the university graduates (.) they are different (1) but (.) exactly similar to the old method we give homework, here it is said there is no homework, it is child centered, by doing and experiencing etcetera etcetera it used to be said (1), there is no such thing (2) that means, the same old thing (.)

As demonstrated in the preceding passages, the teachers (rightly or wrongly) assumed that homework, at least in a specific form, is forbidden according to the new curriculum. Against this rule, they provide the pupils with homework they prepare themselves or download from the "web." The project work, intended to foster the "child centered" approach of the new curriculum, was not even mentioned by these teachers. Dm then concluded this discourse by pointing to the enduring relevance of the "old curriculum" for the majority of teachers in contrast to the younger ones, who were educated at "university" and did not "experience this curriculum." Interestingly, the group here distinguished not only between those who started their career before the introduction of the new curriculum and those thereafter, but also included to the latter group all those who received their professional training at university (that is, most teachers who started studying after 1981). By differentiating between these teacher groups, *Blue* was clearly referring to different professional generations.

The Professional Generation of Experience-Based Lesson Designers

The teacher groups analyzed communicated a variety of opinions regarding the new curriculum, ranging from "principled resistance" (Altinyelken, 2013), to mixed judgments, and to complete endorsement. While these opinions indicate significant discrepancies between teachers concerning their political outlook, especially vis-à-vis the government and the ruling Justice and Development Party (under the reign of which the new curriculum was introduced; see section 3.2), our documentary interpretation of their group discussions has revealed certain commonalities pertaining to their more tacit orientations in instructional practice. It is this tacit dimension of practical orientations that we placed the focus of our analysis and where we could identify generational commonalities of those teachers with a work experience of more than 20 years.

Regarding the *orientations* underlying teachers' actual instruction *practice*, irrespective of positive or negative *opinions* on the new curriculum, all groups analyzed to this point take it as a general frame—but not as an obligatory and detailed lesson plan. This is a significant feature of this professional generation. Even those who agree with the new approach perceive the curriculum as a kind of signpost according to which they design their own lessons. This teaching orientation can easily be traced back to the practices under the old curriculum of 1968: Whereas the new curriculum (amended by the teacher manual) provides each teacher with detailed instructions for his/her lesson, the old curriculum only defined general topics and desired behaviors teachers had to substantiate in weekly and annual plans. In this sense, it was more of a syllabus than a curriculum. This syllabus, as a formal rule, obliged teachers to design their own lessons, which evidently led to a habit that is specific to this professional generation: that of designing lessons within the general frame of the syllabus.

This implies that within this professional generation, the teaching material—originally developed to substantiate and institutionalize the new curriculum (see "Test Results and Competition Among Public Schools" in chapter 6)—is not used as a strict guideline. Rather, these teachers use the teacher manual and other material as a toolbox; where this toolbox proves to be insufficient or inappropriate, these teachers draw on activities and materials developed by themselves or provided from other resources (for example, from the Internet). As such, they command a rich inventory of classroom activities that were developed before the new curriculum was introduced. As indicated, under the old curriculum of 1968, teachers were obliged to design lessons on their own, developing or choosing suitable activities and material by themselves. It is in this sense that we denote these teachers as the professional generation of experience-based *lesson designers*.

A generation such as the lesson designers, especially if constituted within a professional realm, cannot be easily distinguished from the stocks of experience gained by its members throughout their lifetime. This is most apparent in the professional generation at hand, which is profoundly connected to a stock of professional experience gained during a long period of teaching. The *lesson designers* are not only united in the "generational entelechy" (Mannheim, 1972, p. 125); that is, the "clearly distinguishable new impulse" (p. 124) inspired by the syllable-like curriculum of 1968. Being oriented toward perceiving the new curriculum as a general frame and developing one's own lesson plans is also based on a huge stock of teaching experience. This also becomes evident through these teachers' certainty regarding what can be expected from pupils at different levels and grades. It is these expectations toward pupils' capabilities that help the teachers to freely design lessons within the curricular frame. As we see in the following sections, this teaching orientation is unique for the professional generation of *experience-based* lesson designers and cannot be identified among other teacher groups.

4.3   Novices and the Curriculum

We continue our inquiry into the generational dimensional of teachers' organizational milieus with those whose experience and orientation are in maximal contrast with the professional generation of *experience-based lesson designers*. The novice teachers within our sample were all trained at university in a time when the old curriculum had come under heavy criticism and when elements of a constructivist (and multiple intelligence) approach were already taught at the colleges of education. Starting their service shortly before or after the introduction of the new curriculum, these teachers have built up their—albeit limited—professional experience of 2–11 years entirely through the new teaching approach. The specific generational dimension of these teachers' organizational milieus was typified by interpreting five group discussions; two of them with class teachers, three with branch teachers. As previously, we reconstruct the instructional experience of each group before summarizing their typical approach to the new curriculum.

Group Turquoise: Closely Following the MoNE's Annual Plan

The three class teachers of *Turquoise*, two of whom are union members, upon entering school service had already acquired knowledge about the 'multiple intelligence' approach as well as about constructivism at university. Although they welcomed the new curriculum, this group often alluded, during the discussion, to its inappropriateness for the social conditions of their school. Another issue that surfaced in the discussion was the temporal dimension of instruction, discussed during the teachers' account of preparing annual teaching plans:

Sf: └ we plan them in the committee //mmh// most (.) of them we take ready-made we don't prepare plans especially according to the region, // mmh// it should happen like this normally but (.) normally we take over the programs available in the web and then we (.) as the committee, try to implement them //mmh//

Of: °yes, we all do it in the same way°

Em: to finish subjects in there (.) of course (.) subjects unfortunately,

Sf: └surely we finish them

In this interactive discourse it is documented that the group *Turquoise* perceives the curriculum as a set of operations which have to be applied in the classroom. They download the annual "plan" from the Internet and "try to implement" it. When they later admitted that they should "inspect" these plans beforehand, it is not implied that they would evaluate it according to their own educational convictions and experience; rather, the group is concerned about the length and depth of the "subjects," as these teachers are eager to "finish subjects" in the classroom. Doing so, they work on the assumption that they are obliged to tightly obey the curriculum and its contents, an assumption also shared by the teachers' "committee" of their branch, which is also formed by novice teachers.[9] In the following passage, the group describes the way this approach to the new curriculum is translated into classroom practice:

Em: there is actually in the constructivist approach, normally it should be children, well taught child-centered (.), but, in order to make this happen (.) children should have (.) at least a computer at their home or the Internet cafes are preferred for this, (.) but, (.) the surrounding factors indicate that this is not safe, too, when it is like this there is a hindrance there (.) too; you give it, you allow for some time, but in the end of

Sf: └ (° yeah °) ┘

Em: the process mm the number of students who did it was very low (.) //mmh// one of the causes of this, well, it stems from that the socioeconomic situation of that family has actually not been improved yet (.) as a result, you cannot achieve your goals; consequently there is such trouble; (.) in result (.) it is still teacher-centered (.) while dealing with a topic //mmh// mm mostly the teacher is the transmitter ( )

Of: └ yeah, the curriculum is the new system but the actual practice is definitely the old system //mmh// *there is* a curriculum in appearance, there are plans but we cannot *perform* it

Em: └ you see, there is actually something like that when you read it that constructivist approach if it is possible to apply one-to-one, it is really good stuff, (.) well at the point of leading them to the fields appropriate to their skills, this is very important too (.) *but*, the infrastructure must be established for this, the classrooms (.) need to be rescued from this crowd

Without questioning their positive attitude toward the new curriculum, *Turquoise* explained the deficiencies faced during instruction in the school's environment. While the professional generation of *experience-based lesson designers* criticizes and modifies aspects of the new curriculum according to their own experience, these young teachers do not draw on their instructional experience, but refer to their working conditions, that is, to the inability of pupils to complete the necessary homework. This leads to a bifurcation in the way the curriculum is handled: On one hand, this group—via the teachers' committee—accepts the curriculum and its annual plans as a tight guideline for instructional practice; on the other hand, when they face practical problems (which, according to their perspective, originate from pupils' social conditions), these teachers cut back their expectations and apply activities, materials, and teaching methods which they consider as contradictory to the new curriculum and even as part of the "old," "teacher-centered" "system." In contrast to the older generation, these activities, materials, and teaching methods do not originate from the group's own professional experience, tested and refined during years of instructional practice, but from ready-made sources:

Sf: └you see, normally our books are very *empty*, definitely I mean if we look at math, Turkish, there is a reading text, there is no different activity about it, we thus have them bought by the children extra sources this is not legal //mmh// normally it's definitely forbidden, but we have them bought moreover the question banks, here leaf tests and books for lecturing, we teach through them, normally for example we will apply a test in that day or we will make them research a variety of questions or different sources regarding this from the web (and whatever else) we will tackle (.) we

Em: ⌐there may be visual practices, too

Sf: ⌐do visual practices but furthermore (.) I mean °those are the things we are able to do° //mmh// those are things that we are able to practice //mhm// those barely suffice for forty minutes.

Of: ⌐in the same manner, at the beginning of the year in the committee we talk about sources that are supposed to be purchased //mmh// we make all children buy them (.) in this way we arrange the schedule; but in general, (.) we follow mostly the sources, the lesson, for example, I definitely try not to use the exercise pages because I see that they are not very full (.) in general they waste children's time and therefore (   )

Sf: ⌐°unnecessary°⌐

Em: ⌐kill-time (.) for sure⌐

Of: activities are inclined, more of a (.), yeah

Sf: ⌐ you see, if we merely focus on the book, we would not be able to call it an execution of education it's so empty

Of: ⌐we rather give them as homework to use at home, our source books, we use the source books that we prefer and are pleased with at the classroom //mmh//

In spite of their approval of the new curriculum, this group perceives the textbooks distributed by the ministry as "very empty" and as a waste of time, going even as far as seeing these textbooks as jeopardizing the "execution of education." Instead of the prescribed textbooks, these teachers use "source" books, "question banks," and other material which they download from the Internet or have the pupils buy. Although these books are "definitely forbidden" for use in school, such practical orientation voiced by these teachers is not limited to their individual instruction. In the beginning of the year the respective teachers' "committee" decides which books must be bought by the children, implying that all children of a given grade will work with the same book. Hence, the use of these books—the nature of which we attend to further later—is not only an informal rule of this organizational milieu, embossed by a specific professional generation, but also leads to an official decision by an organizational unit of the school, communicated to the children as an obligation.

Group Khaki: Introducing New Teaching Material Into the Classroom

Similar to group *Turquoise*, the members of *Khaki*—three branch teachers with differing political standpoints—do not criticize the new curriculum, although they think that it is not appropriate for the conditions of their school. Thus, the group discussion focused on examples of this inappropriateness and the social conditions of the school. In the following passage, in which the teachers respond to a question concerning their annual plans, important homologies with *Turquoise* come forward:

Bf: └ anyway our annual program is being planned by the Ministry of Education (.) our books too, we have uni:t mm an annual plan, (.) //mmh// we work in harmony according to it of course the impact of the circumstances and the level of the readiness of students:, (.) they help us to (.) stretch the planned hours in this program, because this, you know some hours according to some topics: well the Ministry of National Education has given three hours, (.) we sometimes are compelled to for example teach more than three hours //mmh// since the level of readiness of the children is lower, (.) besides this, we, ourselves, you know, books, since books are provided by the Ministry of National Education, the planning is also submitted by the Ministry of National Education, we just stretch it; we process it through stretching it according to the conditions of the circumstances and the conditions of the readiness of students //mmh// (1)

Ef: there occurs such a distress for me: for example (.) you know, I teach English, see, English is such a class that progresses on the basis of what has been achieved, you know if she/he does not know what came before //mmh// does not know the lower grade, she/he cannot begin from scratch and progress like that, (.) my distress occurs at the beginning of the year, in the beginning of the year for example (.) yes there is something that was pla- planned already; I cannot stick to that (.) I am obliged to summarize the topics of the past year for a little while, //mmh// as quick as possible, since the things I am going to teach this year will be built on those of the past year eee if there is nothing from the past year, I cannot do it I cannot advance the whole year by sticking to the curriculum //mmh// summaries are done very quickly in the beginning of the year (.) it happens like this (you see) //mmh// (3)

Bf declared that the annual plan is made by the "Ministry of National Education" and that the textbooks follow these plans. Similar to the orientation documented in the group *Turquoise*, she takes these formal rules of the curriculum for granted and only "stretches" the topics which her pupils otherwise would not understand. Underlying this statement is the assumption that teachers do not have any freedom, need, or duty to design instruction on their own and to use their own expectations and experience. Ef then declared that her situation as an English teacher is different from Bf's, as her instruction is always based on what the child has learned in the previous year. When she discovers that the pupils have forgotten (or never received) the knowledge of the previous "grade," she feels obliged to provide them with a "summary" before continuing with what has been planned for the current grade. The underlying shared orientation of both teachers, documented in this discourse, is to tightly follow the new curriculum and only modify it as

far as the temporality of learning (previous-knowledge gaps, slower instruction) is concerned. When discussing their daily plans, however, these teachers
disclosed another component of their teaching orientation:

Bf: └Now, to be honest, I first of all think about the classes which I attend
(1) I look at the level of the class, since the number of good students
in some classes is greater and in some classes it is less (.) then I say how
many persons in this class may benefit from the subject that I will teach
today I think like this; (1) afterwards I look at the book to see what it
provides, (1) I see that there are shortcomings everywhere (.) I go to that
of the instruction centers there are surely subsidiary sources @I am sorry
they say do not use them but, @ (.) //mmh// we have to use subsidiary
sources; (.) //mmh// here, we certainly analyze the books published by
the instruction centers or different publishers; because there is also an
exam process; yes, national education provided us with a book? (.) but
when you look in the book, book, you look in the book (.) there is a SBS
exam afterwards; when you teach the books as they asked for, when you
teach in terms of the curriculum the child then veers away from the test
technique, (.) then the failure emerges in the exam; that means, their success in the exam decreases: (.) then they say what does the teacher teach:
(.) but when you take a look, here, when you tell as they asked, the child
cannot manage the *exam* (.) //mmh// system and the subjects cannot
make sense of them (1) solv-

Sm: └ (for example, this term) two *tests*, (.) for exampl-, it says unit evaluation
(.) okay, good, there are various questions //mmh// fill in the blanks, this
and that but as *test*, (.) there are units that have just two *test* questions; there
have put two or three; then the evaluation is made over the test again, I
mean therefore the course books are not suitable to prepare for that

According to the "level" of the pupils—and especially of those who excel
in a certain branch—these teachers evaluate the ministry's textbook and
come to the conclusion that it needs to be complemented (or even replaced)
by the "source" books developed by "instruction centers," private organizations which prepare children to successfully pass standardized tests. Similar
to *Turquoise*, they are aware that the use of these books in the classroom is
forbidden; however, as these teachers make clear, they do not only obey the
curriculum but also feel obliged to take into account the "exam process"
that leads to the high school entrance exam "SBS," since they see the ministry's textbooks as inadequate. When they stated that if instruction would
(solely) follow the new curriculum the children would "veer away from
the test technique," this group disclosed that, along with the curriculum,
there is another expectation and maxim guiding their classroom activities:
the (standardized) tests to which the children are subjected in the course
of their educational career. These teachers do not implicate that the topics
of the curriculum are different from those of the tests. At the same time,

the way these topics are taught according to the curriculum is—according to their view—contradictory to solving tests: They "cannot make sense of them" (that is, of the tests), as one teacher put it. As Sm concluded, the self-evaluative test questions that can be found in the end of each unit are "not suitable" to prepare the children. Hence, the group *Khaki* in their instruction follows not only the new curriculum but also takes the standardized tests into account. In contrast to the generation of experience-based lesson designers, who have their own ideas about a child's level, with the standardized test there emerges a different measure, taken into account only within the younger generation.

Group Gray: Preparing Children for Standardized Tests

While the younger teacher generation groups analyzed up to this point are oriented toward using a *mixture* of both curricular textbooks and test preparation material, group *Gray* (constituted by two class teachers affiliated to a leftist teacher union) attaches the highest importance to their pupils' success in tests, although they do not principally oppose the new curriculum. The ministry's textbooks seem unuseful for practical reasons:

Y: how do you prepare your annual program (.) when you begin the school year?
Cf: °is it necessary to tell the truth?°
Y: ⌐hi:?
Bf: ⌐ @(.)@ our annual program, actually,
Cf: ⌐ shall we tell the truth,
Y: ⌐yes @(1)@
Bf: it was harder in the past, you know (.) we actually had to sit and write. now the annual plans
         come readily to us (.) we just check them if they are right with course books we compare,
Cf: ⌐ do not
         use them
Bf: ⌐(.) i: o it happens like (.) that
Cf: ⌐ If something like that annual comes readily to me, (1)
         then I do that, you know, I even never look at it (.) //mmh// I mean I write in the class
         register from that daily from the guide books anyway (.) I do not feel the need of making
         comparisons; because (.) since I do not use the book provided by the state I do not have to
         do that annual plan (.) to use that I mean. (1) ((coughs shortly)) because mm
Bf: ⌐we normally are obliged
         to @use them@ here
Cf: ⌐ but, I *never* use the book, you know. I have such a thing. because in the
         moment I use the books, the child cannot be successful in the test

In this discussion, a controversy between Bf and Cf seemed to arise. Whereas Bf—in unison with the groups analyzed previously—claimed that the annual plans are prepared by the ministry and are only checked by teachers—if at all—as concerns their congruence with "course books," Cf insinuated that there is an official and a "true" version of instruction, of which she wants to inform the researcher. In practice, as Cf stated, she uses the annual plans (and even the daily plans provided in teacher "guide books") only to complete the "class register" while she teaches the class in a different way, one that obviously appears to her as more adequate for preparing the children for tests.[10] In her objection that they "normally are obliged to use" the curriculum, accompanied by laughter, Bf implied that she knows about the deviating instruction practices and may even pursue them herself. This evidently antithetical discourse then led to a discussion regarding teaching material, which both teachers evaluated in unison:

Cf: if (.) this (.) government and this (.) system demand this from me, I do not, cannot use these
       books, I mean. (.) I once tried it in the past year, (.) //mmh// I only used the books, I mean,
       the books provided to us, those books provided by the Ministry of National Education (.)
       then we entered the SBS exam, we got too low (.) //mmh// I was the ninth, something like
       this, out of maybe ten, eleven classes. (.) but then I realized, you know, I understood after
       this event that the books really did not work (.) I did (.) we purchased the normal books of
       Gendaş in the past year; I began to use the Gendaş' books (.) //mmh// hence, I excelled to
       second, third or something like this rank. in this year too other than the books provided by
       the National Education I finished four or five sources. at this moment we are at second we
       are in the second rank in the SBS; we are in the second, third rank. (1) //mmh// that is, I do
       not find it very healthy (.) *if* we are asked to use those books there must be classes consisting
       of twenty people, not fifty people, (.) and the school must be really well equipped; (.) and
       also there must not be such exams, for the books; because there is *very little* knowledge (.) and
       th- demanded in the tests, we are asked for *too much* knowledge; I mean now
Bf: ⌐ there are too many examples, yeah ⌐
Cf: why do I do this to my children, my students (.) leave them bereft of this topic (.) //mmh//
       anyway there are a lot of fellow teachers who think the same way as me
Bf: ⌐ no no the books are really, very bad, I mean (.) very very
       deficient
Cf: ⌐ very poor, I mean, yeah

In her statement, Cf not only substantiated, based on her own experience, that the ministry's textbooks are not suitable for test preparation; by identifying herself with the pupils' test performance ("*we* entered the SBS exam") she also—implicitly—spoke on the assumption that the pupils' test results are her own: "I was the ninth . . . of . . . eleven classes." In chapters 5 and 6 we further inquire into the nature and importance of these tests. For the present chapter it suffices to note that there is, apparently—along with or in contradiction to the curriculum—another concern which guides young teachers' instructional practice: preparing pupils for standardized tests. As Cf then went on to say, the source books provided by "Gendaş" helped her to prepare the children so well that the class became the "second" or "third" best in the school. Concluding this discourse, both Cf and Bf agreed that the official textbooks are "very bad" and "very deficient."

In the following account of their daily teaching preparation, group *Gray* univocally described their way of combining the curricular expectations and the preparation for tests. The initial antithesis here turned into a synthesis within the group. Bf, who previously had maintained the "normal" obligation to follow the curriculum now stated that she only takes into account the "gain of that day," as stated in the teacher manual, and then uses her own books (presumably for test preparation) to design instruction:

Bf: ⌐you know, from the National Education I only take the gain of the given day; (.) anyway I do not follow the curriculum. The gain of that day for example (1) I make up (.) here if it is the classification of creatures, (.) there are books that I have chosen myself, for example there is Step by Step Mathematics; here, math, I do not know what (.) there are various books from there (.) //mmh// I directly teach from there (.) it never happened that I used the book (2)

In the continuation of this quote, Cf agreed with Bf and indicated that they use the explanations provided by the teacher manual, but then refrain from making the children accomplish the respective "activities" (an important component of the constructivist approach). Instead, they prepare the children for the standardized test, according to whose results the pupil is transferred to high school or—in the specific case of this school—even to a "free-of-charge boarding" school. While the older generation of teachers takes the curriculum as a general frame and then freely designs lessons—mixing textbooks and other teaching material in an unrestricted way—the group *Gray*, similar to other groups of novice teachers, perceives their situation as a "paradox" that imposed on them by the state. As is evident in their discourse, these teachers are not able to dissolve this paradox; rather, they seesaw between the curriculum and test preparation.

Group Yellow: Test Preparation as an Addendum

Group *Yellow*, composed of six branch teachers, agrees with the new curriculum but brought up its intrinsic incongruences along with the testing problem. In contrast to group *Gray*, these teachers stick to the curriculum and use the test preparation only to enhance the lessons for which the teacher manual does not provide enough material:

Hf: we do not prepare daily plans
all: ⌐ we do not prepare daily plans
Am: ⌐ the daily plan has been lifted
Hf: ⌐ it was removed too
      (.) I mean ( ) when I began my service (.) on the term February 2007 (.) I used to do it indeed that is I did it for that term then it was lifted (.) //mmh// it was removed in that year
Am: ⌐it is anyway readily provided within the guide books
Hf: yeah, anyway it is there in the same way too

Am: └when teaching that subject
(1) you know, within how many hours you are supposed to teach (.) what kind of gains
you will cover, those are provided in the guide books

Hf: for how many course hours we are going to teach, they all are already present in it,
after analyzing the guide book (.) it may be different in terms of time according to the
level of classes, when we take a note on the annual plan (.) you know, (.) after making
the explanation we do not encounter any hardship (.) //mmh// the content anyway
might finish before that despite it is very rare if we consider it tackling the subject (.)
//mmh// in the remaining time too for example let's assume that three course hours
are provided if we finish within the two class hours, here, we solve questions in order
to reinforce it, (.) we definitely catch up, I mean, we, you know arrange ourselves in a
way

Am: └ that is, in general, there remains no subject which is not finished at the end of the year,
for everyone

Hf: └ yes ┘

Am: (1) //mmh// SBS well (.) for completed subjects we go into that

Mf: it is not entirely like this in terms of English and mathematics, regardless, it is hard to finish,
you see, it finishes, but (a little) by compressing them a little //mmh// (.) but it finishes

Hf: └ it's hard to finish, yes ┘

Am: └ well, mine is also hard to finish, you know, it finishes
anyway in the end

In this collective discourse it is documented that the group perceives the
test preparation not as a modification of the curriculum, but as an addendum
to it. Without introducing any self-prepared activities or own expectations
into the classroom, these teachers take the curriculum and the teacher manual as a guideline whose topics have to be tackled and whose gains have to be
achieved. As this group—similarly to all other young teachers—never refers
to any maxims other than those of the curriculum and the entrance exams,
we conclude that there is no experience-based point of reference according
to which these teachers could modify the curriculum or use spare time. In
this case, the standardized tests fill the gap and emerge as an important source
for designing the remaining lessons.

Similar to the other groups of novice teachers, *Yellow* oscillates between
the curriculum and the standardized tests. In contrast to the other teachers,
who tend to prefer test preparation to the curriculum, *Yellow* does not see
both practices as contradicting, but as complementary instead. As we reveal
in chapter 5, this difference is sociogenetically based on the socioeconomic
and geographical situation of respective schools. Hf herself, in the following
quote, takes into account the social situation of her pupils when considering
the instruction material:

Hf: now, it is perhaps not right to categorize the children, to be honest mm
I cannot go on parallel with the book sometimes, if I in any way would
attempt to do all activities within the book, as my colleague said, until I
complete an activity in the class, you know, since it will take too much
time till papers, cartons are cut, more, I myself more such, decide on a

point, I do it if helps me regarding that point, (.) if not, further, you know, I give the lesson by using other methods and techniques //mmh// by @ mixing@ with lecturing too, because otherwise it doesn't get finished that is, nothing gets finished (.) then, afterwards we suffer from this (.) the children because most of them cover the missing parts in the instruction center, eee they do not put much trust in school (.) there are also those who trust, those who get support only from the school, they get low scores, this too makes us feel sorrow, (.) because the result shouldn't be depressing we try to take measures from the beginning, I mean.

For Hf, departing from the curriculum and the MoNE's textbooks is related to her concern for children who are not enrolled in private "instruction centers" and who usually receive "low scores" in the standardized tests. However, these children are the minority in the classroom, since most pupils "finish" the respective topic or gain of the curriculum at preparation centers. As we analyze in chapter 5, the opportunity of (and need for) attending a private preparation center varies from school to school; or, to be more precise, from one social milieu to another.

Group Orange: Ease of Following the Teacher Manual

This group, composed of four branch teachers who welcome the curriculum change, perceives the new curriculum and its accompanying teaching material as a thorough guideline that spares the teacher from preparing lessons on his/her own:

Tm: ⌐ this time it
is left to one's own conscience (1) in the past system (.) yes the good teachers (.) the idealist teachers went and worked more prepared (1) the others go without searching too much (.) but in this, (.) even if the other teacher goes without searching, (.) without working she/he can also do something by looking at notes, you know, at the activities (.) //mmh// in the past she/he could do nothing at all; I remember (.) we used to do daily plans, class by class (1) I used to research on the web (.) what can be done, how could I teach this subject, (2) now I do not research this so much (.), you know, since I have more options at my hand (1) and maybe,

Sf: ⌐ yes ⌐
  ⌐ moreover the questions are ready in the book, everything is ready, you see, in the book? (.) that means the unprepared teacher can go on like that; I, for example, used to be like this for a while and I felt myself extremely uncomfortable; but, (.) you know, as there is no topic on the table for me to tell, that is, it consist of one or two piecemeal topics, (1) ee of that, anyway there is no source to search in too //mmh// there is no beginning and no end of the subject, you know; you will create inspirations for the children, (.) well, *because of that* (.) I used to follow the book, if you do not read it, you know, in an exam (.), it will be asked again (.) according to it, due to this, (.) I did in the way of constant reading, (.) questioning and answering from the book for a term-long (2) I mean even if you do not prepare yourself it passes in a more comfortable way in this system. //mmh//

Tm: ⌐ that is, for
example, (1) I got a hoarse voice for two days (.) yes

Sm: ∟ but it was not like this in the old system I mean; I further researched, I further did research on things

Tm: ∟for two days I did not tackle any topics (1) I only did a little bit today (.). two days before, yesterday, I used to do it like this (.) ((shows with hand signs)) I used to say the second (.) activity, here, I used to say do the third unit (.), they did it, you see, I said fourth (.) they did the fourth; I said the fifth and then they did the fifth (.)

Sf: ∟yes like things like are ready, I mean

In this shared discourse, the teacher manual and the textbooks—in contrast to the "past system"—are perceived as detailed directories according to which teachers (and even pupils themselves) may proceed during the lesson without any preparation. The teachers, as documented here, fully rely on the official material, only adding test preparation devices. However, this additional material gains a higher importance for some branches than for others. As a mathematics teacher exposed in the continuation of this discussion, she perceives the curriculum as a guideline for topics but draws on "five or six" test preparatory books during her lessons, using a mixture of their proposed activities. Again, we see that these young teachers have two reference points in their instructional practice: the new curriculum and test preparation, which they balance according to their branch or to the environment of the school.

The Professional Generation That Combines the New Curriculum and Test Preparation

The novice teachers, most of them with 7 or less years of work experience, find themselves in a dilemma: On one hand, they have been made acquainted, already in university, with the new curriculum and its underlying teaching approach; they endorse it and do not know any alternative ways of teaching, be it by experience or in the form of an alternative curriculum. Hence, they are fundamentally and existentially attached to the new curriculum. On the other hand, when describing their teaching practices they paid tribute to another component of the educational sector, that is, to the standardized tests that all pupils who wish to enter a distinguished high school (and later, a university) must pass. Whereas the professional generation of experience-based lesson designers hardly mentioned the standardized tests (and if so, not as a point that modifies their instruction practice), the novice teachers quite often referred to the need to prepare pupils for these exams, both in terms of content and question techniques. Dependent on the social condition of the school, test preparation may become an addendum to the curriculum or replace the teacher manual, the curriculum being regarded only as a guideline for topics and gains. In this sense, the professional generation herein analyzed may be denoted as *curriculum and test preparation combiners*.

The tribute novice teachers pay to test preparation may be more than a significant feature of the professional aspects of this generation of teachers;

the dimension of professional generation in this organizational milieu is intermingled with aspects of a general generation location: Whereas the teachers of the older generation have started school service long before tests were institutionalized at the threshold of teacher training—or, in fact, of high schools—the young teachers all had to pass several standardized tests themselves, from high school entrance exams, to university entrance ones as well as tests according to which teacher candidates are accepted for—or denied— the status of civil servant. Although we did not systematically inquire into the biographies of the teachers in our sample,[11] we may assume that this biographical background, collective as it is, both strengthens the experienced teachers' reluctance to pay attention to standardized tests and boosts the consideration given to it by novice teachers.

There are, to be sure, also aspects of these generations that pertain to their respective professional experience. Whereas the old teachers are able to fall back on long years of instructional practice and to modify the new curriculum, which they take as a general frame, the younger teachers have not yet gained the experience necessary to handle formal rules (curriculum) and unofficial expectations (test preparation) in such a sovereign manner. In other words, they lack the instruction practice on the basis of which they could modify, on their own, the lesson plans proposed by the teacher manual; instead, they rely on another ready-made source: the test preparation material. Moreover, they do not (and are not able to) evaluate their pupils' performance according to their own expectations, mostly relying on the test results with which they identify and assess even their own performance (see group *Gray* and more evidence in chapter 5). In this sense, this professional generation is again enshrined in a certain—even if a very limited—stock of professional experience gained throughout its life course.

4.4   The Intermediary Position Between Generations

The new curriculum and test preparation combiners, on one hand, and the experience-based lesson designers, on the other hand, display maximal contrast, which helped us to typify two distinguishable professional generations. However, there are also teacher groups that bear components of both generations; we denote these groups as the intermediary generation, which we wish to briefly scrutinize, taking into account the remaining three groups. The intermediary position of these teachers is also reflected in their career length, which varies between 5 and 16 years.

Group Black: Commonalities in Practice, Differences in Judgment

Group *Black*, composed of three class teachers with a variety of political standpoints, displayed a differentiated opinion regarding the new curriculum, both lauding and criticizing it from time to time. Whereas the "old" teachers take their own experience (that is, their previous pupils) as the basis for assessing whether a child will be able to learn according to the curriculum, in group *Black* the multiple-choice tests used at the entrance of high schools and universities constitute the principle criteria of evaluation:

Hf: however, when we began to apply this curriculum, at first we also fell into that mistake, I don't know, it perhaps happened to you too, now you start first and we attempted to finish all activities (.) all of them we attempted to do in particular of course the children (.) in

Sf: └ °yes° ┘

Hf: the meantime we since we did not have complete, you know, experience (.) on that, of course it was activity-focused but the child, at this time (.)

Sf: was deprived of knowledge

Hf: └ mm the knowledge was deficient (.), I mean for children who stand in-between that old and new there are some losses (.) now perhaps, the same thing doesn't happen to those who begin from the first grade (.) more a-

Sf: └ that is as I said, we try to cover that gap through additional source books, I think this is its biggest deficiency

Similar to group *Red* of the old generation, *Black* admits to having used the curriculum in a one-to-one manner in the first year, modifying it thereafter. While group *Red* modified the curriculum by drawing on methods and self-prepared activities from their own experiential background, Sf said she resorts to the "source" books which are so popular among the generation of novice teachers and that serve as preparation for multiple-choice tests. She denoted the difference between the curriculum and the test as a "gap"; therefore, she does not interpret it as a contradiction. Consequentially, she perceives the teacher manual's provisions and test preparations as activities that can easily coexist.

Because the group is characterized by an intermediary position, certain orientation discrepancies within the discourse exist. In the following passage Sf, a novice teacher, opposes Hf, who has 16 years of professional experience:

Hf: now, in the old system, a lot of things did not actually go right, it goes rather well in the new system (.) here for example I did not have any hardship in teaching mathematics (.) in the new system. now, the child accumulates [knowledge] by continuously taking a basis according to a certain level, but in the old system (.) one did not teach by tackling the multiplication table but now isn't it true that child receives a good foundation through rhythmic counting? (1) here, the difference between, I think it is settled more easily, you don't encounter that much difficulty-

Sf: └ but there is such a problem, I interrupted your word, my fellow teacher, (.) to me, the books are absolutely not sufficient in this new curriculum (.) if we just depend on the books and this child would enter *one* pilot test, I do not believe that she/he will be successful, we (.) certainly have to take *extra* publications (.) //mmh// at this moment, I let my class purchase three, four different publications in addition to the text-books, either question banks or leaflet tests if there is no support I do not think the books are enough I may even assert that the content of the book for life studies is totally empty

The discrepancy of orientations is not constituted by a teachers' verdict on the curriculum, but by the way he or she comes to a respective conclusion.

While Hf does not take into account any expectation or maxim from outside her own experience but has a self-assured idea of what, when, and in which sequential order a child should learn, Sf only referred to the requirements of the "pilot tests," a preparatory device for the high school entrance exam, as a criterion. While we do not know if Hf's instructional practice is similar to Sf's (who uses source books), their orientations structuring the assessment of children are clearly different: The older teacher displays homologies with the generation of experience-based lesson designers, while the novice teacher is congruent with the generation of new curriculum and test preparation combiners. Such orientation discrepancies prevent these teachers to be affiliated to an articulate professional generation.

Group Green: Following the New Curriculum With Exceptions

Group *Green*, composed of four branch teachers with varying experience and political stances, has welcomed the new curriculum. In the following discussion, the group collaboratively tells the researcher how they follow the "teacher guide book," but do not fully stick to it:

Km: ⌞ mmm just shortly before our colleague said that, she said here (.) there are teachers

Bf: ⌞ I until the beginning of the week, well

Km: guide book- there are guide books

Bf: ⌞ we benefit from our guide book; I mean we have an order there already, (.) but surely well for example let me speak for myself; according to myself you know (.) I allow for a little way for example you know (.) //mmh// what where with what I will begin here you know which order I will follow (.) it is there already in the guide book too, (1) in that way

Km: ⌞ before this system in the past daily plans used to be prepared, besides annual plans (1) since the daily plans were removed, (.) you wholly follow the teacher guide book, you have to (.) //mmh//

Bf: ⌞ yes I ( ) used to write.

Km: that makes you because it guides you like a daily plan (.) //mmh// but, because there are too many *words*, sentences in there, (.) we do it in the style that our colleagues do (.) we take little notes let's say (.) at the beginning of the class, how will I catch their attention (.) how will I motivate the child (.) you write three to five sentences, (.) you take notes that already *direct* you (.) otherwise if you look at all the advices and for example read all the sentences in the teacher guide book, (.) you look into that anyway (.) it becomes very intense, very difficult (1) you take brief, brief notes from there (.) //mmh// what is the gain that the child gets from that text (1) //mmh// for example the gain of reading, does she/he underst- do reading, you see, it finishes if she/he learns to take three to five things as writing making it done (1) in general it is like this I mean we take short notes.

Here, again, we see similarities to both the old and the new generation. Congruent with the novice teachers (the members of group *Green* have only slightly longer periods of service), *Green* closely follows the guidelines of the curriculum and the teacher manual. They only skip content and write their own text where they consider an activity or a text read aloud by the teacher to be inadequate. In this sense, the teacher manual is not seen as

a mere toolbox, but as a compulsory directory from which one only deviates in case problems arise. Conversely, these teachers do not refer to the
standardized tests and the need of preparing children for them. Similarly to
the old generation, the tests seem to be rather unimportant for these teachers. Instead of the standardized tests, the old curriculum (and Km's teaching
experience with it) is decisive for their instructional practice; as Km later
admitted, although the new curriculum has replaced "ex-cathedra teaching" by "activities," they from time to time still resort to this old type of
teaching.

Group Violet: Following the Teacher Manuals

Both class teachers from group *Violet* approve of the curriculum change.
While the female teacher criticized some components of the new curriculum as well as the way it was developed, the male teacher—who did not hide
his sympathy for the ruling JDP—sees such complaints as the consequence
of misinterpretation and of a reluctance to leave old habits. Although the
group's discourse is embossed by such antithetical discussions, both teachers
have a homologous orientation regarding classroom practice. In the following passage they tell the researcher how they write their annual plans:

Mm: our annual plans mm, (.) branches I mean let me say committees, first
        second third fourth until the fi::fth grades we are six classes each //
        mmh// that is we have six second classes, the committee assembles (1)
        over the web (.) we contribute too //mmh// mm on the present tem-
        plate plan I mean we download a plan we make arrangements according
        to ourselves on that plan //mmh// for example if the text book we
        receive begins with geometry we arrange the mathematics annual plan
        according to geometry //mmh// other than this mm I mean since we
        are a central school well throughout Turkey since we are not a rural
        school, since we do not lack anything, the frames of the *general* plan suits
        us //mmh//
Sf: exactly we do it by downloading from the web. (.) //mmh//

Similar to group *Turquoise*, these teachers download ready-made plans
from the Internet and—within their teachers' "committee"—modify it to a
very limited degree. Differently from *Turquoise*, whose members even use the
annual plan despite the school environment's unfavorable conditions, *Violet* is
convinced that the school, as a "central school," is well equipped and that the
pupils are sufficiently well prepared so that the plans of the new curriculum
"suit" them well. The daily lessons are prepared accordingly:

Sf: ⌐ we surely still prearrange, I mean it was also like this before the
        plans changed it is still like this for preparing the next class here what
        is required what is the equipment for example what is the subject in

Turkish, Life Studies, //mmh// iih according to this we first direct the children and make them prepare equipment, here if we make use of newspaper clippings we assign the subject and they bring the newspaper clippings related to that we do it in the classroom //mmh// to ourselves which examples may we give to the children for that subject which activity, well we will presumably come to the evaluation of curriculum we will tell our thoughts about that too there are enough activities in the books //mmh// we will even tell the deficient aspects //mmh//

Mm: you see there is actually something like this (.) in those plans after *2005* for the teachers, some fellow teachers say that there is an obligation a hardship they rather push us to be an operator I personally do not share this criticism, the guide books,

Sf: ⌐ ( ) ⌐

Mm: they were prepared with a logic, as if for a teacher who was just assigned //mmh// that is, our teacher (grind stone) does the gain in the guide book, she/he should take the trouble to read it before the class tomorrow (.) //mmh// they left space on the side of the teacher guide books, she/he would take notes according to herself/himself, that is it. actually, I mean I may say that the daily plan was removed with the guide book //mmh// well my teacher please read the class of tomorrow, the subject that you are going to teach in the guide book, write some notes too on the side according to you; //mmh// that is the guide book actually became daily plan (2) °didn't it°?

These two teachers write not only their annual plans according to the curriculum and the textbooks, but also their daily lesson plans. However, as Mm noted, the teacher manual is not supposed to replace any preparation on the teachers' part. Arguing against the criticism that the detailed character of the new teacher manuals have turned teachers into a kind of "operator" (of the ready-made material), he—without any objection from Sf—claimed that teachers should at least read the teacher manuals beforehand, and decide and take notes themselves on what to use and what not to use. Test preparation, however, does not concern them whatsoever.

The Intermediary Generation: An Amalgamation of Discrepant Orientations

The groups whose members have partly experienced the old curriculum and whose work experience ranged between 5 and 16 years cannot be subsumed under either the old or the new generation; that is, they cannot be assigned to the experience-based lesson designers or to the new curriculum and test preparation combiners. Within these groups we find elements of both generational orientations in various combinations. While in *Green* and *Violet* groups this combination of orientations is a collective product of the group, in group *Black* the different orientations lead to oppositions within the group.

The blend of different generational orientations and—in the case of *Black*—the lack of collective orientations indicates that the intermediary position of these teachers does not constitute a distinct generation. Whereas the *experience-based lesson designers* and the *new curriculum and test preparation combiners* form succinct professional generations which demarcate their respective organizational milieu and, at times—such as in group *Blue*'s discourse—even indicate that they are conscious of their own generational affiliation, the intermediary position is rather unclear and diffuse. Stretching across the old and the new generation, the researchers can only identify these teachers as an intermediary generation.

4.5   Distribution of Teachers and Schools' Prestige

In contrast to the teachers in the intermediary positions, the organizational milieus analyzed in sections 4.2 and 4.3 are embossed by distinct generational aspects of their respective curricular practices. As the comparison of these two professional generations revealed, the new curriculum is perceived and practiced in two distinct ways:

1. The teachers with more than 20 years of job experience see the new curriculum as a general frame, and the teacher manual (as well as other material provided for by the ministry) as a toolbox. These teachers design their lessons both by utilizing this toolbox and, more importantly, by drawing from their own experience with teaching methods and classroom activities. The adaptation of each lesson to pupils' needs is based on these teachers' own expectations toward pupil performance, built up during their extensive career.

2. The teachers with less than 7 years of job experience lack the expertise mentioned earlier, both regarding the assessment of pupils and the experience-based teaching methods and classroom activities. At the same time, they are experientially attached to the new curriculum and inclined to 'implement' it where possible. To a varying degree, the one-to-one implementation of the new curriculum is modified by concerns for the temporality of teaching and learning, and, more importantly, for test preparation. In some groups of this professional generation, test preparation has even become an equally important component of instruction, and test scores constitute the measure for pupil assessment.

On the surface, these findings confirm the assumption that the 'intended' curriculum is different from the 'taught' curriculum (Cuban). More precisely, the newly introduced curriculum has led to curricular practices that differ from one generation of teachers to the other, or more specifically, from teachers socialized in the old curriculum and those who started service with the new one. As shown, neither of these generationally embossed organizational milieus has undergone a transformative change. Whereas the experience-based lesson designers have adapted the new curriculum to their own habits, the new curriculum and test preparation combiners did not have to undergo transformation to comply with transformative change.

This generational divide, however, does not necessarily imply that experienced, older teachers stick to the old curriculum's contents and teaching approach (behaviorism). As our analysis has shown, the generational affiliation of these teachers is constituted by their habit of perceiving the curriculum as a syllabus, that is, as a general frame within which they creatively design their own lessons. This habit of lesson design is then continued even under the rule of the new curriculum. In contrast, the new generation of young teachers has never developed this habit (and capability) of lesson designing; therefore, these teachers are forced to stick to the new curriculum. Thus, closely following the new curriculum turns out to be not particularly a matter of good teacher training, but of a lack of professional experience instead. This becomes most evident where the young teachers, from time to time (or even predominantly), deviate from the new curriculum to prepare their pupils for standardized tests.

The Unequal Distribution of Professional Experience in Turkish Schools

The typification of generations is, first of all, based on teachers' respective professional experience in a certain sociohistorical time, but is also intermingled with aspects of general social generations whose typical worldview also pertains to people outside the teaching profession. But how are these professional generations represented through Turkey's teaching staff? Notwithstanding the fact that reconstructive typologies do not (and do not need to) represent quantitative distributions, it is important to ask whether the age groups and lengths of work experience that constitute the two professional generations are equally represented not only in our qualitative sampling (in which five groups belonged to the new and five to the old generation) but also in the

Table 4.6 Age of teacher workforce grades 6–9

	Percentage of teachers in each age group											
	Teachers aged under 25 years		Teachers aged 25–29 years		Teachers aged 30–39 years		Teachers aged 40–49 years		Teachers aged 50–59 years		Teachers aged 60 years or more	
Countries	%	(SE)	%	(SE)	%	(SE)	%	(SE)	%	(SE)	%	(SE)
Turkey	10.1	(1.47)	33.8	(2.25)	35.0	(1.33)	14.7	(1.35)	6.2	(0.72)	0.1	(0.08)
TALIS Average	*3.0*	*(0.11)*	*12.1*	*(0.19)*	*28.0*	*(0.23)*	*29.6*	*(0.23)*	*23.5*	*(0.21)*	*3.9*	*(0.09)*

Source: OECD (2009), online data supplement.

teaching staff of Turkey. The TALIS survey of the OECD provides some insight into the structure and working conditions of Turkish teachers for grades 6–9, of which three grades belonged to primary education in Turkey at the time of our investigation. Table 4.6 depicts the age structure of Turkish teachers for grades 6–9 vis-à-vis the average of participating countries.[12]

With 43.9% of teachers below 30 years of age, this age class of the teaching staff in Turkey is nearly three times larger than the TALIS average, and the percentage of teachers over 49 years of age differs from the TALIS average even more significantly. While these figures—and especially the discrepancy in relation to the TALIS average—may also be connected to the structure of teacher training and the retirement regulations in different countries, the high percentage of novice teachers in Turkey (with less than 11 years of job experience) is particularly remarkable (Table 4.7).

From these figures we can legitimately conclude that the teachers who belong to the generation of new curriculum and test preparation combiners represent approximately half of the teaching staff of grades 6–9 in Turkey. Conversely, the generation of experience-based lesson designers was identified among teachers who represent only 12% of the teaching staff, leaving a significant percentage of teachers between both generations. Compared to the TALIS average, it is clear that not only the age of Turkish primary school teachers but also their job experience can be considered very low.

This lack of professional experience may be attributed to the massive expansion of primary education after 1997. As we noted in section 2.3, compulsory primary education was extended in 1997, from 5 to 8 grades. Vis-à-vis an increasing population of children to be enrolled, the teaching staff for grades 1–8 subsequently grew from 289,295 in 1996/1997 to 373,303 in 2002/2003 and 515,852 in 2011/2012 (MoNE, 2007, pp. 3–5; MoNE, 2012, p. 11).

However, primary school teachers in Turkey bear not only a high variety regarding professional experience, but this inequality also concerns their distribution to single schools. Teachers' responses in the TALIS questionnaire

Table 4.7 Employment status and job experience of teachers of 6th–9th grade (2007/2008)

	Job experience							
	Teachers in their first 2 years of teaching		Teachers working for 3–10 years		Teachers working for 11–20 years		Teachers working for 20+ years	
Countries	%	(SE)	%	(SE)	%	(SE)	%	(SE)
Turkey	18.0	(1.85)	50.7	(2.11)	19.4	(1.37)	12.0	(1.26)
TALIS Average	*8.3*	*(0.18)*	*29.2*	*(0.24)*	*26.9*	*(0.22)*	*35.5*	*(0.26)*

Source: OECD (2009), online data supplement.

indicated that there is a clear divide regarding job experience between the countryside and cities, as well as among schools, between the majority attended by pupils from the middle classes and those of the lower classes, respectively. Based on a special analysis of TALIS data for Turkey, researchers maintained that "in 2008, 62% of teachers in the countryside had less than 5 years of job experience" (ERG, 2012, p. 87). This means that in the countryside the share of inexperienced teachers by far surmounts their general share in the teaching staff. As an indicator of the social milieus of pupils who attend different schools, the same special analysis has taken into account the highest educational degree of pupils' parents. The authors (ERG, 2012) came to the following conclusion:

> Whereas nearly no teachers with limited experience were appointed to schools in which more than 60% of the parents are university graduates, 9% of the experienced teachers work in such schools. In a similar way, the probability of a teacher with limited experience to start his/her career in a school where . . . less than 40% of children's' parents are university graduates is 85%.
>
> (p. 88)

These figures imply that inexperienced teachers have literally no chance of working in a school predominantly attended by children whose parents are university-educated; it also indicates that these teachers predominantly start their careers in schools with pupils from a less advantaged educational background.[13]

The Profession–Generational Divide in School Organizations

Our data also mirrored the unequal distribution of teachers throughout the country. As Table 4.8 shows, we could not find and interview any teachers with more than 20 years of job experience in the Demirli village school or in the squatter area school of Enver. Similarly, young teachers were non-existent in the middle-class schools of Tahsin and Safran.

Under these circumstances, it was impossible to directly compare groups with small and large job experience within more than one school. What initially seemed to be a research limitation (and hence a limitation of its results) later turned out to be a significant feature of the Turkish educational sector: As we have—based on statistical data—shown earlier, the teacher generations, with their respective curricular practices, are not distributed equally throughout the country. The young generation of new curriculum and test preparation combiners dominates the squatter area school and is also well represented in the village school (where we also have teachers in an intermediary position), while the older generation of experience-based lesson designers dominates the middle-class school in Istanbul and is well represented in the province capital school and in the rural town school. Although our sampling only

Table 4.8 Distribution of professional generations

School Years of Work experience/ professional generation	Dalen			Istanbul	
	Demirli Village school (Lale)	*Tuzlu town school (Sardunya)*	*Safran middle- class small city school (Zambak)*	*Squatter area school in Enver (Karanfil)*	*Middle- class school in Tahsin (Papatya)*
Over 20 years/ experience-based lesson designers	–	*Pink*	Red	–	Brown, Blue, White
5–16/intermediary position	*Black*	–	Green, Violet	–	–
Less than 7 years/ new curriculum and test preparation combiners	*Orange*	*Yellow*	–	Gray, Turquoise, Khaki	–

Note: Groups in italics are formed by branch teachers.

included 13 group discussions with teachers, the correspondence between this data material and the unequal distribution of teachers with small or large job experience across the country (ERG, 2012, pp. 87–88) leads us to maintain that the generational divide in curriculum practice is intimately interwoven with the organization of school education in Turkey.

Bureaucratic Background of the Unequal Distribution of Teachers in Turkey

What appears to be an injustice—leaving village and lower-class children to inexperienced teachers, while middle-class pupils are catered for by experienced personnel—is the result of a staffing policy introduced in Turkey in 1999. Whereas prior to 1999 schools throughout the country had been staffed with teachers in an appallingly unequal way (some schools did not have any teachers at all, while others had an excessively high number of teachers who practically did not work), a decree by the MoNE of 1999 obliged the administrations to define a certain "norm cadre" for every school and to appoint teachers according to this "objective measure" (ERG, 2012, p. 85).

While this decree on norm cadres served to foster equality between the schools of the country, significantly reducing the discrepancies between regions regarding teacher–pupil ratios (ERG, 2012), another decree defined which teachers were eligible to work in which school. As section 20 of this decree declared, "the allocation of teachers who wish to be relocated is made according to openings in the norm cadre of their field and according to the hierarchy of service points" (MoNE, 2010b). This implied that teachers could only ask to be relocated if there was a lack of teachers in the respective school. Their application then was evaluated according to their "service points" (with some minor additional factors also taken into account).

As the same decree stipulated, teachers receive "service points" according to their workplace. Provinces and districts considered similar by the ministry "regarding the degree of difficulty in allocating teachers and employing them" (MoNE, 2010b, section 48) are accorded to one of five classes with a respective number of points (the highest number of points given for the most difficult class). A further differentiation is made between village schools (higher points) and those in a town or city (lower points). These two numbers are then multiplied by the years of service in the respective region, resulting in the present "service points" of each teacher. In 2013, for example, a teacher who worked in the Akkuş primary school of the Işık village in the Hakkari province (at the Iranian and Iraqi border) received 30 service points per year, while a teacher employed in the Maçka primary school of Şişli in Istanbul was only given 12 points. Hence, a teacher who has worked for a long time, or who has worked in a village within a difficult region is awarded more "service points" than a teacher who has only started working in a city school within a good district.

Whereas the decree on norm cadres was evidently meant to distribute teachers according to the needs of the country's schools, the decree on "service points" evidently served to organize teacher allocation in a way that may be considered legitimate by teachers. Both decrees, however, in their combination led to teachers not only gaining their service points according to the varying prestige of schools but also accessing their positions in the following way: The ministry accords the most service points to teachers who work in the most difficult schools to allocate a teacher, that is, the most unpopular schools. At the same time, the most popular schools in the country (that is, to which the highest number of teachers wish to be allocated) have the highest number of service points as a threshold for entry. Thus, a school in a popular district of Istanbul requires a teacher to have far more service points for being accepted than a village school. Accordingly, the popular schools are staffed with the teachers with the highest number of service points; in other words, the most experienced teachers.

As the preceding analysis reveals, the unequal teacher distribution in Turkish schools is not an incidental phenomenon; it is firstly a secondary effect of attempts to staff all schools in Turkey according to their capacity needs, and secondly, the effect of attempting to allocate and relocate teachers according to a legitimate procedure. As a result, the varieties in curriculum practices that we have analyzed within the organizational milieus of five schools are not only a matter of the professional generations of teachers, but are also firmly anchored in the organization of schools themselves. For this reason, the inequality (as regards job experience) and the subsequent variety of curriculum practices are not only an effect of organizational milieus; they are also boosted by formal rules which are the precondition for the constitution of such homogeneous units. Had the bureaucratic organization of teacher allocation/relocation not led to the staffing of a school with teachers who have a similar amount of professional experience (and, hence, service points)—especially if it is a popular facility—neither the village, squatter area schools, or the middle-class school which we have investigated in Istanbul would be dominated by one specific generationally embossed organizational milieu of teachers. In a sense, the MoNE, while struggling with the effects of the differentiated prestige of schools throughout the country, has introduced regulations that both ensure that the teacher–pupil ratios of schools approximate each other and take into account the very problem of prestige (although by doing so, the problem of prestige is also reproduced).

Up to this section, in the present chapter, we have tried to focus only on the generational dimension of teachers' organizational milieus, leaving aside the school organizations themselves. As becomes apparent toward the end of this chapter, this aspect of school organization—together with the general structure of primary education—considerably impacts curricular practices. Therefore, in the next chapter, in which we further inquire into varieties of curricular practices, we shift our perspective from the teachers' organizational milieus and their generational dimension to the socioeconomic and geographical situation of the schools themselves. The issue of prestige and its effects on curricular practices—although in a slightly different form—will, of course, continue to be of concern.

Notes

1 This has been shown by numerous scholars who reconstructed teacher milieus with the Documentary Method (see, among others, Martens, 2010; Zeitler et al., 2012).
2 As an alternative to group discussions we could also have observed instructional practice directly, possibly assisted by videography. Such method of data gathering—usually called participatory observation—produces highly complex visual and audio data and is difficult and very time-consuming to interpret according to the documentary method (see Bohnsack et al., 2014; Wagner-Willi, 2012; for ethnographic instruction research, see, among others, Breidenstein, 2012). Moreover, the comparison of cases which will include pupils' parents is easier if all data are gathered in a similar (such as audio-based) way.
3 Although these problems are well known in the educational sector of Turkey, we could not find comprehensive empirical analyses tackling them. Important indications can be found in ERG (2014) and Çoşkun et al. (2013).
4 To keep this province anonymized, we do not specify the sources used to characterize "Dalen" in the following paragraphs.
5 For determining the individual schools, we conducted informal interviews with school inspectors, local education administrators, and activists of teacher unions.
6 We provide the reader with more detailed information on these schools and the social geographies in which they are situated in chapter 5.
7 After each group discussion, we asked the participants to answer some statistical questions formulated in a short questionnaire.
8 For the rules of transcription, see the appendix to this volume.
9 Within Turkish schools, teachers are grouped into committees according to their branch.

10 This statement very much concurs with the New Institutionalist assumption that organizations tend to adopt expectations institutionalized in their environment but decouple their interior practices from them.

11 The novice teachers of group *Yellow*, for example, compared the great variety of source books available today to their own past situation when they were pupils: "in our time there was one test book and one fascicle, we would sit and work the monthly or weekly pensum and solve it. The test book was the only one, we took it in our hand like the Quran, that is, like the one and only book."

12 The following countries participated in the TALIS 2008 survey: Australia, Austria, Belgium (fl.), Brazil, Bulgaria, Denmark, Estonia, Hungary, Iceland, Ireland, Italy, Republic of Korea, Lithuania, Malaysia, Malta, Mexico, Norway, Poland, Portugal, Slovak Republic, Slovenia, Spain, and Turkey.

13 A similarly (or even more) unequal distribution exists between tenured civil servants and inexperienced teachers who work on a fee basis (Güvercin, 2014).

References

Alacacı, C., & Erbaş, A. K. (2010). Unpacking the inequality among Turkish schools: Findings from PISA 2006. *International Journal of Educational Development, 30*, 182–192.

Altinyelken, H. K. (2011). Student-centred pedagogy in Turkey: Conceptualisations, interpretations and practices. *Journal of Education Policy, 26*, 137–160.

Altinyelken, H. K. (2013). Teachers' principled resistance to curriculum change: A compelling case from Turkey. In A. Verger, H. K. Altinyelken, & M. D. Konik (Eds.), *Global education reforms and teachers* (pp. 109–127). Brussels: Education International.

Ayan Ceyhan, M. (2009). Emergence of individualism, entrepreneurialism and creativity in Turkey's state-run educational system: Anthropological contributions to educational sciences. *Procedia Social and Behavioral Sciences, 1*, 101–104.

Bakış, O., Levent, H., İnsel, A., & Polat, S. (2009). *Türkiye'de eğitime erişimin belirleyicileri.* Istanbul: Eğitim Reformu Girişimi.

Bidwell, C. E., Frank, K. A., & Quiroz, P. A. (1997). Teacher types, workplace controls, and the organization of schools. *Sociology of Education, 70*, 285–307.

Bohnsack, R. (2010a). *Rekonstruktive Sozialforschung.* Opladen: Budrich.

Bohnsack, R. (2010b). Documentary method and group discussions. In R. Bohnsack, N. Pfaff, & W. Weller (Eds.), *Qualitative analysis and documentary method in international educational research* (pp. 99–124). Opladen: Barbara Budrich.

Bohnsack, R. (2014). Documentary method. In U. Flick (Ed.), *Sage handbook of analyzing qualitative data* (pp. 217–223). Thousand Oaks, CA: Sage.

Bohnsack, R., Fritzsche, B., & Wagner-Willi, M. (Eds.). (2014). *Dokumentarische Video- und Filminterpretation.* Opladen: Budrich.

Breidenstein, G. (2012). Ethnographisches Beobachten. In H. de Boer & S. Reh (Eds.), *Beobachtung in der Schule* (pp. 27–43). Wiesbaden: Springer/VS.

Coşkun, V., Derince, M. Ş., & Uçarlar, N. (2013). Scar of tongue: Consequences of the ban on the use of mother tongue in education and experiences of Kurdish students in Turkey. *Language Policy, 12*, 355–357.

Cuban, L. (1992). Curriculum stability and change. In P. W. Jackson (Ed.), *Handbook of research on curriculum* (pp. 216–247). New York: Macmillan.

DiMaggio, P. J., & Powell, W. W. (1983). The iron cage revisited: Institutional isomorphism and collective rationality in organizational fields. *American Sociological Review, 48*, 147–160.

EARGED (T.C. Milli Eğitim Bakanlığı Eğitimi Araştırma ve Geliştirme Dairesi Başkanlığı). (2010). *PISA 2009 Projesi Ulusal Ön Raporu.* Ankara: MoNE.

Edwards, R. (2011). Translating the prescribed into the enacted curriculum in college and school. *Educational Philosophy and Theory, 43,* 38–54.

Erdoğan, İ. (2005). Milli Eğitim Bakanlığı'nın Yeni Müfredat Çalışmaları, *Özel Okullar Birliği Bülteni.* Retrieved January 8, 2013, from http://www.irfanerdogan.com.tr/index.php? 1option=com_content&view=article&id=102:milli-egitim-bakanliginin-yeni-mufredat-calismalari&catid=34:ana-sayfa&Itemid=148

Erdoğan, İ. (2011). *Milli Eğitime Dair.* Ankara: Nobel

ERG (Eğitim Reformu Girişimi). (2012). *Eğitim İzleme Raporu 2011.* Istanbul: Author.

ERG (Eğitim Reformu Girişimi). (2014). *Türkiye Eğitim Sisteminde Eşitlik ve Akademik Başarı.* Istanbul: Author.

Glaser, B., & Strauss, A. (1969). *The discovery of grounded theory.* Chicago: Aldine.

Güvercin, G. (2014). *Informal workplace practices and learning experiences of permanent and hourly-paid teachers* (Unpublished doctoral thesis). Bosphorus University, Istanbul.

Hargreaves, A. (2002). Sustainability of educational change: The role of social geographies. *Journal of Educational Change, 3,* 189–214.

Lewis, T. (2007). Social inequality in education: A constraint on an American high-skills future. *Curriculum Inquiry, 37,* 329–349.

Mannheim, K. (1952). On the interpretation of Weltanschauung. In *Essays on the sociology of knowledge* (pp. 33–83). New York: Oxford University Press.

Mannheim, K. (1968). *Ideology and utopia.* London: Routledge.

Mannheim, K. (1972). The problem of generations. In P. Altbach & R. Laufer (Eds.), *The new pilgrims* (pp. 101–138). New York: McKay.

Mannheim, K. (1982). *Structures of thinking.* London: Routledge.

Martens, M. (2010). *Implizites Wissen und kompetentes Handeln.* Göttingen: V&R.

Meyer, J. W., & Rowan, B. (1977). Institutionalized organizations: Formal structure as myth and ceremony. *American Journal of Sociology, 83*(2), 340–363.

MoNE (Ministry of National Education). (2007). *National education statistics: Formal education 2011–2012.* Ankara: Author.

MoNE (Ministry of National Education). (2010). *Öğretmenlerinin atama ve yer değiştirme yönetmeliği.* Ankara: Author.

MoNE (Ministry of National Education). (2012). *National education statistics: Formal education 2011–2012.* Ankara: Author.

Nohl, A.-M. (2014). *Konzepte interkultureller Pädagogik* (3rd ed.). Bad Heilbrunn: Klinkhardt.

OECD. (2009). *Creating effective teaching and learning environments: First results from TALIS.* Paris: Author.

Schittenhelm, K. (2009). Qualitatives sampling: Strategien und Kriterien der Fallauswahl. In S. Maschke & L. Stecher (Eds.), *Enzyklopädie Erziehungswissenschaft Online. Fachgebiet Methoden der empirischen erziehungswissenschaftlichen Forschung.* Weinheim: Juventa.

Selçuk, Z., Kayılı, H., & Okut, L. (Eds.). (2002). *Çoklu Zeka Uygulamaları.* Ankara: Nobel.

Somel, N. R. (2015). *Education in inequality, unequal education. Educational inequality as a combination of multilevel processes. A Turkish primary school study* (Unpublished doctoral thesis). Helmut-Schmidt-University, Hamburg, Germany.

Supowitz, J. A., & Weinbaum, E. H. (Eds.). (2008). *The implementation gap: Understanding reform in high schools.* New York: Teachers College Press.

Tansel, A. (2010). *Changing returns to education for men and women in a developing country: Turkey, 1994–2005.* Unpublished manuscript.

Tönnies, F. (2011). *Community and society.* Mineola, NY: Dover.

Ünal, I., Özsoy, S., Yıldız, A., Güngör, S., Aylar, E., & Çankaya, D. (2010). *Eğitimde Toplumsal Ayrışma*. Ankara: Ankara Üniversitesi Basımevi.

Wagner-Willi, M. (2012). On the multidimensional analysis of video data: Documentary interpretation of interaction in schools. In H. Knoblauch, B. Schnettler, J. Raab, & H.-G. Soeffner (Eds.), *Videoanalysis* (pp. 143–153). Frankfurt: Lang.

Weber, M. (1949). Objectivity in social science and social policy. In E. Shils (Ed.), *The methodology of the social sciences* (pp. 49–112). Glencoe, IL: Free Press.

Weick, K. E. (1976). Educational organizations as loosely coupled systems. *Administrative Science Quarterly, 21*, 1–19.

Yates, L., & Young, M. (2010). Globalisation, knowledge and the curriculum. *European Journal of Education, 45*, 4–10.

Zeitler, S., Heller, N., & Asbrand, B. (2012). *Bildungsstandards in der Schule. Eine rekonstruktive Studie zur Implementation der Bildungsstandards*. Münster: Waxmann.

5 Instruction and Inequality Between Schools

The variety of ways in which the new curriculum is practiced in Turkish primary schools is structured both by generational differences in the organizational milieus of teachers and by other aspects of the school organizations, which we are yet to define in detail. Therefore, in the present chapter we focus on the school organizations and how their socioeconomic and geographical situation influence curricular practices. This shift in perspective requires the broadening of both the scope of empirical data and of the basic concepts that are used. In addition to group discussions with teachers, expert interviews with school principals will help us understand the organizational dynamics of primary schools. To identify the influence of pupils' social milieus and the significance of social geography we also include group discussions with pupils' parents in our analysis. But before doing so, we also need to define the concept of *social milieu* and how we use it to understand socioeconomic and socio-geographic differences between schools. Furthermore, we draw on a reformulated version of Bourdieu's concept of *capital*, with which we underpin inequality between schools in their social, symbolic, cultural, and economic aspects.

After an introduction to the basic concepts newly added to our study (section 5.1), we structure this chapter according to its focus on the socio-geographic and socioeconomic situatedness of schools. First we consider the curricular practices in schools of middle-class districts in "Tahsin," Istanbul, and the provincial capital "Safran" (section 5.2), which we contrast to the school in the poor "Enver" district of Istanbul (section 5.3). We then attend to the schools of a village ("Demirli") and a small town ("Tuzlu") of the central Anatolian province "Dalen," where the new curriculum is practiced in a different frame of educational expectations (section 5.4). Finally, on the background of a summary of the empirical results, we reflect on the theoretical contributions of the chapter (section 5.5).

5.1 Social Milieu, School Organization, and Resources: Theoretical Considerations

Curricular practices, only loosely coupled with (or even fully decoupled from) the formal rules of the new curriculum, are structured according to several components of the school organization. In addition to the organizational milieus of teachers, characterized, among others, by their affiliation to professional generations (see chapter 4), the practicing of formal rules may also be influenced by the social milieus of those who are members of the respective school organization.

Social Milieus

We speak of social milieus when and where people share commonalities in the "stratification of experience" (Mannheim, 1972, p. 112) within society, that is, where they draw on social experience that is structurally similar or identical. In contrast to organizational milieus, of which only experiences one encounters as a member of a specific (kind of) organization are constitutive (for example, primary schools in Turkey), social milieus are situated in society at large. This experience that connects people—in other words, this "conjunctive experience" (Mannheim, 1982, p. 203)—pertains to people's general social life. In the milieu as a "conjunctive experiential space" (p. 194), those who are affiliated to the milieu perceive their world in a similar way. The individual actor is embedded in the specific perspective of his/her milieu to such an extent that he/she "sees the things of his [or her; the authors] experiential horizon only insofar as they fit into collective meanings" (p. 213) of the milieu.

As we already noted in section 4.1, milieus are multidimensional, rather than monolithic. As much as the generational dimension is only one of several facets in teachers' organizational milieus, social milieus are based on the "overlap of different spaces of experience" (Bohnsack, 2010a, p. 111) such as gender, generation, class, and education. In a milieu, these experiential dimensions superpose and modify each other and can only be differentiated analytically. While gender and generational affiliations certainly have their influence on how parents and pupils of a social milieu perceive school and instruction, in our study we are predominantly concerned with two other "social locations" (Mannheim, 1972, p. 102) that overlap: The "class position" (Mannheim, 1972, p. 526), which in our research is roughly schematized as belonging to a certain income group and—as far as parents are concerned—having a certain educational level, and the geographic location, that is, the socio-graphic space in which one lives. With regard to class location, we contrast parents with a high school degree or above whose annual earnings are considered middle class in Turkey to parents whose highest education level is having graduated from middle school and who earn only the state-defined minimum wage or less. For the geographic location we again use a binary differentiation and compare urban and rural locations. As Karl Mannheim (1972) argued, such social locations limit the "range of potential experience" (p. 106); for example, poor parents, in general, have no chance of sending their children to a private school, and rural parents have only a limited range of schools from which they can choose for their children. Because the social locations only refer to a *potentiality* of experience, in our empirical research we have solely used them as search strategies during the sampling process.[1] Similar to the generational dimension in the organizational milieus of the teachers (chapter 4), the empirical reconstructions then have to reveal whether there are, in fact, spaces of collective experience connected to the geographic or class location and what these collective experiences concern.[2]

In its reference to collective experience, the concept of social milieu has points in common with Bourdieu's concept of "habitus" (see Bohnsack, 2014a, p. 221). As a system of "schemes of perception, thought and action" (Bourdieu, 2010, p. 54) the habitus connects people of a milieu, even if they are not aware of it. Whereas in Mannheim's sociology of knowledge the "atheoretical" (Mannheim, 1982, p. 67) character of experience and *knowledge* is underpinned, Bourdieu's approach helps us to include the aspect of non-reflected *practice* in the analysis (Bohnsack, 2014a, p. 221). Similar to conjunctive experience, which may not be reflected and theoretically explicated by the actors themselves, the habitus, with its foundation in practices, is an "embodied history, internalized as a second nature and so forgotten as history" (Bourdieu, 2010, p. 56). Because of this low degree of awareness the "modus operandi" (Bourdieu, 2010, p. 52) of a habitus (that is, the way patterns of perceiving, thinking and acting work) cannot be directly queried from the research participants; rather, it needs to be reconstructed from participants' products of thinking, perceiving, and acting—in other words, from the "opus operatum" (Bourdieu, 2010, p. 56).

As we already mentioned in section 4.1, milieus—like the habitus—are not necessarily based on real groups (such as peer groups), but on the collective stratification of experience constituted within a shared social location (Bohnsack, 2010b, p. 63). On the basis of this conjunctive experience, a "conjunctive knowing" emerges within milieus, in which people have the cultural creations, occupations and "contents in the way of the existential community, a way which is wholly concrete and perspectivistic and which can only be shared conjunctively" with the other members of the milieu (Mannheim, 1982, p. 265). For instance, those who are affiliated to one milieu immediately understand each other when they use words such as "education" or "test." This knowledge is based on the experience they have created by participating in education or by passing tests, or by having helped their children to do so. In this sense, this knowledge is connected with practices which over time may even have become habitualized. If people within one milieu then talk about education or tests, this conjunctive knowledge, the respective practices, and possibly the habits formed are presupposed among themselves. However, those who do not belong to the respective milieu may not understand to which milieu-specific experiences and habits these words refer. For example, for experienced teachers of the older generation the concept of *test* implies that the teacher has to deliver knowledge, since knowledge enables the pupil to answer test questions. In contrast, novice teachers do not associate tests with knowledge alone, but also with the skill of answering test questions in the fastest way possible; as such, they design their instruction accordingly. In this sense, the word *test* has an experiential and practical meaning and significance that vary from one milieu to another.

   If experienced and novice teachers then communicate (that is, when people cross the borders of their respective milieus), they must enter a "completely abstract relationship" (Mannheim, 1982, p. 265) to their practices and experiences, which then results in what Mannheim coined "communicative definitions" (p. 265). This communicative knowledge conveys the meaning of education or tests in their "general function" (p. 258) and is abstracted from the experiences encountered by them. As human beings always live both within their milieus and act across their borders, the communicative and conjunctive meaning of such words may exist simultaneously; of this, Mannheim spoke of a "duality in the ways" of conduct (p. 265).

   Our inquiry is certainly not solely concerned with the general (communicative) meaning of the new curriculum; we also inquire into the milieu-specific conjunctive experiences connected to it. As such, we need to also comprehend those experiences which are so deeply embedded in the actors' practices that they are unable to explicate it by using communicative knowledge. Such conjunctive knowledge is only disclosed to us if we either observe the practices directly or manage to gain access to them through narratives and descriptions (cf. Bohnsack, 2014a, p. 221). For this reason, we conducted group discussions with teachers and pupils' parents in which they could freely narrate their practical experience with the new curriculum and with school instruction in general.

Milieu References to Organizational Rules

In this inquiry, social milieus are of interest only insofar as they are related to the school organization. As we outlined in the previous chapters, organizations are characterized by explicit rules which, as formalized expectations toward behavior, define roles within the organization; anybody who wishes to become or remain a member of the organization must obey these organizational rules, otherwise she/he would risk exclusion (section 2.2). However, formal rules are not identical to concrete actions, making situations in which a rule applies unclear. In chapters 3 and 4 we elaborated on a *first* mechanism by which formal rules are related to organizational practice: Formal rules (for example, the new curriculum) can be tentatively put into practice from situation to situation. If these new practices that follow the formal rule are based on a reciprocal understanding of the organization members, collectively shared informal rules emerge, along which the formal rule is put into practice. These informal rules may constitute the nucleus of an organizational milieu, as it happened, for instance, with the organizational milieu formed when teachers worked with the curriculum of 1968 and related it to their instructional practice by designing their own annual and weekly lesson plans (see section 4.2).

In the present chapter, however, we are concerned with two other mechanisms which relate formal rules to organizational practice (Nohl, 2014, pp. 183–196). To the extent that the members of the organization (such as pupils and their parents) are at the same time affiliated to a social milieu, these mechanisms are deeply enshrined in the social milieu's conjunctive experience.

Indeed, the milieu-specific habits may be directed at the formal rules of the organization and also break them. In this *second* mechanism, the habits of the social milieu serve to "get around the organization's assumptions" and expectations toward its members (Goffman, 1961, p. 189). Goffman called these practices—which run contrary to the organizational rules—"underlife" (p. 194). This underlife may be based on the shared milieu affiliation of organization members. As Goffman reminded us, organizations tend to adapt to underlife "not only by increasing discipline but also by selectively legitimizing these practices, hoping in this way to regain control and sovereignty even at the loss of some of the participants' obligations" (p. 196).

While we reveal instances of organizations' underlife in our research, the *third* mechanism is more important for our inquiry. If there are organization members who are affiliated to the same social milieu and its conjunctive experience, they may perceive the formal rules from the perspective of their own milieu and handle them as such. The formal rules, explicit in the sense of "communicative knowledge" (Mannheim, 1982, p. 258), are then directly and intuitively understood and given sense to within the conjunctive knowledge of the respective social milieu. In other words, by drawing on the "intuitively available practical knowledge" (Bohnsack, 2010b, p. 195) of their shared social milieu, the organization members embed the formal rules into their milieu's taken-for-granted regularities and habitualized practices. This milieu-affected handling of formal rules, of course, presumes that the organization members who put the respective formal rules into practice belong to the same milieu.

This third mechanism is not only limited to *social* milieus. The same mechanism (that is, the perceiving of formal rules, such as the new curriculum, within taken-for-granted knowledge and habits) also applies to existing and consolidated *organizational* milieus such as that of the experience-based lesson designers (section 4.2). Whereas organizational milieus are constituted by tentatively putting formal rules into practice and thus by establishing informal rules that form the nucleus of an organizational milieu, once they exist, these organizational milieus—similar to social milieus—provide the taken-for-granted knowledge and habits upon which new formal rules may be perceived and practiced.

Embedded in the conjunctive practice and experience of their respective milieu, organization members do not only *handle* formal rules according to their taken-for-granted knowledge; they already *perceive* these rules in a selective way, as only formal rules that can be related to the milieu-specific practices and experience become relevant. In this sense, there is always a "tense relation" (Bohnsack,

Table 5.1 Mechanisms of relating milieus to organizational rules

	1st mechanism	2nd mechanism	3rd mechanism
Reference to formal rules	Tentative and practical constitution of informal rules	Breaking formal rules (underlife)	Milieu-specific handling of formal rules
Milieu basis	Possible constitution of organizational milieus	Based on habits that are specific for social milieus	Based on organizational or social milieu shared by organization members

2014b, p. 44) between the formal rules of organizations and milieu-specific practice. The organizational or social milieu, however, is not fixed but may react to the discrepancy between its own practices and the organizational rules. In its "conjunctive space of experience a conflict with normative demands is acted out" (Bohnsack, 2014b, p. 43). The way in which this conflict is managed again is affected by the valid habits in the respective milieu (Bohnsack, 2014b). On the basis of its encounters and conflicts with new formal rules, an organizational or social milieu may then be reproduced or differentiated, and may even be changed to a certain degree—for instance, when the organizational milieu of experience-based lesson designers was confronted with the new curriculum and the respective teachers had to handle it, albeit according to their own habits. Table 5.1 summarizes the three mechanisms of relating formal rules to milieus.

Milieu Domination in School Organizations

If a school was the place of teachers and pupils from a variety of milieus, as we may hypothetically assume, then the school's formal rules as well as its curriculum could not be easily understood and handled within the taken-for-granted knowledge and habits of a single milieu. Bereft of a common understanding of the formal rules of the organization, its members (most importantly the teachers and school administrators) would then have to tentatively put new formal rules into practice and, by doing so, establish informal rules along which subsequently a new organizational milieu may be constituted.

However, the schools we included in our study are far from this hypothetical situation, as they tend to be dominated by a specific organizational milieu of teachers, that is, either by the experience-based lesson designers generation or by the professional generation of the curriculum and test preparation combiners (see section 4.5). While this domination of the school by a specific organizational milieu was not a sampling criterion and only surfaced during our empirical analysis, we purposefully structured our sampling according to the assumed domination of schools by specific social milieus. We intended to analyze whether and how the new curriculum is put into practice under the conditions of a school that predominantly caters for a specific social milieu.

Assuming that the taken-for-granted knowledge and habits of pupils' social milieus influence the way the curriculum is practiced, we chose to analyze schools that are dominated by specific social milieus in different ways: Based on the warranted assumption that—at least in Turkey—social inequalities coincide with spatial inequalities (Ünal et al., 2010), the two schools in "Tahsin," a district of Istanbul, and in the provincial capital "Safran" were taken into account to see how the curriculum is practiced in a school that is predominantly attended by pupils from urban middle-class milieus. The domination by urban lower-class milieus is then scrutinized in the school of "Enver," Istanbul. Finally, these anticipated milieu dominations are contrasted to the schools of the "Demirli" village and of the small town "Tuzlu," which we assumed to be dominated by rural lower-class milieus. Although we purposefully selected these schools due to a domination by specific social milieus, we had not anticipated that these social inequalities also had effects on teacher recruitment and, hence, on the domination of schools by specific organizational milieus.

Resource and Capital

The three mechanisms of putting formal rules into practice (see earlier) are helpful to explain the *heterogeneity* of instruction practices that are only loosely coupled with, or even decoupled from, the official curriculum. However, the fact that schools may be *dominated* by specific organizational and/or social milieus indicates that it would be insufficient to conceive of practices and their relation to organizational rules only as a matter of habitualization that varies from milieu to milieu. In education—and beyond—we are not only concerned with heterogeneity, but also with *inequality*. Some heterogeneities, indeed, may even turn into inequalities, and vice versa. Thus, the study of education has to be sensitive to the ways in which practices assume and are accorded different (that is, higher or lower) values in society and its sectors. Two important factors that define the value of practices are their availability and their appreciation in society.

The curricular practices that we analyzed in teachers' organizational milieus (chapter 4) and that are—in their connection to social milieus—also the focus of the current chapter, are neither a matter of choice nor freely available to teachers and pupils. As the example of the experience-based lesson designers shows, such practices are based on *resources*, such as the professional experience gained through many years of teaching. Bourdieu (1996, pp. 117–118) saw these resources as both a "technical competence" and as a matter of "social virtue." With his concept of "capital," he has elaborated an approach which helps us to theoretically grasp the unequal distribution of curricular practices in the schools under scrutiny. As is widely known, Bourdieu (1986) differentiated capital

as *economic capital*, which is immediately and directly convertible into money and may be institutionalized in the form of property rights; as *cultural capital*, which is convertible, on certain conditions, into economic capital and may be institutionalized in the form of educational qualifications; and as *social capital*, made up of social obligations ('connections'), which is convertible, in certain conditions, into economic capital and may be institutionalized in the form of a title of nobility.

(p. 243; italics in original)

The fourth form, "symbolic capital," directly refers to and is built on the other three. As Bourdieu (1985) recalled, symbolic capital is "commonly called prestige, reputation, renown, etc.," describing it as "the form in which the different forms of capital are perceived and recognized as legitimate" (p. 724). The instructional practices analyzed in this volume are based on such capital.

Practical Capital Formations in Milieus and Organizations

In the present chapter, our sampling strategy is constituted by a *combination* of anticipated differences in both cultural and economic capital. As indicated, we included schools in our sample which cater for pupils from specific social milieus: Those whose parents have a high school degree or higher and whose annual earnings are considered of middle-class in Turkey, as well as those pupils whose parents have the 8-year middle school diploma or less and earn only the state-defined minimum wage or less.

Such an endowment with resources can be identified by using questionnaires or by directly asking the respective persons. The unequal—and often very obvious—distribution of these endowments hence helped us to structure our sample. However, the empirical identification of these resources does not imply that they are also *capitalized* on in the practices of the respective milieu. The old generation of teachers, for example, must certainly be assumed as very experienced and able in teaching a behavioristic curriculum. As our empirical reconstructions revealed, however, these teachers do not rely on this ability but only use their proficiency in independently designing lessons; otherwise, they follow the topics and goals of the new—constructivist—curriculum. Apparently, actors may not use all of the resources with which they are provided in their milieu. The respective endowment with resources is not directly and totally turned into practice; in other words, only a certain part of these resources are capitalized on.

Whereas Bourdieu did not systematically differentiate between resource and capital, we here propose to speak of capital only when and insofar as a certain resource is drawn upon in practice. In this sense, capital is constituted via the input and investment of resources in practices. Therefore, the empirical analysis should not stop at identifying obvious resource endowments; rather, it needs to reconstruct the *practical capital formations*. As we will come to understand in this chapter, these capital formations are not only dependent on the class location but also on other experiential dimensions, most importantly the geographic location.

Organizational Resources

The ways milieu-specific practices are related to organizational rules are based on a certain resource endowment, which they also reproduce. Moreover, organizations themselves are also equipped with various resources on which they can capitalize. As Emirbayer and Johnson (2008) observed, it is not only "the volume and composition of an organization's capital" (p. 12) but also its "trajectory" over time that is important here, since, for example, a "venerable" organization may draw on its prestige (that is, symbolic resources) and thus outperform less well-known organizations. Section 4.5 has provided us with an illuminating example of how cultural resources are appropriated by schools over time: Prestigious schools are able to attract experienced teachers and thus incorporate and capitalize on their cultural resources, whereas unpopular schools are only able to employ novice teachers. As a mutually reinforcing process, this renders some schools (such as the school in the squatter house area) poor in cultural resources, and they are outperformed by more fortunate educational organizations such as the middle-class schools of our sample.

Studying Instruction in the Contested Educational Sector

The concepts of resource and capital, as elaborated, would certainly be meaningless without the notion of struggle within the field in which a school organization is located. As much as the practical capital formations of organizations determine their position in the contested field, the hard-fought value of various forms of capital is assessed in this very field. As Bourdieu (1985) wrote,

> The active properties that are selected as principles of construction of the social space are the different kinds of power or capital that are current in the different fields. Capital . . . represents a power over the field (at a given moment) and, more precisely, over the accumulated product of past labor (in particular over the set of instruments of production) and thereby over the mechanisms tending to ensure the production of a particular category of goods and so over a set of incomes and profits. The kinds of capital, like the aces in a game of cards, are powers that define the chances of profit in a given field (in fact, to each field or subfield there corresponds a particular kind of capital, which is current, as a power or stake, in that game).
>
> (p. 724)

While in a synchronic perspective Bourdieu's metaphor of the "aces" in the "game of cards" might be suitable, it becomes misleading as soon as one observes the dynamics of a given field over time. The value of a form of capital is not predefined and fixed throughout the competition, since—to stay in the metaphor—it is not always clear from the outset which game of cards is being played and since the players might still fight over the type of game that is taking place. Rather, the field itself is—as Bourdieu (1985) himself reminded us—"the site of a more or less overt struggle over the definition of the legitimate principles of division of the field" (p. 734).

If we add the concept of organization (a concept hardly used by Bourdieu) to this picture we may assume, according to Emirbayer and Johnson (2008), that organizations with their respective formations of capital occupy different "points or positions" in the field and are caught in an ongoing—more or less overt—struggle for power:

> These points or positions in organizational space and the forces binding them together constitute (from a synchronic perspective) a structure or a temporary state of power relations within what is (from a diachronic perspective) an ongoing struggle for domination over the field.
>
> (p. 6)

It is for this reason that an analysis of a given field, with its organizations, must also take into account the genesis of the field. In theoretical terms, it "requires . . . that any such field be conceived of as a terrain of contestation between occupants of positions differentially endowed with the resources necessary for gaining and safeguarding an ascendant position within that terrain" (Emirbayer & Johnson, 2008, p. 6). Empirically, this analysis needs to have a historically informed perspective that is then able to "see how new position-takings become possible within organizational fields—but possible only for some and under highly delimited conditions—and how those possibilities then get acted on and realized by particular organizations" (p. 16).

Although we attempted to give our study some historical depth by inquiring into the history of education in Turkey (chapter 2), our analyses only provide a superficial picture of the struggle of school organizations within the field of education, or, as we prefer to call it, in the educational sector. Still, this historical inquiry renders it possible to situate some of our empirical findings of chapters 3–6 in the social genesis of the Turkish educational sector. However, our inquiry does not serve to analyze the immediate struggles within the educational sector in the sense of a research on several schools directly and overtly competing with each other. Such a research would inevitably be confined to similar schools within one district; instead, we have taken into account five schools whose positions in the educational sector maximally differ from each other. Equipped with different volumes and kinds of capital, as well as catering for different social milieus and attracting different organizational milieus of teachers, these schools—as units within the same educational sector—compete with each other in a rather indirect way.

It is exactly these differences concerning the position within the educational sector that render the sampled schools valuable for our investigation. As each school is positioned in the educational sector in its own way—from the village school to the middle-class school in the metropolis—we are able to shed light on how the instruction practices in a school are affected by these different positionalities. In this sense, the domination of a school by a specific social milieu (middle or lower class; rural or urban) is not only a matter of heterogeneity but serves for analyzing how the capital formations constituted in the practices of the milieus and organizations—as a matter of social inequality—affect instruction.

5.2 Prestigious Schools With Middle-Class Milieus

We first consider the curricular practices in schools of middle-class districts in Istanbul and Safran, the central Anatolian province capital. These schools are dominated by an organizational milieu of teachers who look back to a long-standing career and belong to the generation of experience-based lesson designers or—as some teachers in Safran do—to the intermediate generation (see section 4.5). The teaching orientations structuring their instruction practices converge, as we will see in this section, with both the expectations and attitudes of pupils' parents and the situatedness of the schools in which the teachers work; at times, they even amplify each other. As much as the teachers are able to draw on significant cultural resources (their professional experience), the school organization, with its organizational and social milieus, is endowed with a variety of resources. Although both middle-class schools have many points in common, we first scrutinize them separately before summarizing their shared—and hence typical—features.

Papatya School in Istanbul's Tahsin District

The Papatya school in the middle-class district of Tahsin (where approximately 2.5% of the roughly 14 million inhabitants of Istanbul live) is situated in an area dominated by offices and other business buildings. The school draws attention with the bright color of its walls, its huge yard, and the newness of its sport complex. In the morning and in the afternoon there are plenty of service buses in front of the school to carry pupils from their home to school and back. The school has 1248 pupils and 55 teachers, amounting to a teacher-pupil ratio of 1 to 22.69. In the corridors of the school, paintings made by pupils are exhibited on nicely prepared boards. For instruction, in addition to classrooms, the school reserves rooms for each branch, and there is also a vast auditorium.

The school administration has its own corridor in the building. The principal, Ibrahim Arslan, was trained as a class teacher before he was assigned to different bureaucratic posts within the ministry and in several provinces. In our interview, he introduced his school with the following words:

> This is a very beautiful school in terms of its infrastructure (.) it is the one that has everything [. . .] when people see it here see here in fact

from outside (.) they take pains saying that I wish my child too would be educated here (.) as there are many companies in our area, as family residents are very few (.) a very low number of student fall to our share (.) we register them according to their addresses (.) but when our quota is not full (.) we register students from outside within the time period that the ministry allows (.) we go on together in this way (.) this is more like this. the place of the school is located at the center where affluent families dwell (.) but we register every kind of student from different places (.) this is not a place where only children of affluent people are educated, we take in students from everywhere.

Along with praising the school's extraordinary facilities, the principal drew the interviewer's attention to the specific composition of its pupils. As state primary schools in Turkey are required to first enroll the children who live in the school district, and because only a few families live in the vicinity of Papatya, this school is allowed to accept children "from outside," that is, from other areas. Evidently the school has no difficulties finding additional children, as it has become a desire of many parents. Thus, the school is privileged in two ways: Pupils from the area, who have to be accepted by the school, come from families who are "affluent." Regarding pupils from other areas, the school may define how many and who will be accepted for education. Although Ibrahim Arslan underpinned that they enroll "students from everywhere," these pupils and their parents are at least fortunate enough to afford the costly and privately organized transportation to school.

The school is a full-day school, which implies that each classroom is only used by one class. This results in that the children and their teachers may leave equipment and educational material in the classroom in the evening to resume the next morning. The principal highlighted that the school takes the worries of "working families" into account by offering additional "two hours of study time" in the afternoon, meaning that the children only arrive home in the evening. This provision attracts pupils whose parents both work (and are able to pay the additional study time fees) as well as teachers who wish to earn an additional income when they take care of the children in the afternoon.

The Papatya school is not only attractive to children (and more so, to their parents), but also to the teaching staff. As we already revealed in the previous chapter, this school is so popular among teachers that only those with a considerable amount of service points—indicating the time and level of difficulty of previous assignments—are appointed. The principal stressed that the Papatya school has "definitely no lack of teachers," as even if a teacher is transferred to another school, there are enough "experienced" teachers "who have been lining up" to be appointed at Papatya.

Introducing the New Curriculum

The focus point of our investigation (the curriculum change) has not been a major concern for the principal. Apart from some meetings with

administrative staff and from taking into account the change of bureaucratic regulations, Ibrahim Arslan perceived the curriculum more as a
technical change, one that did not require much of his attention. In the
summer of 2005, when schools opened after the change in curriculum,
according to his view everything was "ready" and it was "clear" which
and "how" "topics." Only when the interviewer reminded him that the
new curriculum had a novel philosophy which was promoting "student-
centered" teaching, the principal went into detail:

> Surely, I believe that this was excellent (.) the talkative teacher in his/her
> class was a good teacher in the past (.) that is, while we as administrators
> wandered around the halls of the school the teacher's voice was heard
> outside the doors with a loud noise (.) and we barely heard the voice of
> students (.) but, since there is a student-centered education in the new
> curriculum (.) now the children (.) eh (1) prepare the subject of the
> curriculum that they are going to tackle at home (.) they come then to
> class (.) they tell it as a project in the class (.) the teacher just fills in the
> gaps there or (.) guides them (.) that is better (.) what becomes of the
> children then (.) they become more hard-working (.) they become more
> active (.) they more eagerly follow novelties in the world (.) in this way
> together (.) that is better.

The principal, declaring that he consents to the new curriculum, provided
an account that is clearly based on his own experience and limited to his
perspective: As the person who has the opportunity to observe (or to listen
to, rather) instruction from the "halls" of the school (that is, from outside) he
declared to have encountered a shift of dominating voices, from the teacher's
to the pupils'. Similar to the style of the ministry's press releases and the
curriculum developers' statements (see sections 3.3 and "Test Results and
Competition Among Public Schools" in chapter 6), he attributed this to the
student-centeredness of the new curriculum, which he praises enthusiastically.

While this account may be interpreted as typical for a principal who
wishes to be in accordance with his ministry, it is interesting for what is *not*
mentioned: Ibrahim Arslan did not refer here or elsewhere to any problems
encountered during the introduction or practicing of the new curriculum.
Even more important for our investigation, he did not relate to the tension
between the new curriculum and the system of standardized tests as some
teachers who perceived the new curriculum as an impediment to pupils'
success in tests did (see chapter 4). Notably, the principal did not mention
the standardized tests, although at the day of the interview mock exams
were carried out in Papatya school. These mock exams were organized by
the district's education directorate. By assigning teachers to other schools
(and other teachers to Papatya school) the directorate attempted to prevent
pupils from cheating and from receiving higher scores than they deserved.
Neither the teachers nor the principal mentioned these mock exams; instead,
when asked at the end of the interview if he wanted to add anything, the

principal chose to tell the interviewer about the "Istanbul-wide" "Olympiad for mathematics" organized by his schools for several grades. This and the total negligence toward the importance of standardized entrance exams in the entire interview documents that this school, at least to the perspective of its principal, has left such entrance exams behind, striving for a good position in more prestigious competitions such as the Olympiad for mathematics.

The Practical Experience of Teachers

The teachers of Papatya school are certainly aware of the importance of the standardized entrance exams, but they do not prepare their pupils for them. Instead, as we already saw in section 4.2, these teachers—who predominantly belong to the generation of experience-based lesson designers—take the curriculum and interpret it according to their own teaching experience.

Group *White* is constituted by branch teachers involved with pupils who prepare for the high school entrance exams (as they only teach in grades 6–8). However, these teachers did not mention said exams as something they should take into account (in the form of preparatory exercises) during instruction. Rather, they delved into a discussion about the difficulties of assigning meaningful homework:

Sf: workbooks, they are basic for us (.) they are the transformation into exercises, of
Dm: └ workbooks ( )
Tf: └ we take workbooks as a basis
Sf: what we have taught (.) hence it is very important that they do them, that is I usually give them as homework. besides, there are those which I have printed you know where I find it *insufficient* or where it was mentioned in the book but if it was not given enough space in the workbook if few exercises were given, then I have photocopies made you see in order to give a more //mmh// detailed thing in that way. (1)
Tf: we give project homework, we give performance homework
Dm: └ sometimes project, sometimes performance
Sf: └ performance homework
((short interruption))
Tf: we give them according to well, I mean according to the themes that we have taught related with sub-themes, main themes //mmh// *what* we covered (.), according to that
Dm: └ but, you know
Tf: (.) we, ourselves, decide over
Dm: └ nowadays: there is this thing such a problem regarding homework, I think let's mention this as well, *ready*-made ones, there is no trust in homework now any longer
Tf: └ yeah ┘

In this passage it is documented that these teachers on one hand follow the curriculum, or rather, the "workbook," but on the other hand have points when they "find it insufficient." At such points they use other means to design the homework in the form of "photocopy." As one teacher highlighted, they decide on which homework to assign: "We ourselves decide." The problem they face, however, is concerned with homework that is presented in a ready-made form from, for example, the workbook: They are "ready" on the Internet, and as such one cannot "trust" that children have really completed them on their own.

The focus on the curriculum and on homework—rather than on the entrance exams—is, however, not only a matter of the professional generation location of these teachers. As is documented in the following passage from group *Blue*, as well as in other group discussions at the same school, teachers are pressured by parents:

Dm:	⌐ no mmm::: like this (.) homework mmm::: you have to give homework according to the curriculum why? (.) the curriculum is *very heavy* (.) the subjects, there are so many subjects that, (.) because mmm it is impossible to analyze that subject in the classroom in detail (.) what do you have to do then (.) you have to give homework; (1) *furthermore* (.) the environment, place is very important for giving *homework* or not, for giving or not, (.) if, (.) the parents (.) are a group of conscious parents , when you have not given homework (.) then you are not a good teacher. (1) you surely
Xm:	⌐ yeah ( )⌐
Dm:	have to give homework; (.) that is, let alone the student the child, the parent forces you. (.) why does the tea- give homework why does the teacher did not give homework; // mmh// if you did not give homework (.) once the parent:: begins to question you (.) why she/he does not give homework (.) why she/he does not, (1)

In this passage one teacher, without a word of protest from his colleagues, argued that it is important to assign homework for two reasons: The curriculum is so loaded that children would not be able to follow the lessons otherwise; and the parents of a certain "environment" pressure teachers to do so. These parents, described as "conscious," then become the focus of the discussion, in which it becomes clear that the teachers perceive such parents as "challenging" and "coercing." This does not necessarily imply that such parents really act like the descriptions; nonetheless—and even more importantly—these teachers of Papatya school grant parents the power to control and guide them. The characteristics of such parents then becomes more evident when group *Blue* contrasted them to parents who live either in the remote "countryside" or in a poor and "peripheral suburb":

Dm:	mmm but, (.) here when you do this in a school in a periphery (.) in the countryside or in the peripheral suburb (.) they do not care too much anyway does their child
Xm:	⌐ give it or not ⌐
Dm:	attend school or not (.) or to which grade does it go there are parents who do even not know this. (1) I mean (.) such a mm my child, prodigy my girl my boy you
Cm:	⌐ and also whether it exists or not whether she/he did it they do not know ⌐
Dm:	know do you have any homework or what you are doing what you are up to (.) mm only, by force maybe (1) there is something at school (.) they do not go to attend the meetings (1) let's assume there was some bad thing that happened (.) mmm at the very

extreme point there was a specific event that happened then you are able to get the parent here (1) //mmh// in the suburbs, (.) here (.) in the center, however:: (.) about homework, the parent groups are very decisive at that point (.)//mmh// on the matter of much homework (.) mmm if the parents are conscious they demand more, they force teachers to work (2) that is, parent mmm parent is actually

Xm: └ well she/he bargains with me, that is the thing (   )

Dm: such a hidden hi- (.) controller, an authority over you (.)

The teachers here directly identified the social geographic location of parents with their concern for educational matters: While parents who live "here" (that is, in the "center") are perceived as "conscious," those from other, more remote places are defined as not only uninterested but as totally ignorant of school matters. In contrast to such parents, who can only be brought to the school if "some bad thing happened" to their children, the members of group *Blue* see themselves as even "forced" to "work" by the middle-class parents of their own school, who have become "controllers" and have assumed an "authority" over teachers.[3]

The Double-Sided Ambition of Parents

The parents of Papatya school who took part in two group discussions perfectly corresponded to the image teachers have of them. The discussion, which we subsequently analyze, was constituted by members of the "school-family-union," which is the parents' council. Two persons are university graduates, and one has finished high school. The male person owns a company; of the two women, one is a housewife and the other a retired teacher. The latter discuss the instruction provided to their children, who attend the fourth grade:

Af: └well I believe he doesn't go beyond the curriculum

Bf: └ yeah (1), it's exactly right (1), exactly right

Af: └ I mean

he does it, you know (.), as a duty

Bf: └ if the curriculum goes so far that's it (.), here if it is seven lines (.) I am completely drawing an analogy (.) he does not say lets make ten lines out of seven and give more knowledge (2), there is no such thing, I mean none (going)

Af: └nope┘   └that differenc-

Bf: (coming)

Af: └he handles the @children@ from the social aspect @(3)@

Bf: └@(1)@yes@ (.) @yes@ if the knowledge consists of five lines, he says I shall give five lines that means that, (1) he says that is true in other words that this the child is able to get five lines, so that those five lines were put in front of us (1) but what kind of things this child will deal with in the future mmm this is a dog-eat-dog world, (1) she/he must be much better, let me extend this to seven lines or (give) ten lines you see, let's push the child further, enlarge it to fifteen lines (1), no such thing

This discourse—as well as the following transcripts—first of all, documents that these parents are well acquainted with their children's instruction and take an interest in it. Although they contend that the teachers keenly follow the new curriculum, they are not satisfied and expect them to raise their children's performance beyond curricular goals—but still in the direction indicated by the curriculum ("make ten lines out of seven"). In this sense, they perceive the curriculum as an insufficient preparation for the "dog-eat-dog" world which they anticipate their children will have to face in the future. However, this does not imply that these parents object the curriculum itself (and demand, for example, the preparation for entrance exams instead); rather, they wish the curriculum to be more challenging for their children. In another regard, they are very content with the general education provided by the teacher, particularly its "social direction." In the following passage, Bf expanded on this expectation:

Bf: (.) even if the class seems to not be able to receive [knowledge; the authors] when we look at other classes::? (.) //mmh// but we look and see that their personal development has become very excellent; (.) I mean if there are thirty people in that class twenty of them, (.) can demand their rights (.) can defend themselves nicely (.) or what do I know (.) get their own idea accepted::, (.) we see these efforts then we say, (.) that maybe they didn't receive the knowledge (.) as completely as many other classes:, (.) but it is a very important (.) skill to be able to (.) defend oneself in society (1) especially in Turkey [. . .] when you know this it means there are two different kinds of education but, (.) mmm here we look at their future conditions; that is (.) related to their personal development; the school may provide a lot of things but if it cannot give the child anything according to this, (.) then the things provided by the school may be in vain; that is, I cannot conceive of everything in education (.) as just knowledge; (.) //mmh// I think all constitutes a whole. (1) knowledge is completed in some way; if there is the will in the child, (.) you can hire a private course to complete it, you can yourself deal with it (.) you can do something according to your knowledge (.) or the child can learn something at his/her own will; (.) the knowledge is somehow given, (.)

As is documented in this account, Bf (and presumably the other parents who did not rebut her point of view) does not consider it problematic that her child's teacher conveys less "knowledge" to the class than others do. She appreciates the general education provided to the children, which fosters their "personal development." The school is here perceived as a place not only for knowledge acquisition (such as in the form of exam preparation) but also for acquiring more personal and social capabilities. Moreover, the parent is confident that her child will easily regain the missing knowledge by additional learning outside the school. She here listed a range of opportunities like "private courses" and assisting her child herself.

Evidently, middle-class, well-educated parents are quite aware of the necessity to acquire knowledge to successfully pass the entrance exams for high school.

However, they do not see the school as the only place where this knowledge can be acquired (or where their children can be prepared for the standardized exams). Rather, they give the school the opportunity to educate their children in a comprehensive way which combines knowledge transfer with general education. As is documented in the discussion, these parents assign great importance to such a general education which helps children in their "personal development." This orientation toward "two different kinds of education," one of which is provided by privately organized knowledge acquisition outside school is typical for the middle-class milieu, to which these parents and their children belong. They have a habitus that values both "knowledge" and "personal development," along with the cultural and economic resources to either assist their children with learning or to sponsor additional private instruction.

As much as these parents are acquainted with instruction at Papatya school, they are also familiar with the opportunities for privately financed additional instruction—and endowed with the necessary resources to use them. They send their children to private instruction centers ("dersane"), and, moreover, make them take part in the Istanbul- or even nationwide mock exams organized by other instruction centers. As these parents stated univocally, "we see where the child stands in overall Turkey" and "in overall Istanbul," and "according to this we try to draw a roadmap" and "make up the deficits." The results of these mock exams are, however, not taken as fixed and objective measurement of their children's performance. Rather, these parents evaluate such results according to the peculiarities of each private instruction center; in other words, they take into account whether a center is well known for its difficult mock exams, and then regard even a moderate result as a success. As is documented in another part of the group discussion, these parents evaluate their children's school performance in a similar way.

Zambak School in a Middle-Class District of the Provincial Capital Safran

Zambak school is located in the very center of Safran (which has approximately 130,000 inhabitants) and has a large campus with four buildings. In its surroundings there are middle-class housing estates and company buildings. At the start and end of instruction time, as well as during the lunch break, minibuses crowd around the campus, indicating that many pupils are transported to this school from outside its direct neighborhood. In the school, each teacher has his or her own classroom, implying that he/she may prepare lessons in advance. All classrooms are well equipped. In contrast to the other schools of our sample, every pupil has his or her own locker in the corridors. There are 2000 pupils and approximately 80 teachers at Zambak school, amounting to a teacher-pupil ratio of 1 to 25.

The principal of the school, Mehmet Uzun, looks back on a long career as a class teacher and then as the principal of a boarding school in the countryside of the province we call "Dalen." In 2008 he accepted the post as a class teacher in Zambak school so that his children would be able to be enrolled in an urban school. In 2012, only some months before the interview, he was appointed principal of Zambak. When asked about how the new curriculum was practiced in the school, Mehmet Uzun who—besides sporadic criticisms—approved of the curriculum change, offered the following account:

> At the moment mm (.) we are in very good condition in terms of equipment (.) I can even say proudly that (.) we are capable of competing with private schools (.) although we have two thousand students (.) [. . .] we have a computer (.) a LCD projector (.) web connection (.) printer in almost all our classrooms (.) classes. (.) it is very very important ( ) (.) all these are present [. . .] (.) since in terms of equipment we have equipment (.) we do not have difficulty in practicing this curriculum (.) plus one of our advantages compared to other schools are the well-educated parents //mmh// if there were no educated (.) educated parents those who care about education who really give importance to the future of their children (.) that is I can say that 95 percent of our parents are like this (.) mmm this provides us with an extra advantage (.) being programmed (.) because the parents follow the children one by one (.) in the result of this following we presumably come to that point later (.) the success of the school //mmh// stands out.

Uzun answered the question concerning curricular practices by drawing the interviewer's attention to the situation of his school. Thus, the principal implicitly connected the quality and even the possibility of curricular practices to the material and immaterial conditions of instruction. Among the material equipment he stressed the importance of IT devices (the use of which is indeed suggested in the new curriculum's teacher manuals); he then elaborated on the parents and underpinned both their good "education" and their close care for their children's future. With this account Mehmet Uzun, again tacitly, put curricular practices within the frame of social inequality: The school is not only as well equipped as "private schools" but its pupils also come from middle-class families, which makes it easier to put the new curriculum into practice.

The principal, later in the interview, came back to this point from another angle, referring to the class background of the pupils' families, who are middle class and "above" regarding their "economic" situation. Moreover, Mr. Uzun drew a strong connection between the relative wealth of the families and their eagerness to invest their financial means in their children's education. This combination of financial resources and educational ambition is most prominently manifested in the enrolment of children in privately financed "instruction centers." The resulting "success" is then perceived by Mehmet Uzun as a "self-evolving" feature of the school, rather than as the product of specific efforts. In a certain sense, he views this success as a reciprocally cumulative process. In the sequel of this transcript, the principal then pointed to the importance of "sponsors" who give both a "lorry loadful of material" and make monetary donations. Mr. Uzun, by narrating the story of a father who originally had intended to send his daughter to a private school, tacitly pointed to one specific mechanism of donation: Parents who have the impression that their children receive the same quality education at Zambak school as in a fee-based private school are ready to donate a part of the money they saved. Therefore, being able to compete with private schools therefore is not only a matter of prestige for Zambak; it is also a means to attract families who are able to give considerable donations. In this sense "success comes with success"; or in other words, success reinforces itself.

The underlying assumption that "success comes with success" is also expanded on by the principal in another regard, namely Zambak school's recruitment of teachers: Similar to Papatya school, Zambak's teachers are— according to the principal—under the surveillance of ambitious parents; thus, only those teachers who are ready to face this difficulty volunteer for this school. When Mehmet Uzun then stated that the teachers only join this school's cadre "after a specific experience" and added that there are enough teachers who apply, he pointed to the attractiveness Zambak poses to teachers. Whereas other schools have to fill their cadre gaps with "fee-based" teachers, Zambak does not need to resort to these teachers and has no long-standing cadre gaps. Moreover, when a teacher goes on a maternity leave, or any other longer leave, "at once a new teacher is appointed" who comes from a "surrounding school" and "who is there replaced by a fee-based teacher." Zambak's teachers usually maintain their position for a long time:

> As a result of teachers being experienced and working in this school for years now (.) of course we have every kind of opportunities (.) our student success is pretty high (.) I mean when comparing with other institutions it is very high (.) the general acceptance ratio to middle school institutions with an exam was of 77% in the last education year (.) //mmh// the acceptance ratio to Teacher High Schools, Science High Schools and Anatolian High Schools was of 54% (.)//mmh// that is, this is a very high score for a public school (.) three of our students who took the exam last year answered all questions correctly (.). they made it full (.) that is, became the first of Turkey at the same time (.).

While in previous sections of the interview the principal had only spoken of the pupils' success in general terms, in this part of the interview he measured success according to the competition for high school enrolment and highlighted that Zambak is "very high" above the average success rates of state schools. When he then also mentioned that "three of our students" have answered all questions of the high school entrance exam correctly and hence were the best in Turkey, this revealed that he views educational success—and that of the school itself—as something measured vis-à-vis competitors; that is, he does not view educational success as an absolute measure. This is then also documented in the principal's praise of non-academic successes such as in sports or "chess." The school is not only proud of such success stories—as is documented in the principal's long and highly committed account—but also selects and purposefully trains promising students to achieve such success.

Teachers' Focus on the Curriculum

Although their principal underpinned the importance of success as measured in competitions, among which are the high school entrance exams, Zambak's teachers are rather concerned with putting the curriculum into practice. In addition to teachers who belong to the generation of experience-based lesson designers (group *Red*) and whom we already analyzed in section 4.2, we have conducted group discussions with teachers who were in the intermediary position of those with a career time of 5–16 years (see section 4.4). In the following part of the discussion with group *Violet*, both the careful following of the new curriculum and the independent use of additional material is documented:

Sf: but there is such a point mm I teach the third class for example, there are questions that can be asked at the level of third class when you look at the curriculum, at the program, it gives two digits, now I am at a school like Zambak, I compare it with the school in Diyarbakır where I used to work, students of fifth class there did not know as much as the students that I teach in the third class here. //mmh// it changes very much according to the environment. and my students here in the third class can very easily solve questions at the fifth level at the other place //mmh//. and this is too at the place the level of readiness, the socioeconomic level, the environment, yes it surely has an impact willy-nilly (.)//mmh//

Mm: Parents demand we push. //mmh//

Sf: because of that we necessarily use sources, because the level of our children is generally good (.) at a school like Zambak, of course we may use them when school books are not enough //mmh//

Comparing the children of Zambak with those of a school in the eastern city of Diyarbakır, these teachers maintained that their pupils are on a far higher level, thus perceiving education as something measured through comparisons. They also confirmed the principal's perspective that the "environment" and "socioeconomic level" of these children's families is important for their success. As a result of parents' pressure, these teachers add some "source" material to the curriculum books; however, these "source" books are not viewed as a means of preparing pupils for high school entrance exams, a topic hardly mentioned by the teachers.

Similar to group *Violet*, group *Green* is formed by teachers who are in the intermediary generation position; however, they are branch teachers rather than class teachers. As documented in a part of the group discussion already analyzed in section 4.4, these teachers had previously experienced the old curriculum, but are not existentially attached to its "daily lesson design" practice.

On one hand, they stick to the teacher manual, while on the other hand they think that its provisions are too "intensive" and subsequently write their own "short notes." Similar to the generation of experience-based lesson designers, these teachers take the "gain" as the "basis" for designing their lesson. In contrast to the older generation, they then structure instruction according to their excerpts from the manual. The preparation for the high school entrance exams does not, however, constitute any concern for the teachers. It is only when they try to add other activities to classroom instruction that they complain about the importance this "exam system" has gained:

Km: the children are more bound to the exam system:: exams:: (.)//mhm// to the private courses today compared to the past. (.) //mmh// they are very bound to them; this is also a trouble for us (.) there are workshops on poetry, no one is joining (.) there are

Af: ⌊yes⌋   ⌊there are

Km: theater workshops (1) no one is participating; (.) science (.) social sciences, if

Af: ⌊few of them who join social activities

Km: projects for mathematics would be organized, (1) there is no participation, the teacher will make an effort, (1) in such an activity, (1) no, the student does not come why? She/he will go to the instruction center, why? She/he will attend private lessons, the big brothers and sisters will come (1) the teacher will come, the private teacher (.) the children deal with those

The teachers highlighted that compared to "the old times," the children are even "more bound" to the standardized "exams" and to the "instruction centers" where they are prepared for successfully passing these exams. As is documented in this complaint, these teachers of Zambak school—similar to group *Violet*—do not perceive the high school entrance exams as something for which they, as teachers, should prepare their pupils. Rather, they distance themselves from these exams and preparation and see the children's commitment as an impediment to their own endeavors, that is, to "projects" and "activities" in different subjects.

Although these teachers complained about children's (and their parents') commitment to exam preparation (which, after all, keeps them from putting extracurricular activities into practice), they—as became clear in another part of the discussion—conceded that the "number of pupils" is high and everyone asks how he or she "can elude" these masses. On the background of high enrolment numbers, the differentiated quality of high schools (which are divided into "Anatolian," "Science," and other high schools), and the numerus clausus for entering each high school type that is also dependent on the respective region ("Dalen"), these teachers understand parents who wish their children to enter the best possible high school. Teachers comprehend the wish parents have of sending their children to better schools, as the "state of young people" in "ordinary high schools" is "so bad." These teachers' identification with parents goes as far as approving of the parents' readiness to invest "whatever they have" in education and private test preparation for the child.

Parents' Parallel Ambitions

The parents with whom we conducted group discussions in the Zambak school perfectly fit into the picture drawn by teachers and the principal. From three group discussions, we chose to reconstruct the one conducted with the school-family-union, who continuously attends the school. In our visits to their room, they were counting money; as they maintained in the beginning of the group discussion, raising financial resources for the school is one of their most important duties. Therefore, they are well informed about the school and the financial situation of the pupils' parents. Three women took part in the discussion: Two of them hold a B.A. and one has a high school degree; all three are housewives married to civil servants or small entrepreneurs. The following part of the transcript shows a discussion regarding their children's workload in a time of test preparation:

Af:	((a meaningful laugh)) honestly, our children, this year, it is same with my friend's, at the
Sf:	└ Yeah
Af:	eighth grade, they are in a very intense work tempo, after school, for example four days a week they have the instruction center after school [. . .] that is, they leave school, now, for example, they went to the instruction center. imagine that they will finish the instruction center at about seven (1) they arrive at home at seven and eat their fill afterwards they are in an exhausted condition @a little television a little computer@ then it is time for bed // mhm// in other words, they are *very* busy indeed [. . .]
Af:	well the children don't live their childhood they take the exam when it is still not clear whether they are 'play children' or adolescents I mean the children could not live their childhood //mhm//
Sf:	like a horse race, from there to there, that is they are already in a triangle school
Af:	└ like horse race. ┘
Sf:	instruction center home. *No* social activities I mean almost none.
Af:	└ yes

In this description of their children's daily routine, Af and Sf complained about the time pressure their children face, but showed no doubt that this "intensive work tempo" is necessary. Moreover, it is documented that they are not willing to cut back their children's duties both regarding school and test preparation. Nevertheless, when they regret the consequent loss of "childhood" and of opportunities for "social activities," certain—disappointed— expectations are revealed toward this age group, which may be interpreted as specific for the middle classes.

The children's situation (as "racehorses") does not, however, only refer to the need of test preparation. As the parents made clear in another part of the group discussion, importance is also given to school instruction—including homework—being delivered according to the curriculum, as Sf addressed:

Sf: they have to do that, surely, they do it
Af: └in our school our teachers never favor students that is they never have leniency @their grades are fixed@
Sf: └ they get what their grade is ┘
Af: └ they get what they get and they absolutely cannot ımm their homework mm there is no such a thing as not doing, well anyway they attend the instruction center two days during the week and two days at the weekend they do it in the remaining time that is they have to //mhm//

In an affirmative tone, these parents talked about the homework assigned by the teachers and underpinned their strictness and non-corrupt attitude. As a consequence, their children are not only obliged to attend school but are also very busy with school homework or test preparation during the whole week. As they highly value the "grades" given by teachers, the parents sometimes even complete the homework themselves if their children lack the time as they admitted in other parts of the discussion.

Typical for their middle-class milieu, these mothers are very familiar with their children's learning efforts and view themselves as the main supervisor of their kids' success. As one mother made clear, there is a continuous struggle between education and the "child's desires": "When you let the child free, the child drops it," *it* here meaning the exam preparation. For this reason she, "as a rule starts 10 days in advance" of the exam. This means that the children are put under pressure not only by the school teachers and the test preparation in private instruction centers, but also by their parents in this middle-class milieu. The children are constantly "followed" and forced to learn by their parents, or more precisely, by their mothers. These parents' engagement with their children's learning success goes as far as identifying their own success with that of their children; as one mother put it: "You receive the reward for your efforts."

As is documented in the group discussion with parents of Zambak school pupils, this school is dominated by a social milieu in which parents attach a high importance to both school instruction and test preparation. Their high ambitions for their children's educational career are accompanied by practical endeavors to supervise and control their children's efforts. Although the parents take this for granted, these endeavors are dependent on certain stocks of economic resources (both the time dispensed by mothers to supervise their children instead of paid labor and the money to enroll the children in private instruction centers) as well as on the cultural resources needed to follow their kids' learning efforts.

Middle-Class Schools: Curricular Practices on the Basis of Cultural, Economic, and Social Capital

There are two schools in our sample which are clearly located in urban, middle-class districts and that serve to scrutinize the typical features of putting a new curriculum into practice under the conditions of a certain parent/pupil social milieu. Our group discussions with teachers and parents, as well as the expert interviews with school principals and our own observations, have revealed the typical way of the respective organizational and social milieus in which the formal rules of the new curriculum are handled. First of all, the pupils' class location directly influences instruction; that is, these children, the offspring of parents who usually have a high school degree or above, perform much better in school than what is expected in the curriculum, forcing teachers to add further teaching material to their instruction. Apart from their activities in the classroom, these pupils excel in various competitions, which among others, include the high school entrance exams. In this regard, these children can obviously capitalize on the cultural resources with which they have been endowed both at home and in school.

However, the class location of these children does not solely influence curricular practices: Their parents, equipped with cultural and economic resources, are able to provide their children with a "second" education; that is, they invest money in enrolling their children at private instruction centers (thus capitalizing on economic resources) and/or help them with test preparation themselves (thus producing cultural capital). Therefore, although very indirectly—and yet so much more effectively—school instruction is kept free from test preparation, and teachers can concentrate on practicing the new curriculum.

Dominated by a middle-class milieu, however, the situatedness of these schools is not limited to the relationship between pupils and their parents. The schools additionally profit from their pupils' family background by capitalizing on the economic and social resources provided by parents, who donate money and equipment for improving the school's infrastructural situation (such as with IT equipment and devices that directly affect instruction). Moreover, the most committed parents, organized in the school-family-union, are engaged in fundraising, thus making use of their social relations (mostly to other parents) to improve the school's endowment and/or prestige. In this sense, primarily due to their position (located in middle-class districts) the school itself is able to attract and make use of economic and social resources that help it put the curriculum into practice.

Zambak and Papatya, as educational organizations whose curricular practices can rely on such a range of families' cultural, social, and financial resources, have become attractive schools for well-to-do parents, donors, and for experienced teachers. In this sense the school itself, based on the resources on which it can capitalize, is endowed with certain symbolic resources, that is, with prestige—even through good high school entrance exam results, for which pupils are prepared outside of school. This prestige is not only capitalized on when attracting wealthy donors and well-to-do parents (who may even prefer Zambak or Papatya to a private school), but also with regard to teacher recruitment. The fact that neither of these schools has to employ (inexperienced) teachers on a fee basis nor are faced with extended periods of gaps in the staff structure reveals that they are also popular among teachers. In this regard, these schools, by capitalizing on their symbolic resources, are able to obtain the cultural resources of their teaching staff and to ensure that they are invested in practicing the new curriculum. Parents expect teachers to use their skills in practicing and, where necessary, exceeding the curriculum in instruction. As we will see, not all schools of our sample are as fortunate as Zambak and Papatya.

5.3 A Maximal Contrast: Instruction in a Poor District of Istanbul

The school "Karanfil" is situated in the "Enver" district of Istanbul, more specifically in an area which was covered with squatter houses starting in the 1970s due to a migration influx that still existed at the time of our empirical research. The area has a mixture of squatter houses and apartment buildings, with construction work taking place in every street. One can observe women working in small custom textile manufacturing workshops, accompanied by Arabesk (a music style especially favored by rural and poor people), on the ground floors of the houses across the Karanfil school. There are also people cleaning carpets, building wooden market stands or dealing with some textile work in the gardens of their apartment houses. Poverty abounds, and one sees mostly old cars and many unfinished buildings. At times one perceives a village-like atmosphere; old women wear traditional headscarves and baggy trousers and there are chicken and sheep in the gardens, which are also used for growing vegetables. The area is predominantly inhabited by Alevites, who have also a sacral building ("Cemevi") in the vicinity of the Karanfil school.

The Karanfil school itself has two buildings: one originally reserved for grades 1–5, and the other for grades 6–8. This differentiation, however, cannot always be enforced due to a shortage of classrooms, which also led to the introduction of education in two shifts; that is, each pupil attends instruction either in the morning or in the afternoon. This implies that two classes use one room and that there is no time available for cultural activities. In contrast to the middle-class schools (section 5.2), there are no service buses in front of the school. Children are not transported to school from long distances, but live nearby. Most of them are taken to school by their mothers or older siblings. The school is attended by 4300 pupils and served by 50–55 teachers, amounting to a ratio of 1 teacher for every 40 children.

The Social Conditions of Instruction at Karanfil School

The school's condition is as poor as its surrounding's. The playground equipment in the garden, as well as the staircases, doors, and the furniture are falling apart, not to mention the inexistence of even basic technological equipment. Because there are not enough toilets and because of the lack of adequate cleaning material and staff, there is an intense smell coming from the school's floors. The schoolyard is too small to accommodate all of the children during the breaks, so they cannot play as they wish.

The expert interview with the principal of Karanfil school, Ahmet Sönmez, was again and again interrupted by people entering the room, many of them children who brought loose change collected in their classroom as a compulsory fee for taking part in preparatory high school entrance exams (mock tests). In contrast to the principals of Zambak and Papatya schools, Ahmet Sönmez is considerably young. He graduated from university as a history teacher in 2000, and then worked for 5 years as a social studies teacher in poor suburbs of Istanbul. He was then promoted and became a vice principal, but always working in poor suburban schools. In 2011 he was assigned to his first post as a principal, at the Karanfil school. When he stated, in our interview, "somehow I couldn't go to a good place," not only his negative opinion of the Karanfil school is shown, but also his desire of being transferred to another school. During the interview the principal was asked the following question, to which he started to give a comprehensive account of the school's condition:

Y: when I came to school in these last couple of weeks, I learned that you were just visiting the classes when I could not find you vice-principals said so (1) what were your observations there I mean regarding the class it might be related to the curriculum ((here the interview is interrupted for a while, the record device is turned off))

Sönmez: (3) Yes (1) I often have to walk around the classrooms (1) because (2) well a lot of fellow teachers mention that they are now afraid of going into class I mean //mhm// mmm (1) especially in the last months when the weather gets warm a little bit (1) the children do obviously not fit into the classrooms anymore (1) in my observations over there (1) my fellow teachers think that it is a benefit it is a profit if I may keep the class calm (1) rather than education (1) if I may finish the lecture without having any trouble if I may leave school at full speed after the ring bells //mhm// (1) that is you go into classes I really pity many teachers (1) I feel sorry for many teachers (1) that is on the one side they are accounted for by the administration (1) in other words why are those students very wimpy here why do those not know how to read and write (1) why do those get zero in math (1) on the other side when a slightest thing is said to students' parents (1) some less-educated parents their reactions might include violence (1) I mean teachers are really (1) in a difficult position here but when I look at the teachers (1) who are in the most difficult position (1) they have not been able to wholly understand the profession of teaching mmm (1) the fee-based paid teachers you are suffering the most hardship with them and the trouble that begins with them continuously lasts the whole day that is when a child breaks from the lesson, it becomes very hard to pick him/her up again //mhm//

The principal here indicated that he perceives himself as the person who has to support his "teachers" vis-à-vis children who misbehave. In his account there is—albeit short and unclear—a hint to the physical conditions of the school, as the children during summertime do not "fit into the classroom anymore." According to the principal, the teachers face not only such problems with pupils, but are also put under pressure by the "administration" (that is, by him) in the case of failing pupils. Furthermore, parents with a low educational level are, in the principal's perspective, uncooperative and may even become violent toward teachers who discipline their children. The principal here differentiated between the permanent teachers who are civil servants and those who work on a "fee" basis. As he added, the latter are in the worst situation, and the school is also in a difficult situation with them as it is difficult to "pick up" a child once he or her has "broken" from the lesson due to—as we have to assume—the incapability or absence of a teacher. Such fee-based teachers are, as we saw in section 5.2, not employed in the middle-class schools of our sample whatsoever, whereas the Karanfil school has to rely on them, with roughly 40% of its teaching staff working on a fee basis.

Although the principal feels obliged to walk through his school "very often" to support teachers, in the specific occasion when the researcher saw him he was trying to collect money from children for the school's expenses. Significantly, he used the word "due" or "membership fee" ("aidat"), implying that this was a compulsory donation rather than a voluntary one. Pointing to the poor financial situation of the school, which goes as far as impeding the delivery of any "service," he both disclosed that the school (unsuccessfully) tries to collect these "fees" from the families—which is strictly forbidden under Turkish law—and said he regrets that most pupils are not able to pay them. That is, in contrast to the principals of the middle-class schools of our sample, who—along with collecting similar "fees"—receive generous donations used for advanced IT equipment and more, the Karanfil school is dependent on semi-compulsory donations that are needed to guarantee the delivery of any service in the first place. As Ahmet Sönmez summed up, he sees his school as "disadvantaged" in "cultural, economic, and educational" aspects. In this sense his résumé pointed to the same direction as our conclusion to section 5.2, that is, that the school is not only affected by the educational and economic background of its pupils, but also by social conditions in a comprehensive sense.

Limited Resources for Curriculum Practice

This difficult situation of the Karanfil school also affects curricular practices. Since the principal has to give "six lessons" per week, he also had something to say about the new curriculum. On the background of his claim that the new textbooks do not contain enough knowledge to be delivered to the children, Mr. Sönmez discussed the new curriculum's focus on pupils' own "inquiries." The principal does not view this focus on "inquiring" as generally problematic, but believes it to be so under the specific conditions of his own school: If people do not have "Internet" access at home and if girls are not able to visit Internet cafes, the children cannot carry out their own research tasks. As Mr. Sönmez made clear, the school has made efforts to facilitate children's access to such knowledge by asking people for book donations, but the books that were donated were, apparently, not useful ("romance novels"). At this point of the interview the principal suddenly introduced an alternative into his discourse, which had not been previously mentioned and which does not appear to be compelling: According to him, the knowledge needed can only be taken from private "instruction centers" or from the books they provide. As he underpinned, such books from "outside" the ministry are used, even though this is "forbidden."

The group discussions we conducted with parents of Karanfil pupils provided further insight into the social conditions of putting the curriculum into practice. One group was formed by members of the school's family union, women are either housewives or work with cleaning and whose spouses are unqualified workers earning minimum wage—if they are at all employed. As is documented in the following passage, these women see education in direct relation to their own social condition:

Af: if today I depend on my spouse and see the pittance earned by him my child should not live in this situation (.) that is I clearly wish that my child will really get her economic freedom, (.) //mmh// ee at this moment for example there is my bedridden mother-in-law at home I look after her you know I want my child not to fall into these conditions (.) she shall gain her own freedom she shall not be dependent on either her spouse or anyone else, (.) if it goes on with this system I do not know; (.) let her either go with a wealthy husband and save herself.

Sf: @indeed@

With Sf's approval, Af here described her own situation—dependent on the scarce money earned by her husband and obliged to take care of his ailing mother—and, on this background, legitimized the ambitions for and worries about her child's educational performance. However, she does not see in the Karanfil school an opportunity through which her child could flee these social circumstances. Evidently, her educational ambitions are not met by appropriate opportunities.

While Sf has finished high school in an eastern province, Df, who started the next topic of discussion, has only recently been alphabetized in a "course" through an Alevite association. As she complained, the homework given to her children is above her capacity, and she is unable to help them:

Df: ⌐additionally,
   homework is brought home (.) always brought home (.) nothing is being done at the
   school that is to say; (.) we rea- homework at home (.) for example I ca::nnot read and
   write (.) I joined a course here (.) what can I provide for that child at home (.) he comes
   from school for example I say that; (.) I say to my boy say check tests or other things that (.)
   the teacher (said) which one shall I (go to) you know.
Af: ⌐you see, the classrooms are *crowded,*
   I mean classes with fifty persons; that is with whom should the teacher deal with you feel
   sorry for them, too
Sf: ⌐well the teacher is right too this is certainly still of the state let public
   schools be multiplied, (.)I mean the class sizes shall be decreased,
Df: ⌐we revolt also (1) we revolt but no one hears our voice. (1) sometimes I say that let's
   go out and scream like this @but no one hears @ @(2)@ well:: (1)

In her first contribution, Df addressed her own specific situation, which refers to her poor endowment with cultural resources. Although Df is not able to help her "boy," she is at least very well acquainted with the expectations of the teacher, who asked them to "check" the "tests." However, the other participants of the group discussion, certainly better equipped with cultural resources, did not engage with Df's personal situation; instead, they drew attention to the difficult situation of the class, which is "crowded" with "fifty persons," resulting in that the teacher is unable to individually help the children (and check tests him- or herself). The group then found its collective standpoint in "revolting" against this situation and demanding the opening of more schools. However, they also agreed in the futility of this endeavor: "No one hears our voice."

Parents' Ambitions for Test Preparation

Despite their pessimistic outlook, these women take pains to foster their children's educational career. Df is ready to take up cleaning jobs to finance her child's enrolment in a private instruction center, and Af spends all the time she can spare from caring for her mother-in-law in the school, working voluntarily in the school-family-union. With their children in classes 1, 2, and 4, these women view these first 4 years of school life as the "basis" that also defines the children's success in the following, higher grades. They believe that their school is unable to provide this foundation for their children, and struggle to compensate this failure by giving their children a "list of questions" and "a lot of books." These books and question lists constitute, as we can infer from the following passage, an alternative to the new curriculum and its textbooks, which these parents see as unhelpful with regard to what they consider "education":

Af: My two daughters (.), one is in the first grade one is in the second grade (1) //mhm// we are something as such about the education issue to be honest I am like this I do not know extremely picky shall I say (1), I am very afraid very

Sf: └ worried ┘

Af: worried I mean I can feel like fighting with teachers about even anything, (.) on education I mean. (.) you know there is really *nothing* in the present state books education-wise and I do not want them to teach anything (.) from the state books (.) sometimes I say you know let me go to school even if they do the state books (.) if they do lectures about them then I shall not send my child to school I shall fill in the blanks in those state books together with my child at home, (.) bring and show (.) I should not deal with the school at all sometimes I think because (.) there are such teachers (.) who well you know they keep to the state books and only follow that procedure.

"Worried" is the word through which these women's collective orientation toward education at the Karanfil school is metaphorically expressed: As shown with the example of Af, they object to teachers who "keep to the state books and only follow that procedure" (of the new curriculum), and actually threat these teachers to no longer send their children to school. Such teachers are in the minority, though, as is indicated through the use of "even." Thinking that their children do not learn anything with the textbooks provided by the ministry, they implicated that "education" is provided elsewhere. Although they did not openly say so, these parents assume that there is an alternative to curricular instruction, and that it should be implemented.

When the researcher asked how they assess their children's performance, the parents made clear that they fully trust the "mock tests" prepared throughout the school:

Df: └° mock test °┘

Af: mock test etc. was done; (.) throughout the school, (1) //mhm// by evaluating this the class is already crowded the school (1) mmm it was done for three times four times; (.) you know according to the trend of these exams

Similar to the parents of middle-class school pupils, these inhabitants of the squatter house area take the "trend of these tests" as a measure for their children's performance. In contrast to the middle-class parents, however, they do not compare different mock test providers, using these mock tests as the only standard according to which they assess their children's educational performance (whereas the middle-class children are also judged according to their general education). As we mentioned in section 5.2, these mock tests are a form of preparation for the high school entrance exams and are organized as a multiple-choice test. When the interviewed women complained about the permanent teachers (who have passed the exam to become a civil servant), who—to their perception—do "not teach anything," it is documented that they were not only dissatisfied with teachers' performance but also were "angered" by it, as seen in the following passage:

Df: └furthermore teachers for example (.) since they are working on a fee basis they more often do that is (.) they are very interested in the children for example our teacher (.) was like this, (.) our thi- third year (.) this year it was a tenured civil servant I see that she/he became more that is to say. (.) this year for example all parents are always angered (1) //mhm// I mean she/he does not teach anything:: (.) she/he always makes them play in the classroom; always makes them play,

Af: └well because they are at ease, (.) you know they are tenured I mean you cannot do anything you send them away she/he will go to another school (.) the fee-based ones have some fears (.) perhaps she/he would be dismissed (.) you see, in the end they are like paid workers or something like that

In the preceding, Af and Df differentiated between permanent teachers who are "at ease," "play" with the children (which is seen as synonym to curricular practice) and do not pay attention to parents' complaints, and the "fee-based" teachers who may be threatened with job loss if they do not teach according to parents' wishes. Similar to previous passages from this group discussion, this discourse reveals that these parents, albeit endowed with only very limited cultural and economic resources, are very ambitious with regard to their children's education, which is seen as a means to be able to obtain a certain social position. In addition to their ambition, they also actively interfere in the school, a point also experienced by the teachers.

The Inappropriateness of the Curriculum

At the Karanfil school we conducted three group discussions with teachers. These teachers, belonging to the younger generation, follow the new curriculum only to a certain degree. Whereas their generation, in general, is constituted by teachers who combine the curriculum and test preparation (see section 4.3), the teachers of Karanfil tend to focus on test preparation only. As we will show, there are a number of points connected to the situatedness of the school that push these young teachers in the direction of test preparation. In group *Grey*, for example, two female class teachers talk about the inappropriateness of the new curriculum as concerns the "stimuli" used in the textbooks:

Cf: └ now, it is about experiences, I mean
how much visual things the child sees around, that much
Bf: └ surely, the abundance of stimuli
Cf: └ that much yeah the abundance of
stimuli of the children here is debatable (.) within those books, (.) we were even talking
about this issue with our science teacher an example was given in the text book (.) there
was a trampoline (.) something like that in someone's grandpa's time at home, (.) we even
laughed a lot, you know (.) in his time (.) I am talking about the father's about the grandpa's
time, (.) it is discussed whether there were trampolines at home in his time. that is, there is
such information in the book now. now which one of these families here? normally there
is no trampoline at home at the moment that that is let alone they could see a trampoline at
the time of their grandpa; (1) I mean when some things were being prepared it was being
prepared for certain sections without considering Turkey in general (1) this is a very big
mistake that is to say;
Bf: └ yeah ┘
Cf: in the books there is no such a thing as harmony with the surroundings (.) //mhm//
Bf: └ with
those here (.) it won't go with those books I mean
Cf: └ no use (.) yeah, no use

The two teachers here agreed on the assumption that the textbooks provided by the ministry expose pupils to "stimuli" that are meaningless for them, as is exemplified with the "trampoline," which—as these teachers assume—the children of Karanfil have never seen before. They concluded that the textbooks were prepared only for people from "certain sections" of society and that the books do not work for "those here," that is, for children who live in the squatter house area.

Another problem when practicing the new curriculum is the size of the class. As one English teacher from group *Khaki* described, in a class of "fifty" pupils, the teacher is concerned, from the first minute, with enforcing discipline in the classroom, beginning with "silencing" and counting pupils and continuing with interfering in "fights" between the youngsters. The remaining time—about half of the lesson—is then used for "giving a lesson." The lesson then does not follow the new curriculum; rather, it uses "source books" (provided by private instruction centers) and prepares for the high school entrance exam. In tacit agreement with the principal's statement, the teacher concluded this description by pointing to their "first goal," which is to prevent fights and hence to preserve discipline. As the teachers from group *Khaki* discussed, the problems with pupils' discipline also originate from the low motivation some eighth graders have. These children are forced to attend school by law, but do not intend to continue their education at a high school after the eighth grade. As the group argued, some children attend primary school "only to receive a diploma" or so they will not be sent to "work" by their parents.

Group *Turquoise*, comprising class teachers—one of whom is paid on a fee basis—confirmed the complaint about crowded classes, adding that even if the equipment of Karanfil school was better, they would still not be able to use it:

Em:	save that, the classrooms should consist of twenty people, (.) //mhm// or twenty-five people in this constructivist approach, but this too, when we look in a district like ours some classes consist of forty, forty-five, fifty people today if this is the case //mhm// you, there, I mean you
Sf:	⌐ at least double ⌐ ⏐
Of:	⌐ certainly ⌐
Em:	cannot apply the work for pupils' work one-to-one (.) there needs to be team work for this there must also there must be an infrastructure in the classrooms and the school, (.) now (.) although classes began to be newly formed a music laboratory was formed, there is a distinct place for visual arts (.) but, mostly these do not exist at the moment (.)
Of:	but these always are for show because the classes are too crowded (.) //mhm// you see there is such an area but: (.) for certain we cannot
Em:	⌐ only for show
Of:	use this within the curriculum can we, (.) it *exists* but cannot be used
Em:	⌐ certainly ⌐

As the teachers acknowledged, the ministry has recently begun to equip the school with new classrooms and laboratories, which are, however, not yet finished. Nonetheless, they are convinced that they will not be able to "use" them "within the curriculum" due to the size of the classes; using the new facilities, particularly in activities in which pupils become active, such as "team work," seems impossible. As the teachers of *Turquoise*, in a subsequent section, pointed out, this and the limited resources of the pupils' families impede a "student-centered" education. Due to the "socioeconomic structure" of their families, the pupils are not able to complete their homework, for which they would need access to a computer; as they do not have computers at home and with no "safe" "Internet cafes" in this area, only very few children complete their homework within the assigned time limit. Such limitations make teachers—as group *Turquoise* stated—fall back on "teacher-centered" education and consequentially to the style of the "old system," that is, ex-cathedra teaching.[4]

Preparation for the Standardized High School Entrance Exams

Although the members of group *Turquoise* experience this inappropriateness of the new curriculum in relation to the Karanfil school, they do not principally object to it. As we showed in section 4.3, these teachers do not fully comply with the curriculum's provisions and expand on it by introducing "sourcebooks" and "question banks" into instruction. By doing so, they prepare children for the standardized high school entrance exams, for which this material has been developed in the first place. The teachers of group

Khaki, likewise, do not generally object to the new curriculum, but feel obliged to use the "sourcebooks" prepared by private instruction centers so that their pupils do not "veer away from the test technique"; otherwise, they argued, their "test success" would "drop." Group *Grey*, in a passage quoted in section 4.3, described how they only nominally observe the formal rule—the curriculum—by making the respective entries, taken from the teacher "manual," in the "class book." Apart from this, Cf—with Bf later admitting that she agrees—prepares pupils for the standardized high school entrance exams, here called "SBS":

Cf: └ but, I *never* use the book you know. I have such a thing. because in the moment that I use the books, the child cannot be successful in the test, (.) if this (.) government this (.) system demands that from me, I cannot tea- teach with those books. (.) I once tried this in the past year, (.) // mhm// I taught with just the books that is (.) with the books provided to us, I used those books provided by the Ministry of National Education, (.) afterwards we took the SBS exam, but we got too low (.) //mhm// I was the ninth something like this out of maybe ten eleven classes. (.) but then I realized you know I understood after this event that the books really did not work, (.) I did (.) we purchased the normal books of Gendaş in the past year; we began to teach with the Gendaş books, (.)//mhm// by doing so we climbed over to second, third or something like this row in this year, in other words. in this year, other than the books provided by the National Education I finished four or five sources. at this moment we are at second we are in the second row in the SBS; we are in the second third row. (.). that is, I do not find it very good; if we are asked to teach with those books, there must be classes consisting of twenty people, not fifty people, (.) and the school must be really well equipped; (.) and plus there must not be such exams for the books; for there is *very few* knowledge and what is demanded in the tests is *too much* knowledge;

In this quote the teacher admitted to an instructional practice that is contrary to the official, formal rules. This "underlife" (Goffman, 1961, p. 194; see section 5.1) is legitimized by her experience with her previous use of the ministry's textbooks, which caused a significant decline in test results. This practice on behalf of group *Grey* (and of other teacher groups at Karanfil school) is the rare instance of an underlife performed by an organizational milieu which evolved in the very collective practices of the formal rules of this organization, instead of by members of a social milieu who are subjected to organizational rules. However, group *Grey*'s—and the other teachers of Karanfil's—interest in test results is more than just a point of concern for their pupils' educational career. As the group discussion documents, teachers themselves are judged according to their class' test results. Whereas Cf and her class had previously (when she worked with the official textbooks) been one of the last in the rank order, the class excelled and went up to the "second" rank after she began to use a private instruction center's sourcebooks.

Whereas in the schools dominated by middle-class milieus the preparation for standardized tests is completely left to the families and their financing of private instruction center enrolment, in Karanfil school test preparation is clearly a matter to be accomplished by the school itself. The parents expect teachers to foster their children's success in high school exams, not least because they do not possess the cultural and/or economic resources to provide for the preparation. Thus, the teachers are put under pressure not only by parents' expectations but also by an annual ranking organized within the school; only teachers whose classes turn out to be successful in the entrance exams are appreciated.

The middle-class schools analyzed in Istanbul and Dalen (Papatya and Zambak) also pay attention to their pupils' achievements in this competitive test. However, they do not make any efforts to foster their pupils' performance, and only pride themselves for their excellent results. The Karanfil school, dominantly attended by pupils from poor milieus of the squatter area in Enver, Istanbul, pays equivalent attention to test results, but sees no reason to be proud of its endeavors. Paradoxically, even though the Karanfil school—in contrast to the middle-class schools—is *expected* by parents, teachers, and the principal to provide test preparation, it fails to do so, and even when pupils are successful the parents and the principal attribute such success not to the school's efforts but to the work of *other* organizations, that is, to the work of instruction centers. After a visit to a private instruction center, which is attended by some pupils of Karanfil, the principal, Ahmet Sönmez, described the situation as follows:

> ((deeply breaths out)) (1) now the eighth graders of this year (.) when you make estimations (2) they will be slightly better than those in the past mmm (1) if @you ask why@ if this is not related with the curriculum mmm there is a serious ratio of those who attend instruction centers //mhm// (1) on the way back I visited the Bilim-Yön instruction center (1) I was invited (1) I visited them for five minutes (1) we have sixty-five students attending there (1) they told me that twenty of them were so good (1) that they can be admitted to Anatolian high schools (1) when you look at whether it is *good* to have twenty for the Anatolian high school out of 450 students it is very very bad but when I asked my older friends who work here I get a reply that well this class is very good very good. but when I look at the sixth seventh grades I see that there will be a decline in the future, that is these eighth-grade classes are those who may graduate without being too much involved with the curriculum that is to say those who will be involved with the curriculum will be worse (1) according to me (1) that is in my conversations with all my fellow teachers they say the sixth, seventh graders are getting worse //mhm//.

As the principal of Karanfil underpinned, the success (to "be slightly bet-ter than those in the past") of the eighth graders of the present year is not due to the "curriculum," but to the private "instruction center" attended by a "serious ratio" of pupils. What he declared to be a significant proportion (that is, 65 pupils out of 450 eighth graders) shows that being enrolled in an instruction center is an exception at the Karanfil school, whereas in the middle-class milieus of Papatya and Zambak, the exception is non-enroll-ment instead.

Furthermore, it is documented in Mr. Sönmez's narration that he takes the information provided by the instruction center as an absolute measure for his pupils' anticipated success in the entrance exams. Rather than relying on his own teachers' information, he takes into account only the instruc-tion center's impression, therefore considering this organization as the only competent authority. Consequentially, he anticipates that all those pupils who do not attend the instruction center will have no chance of accessing one of the prestigious "Anatolian high schools." In other words, he tacitly views his own school as incapable of preparing children, on its own, for the standardized tests.

Finally—and most importantly—in the principal's account it is docu-mented that according to his views (and also to those of teachers and parents; see earlier) the new curriculum is perceived as an impediment to test success. Whereas the present eighth graders have finished primary school "without being too much involved" with the new curriculum, the principal antici-pates and is afraid that lower grades, in which the curriculum is put into practice more systematically, will be less successful in the entrance exams. Although we do not know if all teachers with whom he has spoken attribute this decline to the new curriculum, Mr. Sönmez is convinced that his school will experience a setback in the high school entrance exams. With this con-viction he also legitimizes the underlife of the organizational rules (that is, of the curriculum) on the part of teachers and their organizational milieu.

Summary: How the Lack of Cultural, Economic, and Social Resources Influences Curricular Practices

The Karanfil school, situated in a squatter area of Enver, Istanbul, is predomi-nantly attended by pupils from poor social milieus. However, to the extent shown by our group discussions with parents and teachers as well as by the expert interview with the principal, there is a certain amount of pupils (or their parents, rather) who strive to be upwardly mobile and view education as an important means for a successful career.

The school itself offers only few opportunities to foster one's educational success. Situated in an area which continuously receives migration (even from other parts of Istanbul, where rent prices have risen), the school is so overcrowded that classes still comprise approximately 50 children, even though pupils are taught in two shifts, This adds to the poor equipment of the school, only rarely and minimally improved by moderate (and at times compulsory) financial contributions from the children's families.

Given this situation, the school is unattractive both for families beyond the poor milieus in its vicinity and for experienced teachers who, equipped with a higher amount of service points, are able to choose their workplace among a wide range of schools. Karanfil school, in this sense, has very few symbolic resources; therefore, it struggles with a severe shortage of staff and is compelled to hire fee-based teachers who are usually inexperienced and very often change their work place. In other words, the school itself is not only endowed with poor economic resources, but the cultural resources on which it can capitalize are also very limited.

Under these circumstances, the new curriculum is perceived as an impediment to test success by parents, teachers, and the principal. The pupils' parents, who come from social milieus which are poor but who also strive for upward mobility, pressure the school and its teachers to prepare their children for the high school entrance exams. Viewing these multiple-choice tests as the only real education, these parents disapprove of the new curriculum and urge teachers to orientate their instruction toward exam preparation. As they lack the economic resources to send their children to private instruction centers (only one seventh, approximately, of all eighth graders are enrolled) and usually are not endowed with the cultural resources to prepare their children on their own, school is the only place where children can receive the training for exams.

The teachers, who are themselves convinced of the priority of exam preparation due to their generational affiliation (see section 4.3), easily bow to the parents' wishes. Besides, given the poor equipment of the crowded school, instruction according to the new curriculum is not perceived as feasible. While other teachers belonging to the same generation combine test preparation with the curriculum, the teachers of Karanfil are inclined to prioritize the former. Being poorly endowed with cultural resources on their own, they are also unable to freely design their lessons, and hence resort to the "source-books" prepared by private instruction centers, only superficially attending to the new curriculum. This general inclination toward multiple-choice test preparation—and, therefore, toward an "underlife" of the formal rules of the curriculum—demanded also by ambitious but poor parents, is reinforced by an informal competition among teachers, evidently boosted by the school administration through the ranking of teachers according to their pupils' standardized test results. We focus on the competition based on standardized test results in chapter 6. Before we do so, however, we shall give attention to the instructional practices in the countryside schools of our sample, where the curriculum—and test preparation—have yet another meaning.

5.4   Rural Schools With Poor Milieus

Our comparison of instructional practices in Turkish primary schools does not stop at class differences; that is, at the analysis of schools dominated either by poor or middle-class social milieus. We also included schools which vary in their socio-geographical situation: Whereas the previously analyzed schools are situated in cities, we subsequently pay attention to instruction in rural schools. Our main question again is how the new curriculum has been put into practice in these schools, which are dominated by pupils who originate from social milieus characterized not only by a lower (albeit not necessarily poor) income situation but mainly by their rootedness in the countryside.

Under the conditions of a continuing migration from the countryside to the cities (see chapter 2), being located in the countryside implies that schools as well as pupils and their families are confronted with an inverted version of the pressure faced by the Karanfil school in Istanbul: Whereas Karanfil school has to cater for an ever-growing number of pupils (resulting in crowded classes and double shifts), both schools investigated in the countryside of Dalen struggle with a decreasing number of pupils; Lale school, in the Demirli village, even approaches the possibility of closing down because of the problem.

The low population density is also manifested in the fact that both schools cater for pupils who are transported from other villages. Whereas 131 of a total of 148 pupils are transported to Lale school from eight villages, the school in the small town of Tuzlu caters for 71 pupils carried from surrounding villages. We may compare this student transportation scheme to the middle-class schools in Safran and Istanbul: There, pupils whose parents find these schools attractive are transported—at the parents' expense—to school. The villagers' children are taken to school at the expense of the state because there are no schools in their area; in other words, they have no other choice.

The village school is the only one in its location, while in the small town there are three primary schools. All these schools cater for pupils on a full-day basis and their classes, compared to city schools, are rather small. These favorable conditions for instruction, however, are clouded by a lack of branch teachers. Whereas the ministry appoints a class teacher to every class, only one branch teacher for every 21 children is sent to the respective school. Hence, in the village and town schools of our inquiry (both of which struggle with low pupil numbers), some branches are not taught by a specialized teacher.

All of the mentioned conditions in the rural schools have their effects on instructional practice. However, there are even more important common features shared by these schools, which we summarize as soon as we have scrutinized these educational organizations one by one.

Sardunya School in Tuzlu Town

Tuzlu is a town of approximately 5000 inhabitants, situated in the province of Dalen and 35 km from Safran, the province capital. The Sardunya school has been constructed through the financial donation of a rich entrepreneur living in the district. It has two buildings and a gymnasium. Although it is relatively well equipped, its technical infrastructure is still behind that of the middle-class, urban schools. For example, only one classroom is equipped with a smart-board and a data projector, and the two eighth-grade classes constantly compete over the right to use it.

The school has 446 pupils; classes have approximately 21 children, and 30 teachers are appointed to this school, leading to a teacher-pupil ratio of 1 to 14.87. As there are several state institutions (including the military) as well as—due to the nearby motorway—car repair shops in town, the pupils come from civil servant and worker families, and the villagers come mainly from farmers.

The Teaching Conditions of Sardunya School

The principal of Sardunya school, Ali Akbaba, was born in 1964 and graduated from a teacher high school. He has worked as a teacher since 1986, and as a school administrator since 2008. After several positions as teacher and administrator in the district of Tuzlu, he became the principal of Sardunya in May 2011. He described his workplace with the following words:

> Tuzlu, as much I see (.) having worked in Dalen might have been a chance for me (.) let's say so (.) of course there are very good schools in Dalen too (.) as concerns schools the three schools of Tuzla all three of them are to my observation of higher quality //mhm// that is (.) we all know schools with a high parent profile anyway (.) it is not necessary to name them (.) I see that in this school more value is given to teaching and education (1) but that the parent side is not wholly settled (.) what I can see is that that is to say the parent side is not completely settled here in the Tuzlu region (.) it is more done by the effort of teachers // mhm// by the intense effort of teachers and school administrations. (2) if we can advance the parent profile some more (.) and anyway in this regard we are doing parent visits (.) [. . .] that is if we can move the parents a little bit more of Tuzlu it already comes first in Dalen as a district in general sense //mhm// I guess we can keep this constant in terms of SBS's averages.

In this quote, the principal clearly distinguished town schools from city schools by drawing attention to the different "parents profile" or, more precisely, to the "value given to teaching and education." Drawing from our own analysis of how parents of city schools value education, we may assume that the principal here is complaining not only about parents' low expectations toward their children's educational performance, but also about the consequential scarcity of donations and the low enrollment in private instruction centers.

Similar to all other principals, Mr. Akbaba uses the high school entrance exams as a measure for school performance. However, he did not compare his school to the ones in the city (such as in Safran), but alluded to the competition between town schools; that is, the competition with schools from other districts in the province of Dalen. Evidently, parents' low educational expectations of their children here go hand in hand with the principal's low expectations of his own school. One manifestation of parents' low expectations is their reluctance to financially contribute to the school. As the school is not able to raise any funds, the principal has to "manage the school with zero income." Even donations in kind ("coal") are not feasible, as Mr. Akbaba made clear. The lack of financial contribution to the school is not necessarily due to parents' absence of economic resources (who are, in average, better off than the squatter area parents of Karanfil school). These parents, however, are not used to giving financial donations to the school. In contrast to his impression of parents, the principal portrayed a cooperative atmosphere in his account of the teaching staff:

> In particular our meetings take a very beneficial course (.) that is everyone can honestly say everything in our teacher committee meetings (.) of course (.) we have the opportunity to go into classrooms and control them (.) we go in (.) look (.) here different tests (.) the works of pupils sometimes we reward them upon the proposal of our teachers (.) there are also projects that we are doing (.) various projects as a school (.) when we get together during them (.) we have an exchange of ideas (.) that is there is no trouble in this issue (.) everyone is open (.).

In this account it is documented, on one hand, that the principal does not view the teachers as competing with each other vis-à-vis their pupils' performance in standardized tests; conversely, he does not distinguish between "tests" and other teaching methods, such as the "various projects" mentioned. The principal evidently favors the general atmosphere to the educational success measured by standardized tests.

Experienced and Novice Teachers' Instruction

In contrast to the schools we have examined so far, Sardunya school has a mixture of teachers from different professional generations. The class teachers— belonging to the generation of experience-based lesson designers—originate from the villages of this province and have returned here to work. They know the region and its people very well and are perceived by parents as the permanent staff of the school. Whereas these teachers live in the town, the young branch teachers—of the generation of new curriculum and test preparation combiners—have chartered a minibus to commute from the provincial capital in which they live. As this constitutes an additional (financial) burden, these teachers try to move (by appointment) to urban schools; parents, accordingly, view them as temporary staff.

By conducting a group discussion with experienced teachers and one with novice teachers, we have captured the variety of teachers in the Sardunya school. Group *Pink* is constituted by four experienced class teachers, two of them females. Conversing about the new curriculum, these teachers thematize the adverse attitude of their pupils' parents. Whereas the "old curriculum" did not expect parents to participate and assist with education, group *Pink* is convinced that parents must help their children (with building a "birdhouse," for example) to learn according to the expectations of the new curriculum. Parents in Tuzlu, however, have not changed their participation and assistance in education: Those who are active are the same ones who had previously been so. In a sense, the teachers here confirmed their principal's account of Sardunya parents. To the extent that the new curriculum does not seem to be suitable for parents who, coming from rural milieus, are not used to engaging with their children's school education, the new curriculum itself seems to be adapted only to the conditions of a city:

Fm: our environment can be different (.) you adapt to the environment; you change the
       instruments
Bm: ∟ mm ⌐
       ∟ for example, (1) life studies the one who prepared this (.) or
       in science in social sciences here a visit to be made to a museum
Rf: ∟ yes ⌐
Bm: there is such an activity, (.) ee since there is no museum here, (2) //mhm//
Rf: ∟ (here, museum) ⌐
Bm: if I take this (.) it will be meaningless. (.) what may I do with this in my environment
Fm: ∟ you replace it with another activity ⌐   ∟ or
       forming a museum in the class
Bm: ∟ °mm° (.) something like this, (.) I cannot arrange a visit
       to a museum but I say that I will show them videos of a museum from the web. (2) [. . .]
       the main subject does not change, (.) the activity that you will do may be different.
       (1) //mhm// we want revisions in these
Rf: ∟ the curricula become elastic, (adapted) to the
       environment

The teachers not only consider the new curriculum as developed for the "environment" of the city, they also criticize that the teaching material does not allow for the adaptation of instruction to the circumstances of the respective school. Despite these complaints, the discussion documents that these teachers—in accordance with their generational affiliation—agree that one has to "adapt" the new curriculum "to the environment" and to "change the instruments." This was then illustrated with the museum example: As there are no museums in Tuzlu, the teachers then replaced them with virtual pictures. Nevertheless, such adaptations are more difficult now, as the teacher manuals include detailed requirements on how to put lessons into practice.

Group *Yellow* is formed by six branch teachers, four of them females and all of whom belong to the younger generation of new curriculum and test preparation combiners. As we showed in chapter 4, these teachers use both the new curriculum and the preparatory material for standardized high school entrance exams, as they feel ethically obliged to train pupils for the tests and also think the school administration expects them to do so. When we asked group *Yellow* if they are able to implement the student-centered approach of the new curriculum, the following discourse unfolded:

Nf: we become tired (.) in other words (.) is this student-centered on the contrary she/he would do the student who has a feeling of responsibility does something if she/he will do anything (.) the others are in the same situation, (.) there is no such situation that they shine out

Hf: └ but here that is (.) when it is used, it is perhaps it varies from class to class or from place to place too I for example very different things may happen (1) in a city center at the moment, even here, with a good class, between a class with a good grade, and a bad class there are many differences for example when I go into a good class I am not 100 percent a teacher (.) // hmm// they become sometimes teachers themselves; because they direct it because; but among weaker students the children think directly with the old logic that everything coming out of the teacher's mouth is important and required to be listened it is very different from child to child (.) but here there is that is if I have to confess, I can observe that a lot of gains that I memorized, as memorizing, unaware of what I am doing, just memorizing and become successful, today the children wholly get them themselves and find it like a scientist //mmhh// how does this happen, it is completely related to the class's character

Similar to group "*Pink,*" these teachers perceive the curriculum as being prepared according to urban environments. Whereas in the "city center" (that is, in the province capital, Safran) the curriculum and its student-centered approach might possibly work, in Sardunya school the teachers are able to follow this approach only with certain pupils and classes that are described as "responsible" and "good." Other, "bad" children virtually make teachers follow a teacher-centered approach; that is, they motivate them to teach ex-cathedra. The curriculum developers, however, seem to wish there to be a "single type student," as these teachers critically remarked in the sequel of this quote.

The orientation of group *Yellow* toward the new curriculum is ambivalent. On one hand, they praise the success of children who take over the "teacher" role and act like a "scientist"; on the other hand, they are convinced that this curriculum, with its student-centered approach, is only suitable for specific (more urban) environments. Contrastingly, group *Pink* complained about the lack of material and about the need to adapt the new curriculum to the circumstances of the small town, but was also capable of mastering these challenges. The younger teachers of group *Yellow*, conversely, do not perceive themselves as capable of adapting the curriculum while staying within its student-centered approach. Thus, they surrender to a teacher-centered approach as soon as they are confronted with pupils who do not seem able to learn to the standards of the new curriculum.

The Parents' Perspective

At the Sardunya school we conducted discussions with three groups of parents. In the following, we analyze the group discussion with five mothers, three of whom have graduated from high school, one from vocational college, and one from primary school. They all work as housewives and some of them are members of the school-family-union, which is less organized in the town school than in urban contexts. Still, these parents visit the school more often and help with fundraising and cleaning the school premises. In the following passage, the group discusses their relation to teachers:

Df: I came for a meeting with teachers (.) last year for the last time; and there used to be a private meeting in our thing school, (.) //mhm// each teacher in a classroom everyone you know could go and ask the child's situation; (.) that time some teachers for example told me that

Af: └ we could meet them (.) separately ┘

Df: your child has no problem at all; @you do not need to come and *ask,*@ (.) //mhm// if there would be any problem we come and find you anyway; (.) when it is said so I did not either come or ask, (1) only last year teacher Burcu came to visit houses us, (.) and to a friend then presumably she could not go to anyone else, (1) somehow it is something like that ((conversation moves out of the topic))

Ff: she is said to have said for this year

Df: └ but this year is guaranteed that

Ff: she is said to have said (.) I just want tea

Df: └ yes it was tea

Although these mothers are certainly interested in the instruction provided to their children and, like Df, visit the "meeting" with the class teacher, they did not mention any issues or concerns they wished to share with the teacher. Instead, their discourse—starting with the home visits of the teacher called "Burcu"—turned into a discussion of what should have been served to the teacher ("tea" only, and nothing to eat). In this discourse it is documented that these mothers view the teacher's visit as a social event, rather than as an opportunity to talk about the educational career of their children.

The parents then talked about their children's future. Similar to the previous transcript they here view education in terms of social relations and positions instead of elaborating on teaching methods or contents (which were topics on which parents of both poor and middle-class milieus focused):

Ff: *my child,* (1) if you get married your husband shall have a job you shall also have a job
      you live in (.) ease you go on holiday together you have a car (.) a house (.) you
?f: └ we tell the same too ┘
Ff: will lead a comfortable life if you like you send your child to an instruction center or
?f: └ yeah ┘
Ff: you sent it to a private school (.) that is you shall have *opportunities* (.) you see us;
Df: └ yes ┘   └ of course ┘
Ff: this is a small place (.) our opportunities °provide just that much°
Df: └ mm (.) of course my husband is a driver (.) he goes and does not come
Ff: └ our ┘
Df: for *two months* (1) my husband goes to Kazakhstan. (.) I am with my children I say
Ff: └hea:::┘   └ that much ┘
Df: look I am waiting for my husband his money (1) but you will not wait for him (1)
Ff: └ nothing
Df: you will reach to a good position (1), of course you become a teacher that and your
Ff: └° that is °
Df: husband won't become a driver (1) you will get married to someone at your level (1)
      more comfortable (.)

Here, education is viewed as a means for a better social position and for a better life in general. These mothers particularly wish this future for their girls, who they want to have the economic and other opportunities which they—the mothers—lack. Such a life would, according to these mothers' hopes, not be led fully independently, but within a marriage; at the same time, backed by a good education, their girls should be on equal terms with their spouses, based on their own income.

Moreover, these mothers imagine the future of their children by negatively drawing from their own life experience. Whereas they—also due to living in a "small place"—could not send their children to a "private school" or a private "instruction center," they hope that their children will live in a place with more opportunities of this kind. In this discourse it is, thus, documented that these mothers do assign importance to education in private schools or instruction centers, and would send their children to those if they could. However, lacking the necessary financial means and residing in a small town, it is not possible for them to provide (additional) private education for their children.[5]

When these mothers were asked what plans they had made for their children's high school education, they delved into a discourse that again pointed to the restrictions experienced in the countryside:

Ff: now the science high school too (.) actually you know (.) everything is limited now also
      because she is a girl (.) how can you send her let's say (.) she won in Ankara or in Bartın
      or Çaycuma
Df: └ yes:: (1) I don't send anywhere else (.) except Safran, this time

Ff: ⌐moreover (.) because she is small
Df: go to the teacher high school or Anatolian high school
Ff: (.) I mean everyone all those in Tuzlu generally have to prefer Safran (.) you see

These women are ambitious regarding the educational success of their children, including the girls. As we know from other parts of the group discussion, they make their children engage in test preparation and help them with homework. But even if their children "won" a place at a high school in "Ankara" or "Çaycuma," they would not send them there, especially in the case of a girl. The most distant place where they would send their children for high school would be the province capital, "Safran," which also implies that the child would only attend a "teacher high school" or an "Anatolian high school," but not one of the prestigious "science high schools."

It is on this background of geographically restricted opportunities, to which gender concerns are added, that these parents' expectations of the school are low regarding test preparation. Although they help their children to prepare for the high school entrance exams and some even send them to private instruction centers in the province capital, these parents do not make full use of their economic and cultural resources. As our empirical data reveals, the reason for this reduced investment in education—which is even noticeable in the principal's and teachers' discourses—is the geographic situation of Sardunya school and its pupils: Being located in the countryside, the school does not compete with other educational organizations. Moreover, the range of high schools for which its pupils can prepare is rather limited, resulting in a low need for engaging in test preparation (and for investing economic and cultural resources in this direction).

Lale School in Demirli Village

Lale school is situated in a village with approximately 380 inhabitants and located 20 km from the city of Safran. There is one class at each grade; classes have between 13 and 24 children and are taught by 16 teachers, resulting in a teacher-pupil ratio of 1 to 9.25. The school has two buildings, an additional cafeteria, and a small staff house, where one teacher lives with his family. All other teachers commute from Safran, with the exception of the vice principal, who lives in a nearby village. In addition to the children of Demirli village, pupils from eight nearby villages are transported to the school at the state's expense.

Lale school offers full-day education and has separate classrooms for special branches (such as social studies), which, however, have only limited equipment (such as maps), if any whatsoever. The only branches served by specialized teachers are English, Social Studies, Mathematics, and Turkish, whereas other branches (life studies and others) are taught by non-specialized teachers. Lale's principal, Mr. Ata Vergin, was trained in Istanbul University at the Institute for Education Administration and started his career in 1995. He has worked at the Lale school for only "two years." In his interview, the principal differentiated between "education" and "teaching" and made clear that, to his regret, social expectations are only concerned with the latter, as measured by the standardized entrance "exams" for high schools. In contrast to the schools investigated in the urban contexts of Safran and Istanbul, the principal measures his school's success not by its pupils average entrance exam results, but by the most successful students' ranks, referring, however, to the standardized tests. According to this perspective, the school is successful because "twelve years" ago, as well as in the previous year, there were a total of three students from his school among the best of the province. Apparently, such success is not permanent and the principal's (and presumably the educational administration's) expectations of Lale school are considerably low. Similar to the principal of the town school ("Sardunya School in Tuzlu Town" in this chapter), Mr. Vergin in his interview did not compare his school to urban ones, but to the one in the village in which he had previously worked.

Differently from village schools where he had previously worked, Mr. Vergin perceived Lale's teachers, pupils, and parents as motivated. The difficult conditions of the school (the considerable distance to the city, problems in "transporting" children to school, and providing them with a "meal") considered, he then evaluated the school's performance as a "superb success." He added that there would be even more successful students if parents were able to send their children to private instruction centers, but that "because their parents are not that powerful economically they cannot benefit from instruction centers (.) of course this inevitably reflects on education and teaching." In these words it is documented that the principal views the success of pupils of the school as directly connected to the enrollment in instruction centers; notably, all successful students of Lale had been prepared in such centers. Nevertheless, similar to all other principals, he perceives—without hesitation—high test scores as the school's success, although he does not expect his school or its teachers to prepare pupils for such exams. The principal also did not express any expectation toward or concern for practicing the new curriculum in his school, leaving teachers with a considerable leeway in their professional practice.

As we will later understand, the principal is not alone in his low expectations of Lale school and its pupils. The parents, too, although wishing their children to attend high school, do not see education as the only means for a socially secure life. As the principal recalled, the province is one of the richest in Turkey: "If you are in need then you learn (.) but if not you do not learn (.) this person receives when she/he becomes eighteen a car thanks to the father." The student, therefore, "doesn't see the need for studying anymore." These words point to a social milieu which, similar to the one of Sardunya school, is economically situated between the social milieus of Karanfil and those of the urban middle-class milieus; more importantly, this milieu is more distant from educational careers than all other urban social milieus investigated.

Given these circumstances, Mr. Vergin did not see any major impediments to practicing the new curriculum, only some minor deficits in the technological equipment of classrooms. However, he was also not very knowledgeable regarding curriculum practices and did not even mention the teachers' complaints about parents' inability to help their children with homework (see later). For the principal, apparently, the fact that a school exists in Demirli is already an important asset, and he considers all teachers who put up with the difficulties and commute to the village daily as "willing to make sacrifices."

The Mixed Generations of Teachers

We interviewed two groups of teachers at the Lale school. In group *Black,* three class teachers with differing professional experience talked about working at Lale school. According to them, the children have a lack of knowledge when they start their school career, as they have not attended pre-school and their parents' participation in education is insufficient. Given these conditions, which are considered "medium" and "between good and bad," the teachers still maintained that they "give their best."

Apart from their collective perspective on the educational situation of Demirli village and its people, these teachers have different and, at times, even discrepant orientations toward teaching. In a part of the group discussion (already quoted in section 4.4), Hf, who had previously worked with the old curriculum, praised the new curriculum for the sequentiality of its topics and gains, which facilitate learning and teaching; Sf opposed her by declaring the curriculum and its books as "insufficient." Similar to the teachers of the generation of new curriculum and test preparation combiners, she underpinned the need to add other books and "question banks" to the instruction material listed in the teacher manuals, clearly referring to test preparation. In contrast, Hf perceives the curriculum as a matter of certain educational goals.

Sf's reservations do not solely imply that she disagrees with the curriculum as such. In the following part of the group discussion she even praised the curriculum as facilitating teachers' work and as being "activity"-based. However, now it was Hf's turn to show opposing views:

Sf:	⌐ but I think like this my colleague, the young teachers in this method system (.) I mean I think they are very (.) *lucky* because what we actually
Om:	⌐° yes because °⌐
Hf:	⌐ very practical ⌐
Sf:	got from university we always prepared activities I recall in the teaching of subjects however mm when I became a teacher I realized that there was no activity in the books in the old curriculum (.) then when we changed over to this curriculum I understood that we actually gave lessons according to this I learned this (.) this is my opinion
Hf:	⌐ but in the old system we rather had to do it by ourselves (.) in the old system the teacher had to do everything in the old system there was nothing there was no source

In this transcript it becomes evident that Sf only knows the old curriculum from her reading of text-"books," whereas Hf had gained her own teaching experience. Sf was trained in a time when the old curriculum was still valid, so she learned how to develop "activities" on her own. However, when she started working, the new curriculum was introduced and she found ready-made activity suggestions in the teachers' manuals and textbooks. Hf, in contrast, disapproves of Sf's suggestion that the old curriculum was not activity-based; in accordance with the teaching orientation of the older generation of experience-based lesson designers, she highlighted that they "had to do everything" by themselves, a capability and habit these teachers still employ when putting the new curriculum into practice (see chapter 4).

In contrast to group *Black*, group *Orange* is formed by all branch teachers of Lale school. They are young and combine curricular activities with test preparation according to the circumstances of their respective branch and classroom situation. In the following part of the group discussion, these teachers talk about the differences between classes and pupils with which—inexperienced as they are—they have difficulties to cope:

Tm: a class is sometimes very lucky in a certain year (1) that is it gets through with one or two teachers (1) for their luck a good teacher comes (1) but another class goes (.) on with five teachers (2) they sometimes do not see any teachers for a month (1) now when they get into the sixth of course (.) they come with great disadvantages //mhm// (3) I will go back to the starting point (.) then there is the family; the family ( ) too many- issues a too complex situation //mhm//

Mf: it happens like this for example there are friends who work in the *center*, I talk about the same issue sometimes because I do not have a committee, //mhm// I try to follow up with friends in other schools, I say what did you do she/he says the nat- numbers are finished I say how did you finish? (.) we still work on multiplication or something else (.) she/he says we go to the instruction center or take private lessons, you know I get stuck there; no one of ours goes to the instruction center or takes private lessons (.) //mhm// it is like an effective factor I think, you know, that level of readiness (.) makes a big difference

Tm: ⌐ yes ⌐

The teachers here assess their pupils' performance by comparing them with each other and with those who are educated in the schools of the province's "center," that is, of Safran. In contrast to the dominant perspective in the urban schools of our sample, such comparisons are not elaborated as competition: Whereas in the city schools the difference between classes usually refers to the competition between classes of the same grade, and thus between teachers, due to the lack of classes of the same grade Tm here complained about the variation in the performance of classes of different years when they enter the sixth grade and hence are taught by the branch teachers of group *Orange*. These differences were then explained with the disadvantaged situation of certain pupils, such as having had no teachers or not ever changing teaching staff, or—as compared to pupils in Safran—having no access to private "instruction centers."

By viewing the training received in these instruction centers as helpful and necessary for a successful school education, these teachers, in accordance with other members of their professional generation, combine curricular instruction and test preparation and admit that the school is insufficient in providing the children with this kind of teaching (test preparation), a significant contrast to the teachers of the older generation, who are self-assured about the quality of their teaching and did not even mention the instruction centers in their discussions. With regard to the new curriculum, these teachers think that its expectations exceed the capabilities of children in the village. By turning teaching to a "student-centered" mode the pupils are first of all overstrained, leading to a "parent-centered curriculum" (as they put it), since parents have to help their children prepare for instruction. Whereas group *Orange* is sure that, in general, there are pupils who are "lucky" to have parents who are able to help them, this is not quite the case in Lale. For this reason these teachers maintain not only that the student-centered teaching approach has failed, but also that additional weight has been put on teachers, who have to turn back to the "old fashioned methods," that is, to teacher-centered education.

The teachers, therefore, consider themselves alone in their struggle to put the curriculum into practice and to prepare children for standardized entrance exams at the same time; as one teacher stated, "everything is on you." However, in their discourse they did not refer to anyone who had put pressure on them or to respective educational expectations, neither with regard to the school administration nor to the parents. This radically contrasts with the squatter area school of Karanfil, where teachers complained about the expectation of parents and administration. In Lale, neither the principal (see earlier) nor the parents raise such expectations toward teachers.

The Care by Parents

Six group discussions with parents were conducted in the village. They took place outside the school in a family house, a communal house, and in the mosque. For our analysis we have chosen a group of five mothers (accompanied by children and grandparents), all of which (along with their own parents) graduated from primary school (in their times a 3- or 5-year education). In the following part of the discussion, they were asked if they help their children with the "homework," a point of complaint on part of the teachers:[6]

Y: Do you help with homework? Do you look at the notebook, book to see what she/he has done?

Df: When she/he does not know we help of course

Kf: What we know of course. For example she/he goes to the third grade I do not know everything. I graduated from the primary school, in general you cannot know most of it. But I try to help as far as I know

Sf: └ compared to those of the last year this year's lesson has become more like,

Kf: └ in the future we won't understand anything

Sf: └ Beyza says our subject she/he gives what we have treated. she/he gave as test

Kf: └ this teacher teaches very well. this teacher is very good.

Sf: I mean the kids do what they could not know, she/he says the child must repeat the lesson they did in school but they just do their lessons. She/he says on purpose she/he says for this reason you give a lot of homework she/he shall do it and not complain. The other Ali Öztürk usually did not give homework

Kf: └ His/Her discipline is fine

Sf: └ Discipline, I mean his thing is fine

Kf: └ God I wish she/he stays with us

Sf: └ It is said she/he will not, she/he will leave next year, appointment or something else

Kf: └ she/he won't. really.

Df: She/he actually came from from there far away, from Şırnak, just to stay here for a while.

While these parents, in the first lines of this transcript, confirmed the teachers' complaints that their assistance with homework is very limited, they also made clear that this is not due to unwillingness or neglect, but because of their own limited intellectual capacities (Kf stated, for example, that she does not completely understand grade 3 topics). Conversely, these parents complained about the frequent change of teachers, all of whom have a different teaching attitude, ranging from assigning to refusing to assign homework, keeping "discipline" or not. This also documents that these parents are not so much concerned with the content of homework or with their children's educational success, but primarily with the teachers' influence on their children's general behavior ("discipline," as they put it).

Compared to parents in urban schools, these mothers perceive themselves as subject to the change of teachers (whereas in the squatter area school of Karanfil parents talked about changing teachers with whom they were not pleased). Moreover, they have no possibility of comparing a teacher to others of the same grade, as there is only one class in each grade. All in all, these parents are less concerned with what happens in the school and in the classroom (the methods and the activities used by teachers) than their counterparts in urban environments. For them, the repercussions of school instruction on family life (such as "homework") are important. Being unable to assist their children with homework, these parents delved into a discussion about other ways of caring for their children:

Tf: also if we wouldn't have the meal problem we will be the very first ((general laughs)) we @have the meal problem here if it wouldn't the school is actually the very first@ ((from the back, a child says "they do not give me food"))

Mf: └ they do not give food to him ┘
Tf: and there is also a vehicle problem. if the food problem, vehicle problem didn't exist the
         school is the very first to my opinion.
Mf: └ it's with money ┘
Tf: for example the vehicles are sent by the state, to the distant places. for example there
         is too much between us and the school, isn't it? we talk with the drivers, whatever the
         driver asks for, whether he asks for thirty or for forty

These parents are concerned with their children's nutrition—there is a problem with the regular dishes served at the cafeteria—and their transportation, which is only provided by the state for children living in remote villages. On one hand this indicates that the parents leave school education entirely to teachers. On the other hand, they are, nevertheless, motivated to send their children to school even if this is costly. This indicates that the dominant social milieu of Lale school, bearing many similarities to that of Sardunya, maximally contrasts with the social milieus of the urban schools investigated: While nourishing aspirations for children's education, in this social milieu education is something with which parents are not intimately involved, something that is distant and external to them. Moreover, these parents—as already indicated in the principal's interview—motivated as they are for their children to be educated in school, still do not expect much from the school which they consider very good and with which they are very pleased (apart from the transportation and nutrition problems). Similar to the mothers of pupils at Sardunya school, these mothers develop their ideas about their children's—and especially their girls'—future by comparing it to their own lives; that is, they do not imagine for their children a life that is detached from their own, only one that is slightly better and more self-determined. Even if their children would not be able to attend university, they would—girls included—receive a driver's license and IT knowledge that are useful to obtain a moderate but solid desk job.

These mothers certainly attempt for their children to be prepared for university entrance exams, including by sending them to a private instruction center. However, some children, especially girls, are excluded from this opportunity due to the lack of convenient transportation and transportation that is considered safe by the parents. The way these mothers discussed the issue of university entrance exam preparation also reveals that they have no idea about specific academic disciplines or professions to which their children should aspire, leaving it up to the instruction center and the results of the exams. This again documents that for this rural milieu, education is just as important as it is also a 'black box' of whose contents and details they are ignorant.

Rural Schools: Education as One of Several Means of Social Reproduction

The rural schools of our sample are dominated by social milieus in which education is certainly a highly estimated but also an alien asset of children's lives. Moreover, there is an alternative to education: Children are able to reproduce their parents' social position without excelling in school. In this sense, these rural schools are educational organizations in which education, to pupils and their parents, is not viewed as such an important and valuable capital as it is perceived in the urban schools of our sample. The moderate resources available in these rural milieus, thus, are not fully taken advantage of, as parents do not perceive a higher investment in education as a yield on capital.

The school administrations seem to have taken into account such low capital expectations toward education. Putting no pressure on students or teachers regarding good results in high school entrance exams, their only concern is that their educational organizations work, that is, that they are able to include all children and deliver education. Under such conditions, the high performance of only one or two pupils in the standardized entrance exams is seen as a great success of the respective school.

Given these conditions, the teachers of Lale and Sardunya schools, mixed in their profession generational affiliation, are free to follow their own teaching orientations in instruction. In other words, the older generation takes the new curriculum as a general frame within which teachers design lessons, working in an experience-based manner and according to the limited opportunities of rural schools, while the younger generation—as well as those in the intermediary position—combines the application of the curriculum with test preparation.

5.5 Reciprocally Amplifying Resources in Instructional Practices

As the present chapter makes clear, the profession generational dimension of organizational milieus is not the only factor to influence the way the new curriculum is put into practice. The situatedness of schools also plays a major role in curricular practices. As the comparison of five different schools, dominated by either middle-class or poor urban milieus, or by rural milieus revealed, the situatedness of a school, combined with the generational factor among its teachers, is crucial for the ways in which the new curriculum is made practical.

There are two schools in our sample, Papatya and Zambak, which are dominated by pupils and parents from middle-class social milieus. This milieu domination does not manifest itself only in the good educational performance of pupils (who, as the offspring of parents with a high school degree or above, exceed the expectations formulated in the curriculum and excel in various competitions, most importantly the high school entrance exams). As the parents are financially able and also motivated to provide their children with a "second" education—that is, through preparing them for the high school entrance exams outside school—they thus allow school teachers to focus on practicing the new curriculum in school. The parents not only invest in their children's enrolment in private instruction centers, but also capitalize on their economic resources by making donations to the school, thus significantly fostering its infrastructure, an important feature for curricular practice. Zambak and Papatya, as educational organizations which can rely on such a range of cultural, social, and economic resources of the middle-class milieu, have become attractive schools for well-to-do parents, donors, and experienced teachers who are appointed to these schools with a high amount of service points. Relying on their long-standing professional experience, these teachers can handle the formal rules of the curriculum, conceived of as a general frame, according to their own organizational milieu's teaching orientation, that is, within their ability of designing lessons on their own.

Whereas the urban schools, dominated by pupils' middle-class milieus and the organizational milieu of the older generation of teachers, can capitalize on a variety of resources, Karanfil school, situated in a squatter area of Istanbul, is predominantly attended by pupils from poor social milieus. Although these pupils' parents, to a certain degree, strive for an upward mobility of their offspring and view education as an important means for a successful career, they have little cultural and economic resources to help their children, let alone to enroll them in private instruction centers. Consequently, these parents exert pressure on the school and on teachers to prepare their children for the high school entrance exams, which they view as the only real education form, while they disapprove of the new curriculum for the same reason. The schools' conditions are not convenient for practicing the new curriculum, as the school is overcrowded due to continuous migration and very poorly equipped. Based on this situatedness, the school is unable to attract both pupils from wealthier milieus and teachers, especially those from the older generation. Given the school's poor economic and cultural resources, the teachers—who have themselves passed many standardized exams—bow to the pressure of parents and prepare children for the high school entrance exams, thus pushing the stipulations of the new curriculum aside in a kind of "underlife." This general inclination toward multiple-choice test preparation is reinforced by an informal competition among teachers.

Despite the contrasts between schools dominated by either middle-class or poor social milieus, these schools share two features which are dependent on urban life: Education is seen as a major means of reproducing or fostering one's social position, and it is also a highly competitive sector in which pupils compete for entering the most promising schools. These features become even more evident when the rural schools of our sample are included in the picture.

The rural schools (Sardunya, in Tuzlu town, and Lale, in Demirli village) cater for children who originate from lower civil servant, worker, or farmer milieus. Although parents wish their children to gain a better social position by successfully graduating from high school, they invest only very limited economic resources in school or private instruction centers. In contrast to the urban schools, neither parents nor the school administration or teachers here view education as an issue of fierce competition. Regardless, in these rural environments pupils do not have the choice between "good" or "bad" primary schools, or even between high schools of diverse quality; hence, they must enroll in the only school available. Therefore, the expectations toward educational performance, as measured by standardized test scores, are low on both sides. Given this situatedness, the teachers who originate from both the older and the younger professional generation are able to put the new curriculum into practice according to the teaching orientations of their respective organizational milieu. Although rural schools are not appealing for teachers, along with young teachers (who could not find an appointment in more attractive schools), there is a range of more experienced teachers who originate from the province of Dalen and have always lived in the countryside. Therefore, these rural schools, in spite of their lack of appeal, can still capitalize on the teacher's mixed cultural resources.

The comparison reveals that the urban schools in our sample are not only dominated by specific social milieus (poor vs. middle class), but also that these social milieus' expectations toward school education (test preparation vs. curriculum) are very close to the teaching orientations of the generationally embossed organizational milieu (experience-based lesson design vs. combining test preparation and curriculum) prevalent in each school. In contrast to these schools, which are dominated by congenial social and organizational milieus, the rural schools feature a relative heterogeneity, especially with regard to organizational milieus: There are teachers from the professional generation of test preparation and curriculum combiners as well as from the generation of experience-based lesson designers, along with teachers with an intermediary generational location, who work in the same schools and who cater for pupils from rural milieus ranging from lower civil servants to workers and farmers. Accordingly, a higher heterogeneity of instructional practice exists in these schools (see Figure 5.1).

The situatedness of schools, dominated by different social and organizational milieus, made it necessary to introduce new basic concepts into our investigation: As our empirical analyses have shown, the endowment with cultural, economic, social, and symbolic resources (on the part of parents, teachers, and schools) is crucial for instruction practices on which they are capitalized. Our group discussions with teachers and parents, amended by expert interviews with school principals, unambiguously made clear that practicing the new curriculum is dependent on a certain endowment with various resources: To pay attention to the provisions of the new curriculum in a particular way, the class size must be of less than 30 pupils; the classrooms must be equipped with certain IT devices and be used by one class only; families need to have access to IT and be able to help their children with home or project work. Furthermore, if they—in urban contexts—strive for educational success, families have to be wealthy enough that they are able to additionally send their children to private instruction centers for high school

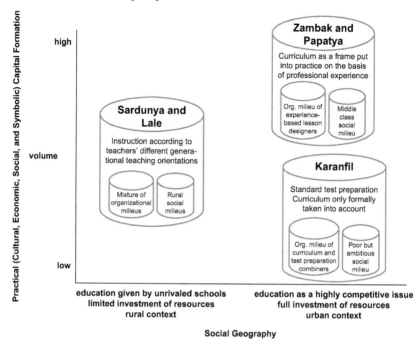

Figure 5.1 Schools, resources, and social geography.

entrance exam preparation. Otherwise, the schools (and teachers) are put under pressure to favor test preparation over the curriculum in the classroom.

This dependence on various resources is further complicated by two points: There is a considerable inequality among schools regarding their own resource endowment, and these resources (or the lack thereof) amplify each other. As Pierre Bourdieu has made clear, resources are not an absolute property, but are relational in constitution. The value of a resource (that is, the degree to which it can be capitalized on) is dependent on the resource endowment and practical capital formations of other (corporate) actors. The following quote by Bourdieu (1985) can be applied to both individual and corporate agents (that is, to organizations):

> The position of a given agent within the social space can thus be defined by the positions he occupies in the different fields, that is, in the distribution of the powers that are active within each of them. These are, principally, economic capital (in its different kinds), cultural capital and social capital, as well as symbolic capital. . . . One can thus construct a simplified model of the social field as a whole that makes it possible to conceptualize, for each agent, his or her position in all possible spaces of competition.
>
> (p. 724)

Putting the competition among organizations into focus, Emirbayer and Johnson (2008) spoke of "the structural tension between the dominants and the dominated within any (organizational) field" (p. 6). When we analyze how the new curriculum is practiced in each school of our sample, we therefore need to view the school within the field of its competitors; that is, within the field of other schools. This requires the educational field or—as we prefer to call it—the educational sector to "be conceived of as a terrain of contestation between occupants of positions differentially endowed with the resources necessary for gaining and safeguarding an ascendant position within that terrain" (Emirbayer & Johnson, 2008, p. 6).

This competition is most fiercely reproduced where several schools, with their respective resources, compete over the same pupils and teachers. As we have seen, among the rural schools there are also educational organizations for which such competition is less significant than for others, as there are no alternative schools to which parents could send their children. However, with regard to the high school entrance exam results of their pupils, these schools are still considered—and consider themselves—within a nationwide competition (although expectations are less ambitious). Such a nationwide competition is also relevant in the assignment of teachers.

In contrast to the rural schools, the urban schools of our sample are caught in a severe struggle within the educational sector. These schools capitalize on resources to boost their prestige (that is, their symbolic resources), which is again used to open up new resources by attracting pupils and teachers. This competition among schools is not limited to one resource, or to pupils, or to teachers: As we showed in sections 5.2 and 5.3, the urban schools of our sample are endowed with several resources, provided by pupils, teachers, or by the schools themselves. These resources may amplify each other, such as in the case of schools dominated by middle-class milieus; the lack of such resources may also be reciprocally intensified, as in the case of Karanfil school, dominated by poor milieus. Figure 5.2 depicts how the economic, cultural, social, and symbolic resources are related to each other and, in their combination, how they influence instructional practices within a single school.

This graphic only captures resources, leaving aside how social and organizational milieus influence instructional practice otherwise. It also simplifies the resources of the organization in two ways: It does not depict the competition between schools (for example, in recruiting pupils from a well-to-do milieu or in raising funds from private donors) and it assumes that there is only one dominant social milieu from which the school's pupils are recruited as well as only one organizational milieu of teachers, as was the case with the urban schools of our sample. However, the resource relations between milieus and the organization depicted in this graphic may be multiplied for other, more complex cases, as for example, in the cases of rural schools where we have identified different organizational milieus, none of which able to dominate the organization. Following the arrows in the graphic, marked by

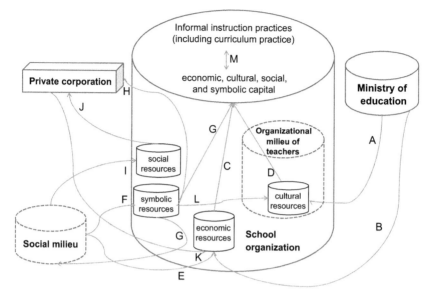

Figure 5.2 Resources of the organization.

characters, we subsequently describe the possible resources of educational organizations.

A. The ministry of education employs teachers and allocates them to schools according to its formal rules. The teachers differ with regard to their knowledge and skills, that is, their cultural resources. By being appointed to a specific school, these cultural resources are incorporated into this educational organization. These cultural resources are not only important as concerns their volume, but also regarding generational structure (to be professionally socialized before or after the introduction of the new curriculum) and professional experience. According to the formal rules of the ministry, teachers with a longer career and who have previously served in unpopular schools or areas (such as in the southeast of Turkey) are more privileged in choosing a school where they wish to teach because they have earned more service points. According to their prestige, schools vary with regard to the amount of service points needed for assignment.

B. The ministry of education allocates economic resources to each school, with which the maintenance of the school is financed (limited to heating, electricity, water, and Internet expenditures, as well as teacher salaries) and which includes instruction material for pupils, such as textbooks (itself a manifestation of cultural capital).

C. The economic resources (for which there are also providers other than the ministry) turn into economic capital only if and insofar as they are used in the (informal) practices of the school. While it seems impossible for schools to save these resources instead of using them, the school can still invest them in different ways: The economic resources may only suffice to maintain ordinary instruction (as in the squatter area school), but they may also be so splendid that the school building can be improved, the equipment of classrooms expanded and extracurricular activities supported (as in the urban middle-class schools).

D. The cultural resources provided by the teachers appointed to a school are only turned into capital if and insofar as these teachers are part of the (instructional) practices of the school. The cultural resources of teachers on a sick leave or for whom there is not any demand are hence not capitalized on. It is also important to consider how these cultural resources are used in practice; for example, if teachers are allocated to classes according to their expertise or if a mathematics teacher gives lessons in biology or music (as we observed in the village school).

E. Each school receives economic resources (mostly money) from pupils' parents. While this is not required by law (and the enforcement of donations even forbidden by the ministry), raising funds among parents is a common practice. Particularly because the school is only rudimentarily financed by the ministry of education, parents' donations are highly important, both if they lack (such as in the squatter house area school and in rural schools) and if they are abundant (as in the urban schools dominated by middle-class milieus).

F. Whether a pupil originates from *this* or *that* social milieu makes a great difference. In contrast to a poor milieu, the enrollment of pupils from a (upper) middle-class milieu may constitute a symbolic resource which virtually is automatically available to the school (and which can be turned into symbolic capital if these pupils excel in competitions such as the high school entrance exam).

G. As soon as the school puts these symbolic resources into effect within its own practices (for example, by praising children's success in high school entrance exams), such resources turn into capital with which the school is able to operate. First of all, this symbolic capital improves the attractiveness of the school among potential pupils (and their parents) so that the school has an even greater opportunity to select the children they prefer to have as pupils. If, however, the school is not able to raise symbolic resources, its ability to select its pupils from a broader range of children is very restricted.

H. The school may use its symbolic resources (which, in addition to the inclusion of pupils from well-to-do milieus, may also be constituted by other means) in the communication with private corporations and entrepreneurs who are approached as potential donors.

I. By recruiting pupils from specific social milieus the school can also utilize their social resources. In this regard, schools dominated by poor milieus significantly differ from those dominated by well-to-do milieus (where the social resources of parents may even be mobilized to raise funds from private companies).

J.   As far as the social resources are capitalized on (by contacting donors etc.) they are turned into capital.

K.   Private corporations, which may have been contacted by means of the social capital of the school and may be attracted by its symbolic capital, may contribute to the economic resources of the school in the form of donations in kind or in money.

L.   The symbolic resources are also capitalized on when the school becomes attractive for teachers. In this sense, the school gains symbolic capital due to its geographical situation (for example, Istanbul versus an Anatolian village) and through the social milieus from which pupils are predominantly enrolled. Teachers then choose the school according to its symbolic capital; therefore, experienced teachers (with many service points) are appointed to attractive schools while unpopular schools are left to novice teachers (see A.). There may be—this needs to be noted—differences between teachers and pupils/parents in the perception of what makes a school attractive.

M.   The practices on which resources are capitalized (first of all, the instruction given), including the practice of the new curriculum, differ from one educational organization to the other. In addition to and intermingled with the orientations prevalent in social milieus (parents who address their expectations to teachers) and organizational milieus (of teachers), the schools are equipped with and capitalized on economic, cultural, social, and symbolic resources in different ways.

In their practices, schools are in a continuous struggle over these resources and the diverse ways of securing them. As symbolic resources are important to attract promising pupils, experienced teachers, and private donors (and as these resources are again boosted if the school succeeds in doing so), they are "especially significant as both a stake and a weapon in these dynamics of contestation" (Emirbayer & Johnson, 2008, p. 12). The rules of this (often tacit) contestation (and also of the underlying contest), however, are not static or imposed on the schools by an outside power alone. The corporate actors (that is, the schools themselves) take part in this struggle. As Bourdieu (1985) wrote, "in the struggle to impose the legitimate view of the social world, . . . agents yield a power proportionate to their symbolic capital, i.e., to the recognition they receive from a group" (p. 731). This "symbolic struggle over the production of common sense, or, more precisely, for the monopoly of legitimate *naming*, that is to say, official—i.e., explicit and public—imposition of the legitimate vision of the social world" is fought not only by individual schools but also by other corporate agents of the educational sectors, among them the ministry of education itself. As we have shown in the present chapter, this struggle focuses on the "legitimate vision" of what education represents; for example, whether it is manifested by the curriculum or by standardized tests. Thus, in the following chapter, we analyze how such visions of education become institutionalized.

Notes

1 Large-scale analyses of school performance like PISA and TIMMS take into account the social background of pupils in a very sophisticated way. They, however, usually limit their analysis to identifying the social locations in an objectivist way, falling short of reconstructing the respective experiences of the research participants.
2 As our empirical comparisons only comprise binary and maximal contrasts, they will not suffice to identify details of each experiential space, sophisticatedly differentiated within a broad range of class and geographic locations. Rather, they help us to understand the variability of curricular practices in the schools of the country under the influence of social milieus and their respective collective experience.
3 For the third group of teachers in Papatya school, *Brown*, see section 4.2.
4 Another problem mentioned by group *Turquoise* is that migration continues in this area, leading to an influx of new pupils during the school year who are even behind the Karanfil students regarding their school performance.
5 There is only one private instruction center (for standardized test preparation) in the town, but parents are not satisfied with its quality. Those who are able to do so send their children to instruction centers in the provincial capital, Safran. Therefore, Sardunya school pupils, if at all, visit either the Tuzlu or Safran instruction center.
6 Many people, including those who were not engaged in the discussion, were present and made it difficult to transcribe the discussion. Therefore, in this transcript, the side talks were deleted for the sake of readability.

References

Bohnsack, R. (2010a). Documentary method and group discussions. In R. Bohnsack, N. Pfaff, & W. Weller (Eds.), *Qualitative analysis and documentary method in international educational research* (pp. 99–124). Opladen: Barbra Budrich.

Bohnsack, R. (2010b). *Rekonstruktive Sozialforschung. Einführung in Methodologie und Praxis qualitativer Forschung.* Opladen: Budrich.

Bohnsack, R. (2014a). Documentary method. In U. Flick (Ed.), *Sage handbook of analyzing qualitative data* (pp. 217–223). Thousand Oaks, CA: Sage.

Bohnsack, R. (2014b). Habitus, Norm und Identität. In W. Helsper et al. (Eds.), *Schülerhabitus* (pp. 33–55). Wiesbaden: Springer.

Bourdieu, P. (1985). The social space and the genesis of groups. *Theory and Society, 14,* 723–744.

Bourdieu, P. (1986). The (three) forms of capital. In J. G. Richardson (Eds.), *Handbook for theory and research for the sociology of education* (pp. 241–258). New York: Greenwood.

Bourdieu, P. (1996). *State nobility.* Cambridge: Polity Press.

Bourdieu, P. (2010). *The logic of practice.* Cambridge: Polity Press.

Emirbayer, M., & Johnson, V. (2008). Bourdieu and organizational analysis. *Theory and Society, 37,* 1–44.

Goffman, E. (1961). *Asylums: Essays on the social situation of mental patients and other inmates.* Oxford: Anchor Books.

Mannheim, K. (1972). The problem of generations. In P. Altbach & R. Laufer (Eds.), *The new pilgrims* (pp. 101–138). New York: McKay.

Mannheim, K. (1982). *Structures of thinking.* London: Routledge.

Nohl, A.-M. (2014). *Konzepte interkultureller Pädagogik* (3rd ed.). Bad Heilbrunn: Klinkhardt.

Ünal, I., Özsoy, S., Yıldız, A., Güngör, S., Aylar, E., & Çankaya, D. (2010). *Eğitimde Toplumsal Ayrışma.* Ankara: Ankara Üniversitesi Basımevi.

6 The New Curriculum in Competition With Other Institutionalized Expectations

As we showed in the previous chapter, instruction varies according to the situatedness of the school in which the curriculum is practiced. The cultural, economic, social and symbolic resources on which the school, its pupils, and teachers can capitalize are crucial for the manner in which the curriculum is put into practice; they are also decisive for the question of whether the curriculum is perceived as a relevant and important formal rule of educational organizations at all. Another issue, in addition to the new curriculum, troubles pupils, their parents, and sometimes also teachers in Turkey: the standardized multiple-choice tests, which one must pass if he or she wishes to be transferred to a (prestigious) high school. There are certain differences between schools as to how these standardized entrance exams are regarded—and if at all. In general, however, it is evident that these entrance exams constitute an important expectation within the educational sector.

Although the new curriculum is the only *formal* rule that is supposed to guide instruction in primary schools, such schools are also confronted with other—and rather *informal*—expectations. Our empirical analyses in chapter 5 indicate that these non-curricular expectations are, in some cases, taken as even more self-evident and important than the curriculum itself. Moreover, if parents (and the principal) expect teachers to prepare children for the standardized high school entrance exams (informal expectations) instead of teaching them according to the curriculum (organization's formal rule), as we have seen in Karanfil school dominated by poor urban milieus, then one can argue that these informal expectations (test preparation) are more institutionalized than the formal rule (new curriculum).

As we discussed in section 3.1, institutionalization takes place if "habitualized actions" (curricular instruction or test preparation) are reciprocally *typified* by "types of actors" (parents, teachers, principals) (Berger & Luckmann, 1991, p. 72). Such an institutionalization, to be sure, is not limited to the level of individual schools but takes place in the educational sector and, at times, in society at large. According to Meyer and Rowan (1977), organizations such as schools tend to "incorporate the practices and procedures . . . institutionalized in society" (p. 340), thus increasing their legitimacy. As we saw in chapter 5, schools may accommodate social expectations even at the expense of formal rules, implying that instruction is tightly coupled to some institutionalized expectations while being only loosely coupled to formal rules that may be less institutionalized. Seemingly, a contradiction may exist between different institutionalized expectations toward the school and its formal rules (in our case, between the curriculum and the standardized entrance exams for high schools). Each school copes with this contradiction according to its situatedness, that is, according to its resources and organizational and social milieus.

In the present chapter we leave the level of individual schools (with their organizational and social milieus) aside and inquire into the competition between the new curriculum and other institutionalized expectations of education entertained in the schools' environment. Such an inquiry is difficult in methodological terms: It is relatively easy to empirically examine individual schools and their organizational as well as social milieus; however, institutions pertaining to social sectors and the society at large are difficult to grasp, empirically, because a very broad and sometimes vast empirical basis is needed to produce reliable results. Our investigation here can only rely on empirical indicators such as the expert interviews conducted with curriculum developers and educational administrators, or on analyses of public discourses and documents of ministerial units.

In a first step of our inquiry, we go back to the time when the new curriculum was promulgated, scrutinizing the way it was explained to the public and the way its developers and ministerial bureaucrats tried to get this formal rule institutionalized within the educational sector (section 6.1). Then, in a second step, we shift our perspective to the high school entrance exam and show how the extent to which it has become a habitualized action pattern reciprocally typified in society and in the educational administration (section 6.2). Finally, the competition between the new curriculum and test preparation makes it possible to theoretically study the intriguing relation of loosely and tightly coupled institutionalized expectations and formal rules within educational organizations (section 6.3).

6.1   Institutionalizing the New Curriculum

The new curriculum, until it was approved and promulgated by the Turkish Board of Education on July 12, 2004, had been the product of a rather homogeneous and small organizational milieu of academics around Ziya Selçuk, the president of the Board. Although the small number of people involved in the process up to that point had helped make the curriculum relatively coherent in its constructivist approach, the process needed to become more inclusive for the subsequent stages of the curriculum change both with regard to informing the wider public and integrating the ministry's bureaucracy and school teachers in the process. In other words, to establish the new curriculum as an institution in society as well as in the educational sector, the curriculum development process had to be shared with many other people. Therefore, after the promulgation of the new curriculum, the ministry of education started a press campaign to promote the new teaching approach to the wider public (see the following section "The Ministry's Press Campaign"). During the subsequent piloting process, carried out in six provinces in 2004/2005, the Board of Education developed teaching material and members of the curriculum commissions started to train teachers in an endeavor to institutionalize the new curriculum (see "Substantiating the Curriculum" in this chapter).

The Ministry's Press Campaign

Starting with a press conference on August 11, 2004, Minister of Education Hüseyin Çelik and the president of the Board of Education, Ziya Selçuk, gave interviews to television and newspapers. Although there are certain differences between these interviews, six messages were repeatedly stressed. In the following paragraphs we summarize and give empirical evidence for these messages and discuss them. Whereas we refrain from examining the degree of truth in these messages,[1] we formulate some cautious assumptions regarding their function.

1. 'The old curriculum was no longer appropriate for the country, which had undergone significant social change': In his press release, Mr. Çelik declared that the "change of the curriculum is required so that it accommodates the necessities of the age."[2] This reference to the temporal state of society was specified when, in an interview, he said that "our education system is not sensitive to the economy, it is not sensitive to democracy, it is not sensitive to production, and it is, in sum, not sensitive to promote the individual."[3] With these references to the political realm, to the economic sector, as well as humans' place in society, the minister both imposed a range of tasks on the school and appealed to different sectors of society, bidding for their approval.

2. 'The need for a new curriculum was felt by everyone, irrespective of political affiliations.' This message was expressed, for example, in the words of Hüseyin Çelik: "*Everybody* agreed that our children do not deserve the existing system."[4] Out of the six messages, this one was voiced least, indicating that both the minister and the president of the Board of Education took the unanimous disapproval of the old curriculum as a matter of course. Connected with the first message, the claim that the old curriculum was unanimously refused by society serves to build the legitimate basis for changing the curriculum in the first place.

3. 'The ruling Justice and Development Party did not interfere in the curriculum development process': Hüseyin Çelik and Ziya Selçuk univocally underpinned that the ruling party was kept out of the curriculum development. As the minister said, "when we took this problem [the curriculum; the authors] in our hands, we saw it more from a scientific than from a partisan point of view."[5] The president of the Board of Education stated that "The minister of national education Hüseyin Çelik never said 'the JDP has some

goals, we as a member of the party wish that something like this goes into the curriculum.'"[6] This non-partisan development of their work was also voiced by leaders of the curriculum commission.[7] This approach anticipates a strategy of criticism often used for governmental measures and thus serves to 'take the wind out of the critics' sails.'

4. 'The curriculum was developed through a comprehensive consultation process that included stakeholders from civil society and education science': Ziya Selçuk declared that during the curriculum development "we have ensured an environment which was open for every kind of criticism" and which enabled the participation of "universities" and "civil society organizations."[8] In an interview, the minister added that "trade unions," "especially teachers' unions" as well as "stakeholders in education from teachers to pupils, from parents to inspectors" were included in the consultation process, in which they could voice their "expectations" of the new curriculum.[9] With this message, again, the legitimization basis of the new curriculum is broadened, especially on the background of possible accusations that the curriculum had been developed by a small clique.

5. 'Those who opposed the new curriculum are ideologically bound:' In general, Ziya Selçuk underpinned that, to his view, "one cannot approach science ideologically."[10] More specifically, Hüseyin Çelik, talking about the feedback received from social groups, divided it into the approval they received by the majority and the criticism on part of "ideological groups": "There are some political cadres who view us in a prejudiced way, there are some ideological groups . . . They are persons who are the minority of a minority in Turkey. But the broad masses of the people saw that what we are doing helps their children and that this is good work for the benefit of our society and its future, and they supported us in this issue."[11] By declaring education as a non-ideological issue and by delegitimizing criticism as ideologically biased, the advocators of the new curriculum render the criticism manageable: Those who generally approved of the curriculum but raised minor concerns were taken into account, whereas more radical critics were marginalized as irrelevant and irrational. With this division, Ziya Selçuk and Hüseyin Çelik tried to both ensure a participative appearance and render irrelevant and illegitimate any criticism on the constructivist approach of the curriculum.

6. 'The new curriculum aims at educating competent members of the contemporary society in a globalized world': Claiming that the new curriculum "is based on a good individual, a good human being, and a good citizen," the minister of education situates education in a comprehensive social realm (similar to the first message). In a more detailed way, he also stated that "with the new curriculum we have moved from a strictly behavioristic curriculum to a cognitive, constructivist approach. [. . .] Eight skills deficient among our children have been identified. Those are critical thinking, problem solving, scientific inquiry, creative thinking, initiative, communication, use of information technologies, and the skill to nicely use the Turkish language."[12]

Among the messages disseminated by the minister and by Ziya Selçuk, those who were directly concerned with the curriculum's new teaching approach were rather negligible. The minister here only denoted the change of the teaching approach, but did not explain it or even connected it to the "eight skills" mentioned previously. Ziya Selçuk, similarly, hardly mentioned the constructivist approach of the new curriculum and its foundation in multiple intelligence theory in his public interviews. As it seems, the two protagonists of curriculum change did not make greater efforts to highlight the background philosophy of the curriculum.

Hüseyin Çelik and Ziya Selçuk, as the politically responsible persons, in their endeavors to link the new curriculum to the public debate underscored specific aspects of its development while downplaying others, as the six preceding messages reveal. They utilized the existing criticism in society toward the old curriculum and presented the new curriculum as something which anybody else would have developed in the same manner and direction. By doing so they avoided any major discussions on the new curricular approach, that is, discussions concerning constructivist teaching.[13] Moreover, they presumably enlarged the legitimation basis of the new curriculum and, in general, mitigated criticism in society. However, the society at large may have remained unaware of the radical change from behaviorism to constructivism which school education was meant to undergo.[14]

Substantiating the Curriculum

The institutionalization of the new curriculum pertained not only to informing and convincing the public, but also to a necessity within the educational sector. When the curriculum change turned from an issue of a small organizational milieu within the Board of Education to an affair of the entire educational sector, the difference between organizing (that is, writing new formal rules for instruction) and institutionalizing a new curriculum (turning these rules into reciprocally typified actions) also emerged. The new curriculum, even before it was put into practice by generationally different organizational milieus (chapter 4) in schools under the domination of various social milieus (chapter 5), produced by a narrow organizational milieu of academics, met a wide range of educational orientations and attitudes in the bureaucracy of the ministry of education and its field organizations. At this point in time the formal rules of the new curriculum were still rather abstract and had yet to be made feasible for classroom instruction. This concretization and substantialization of the new curriculum was accomplished by developing teaching material and by informing teachers. These activities, however, did not solely help to bridge the gap between abstract formal rules and concrete classroom practice; they also served to link the new curriculum to the existing educational organizations, schools (that is, district and province administrations of education). In this sense it fostered the institutionalization of the new curriculum. However, as the subsequent analysis will show, only certain understandings of the new curriculum—in lieu of others—were institutionalized.

Curriculum Developers and Their Relation to the Ministerial Bureaucracy

As we saw in chapter 3, Ziya Selçuk, even before being appointed president of the Board of Education, perceived the "nearly 600 persons" employed in the organization as "protesting" the new government and refusing to work effectively.[15] When he then also faced the passive resistance of other ministerial units as well as other state agencies (universities, the Higher Education Council), and when he, additionally, was able to secure the financial budgets from the Support to Basic Education Project (SBEP) of the European Commission, he appointed close colleagues as leaders of the curriculum commissions, who then formed a homogeneous organizational milieu that was inserted into the Board of Education.

However, our interviews with several lower- and medium-rank bureaucrats of the Board revealed that its president may have misinterpreted the attitude of his staff. Seemingly, the staff of the Board was generally convinced that the old curriculum was insufficient and needed to be changed. As a department head admitted, "it is the duty of a government to change the curriculum." Regardless of whether Ziya Selçuk was mistaken, his perception led to the formation of an organizational milieu of like-minded curriculum developers, but for piloting the curriculum and for developing the teaching material for all Turkish primary schools, the curriculum developers—particularly as they were only given 1 year for this task—had to rely on the cooperation of other educationalists within and outside the ministry. For example, new commissions had to be constituted for the development of textbooks, to which personnel from different departments of the ministry were appointed. Furthermore, the teaching material, which was prepared by private publishing companies, had to be controlled and approved by the Board of Education within a very short time, a task accomplished by personnel who previously had not been involved in the development of the new curriculum.

As soon as other ministerial departments and bureaucrats outside of the original curriculum commissions became involved in the curriculum change, the members of the organizational milieu around Ziya Selçuk started to gradually loose control of the process. For example, one commission leader, Prof. Dr. Aydın, described his relation to a department that prepared "teaching tools" with the following words:

> For example here there is this Eğitek there used to be teaching tools or whatever else I do not know if it still exists (1) from them we ordered some visual things for Social Studies some of them were made (1) I see in some schools in some units of the Ministry of National Education for

example we proposed chronologic thematic maps //mhm// I saw that some of them were made.

Here it is documented that the commission leader was not familiar with this ministerial unit for educational technologies, and that he did not have the power to guide its operations: He only "proposed" a specific kind of "maps" and later understood that only "some of them" had been prepared. This and similar accounts of other commission members indicate that they only had limited control over the process of substantializing the curriculum with teaching material. Consequently, some of the teaching material did not meet their expectations but was nevertheless published.

Informing Teachers

Along with developing teaching material, the teaching staff of primary schools—389,859 persons at the time (MoNE, 2010, p. 11)—had to be persuaded into the new curriculum and trained accordingly before the start of the school year of 2005/2006, when the curriculum became obligatory throughout Turkey. Given this narrow time frame and limited financial resources, the curriculum developers around Ziya Selçuk, with their lack of confidence in other ministry personnel, decided on three strategies: (1) Under the catchword "training the trainers," a number of voluntary teachers, administrators, and school inspectors were trained; they were supposed to subsequently inform other teachers about the new curriculum; (2) in many provinces of the country, the commission leaders themselves gave information lectures for teachers; (3) in addition to textbooks for pupils, manuals for teachers were written. In the following paragraphs we analyze these strategies:

1. The curriculum developers invited administrators, school inspectors, and teachers from all over Turkey to take part in more intensive training (such as a 2-week seminar in Ankara), in which the new curriculum was conveyed to them. One Zambak school teacher in Dalen was among those invited, and narrated the following:

we were informed about this process like this; a new curriculum is being prepared (.) //mhm// an invitation was made that teachers' opinions and contributions are also required (.) for preparing that curriculum, [. . .] when we arrived there we saw that (.) we saw people who had seriously been dedicated to that task; in fact they had prepared templates. they just presented the curricula with key features to us, they said do you have any criticism or something (.) maybe they revised one or two things due to our opinions (.) but they had very well known what they would do, they had already decided what they would do anyway. (.) // mhm// when we, there that is (1), when we met with the curriculum developers we saw them as enough equipped (.) //mhm// and we saw them as willing (2) [. . .] they were the pioneers of a trend; (.) and they were very enthusiastic that an approach will develop according to our thinking.

As documented, this teacher expected the seminar to be an opportunity to take part in "preparing that curriculum," only to discover that its "key features" had already been drawn by a group of "dedicated" people. Although such people may have taken into account some criticism from teachers, in general it became clear that the seminar, rather, served to talk the participants into the curriculum and to enable them to inform their colleagues about it.

However, the teacher did not feel prepared to train his own colleagues after the seminar. When he returned from a similar seminar on the curriculum for music, he was appointed to train his colleagues at Zambak school in Safran:

> An official letter arrived, what will Mehmet Uslu do in Zambak school? (.) today he will give information about the music curriculum for four hours (.) all fellows in front of me are music teachers (.) I told them friends are we going to sell snow to Eskimos (.) they gave us a CD (.) here they have defined the annual plans with their key features; (.) those books had not arrived yet. (.) //mhm// they decided like this, *voilà* (.) I said let's share this information together here, (.) we projected them to the wall what is asked from the first grade:: what is asked from the second:: we are still doing wrong we make our students in the first second and third grades (1) sing the *national anthem*. singing the national anthem does not exist in the music plan of the first grade.

This account reveals that this class teacher not only refused to view himself as more knowledgeable than his music teacher colleagues and to train them accordingly, but also that when he subsequently watched the CD slides with his colleagues, he was only interested in the order of curricular content and apparently did not touch upon its teaching approach.

2. In addition to training the trainers, the commission leaders took part in short teacher information campaigns. As Prof. Aydın (the commission leader) described, there was an "institute for internal training" in the city of Yalova, where "5600 participants" could be trained at a time. In groups of "400," the curriculum was "presented" to teachers, the commission leader having one day each week to talk about the part of the curriculum he himself had developed. Additionally, he was also invited to present the new curriculum in other provinces such as "Van," "Izmir," "Batman," and "Istanbul." Ziya Selçuk, who was also present at the Yalova training center, gave his account of this presentation campaign:

> We travelled 58 provinces and talked (1) //mhm// I mean here we did not say let's sit in Ankara and do something from here teachers came up and said that what do you think who you are you manage from Ankara

she/he was angry and yelled //mhm// she/he said you did this wrong, mm you could be right, come and sit, let's drink a cup of tea and talk you are right, what we can do look you misunderstood this through dialogues like these we enforced our discourse travelling 58 provinces.

The lectures, given in "58" of Turkey's 81 provinces, served to reach the highest number of teachers in the least amount of time and aimed to "enforce our discourse," that is, the cause of the new curriculum. As is documented in the instance when Mr. Selçuk was confronted with harsh criticism by a teacher who apparently accused the curriculum developers of imposing something on the teachers in a centralistic way, these lectures were not intended to discuss the new curriculum but to persuade teachers into it: Mr. Selçuk tried to convince the teacher by establishing a personal relation ("let's drink tea and talk"), ultimately telling the teacher that she/he had "misunderstood this."

The accounts from commission leaders and Prof. Selçuk document that the teachers were *informed* about the new curriculum, rather than *trained* on it. There are also no reports of any practical sessions in which teachers could actually use the teaching material or discuss issues of their instruction practice. The teachers themselves, in our group discussions, complained that they didn't receive any information on how to use the new curriculum in practice. Moreover, the communication with teachers was rather unidirectional and aimed at persuading the teachers (for example, the conversation between Selçuk and the teacher). As a matter of fact, those who were trained as trainers also seem to have perceived the communication as unidirectional. This also implied that the curriculum developers were not able to thoroughly inquire into how teachers would use the new curriculum in school. The following account reveals that, being limited to communicating the curriculum without insights into teachers' practice, Prof. Aydın only perceived a difference between "new" and "veteran" teachers:

> Novelty is an advantage for new teachers. they can understand better what you mean. the veteran teachers for example developed a resistance to the change saying that are you bringing new tricks to old dogs, we used to do this also like that and we used to do it well. it was hard to break this resistance. they developed many mechanisms in this sense. for example there was a resistance mechanism which I called 'the we already know this syndrome.' whatever you say, they say we knew this. this is actually a cognitive bias.

Whereas the young teachers seem intellectually able to "understand" the new curriculum, the older teachers were described as prejudiced in a certain way: Rather than objecting to the new curriculum, they supposedly ignored its novel character. This is perceived as a "resistance" which the curriculum developer intended to "break." At the same time, this attitude of "veteran" teachers is not presented as a valid claim, based on their professional experience, but as an intellectual deficiency, and thus delegitimized as a "cognitive bias."[16]

3. When it became clear that it was impossible to inform all primary school teachers about the new curriculum through face-to-face communication, let alone to thoroughly train them, it was decided to publish teacher manuals. Prof. Dr. Kaya, a commission leader, narrated this process as follows:

> We understood that we cannot reach teachers //mhm// do you know what I mean as concerns education (1) then we said that however this is a new thing so there shall be a new thing for teachers (.) a book like a guide (.) guide (1) [. . .] it was actually inherent in the structure of this system //mhm// there was a debate on whether to give it before or after the training since we could not organize training we said before the training let's prepare a book (1) we anyway could recommend that to our teachers but we could not do anything else in terms of training.

The commission leader here maintained that the teacher manuals were developed when they "understood" that they could not "reach teachers" in terms of "education," that is, in terms of a more thorough training.[17] However, there is also other evidence that the idea to publish teacher guidebooks, previously unknown in the Turkish educational sector, was introduced by international consultants of the SBEP of the European Commission. These manuals, which not only gave very detailed descriptions and advice for each lesson (as we mentioned in chapters 4 and 5) but also provided information about the teaching approach of the new curriculum, were intended to bridge the gap between the developers of the curriculum and its formal rules and those who are seen by the commission leader as its "users" (as he said later), that is, as the teachers who only apply it (and thus apply the practicing of these rules).[18] However, these teacher manuals considerably limited the degree of freedom for individual teachers who used them. Quite contrary to the constructivist teaching approach, the teacher manuals virtually defined teachers' behavior.

Involvement of the Educational Administration

Although the bureaucrats in the province and district directorates of education, as well as the school principals, were informed about the new curriculum, their respective knowledge remained cursory. As an interview with Mr. Özkan (a school inspector whose task was to guide and control teachers in a province where the new curriculum was piloted) indicates, such administrative personnel were not especially interested in the curriculum change:

> now they [the directors of the province and the district directorates for education; the authors] used to say to me you exhaust us very much

(1) //mhm// well my brother your school (1) your province (1) was chosen by the ministry as a pilot (1) Turkey will take a shape according to the conclusions you draw so we have to get exhausted a little bit (3) I take him by force (1) //mhm// this district director of national education (2) did not understand that anyway (2).

According to the inspector's perspective, the local education administrators (the "district education director") neither saw themselves as responsible for piloting the new curriculum nor "understood" the intention of the curriculum developers. This is in agreement with the expert interviews we have conducted with provincial and district education administrators both in Dalen and in Istanbul: They were not intensively involved in putting the new curriculum into practice. However, this may not solely relate to administrators' reluctance to concern themselves with instruction practice; seemingly, the curriculum developers were not eager to let the provincial and district administrations participate in the curriculum change as well. For this reason, the new curriculum did not become institutionalized among education administrators on the local level. Even the principals of the schools of our sample, as our analyses in chapter 5 reveal, were not very interested in the new curriculum; if at all, they were concerned with the equipment necessary for practicing this curriculum or with effects that might be directly perceived by the principal (such as the voices of pupils being heard in school corridors, instead of teachers' voices). Among them, hence, the institutionalization of the new curriculum was also very limited.

The Practice of Piloting: Mixture of the Old and the New

As mentioned earlier, Ziya Selçuk and his colleagues were given 1 year to pilot the curriculum in selected schools of six provinces during the 2004/2005 school year. For this endeavor, the curriculum developers had to cooperate with school inspectors and teachers of the respective provinces. Inspector Özkan, who supervised a piloting province, had taken part in a 2-week seminar, of which he gave us the following account:

They said to me we know the theory of this job but we do not practice it (1) yes I have graduated from some faculties but I have actually graduated from the teacher school and I am the last graduate (1) //mhm// we this in the school our teacher, our teacher for professional courses Mehmet Ali Türk (1) and another teacher taught this very well (1) they said what will we do I said my colleague let's do like this (2) you provide us with the theoretical parts (2) we see at what is this what is happening and such (2) I go and apply this in my region (2) and bring you the written results (1) I went (2) and applied it in my region (2).

In this account it is documented that the inspector did not perceive the seminar as an occasion in which he should learn something new. Rather, he views himself as a stakeholder who is distinguished by his education in a "teacher school," that is, in a vocational high school in which teacher candidates had been practically trained before teacher education was transferred to universities in 1982 (see section 2.2). On one hand, he does not object to the new curriculum but evidently is eager to take part in the process of curriculum change; on the other hand, it is documented that he takes the new curriculum as something that he can easily apply on the basis of his practical teacher education, which he clearly separates from "the theory of this job." Together with the fact that Mr. Özkan, who had previously worked as a teacher for many years, highlighted his graduation from a teacher school, this account indicates that he perceives the new curriculum as something that does not need to be *understood,* but something that must be put into practice instead; that is, as a problem that he can tackle with his existing knowledge (both theoretical and practical) rooted not least in his training and experience with the old curriculum of 1968. Indeed, to develop examples for practicing the new curriculum in school the inspector then chose teachers who were also "raised with the curriculum of 1968" and who "had captured the spirit of this work." Evidently, rather than trying to understand the 'spirit' of the new curriculum, Mr. Özkan relied on a broad and experience-based understanding of teaching ("work") as such. Within this cooperation with teachers from the generationally embossed organizational milieu of experience-based lesson designers (see section 4.2), this inspector also likened the new curriculum to the old one:

> We after studying for 30 years 20 years derived something belonging to us (1) here to me one of the good aspects of those the similar sides there is teamwork group work in both curricula.

In this quote he referred to "something belonging to us," which he himself had developed. One example of this experience-based instruction practice for which the old curriculum gave broad leeway is the "group work" which the inspector also welcomed within the new curriculum. By doing so he created a synthesis of the teaching approach, on one hand of the older generation of teachers, and on the other of the organizational milieu of curriculum developers, who saw this older generation as the most problematic one.[19]

Inspector Özkan's case indicates that during the piloting process, even before it had been put into practice by individual teachers, the new curriculum may have been filtered according to the teaching approach of the organizational milieu of experience-based lesson designers, rooted in the curriculum of 1968. This inspector continuously shared his work with the curriculum developers and even caused changes in the curriculum, as well as in textbooks. Furthermore, he wrote a book on alphabetization and prepared teaching material as well as mock tests according to the new curriculum. In this sense, he was very influential in substantiating the new curriculum 'on the ground.'

Institutionalization of a Partially Mutated New Curriculum

Originally, the new curriculum had been the relatively homogeneous product of an organizational milieu of like-minded academics and had radically adopted a constructivist teaching approach, combined with the multiple intelligence theory. However, when the curriculum had to be substantiated by developing teaching material and when it was to be presented to teachers, the original developers had to go into cooperation with ministerial bureaucrats as well as educational administrators, school inspectors, and teachers on the local level who re-interpreted and gave sense to the formal rules of the new curriculum from their respective viewpoints (for example, from the outlook of their professional generation). Whereas the academic milieu of curriculum developers perceived this reinterpretation as "resistance" or distortion, the administrators we interviewed did not display the same attitude. Rather, the new curriculum was embedded and incorporated into their existing teaching experience and approach. The perspective of curriculum developers on this process is well captured by commission leader Prof. Kaya, who likened the curriculum to an orphan:

> those coming afterwards too (1) they made some changes this and that that is those that were criticized very much but (1) this looks like very much whether it is very true I don't know but (1) I am having a baby I as mother or you that baby you want someone else to raise that baby // mhm// I mean can she/he give the love, the feelings of a real mother (1) whoever it is, whatever is it.

Referring to the "changes" made after his own input, the metaphor of a "baby" who is "raised" by "someone else" gives him the opportunity to paint a powerful picture of how the new curriculum mutated and was neglected after it had been taken from his hands. The commission leader here alluded to an inevitable situation, for which he does not blame anyone. Indeed, Prof. Kaya is sure that even this orphan conserved his "essence," saying, "Because the basis of the system was not played with, this baby grew without loosing its essence." Despite his skeptic attitude toward the ministry's bureaucrats and toward his successors, this commission leader hence was sure that the curriculum endured.

Closure of a Window of Opportunity for Change

While Mr. Selçuk, with the political support of the minister and the financial sponsorship of the European Commission, had succeeded in pushing through the new curricula for grades 1–8 and in initiating their implementation in schools (including the provision of instruction material), he admitted to having failed to organize a more comprehensive transformation of the educational sector. When he understood that the Ministry of National Education and other bureaucratic and political institutions would not allow him to change teacher education and the funding system for schools, he resigned from his presidency at the Board of Education in May 2006, only to be followed by İrfan Erdoğan, a professor who had previously not hidden his discontent with the new curriculum (see Erdoğan, 2005). The commission leaders stepped down as well; as one of them told us, "we weren't convinced that what we had achieved would be appreciated and continued."

The ending of this educational reform period coincided with a temporary slowing-down of political reforms in the country.[20] Whereas until 2006 the JDP, against the resistance of the military, bureaucracy, and judiciary, had pushed through some important laws toward democratization (such as according some rights to minorities), with ever-improving election results it began to install its own authoritarian rule. The acclaim the party had received from liberals (whom it had attempted to include within its own ranks, a result of which was the appointment of Erkan Mumcu as minister of education) and even leftists in its early years in power turned into disappointment and criticism.[21] The window of opportunity that had been widely opened to a certain community of education scientists was closed again.[22]

The appointment of Prof. Erdoğan as the new president of the Board of Education was perceived by some NGOs as the end of the reform. Indeed, Mr. Erdoğan, a renowned critic of the new curriculum (see Erdoğan, 2005) first tried to constitute a group of academics who were to change the new curriculum again. As he stated in our interview, he organized a 2-day "workshop" that turned out to be unsuccessful, producing nothing "worthwhile" and no "contribution" whatsoever. Upon this disappointment the new president of the Board of Education started to embrace the new curriculum developed by his predecessor and tried to "put it in order," as he coined it. Without changing the essential approach of the new curriculum, he linked it to other components of the educational sector, such as the official student evaluation criteria or the standardized exams.

Although the organizational milieu around Ziya Selçuk was not able to continue its work on the new curriculum, it was apparently not possible to trim the curriculum change; as the curriculum commission leader Mr. Kaya maintained, this "baby" did not loose its "essence." The sustainability of the new curriculum is also manifested in the appointment of Prof. Dr. Emin Karip—once an assistant of Ziya Selçuk and a member of the organizational milieu of curriculum developers—as the president of the Board of Education, from 2011 until the day these lines were written.

The Partial and Mutated Institutionalization of the New Curriculum

Whereas the development of the new curriculum by a small organizational milieu of like-minded academics rendered it radical and homogeneous in its teaching approach and, hence, led to a transformative change of the formal rules of school organizations, this strength turned into weakness as soon as the new curriculum had to be announced to the public and had to be substantialized within the educational sector. In other words, the new curriculum could be organized—that is, formulated as a set of formal rules—by a small group of curriculum developers, but when it then needed to be institutionalized, the process needed to include a broad range of actors with heterogeneous ideas and approaches to education.

To win over the public, Minister Hüseyin Çelik and President of the Board of Education Ziya Selçuk chose to underpin the social change Turkey had undergone and which rendered the old curriculum outdated. Thus legitimizing the need for a new curriculum, these protagonists only in passing mentioned its new teaching approach (constructivism; the multiple intelligence theory was not mentioned whatsoever). Although the public was informed that there was a new curriculum in primary schools, its teaching approach was not made a major issue of discussion—and subsequently no public debate on teaching emerged. In this sense, the new curriculum was only weakly institutionalized in society.

Regarding the educational sector, the new curriculum had to be substantialized by developing teaching material and by linking it to teachers' instruction practice. The teaching material, as we have seen, was produced in a cooperative endeavor between the original curriculum developers and other units of the ministry which were not under the developers' control. In this sense, the teaching material already did not fully reflect the pristine ideas of the curriculum change, but synthesized it with the various teaching approaches entertained within ministerial units. As much as this teaching material then helped to institutionalize the new curriculum, the curriculum had already mutated and was embedded in the existing approaches of the ministry.

Given the limited resources for training all primary school teachers, and given their distrust in other governmental units and local education administrations, the curriculum developers chose to inform teachers in the provinces of the country by giving ex-cathedra lectures themselves. While this strategy ensured that the teachers were informed about the curriculum in an undistorted way, the problems and opportunities they would encounter when putting the curriculum into practice were not taken into account. Rather than training, this was an information campaign reaching out to a huge number of teachers. However, this campaign left teachers unaided when they went back to their schools and tried to practice the new curriculum; hence, it gave broad leeway for instructional practices according to the teaching orientations of the respective teachers' organizational milieus (chapter 4) and to the educational expectations of the schools' dominant social milieus (chapter 5).

Where the new curriculum—during the pilot year—was transferred to individual schools with the assistance of ministerial inspectors, this implied that those with teaching experience according to the old curriculum of 1968 were included in its substantialization. As we have shown, the result of this was a synthesis of the new curriculum with the teaching experience based on the old curriculum. In other words, as much as teachers and inspectors of the generation of experience-based lesson designers (see section 4.2) participated in substantializing the new curriculum (by giving feedback and developing teaching material), the new curriculum was synthesized with the previously valid instruction practice.

Thus, the institutionalization of the new curriculum was partial in that its teaching approach was neither intensively discussed with the public nor with local education administrations, which were only informed about the new curriculum in general but scarcely notified about its constructivist character. The new curriculum was certainly institutionalized as far as teachers and school inspectors were concerned, but this institutionalization was realized at the expense of the radical and transformative change envisaged by its original developers. Hence, to a certain degree, it was a mutated curriculum, already linked to the teaching orientations and professional experience of experienced teachers; that is, to the "historical curriculum" (Cuban, 1992, p. 223) that was institutionalized within the educational sector, thus, muting the transformative character of this change.

6.2   The Informal Institutionalization of Standardized Tests

Whereas the new curriculum was organized as a formal rule of the primary school and only subsequently institutionalized, the standardized entrance exams for high schools—although they formally regulate the career of pupils—are not part of the formal rules that organize primary school. Additionally, there are even by-laws that forbid the use of teaching material for exam preparation in the classroom.[23] Nevertheless, test success turned out to be important for all primary schools of our sample, and in specific cases such as in Karanfil school, dominated by an urban poor milieu, test preparation was even important in instruction itself. Evidently, there are competing and at times even contradicting institutional expectations which the schools must handle.

In this section we inquire into how the standardized entrance exams for high schools have become an institutionalized expectation both within society and among public primary schools. In contrast to the new curriculum, which was only scarcely discussed with the public, the entrance exams are a continuous public issue that is closely followed by the media. This media coverage reflects a social demand: As we showed in previous chapters, success in the entrance exams is decisive for the individual pupil's educational career (see "Success in Tests as a Public Expectation"). While these educational careers of individual pupils are shaped according to formal rules, the competition among primary schools, districts, and provinces (which results in a ranking as to where the pupils with highest entrance exams scores are educated) is only informally embedded in the educational sector. However, as we see in "Test Results and Competition Among Public Schools" further on, this informal competition is very effective.

Success in Tests as a Public Expectation

In section 2.3 we highlighted that following the university entrance exams, which had been organized since 1974, access to high schools started to be regulated by centralized tests in the 1990s. The quality and prestige of high schools has varied considerably and these variations have even been promoted by the ministry of education, which introduced different types of high schools, ranging from ordinary ones to the prestigious "Science" and "Anatolian" high schools. The informal ranking among different types of high schools is evident in the fact that, between 2003 and 2011, 85.84% of the most successful 1% of students on entrance exams chose science-focused or highly estimated 'Anatolian' lyceum types of high schools that between 1990 and 2010 catered to only 7.05% of all students. The remainder of the pupils predominantly attended normal general and vocational high schools (see MEB, 2012, pp. 12–15).

This competition between pupils who wish to attend a prestigious high school and who have the opportunity to choose between different high schools turns the centralized and standardized entrance exam (whose results are not the only factor for getting accepted in a high school, but are the most important) into an important threshold within the educational career. In this sense, the high school entrance exam is formally organized and pupils are subjected to it by official rules.

This exam, however, is also an important public issue. Some newspapers publish pages or supplements which are solely or predominantly concerned with such centralized exams, offering practical information for their readers.[24] Every year, around the time when this exam takes place, newspapers report which schools' and which districts' pupils have turned out to have the best scores. The newspaper Hürriyet, for example, identified the three "most" and "least successful" primary schools of each district in Istanbul. Table 6.1 provides an example of how this newspaper presented these results for the district of Bakırköy.

Additionally, Turkish newspapers report the approximate scores needed for entry into the most prestigious schools.[25] For less known schools and for more technical information on each province, there are also specialized sites on the Internet.[26]

As we indicated in section 2.3, a growing number of pupils are trained for the entrance exams in private instruction centers ("dershane"), amounting

Table 6.1 The "most" and "least successful" schools in the district
of Bakırköy according to the Hürriyet newspaper

BAKIRKÖY

Name of the school	Number of students	Average points in secondary school placement
Most successful schools		
Private Taş	55	446.399
Florya Final	44	427.509
Bakırköy Fatih	42	421.448
Least successful schools		
İbni Sina	105	319.858
Şenlikköy İlköğretim	115	321.158
Pilot Cengiz Topel	103	321.321

Source: http://fotogaleri.hurriyet.com.tr/galeridetay/25451/2/7/istanbulda-sbsde-basarili-ve-basarisiz-okullar (retrieved January 1, 2014).

to 1,174,000 in 2009 (Özoğlu, 2011, p. 7). According to a survey-based research among 3870 pupils of grades 6–8 and 1895 parents, TED (2010) reached even higher figures, concluding that 50% of sixth-graders, 57% of seventh-graders, and 71% of eighth-graders attended private preparatory courses (TED, 2010, p. 40). In the months prior to the entrance exam, many pupils go on a sick leave from primary school to prepare. In this survey, 14% of sixth-graders, 25% of seventh-graders, and 42% of eighth-graders stated that they had either skipped school or obtained a sick certificate to prepare for the high school tests (TED, 2010, p. 39).

The private instruction centers, which are organized through four lobby associations, have developed their own teaching material and methods whose only goal is to qualify pupils to answer as many multiple-choice questions correctly, as quickly as possible. To this purpose they have transferred the respective curricula into multiple-choice questions and published a broad range of "source books" with which the pupils can prepare for the tests and which, as we showed in chapters 4 and 5, are sometimes also used in the classroom.[27] There is, to be sure, a fierce competition among private instruction centers. With the inscription fees (ranging from 400 to 2400 USD per year; see Tansel & Bircan, 2008, p. 25) as one competitive parameter, the centers first of all advertise their students' success in the entrance exams. During summer, when results from the previous central exams have been published and new students enroll for the next school year, one often comes across advertisements in television and newspapers as well as on huge banner ads on the centers' walls.

The empirical data presented here do not conclusively unfold that the centralized and standardized entrance exams for high schools have become an institutionalized expectation in Turkey. Such an analysis would demand a far broader empirical basis and more thorough interpretation. However, even the few insights into newspapers' discourse on the exams as well as into the ranking of high schools and the prospering of private instruction centers strongly indicate that the standardized entrance exams for high schools are an institutionalized expectation in Turkish society, as far as education is concerned. In the next section we reveal that this institutionalized expectation is not confined to society in general (and to private instruction centers), but also entrenched into public primary schools and their administration.

Test Results and Competition Among Public Schools

The importance of test results for the schools of our sample was, first of all, underpinned by the principals we interviewed. Whereas only some of them endorsed the new curriculum (the principal of Karanfil school particularly saw it as a burden), all principals highlighted the importance of their pupils' success in the high school entrance exams. Even the schools that most evidently did not prepare their pupils for these exams (because as members of middle-class milieus they were sent to private instruction centers by their parents) perceived and presented success in these exams as an asset of their own organization (see chapter 5). Whereas only some schools in the country publicly advertise such successes on their websites, it must be assumed that it is well known, in society, which schools' pupils are successful in the exams and which are not; the ranking of schools reported in the Hürriyet newspaper (see "Success in Tests as a Public Expectation") already alluded to this.

The districts' and provinces' directorates of education, as a standard, publish their position in the respective ranking on their websites. On the left bottom of these websites one finds a column titled "province statistics" or "district statistics," with information on the number of schools, teachers, and pupils in the district and, in the second row, the position of the district in the entrance exam ranking of the province or of the province in the country.[28] The entrance exam ranking has become a palpable and important parameter of the competition not only between schools but also between district and provincial directorates of education. Whereas for the individual schools the position in this ranking may be seen as an important information for parents who have to choose a facility for their children (and, if they do not live in the countryside and if they can afford transportation, may choose among several schools), the average ranking of the districts or provinces does not seem to be an information directed at parents and future pupils; rather, it is part of the internal communication and competition between different educational organizations.

This competition is also alluded to in the strategic plans each district and province directorate has to write and publish periodically. In the strategic plan of the Istanbul province directorate it is written that "in addition to the evaluation works within the school and class in to assess and develop the academic success of pupils, the SBS [high school entrance exam; the authors] and ÖSS [university entrance exam; the authors] which have the aim to allocate to the upper education, give an idea of the academic success of the pupils" (Istanbul MEB, n.d., p. 30). Accordingly, one of five different performance indicators for the strategic goal of improving the success of pupils is the "mean result of the school, differentiated in classes, in the high school entrance exam" (Istanbul MEB, n.d., p. 68). Although in the strategic plan the exam results appear as one of several equally important performance indicators, a regulation of the provincial directorate which foresees how the performance of district directorates should be evaluated accords the directorate's results in centralized tests 34.8% of the points given to the district's schools, whereas the other five criteria, combined, only receive 65.2% (MEB, 2012, p. 17). The district directorates receive such performance points for their position within the provincial ranking, differentiated in the number of pupils who entered the exam, those who failed, and the average success of the district within the province (MEB, 2012, p. 18).

This emphasis on the standardized exam results is also reflected in the strategic plans of district education directorates. The strategic plan of the "Enver" district in Istanbul (where we have studied the Karanfil school in the squatter neighborhood) states that the district does not occupy the position it desired in the provincial exam ranking; therefore, it envisages to assist all those children who are not enrolled in private instruction centers. Furthermore, the plan states that all exams of this kind should be analyzed by the branch teacher commission, and that each year new goals should be defined by all teachers of the school.[29] It is striking that the strategic plan of the middle-class "Tahsin" district in Istanbul only states that it occupies one of the best positions in the province's high school entrance exam ranking. In its strategic goals, however, these exams are not even mentioned, while ample space is given to goals connected to the new curriculum.

In the strategic plan of the province of "Dalen," we find similar provisions under the title "Improving the academic success of pupils," which looks to increase the number of pupils who find access to a high school and to improve the position of the province in the country-wide high school entrance exam ranking. The strategic plan of the "Tuzlu" district then provides detailed provisions regarding how much the average high school entrance exam results should be improved over the years and how this should be accomplished.

The strategic plans analyzed here reveal not only that the provinces and districts inform about their position in the high school entrance exam ranking on their website, but also that this ranking is the medium through which a fierce competition between provinces and between districts takes place. Interestingly, we did not find any reference of the kind (to the high school entrance exams) in the strategic plan of the ministry itself (see MEB, 2009). On the local level, however, this competition extends to the individual schools. The school principals we have interviewed are more than just proud or disappointed of their school's position in the district ranking—the principal of Karanfil school even reported how this competition was fueled by the district directorate:

> In the district meeting of principals on the one side it is mentioned that children are not race horses (1) and their frequent participation in social and cultural tours ((a voice coming from his throat)) (1) or learning by researching through projects, at the *same* meeting after an hour half an hour forty-five minutes the list of success evaluation exams organized throughout the district is being- Karanfil Primary School, your children are very bad in the high school entrance exam, (.) why is this so (1) // mhm// eee for another school you are superb your children answered such a number of questions (1) mmm which one is that now shall we keep the children racing (1) or shall we extend this over a period of time and I mean make kids relaxed mmm and foster their research and self development I mean, @which one@ there may emerge different things even in the same meeting.

In one of the regular conferences in the district directorate of "Enver," the principals were asked to both foster out-of-classroom activities like "social and cultural tours" and to improve their position in the exam ranking. In the principal's account it is also documented that, on one hand, it is a matter of course that the principals and their schools may be evaluated according to these exams ("your children are very bad in the high school entrance exam"), and that, on the other hand, this evaluation is not linked to any sanction mechanism. Similarly, we showed in chapter 5 that teachers in the school are evaluated according to their class' position in the school's ranking, but face neither material sanctions nor rewards. The competition, fierce and important as it is, is fueled and fought on a symbolic level.

However, even if this competition remains on the symbolic level, mean results in the high school entrance exams are the most important criterion for this race between schools, districts, and provinces, which boosts and reproduces the importance given to these standardized exams. In addition to the public attention given to these exams and their institutionalization within society (see "Success in Tests as a Public Expectation" in this chapter), the educational sector itself, and most importantly, the educational administrations of districts and provinces, thus institutionalize the exams by elevating them to the post of most important performance indicators. Here, we see that what at first glance only seems to be the "technical output" of school organizations (that is, the exam results) is also "socially defined" (Meyer & Rowan, 1977, p. 354).

6.3   The Competitive Combination of Loosely and Tightly Coupled Institutions

As we have shown in this chapter, the new curriculum and the high school entrance exam are more than just issues taken into account and tackled by teachers, principals, parents and pupils of the schools we analyzed in chapters 4 and 5; they are, albeit to different extents, institutionalized in the educational sector and in society in general. Although the curriculum developers aimed at substantializing and disseminating the new curriculum to make the public—and, more importantly, the teachers—aware of its break with the old behavioristic curriculum, the institutionalization of the new curriculum was not only threatened by the continuing efficacy of the behavioristic approach, but far more by the standardized exam which pupils need to pass to find access to a (prestigious) high school. As we have seen, this exam is at least equally institutionalized in the educational sector and in society, although it is not forced upon primary schools and educational administrations by by-laws (that is, by formal rules). The new curriculum, in contrast, although formulated as a set of formal rules, has only been partially institutionalized. Moreover, the curriculum mutated during this process of practical substantiation and institutionalization; this means that on the level of primary schools and educational administrations, we are concerned with the competition between two institutions: one enforced on these organizations as a set of formal rules; the other only informally established as a criterion with which educational success is measured.

For all primary schools investigated in this volume, both the new curriculum and the exam results were important institutions of their environment. However, in accordance with the assumptions of New Institutionalism, one of them was at times only loosely coupled to the instruction practically given in the schools, while the other was tightly coupled. In his seminal work on "loose" and "tight coupling," Weick (1976) already assumed that "a tight coupling in one part of the system can occur only if there is loose coupling in another part of the system" (p. 10). Therefore, he spoke of a "distribution of tight and loosely coupled systems within any organization" (p. 11) and proposed to analyze these "patterns" (p. 16).

In the urban middle-class schools the curriculum and test preparation were not perceived as contradicting institutions because pupils were prepared for the high school entrance exams in private instruction centers. This led to a tight coupling of instruction to the curriculum, whereas instruction was only loosely coupled to test preparation. In the poor urban school we found a different pattern, in which the curriculum and test results are perceived as contradicting institutions because pupils are not prepared for tests outside of school. In this case, upon the pressure by parents and due to the teaching orientation of the younger professional generation, instruction is tightly coupled to test preparation and only loosely coupled to the curriculum; that is, the loose coupling of the curriculum allows for the tight coupling of test preparation. In the rural schools the curriculum and test preparation were not perceived as contradicting institutions, although test preparation was not provided by private instruction centers and although the average test results of the schools were not high. Given the low degree of competition among schools and the relatively low importance parents give to education in terms of social reproduction, both the curriculum and the tests were loosely coupled to instruction. Here, instruction was predominantly structured according to the different organizational milieus of teachers and their generational affiliation.

These empirical results of our investigation reveal that the loose coupling of one institution (for example, the loose coupling of tests) does not inevitably imply that the other institution is tightly coupled to instruction. In other words, Weick's assumption that "tight couplings in one place imply loose couplings elsewhere" (Weick, 1976, p. 10) does not hold true for the opposite direction. Additionally—and evidently—the "trend toward test-based accountability systems" (Rowan, 2006, p. 22) manifested in the informal institutionalization of high school entrance exam results as a performance criterion for teachers, schools, district and province directorates does not directly lead to "a shift to more tightly coupled and narrowly controlled practices in organizations that were once exemplars of 'loose coupling'" (Rowan, 2006, p. 2). First of all, the instructional practices of the educational organizations we scrutinized were—tightly or loosely—coupled to two possibly contradicting institutions, the tests in the urban schools competing with the curriculum. Secondly, the accountability system informally institutionalized in the Turkish educational sector (at least as far as provincial and district directorates as well as public schools are concerned) takes effect only in the urban contexts where there is a competition between schools. In the countryside, where such an informal accountability system certainly exists, such system does not qualify for fueling the fierce competition to which the urban schools are subjected.

In view of the three patterns in which the new curriculum and the centralized and standardized exams are coupled to school instruction (from the urban middle-class schools to the poor urban school and the rural ones), we may draw the following conclusions:

1. Institutionalized expectations which are also defined as formal rules imposed on the school organizations (for example, the new curriculum) are not necessarily more tightly coupled to instruction than institutionalized expectations that are only informal (for example, the test results).
2. The opportunities for controlling the organization's practices, if the organization has taken into account any institutional expectation, are also decisive. Although the formal rules of the educational organization forbid its members to teach in a way that disregards the curriculum (such as by using "source books" from private instruction centers), the organization has only limited means to control the compliance with

these rules, since the control is based on self-reporting (the teachers themselves note the content of their instruction). Conversely, control can be easily exerted if the pupils of a class, school, district, or province have been well prepared for the standardized entrance exams, as their results are published in a detailed and comparative way. Moreover, the quantitative nature of exam results renders their comparison over years and among organizations very easy. However, there are only symbolic sanction mechanisms in place for educational organizations whose pupils show poor exam results.

3. As far as the three patterns of loose and tight coupling detected in the schools of our sample are concerned, it is empirically evident that each pattern is strongly connected with the situatedness of the respective school; that is, whether school instruction is loosely coupled to the curriculum or to the standardized exams (or even to both) is determined by the school's own resources, as well as by its dominant organizational and social milieus and their respective resources. Therefore, although both the new curriculum and the standardized entrance exam for high schools are institutionalized in society and in the educational sector, their relevance for practical instruction is mediated and structured by the resources and milieus of each school.

Notes

1　The reader may, however, compare the messages to our own analysis of the curriculum development process and its summary in section 3.5.

2　Unfortunately, Çelik's press communique could not be found on the Internet. However, the following quotes are confirmed by articles in the Hürriyet (http://arama. hurriyet.com.tr/arsivnews.aspx?id=248657) and the Radikal (see http://www.radikal. com.tr/haber.php?haberno=124730) newspapers on the August 12 and 11, 2004, and by a press bulletin of the ministry issued on August 12, 2004 (see http://www.meb. gov.tr/haberler/haberayrinti.asp?ID=5821) (retrieved June 1, 2015).

3　Ergüder: Her yönüyle yeni müfredat (1). Radikal, 26.8.04. http://www.radikal.com. tr/haber.php?haberno=126079 (retrieved June 1, 2015). A similar justification was given by Ziya Selçuk in his expert interview (see section 3.2).

4　Italics ours. http://arama.hurriyet.com.tr/arsivnews.aspx?id=248657 (retrieved June 1, 2015).

5　Ergüder: Her yönüyle yeni müfredat (1). Radikal, 26.8.04. http://www.radikal.com. tr/haber.php?haberno=126079 (retrieved June 1, 2015) "biz bu meseleyi ele alırken, meseleyi parti bakış açısından ziyade, bilimsel bir açıdan gördüğümüzü ifade etmek istiyorum."

6　http://haber.gazetevatan.com/0/36887/1/Gundem#.UEhofyLN6uI (retrieved June 1, 2015).

7　See http://arama.hurriyet.com.tr/arsivnews.aspx?id=254969 (retrieved June 1, 2015).

8　http://haber.gazetevatan.com/0/36887/1/Gundem#.UEhofyLN6uI (retrieved June 1, 2015).

9　Ergüder: Her yönüyle yeni müfredat (1). Radikal, 26.8.04. http://www.radikal.com. tr/haber.php?haberno=126079 (retrieved June 1, 2015).

10 http://haber.gazetevatan.com/0/36887/1/Gundem#.UEhofyLN6uI (retrieved June 1, 2015).

11 Ergüder: Her yönüyle yeni müfredat (1). Radikal, 26.8.04. http://www.radikal.com. tr/haber.php?haberno=126079 (retrieved June 1, 2015).

12 http://arama.hurriyet.com.tr/arsivnews.aspx?id=248657 (retrieved June 1, 2015).

13 The constructivist approach was discussed intensively neither by teachers' unions nor by NGOs or in the newspapers.

14 As far as a broad investigation into the newspapers of the time revealed, the curriculum reform, apart from some news articles, was not met with much response. Particularly, the opinion-forming columnists did not address this topic in their articles very often.

15 These and the following quotes have been taken from the expert interviews with the respective actors. See the appendix for a list of the expert interviews.

16 As we showed in chapter 4, there are certain differences between younger and older teachers regarding their practical instruction that led to different attitudes toward the new curriculum, but they cannot be described in terms of as a positive versus a negative attitude toward the new curriculum; rather, they are based on the teachers' different professional and generational experiences.

17 A similar account was raised by a member of the Board of Education, who told us that the "internal training" for teachers was "not sufficient" and thus "teacher guidance books" were published with which the teacher, "when she/he entered the classroom very well knew what to do."

18 In contrast, our empirical analyses reveal that teachers not only apply the new curriculum but also may refuse it or design their own lessons based on different curricular goals and their own teaching experience. When characterizing the way teachers deal with the new curriculum, we therefore avoided the terms 'application' or 'applying.'

19 Such a synthesis was also tacitly promoted by the bureaucrats who underpinned the continuity between the old and the new curriculum. One member of the Board of Education informed us that they told ministerial bureaucrats and teachers "what the approach will bring, what the gains are (1) the reasons for this change and that it did not imply a radical break, and that ultimately specific aspects of our previous curriculum have been preserved anyway." Indeed, even Ziya Selçuk, in a journal for teachers and education bureaucrats, denied that the new curriculum implied a radical break and underscored that the curriculum developers had "very much cared about the accumulation of previous [curriculum; the authors] work" (Karaçalı, 2004). There had also been times when the curriculum developers underscored the radical character of their endeavor to make stakeholders aware of it. Apparently, the radicality of the new approach was *either* disguised *or* underpinned according to the respective audience.

20 Beginning in 2011, the JDP government, equipped with ever-increasing seats in parliament, started further reforms by restructuring the primary and secondary school system as such and changing the central structure of the MoNE. This second period of education reform, however, is out of the scope of this volume.

21 The following articles in leftist Internet outlets both depict the disappointment of the liberals and mirror different leftist positions very well: http://haber.sol.org.tr/medya/bir-donem-birbirimizi-kullandik-ama-haberi-38406 (retrieved March 27, 2013) and http://www.turksolu.org/175/ozsoy175.htm (retrieved March 27, 2013).

22 Like some other interview partners, a ministerial inspector stated that the government had originally included Minister Erkan Mumcu as well as Ziya Selçuk to solve the problems the Justice and Development Party faced in the beginning. When these

problems with the bureaucracy and the president of the republic had been solved, Mumcu and Selçuk were not needed anymore and hence crowded out of the ministry.

23 The "by-law on schoolbooks and educational devices" stipulates that pupils may only be required to buy books and material approved by the ministry.

24 See, for example, the respective websites of three newspapers with the highest sales volume: http://sinav.zaman.com.tr/, http://www.hurriyet.com.tr/egitim/, http://www.sabah.com.tr/Egitim (retrieved January 2, 2014).

25 See, for example, http://www.hurriyet.com.tr/gundem/24465911.asp; http://www.sabah.com.tr/Egitim/2013/07/17/sbs-tercihinde-puan-degil-sira-onemli; http://www.sabah.com.tr/Yasam/2011/08/02/kolejlerin-taban-puanlari-aciklandi (retrieved January 2, 2014).

26 See, for example, http://www.okulsecim.com/ (retrieved January 2, 2014).

27 In 2008 the centralized exams were adapted to the new curriculum with regard to content, Furthermore, the ministry tried to reduce enrollment in private instruction centers by dividing the high school entrance exam, previously held at the end of grade 8, into three: one after each school year from grades 6 to 8, and by including school grades as a relevant part of the exam. When it turned out that upon this measure the number of private instruction centers actually grew and its pupils became ever younger, the ministry returned to the single exam format (at the end of grade 8). Ultimately, it became evident that the private instruction centers always adapted their courses to the respective conditions, and thus could survive.

28 See, for example, the following websites: http://amasya.meb.gov.tr/, http://istanbul.meb.gov.tr/, http://tuzla.meb.gov.tr/ (retrieved January 2, 2014).

29 Due to the anonymization of the location of our field research, this and the following statements, for which the respective strategic plans of the districts and the province of Dalen have been used, are left without any reference.

References

Berger, P. L., & Luckmann, T. (1991). *The social construction of reality*. London: Penguin.

Cuban, L. (1992). Curriculum stability and change. In P. W. Jackson (Ed.), *Handbook of research on curriculum* (pp. 216–247). New York: Macmillan.

Erdoğan, İ. (2005). Milli Eğitim Bakanlığı'nın Yeni Müfredat Çalışmaları. *Özel Okullar Birliği Bülteni*. Retrieved January 8, 2013, from http://www.irfanerdogan.com.tr/index.php? ıoption=com_content&view=article&id=102:milli-egitim-bakanliginin-yeni-mufredat-calismalari&catid=34:ana-sayfa&Itemid=148

Istanbul MEB (T.C. İstanbul Valiliği İl Milli Eğitim Müdürlüğü). (2012). *İlçe Milli Eğitim Müdürlükleri Performans Değerlendirme Kriterleri*. Istanbul: Author.

Istanbul MEB (T.C. İstanbul Valiliği İl Milli Eğitim Müdürlüğü). (n.d.). *2010–2014 Stratejik Plan*. Istanbul: Author.

Karaçalı, A. (2004). Talim ve Terbiye Kurulu Başkanı Prof. Dr. Ziya Selçuk'la Söyleşi. *Bilim ve Aklın Aydınlığında Eğitim Dergisi*, Nos. 54–55. Retrieved October 1, 2010, from http://dhgm.meb.gov.tr/yayimlar/dergiler/Bilim_Dergisi/sayi54–55/soylesi.htm

MEB (T.C. Milli Eğitim Bakanlığı Strateji Geliştirme Başkanlığı). (2009). *2010–2014 Stratejik Plan*. Ankara: Ministry of National Education.

MEB (Milli Eğitim Bakanlığı). (2012). *İlköğretimden Ortaöğretime Ortaöğretimden Yükseköğretime Geçiş Analizi*. Ankara: Author.

Meyer, J. W., & Rowan, B. (1977). Institutionalized organizations: Formal structure as myth and ceremony. *American Journal of Sociology, 83*, 340–363.

MoNE (Ministry of National Education). (2010). *National education statistics: Formal education 2009–2010.* Ankara: Author.

Özoğlu, M. (2011). *Özel Dershaneler: Gölge Eğitim Sistemiyle Yüzleşmek.* Ankara: SETA.

Rowan, B. (2006). The new institutionalism and the study of educational organizations: Changing ideas for changing times. In H.-D. Meyer & B. Rowan (Eds.), *The new institutionalism in education* (pp. 15–32). Albany: SUNY.

Tansel, A., & Bircan, F. (2008). *Private supplementary tutoring in Turkey—Recent evidence on its recent aspects* (Working Papers in Economics No. 08/02). Ankara: ERC.

TED (Türk Eğitim Derneği). (2010). *Ortaögretime ve Yükseögretime Geçis Sistemi.* Ankara: Author.

Weick, K. E. (1976). Educational organizations as loosely coupled systems. *Administrative Science Quarterly, 21,* 1–19.

7 Conclusion

Change, Education, and Society

"Modern education," as Karl Mannheim (1968) suggested, is "a living struggle, a replica, on a small scale of the conflicting purposes and tendencies which rage in society at large" (p. 138). In the change of a curriculum this struggle can be observed through a magnifying lens. It is for this reason that we analyzed the relation of education and social dynamics through a case study on the curriculum change experienced by Turkish primary education in the new millennium.

A comprehensive understanding of the curriculum needs to include the social dynamics within which the curriculum is both constituted and practiced. In the face of heterogeneous social change, which captured social groups, strata, and milieus of society to a varying degree and led them into different directions, the curriculum is an attempt to homogenize and mainstream the people who are subjected to it. This is as much the case where the validity of a curriculum is limited to a single school (Kliebard, 2002) as where it is mandatory for a whole nation. However, given the heterogeneity of society, the curriculum itself does not and cannot reflect the expectations, convictions, and taken-for-granted assumptions of all social groups and milieus. Rather, the curriculum is "part of a selective tradition, someone's selection, some group's vision of legitimate knowledge" (Apple, 1993, p. 223; see also Bourdieu & Passeron, 1990; Whitty, 1985). But even though the curriculum, as the generalized expectations of some milieu(s), is meant to mainstream an otherwise heterogeneous society, the various milieus and dynamics of society influence the curriculum as soon as it is put into classroom practice. In instruction, the curriculum is altered not only by the "organizational routines" of teachers (Spillane et al., 2011, p. 586), but—at times—also by the educational expectations of social groups whose children dominate the respective school (as our research reveals). It is in this sense that the curriculum is both constituted and practiced vis-à-vis the dynamics of society. Therefore, curriculum studies should not be confined to inquiry into education policy (for example, into the curriculum as a 'political text'); it must extend to educational practices in society and its schools (Cuban, 1992; Tyack & Tobin, 1994). Primary education allows for the broadest possible analysis of the curriculum practices' social contexts, as children from nearly all social milieus—rural or urban, poor or middle class—attend primary schools.

The present volume has sought to base its theoretical and empirical inquiries on such comprehensive understanding of curriculum change. With this end in view, we did not focus our observations and interpretations by ex-ante hypotheses, but introduced basic theoretical concepts which help us order and arrange the complex relation of education and social dynamics. The evolving frame of these basic theoretical concepts structured our empirical analysis of curriculum change in Turkish primary education. Likewise, the unanticipated empirical results of our investigation into how a new curriculum was constituted by the ministry of education and subsequently practiced in primary schools instigated us to challenge and further develop our basic theoretical frame. Hence, the case study of curriculum change in Turkey has been more than an opportunity to demonstrate the usefulness of our general concepts; it has also been valuable for further developing or sharpening some of those concepts in the first place. Of course, such an ambitious endeavor cannot work without a thorough methodological basis that both steers empirical inquiry and defines the place of basic theoretical concepts. This final chapter serves to comprehensively discuss our empirical results vis-à-vis their basic theoretical frame and the underlying methodology, and to highlight the broader implications of our research that carry it well beyond the confines of our case study.

7.1 Education and Social Change in Turkey

The foundations of the curriculum change that came about in the beginning of the new millennium go back as far as the 19th century, where the origins of a modern educational "sector"[1] in Turkey can be retrieved (chapter 2). In the course of the social change undergone by the Ottoman Empire since its armies started to loose wars and its territories shrank, a new educational sector emerged in the 19th century which was, albeit not country-wide, differentiated into consecutive levels (primary, secondary, and tertiary level) and which paralleled the traditional facilities of religious education that had long since constituted a—albeit basic—*religious* educational sector. The *secular* educational sector only aimed at training the staff needed for modernizing the state apparatus; however, it did not target society in general, that is, the whole population of the Ottoman Empire (Fortna, 2002; Somel, 2001). The secular educational sector, after the decline of the Ottoman Empire in World War I and the emergence of the Turkish Republic (1923), then became the starting point for the Kemalists to enlarge a country-wide *laicist* educational sector, which served not only to qualify the population of the new nation state but also to provide it with citizenship education.[2] Both qualification and citizenship education were meant to include all parts of the population into the social change (modernization) that had already captured the urban middle classes. In this educational sector, therefore, the unifying mechanism of the nation state was brought forward (Üstel, 2004). According to our analysis, the very emergence of a secular educational sector in the late Ottoman Empire, as well as the enforcement of a country-wide laicist educational sector in the Turkish Republic, were instances of transformative change in the sense of a "second-order change" that "changes the system itself" (Watzlawick et al., 1974, pp. 10–11). In contrast, until it was totally closed down in 1924, the religious educational sector only went through reproductive variations ("first-order change"; Watzlawick et al., 1974), which only altered some of its procedures and practices.

The Kemalists, successful as they were regarding the foundation of modern Turkey, only partly succeeded in unifying the people by the means of education: On one hand, not all social milieus which were supposed to change according to the requirements of a nation state could be reached (Zürcher, 2005, pp. 186–187); on the other hand, since 1945, due to ongoing social change (industrialization, the rapprochement with Western NATO countries, and growing political importance of religious-conservative milieus), the educational sector itself was internally differentiated (Günlü, 2008; Okçabol, 2005) and, hence, underwent reproductive variation in the sense of "correcting deficiencies" (Cuban, 1992, p. 218). Nevertheless, education, at least as far as primary education was concerned, had turned into a comprehensive system with which the state had access to the young population in its full breadth.

With the extension and internal differentiation of secondary education after the 1980 coup d'état, the instrument of education became even more powerful. The political dimension of education (as a means of integrating a national society) went along with the growing importance of education for social reproduction: More and more positions in the growing industry and in the service sector (although not in other parts of the economy, such as in agriculture) were assigned according to educational grades (Kepenek & Yentürk, 2007, pp. 492–493; Tansel & Bircan, 2008). The growing importance and internal differentiation of secondary education, which distinguished not only between vocational and general high schools but also according to the varying prestige of schools, also constituted an important background for the functionality of primary education. As we discuss in the following pages, the competition between the new primary school curriculum and other institutionalized expectations, most importantly the standardized entrance exams to high school, is only understandable vis-à-vis this historical background.

Change was not limited to the educational sector. Since the 1950, Turkey saw an ever growing migration from the countryside to its emerging metropolises, where 64.9% of its population (who previously used to be overwhelmingly constituted by rural peasants) lived in the year 2000 (State Institute of Statistics, n.d., p. 46). After 1980, "ever-widening income disparities" (Buğra, 2002, p. 120) also led to a further differentiation and drifting apart of social milieus. As we show in what follows, both the internal differentiation of the educational sector and the gap between social milieus heavily influenced schools and their curriculum practices.

7.2 The Making of a Curriculum

When the primary school curriculum was changed (starting in 2003), the reformers related their endeavor to social dynamics that had captured parts of—although definitely not the entire—society in different ways. Most importantly, the new curriculum referred to the developments in the economy (growing industrial and service sector) and in the social milieus (first of all, the educated middle classes) connected to them. Hence, the curriculum change was inspired and legitimated by a selective reference to social change insofar as it took into regard only certain social trajectories.

To generalize the educational expectations of specific social strata; that is, to turn the orientations and knowledge of *specific* (educated middle-class) milieus into a standard to which *all* pupils henceforth shall be subjected may, on one hand, be viewed as an illegitimate and unjust privilege for those affiliated to this social strata (Apple, 1993; Bourdieu & Passeron, 1990; Whitty, 1985). Accordingly, the new curriculum in Turkey was criticized for being individualistic, neo-liberal, and economy-minded (İnal et al., 2014; Ünder, 2012). On the other hand, however, one may argue that on the background of the growing importance of education for an ever-broader spectrum of the populace, the new curriculum was intended to provide all pupils with "powerful knowledge" (Young, 2008, p. 14) that brought the accomplishments of social change to previously unprivileged groups. It was for a reason that the *declared* goal of the ministry of education was to teach all children "critical thinking, problem solving, scientific inquiry, creative thinking, initiative, communication, use of information technologies, and the skill to nicely use the Turkish language" with the new curriculum.[3] In this sense, the curriculum was declared to provide the new generations in their entirety with competencies previously only consolidated in certain parts of society and its economy.

At this point a distinction has to be made between the espoused claims from the curriculum developers who sought for public legitimation on one hand and for the social genesis of the new curriculum on the other. Although there is enough evidence of a "misalignment" (Waks, 2007, p. 289) between the educational sector and the rest of society, and most importantly of the dissatisfaction that had grown prior to 2003 with the previous, behaviorist syllabus among a broad range of people interested or involved in education, the new curriculum for Turkish primary schools was not developed in a broad consultation process in which many different social groups, educational activists, and academics with different standpoints participated. As we revealed in chapter 3, the teaching approach adopted for the new curriculum—that is, a mélange of constructivism and "multiple intelligence" theory (Gardner, 1983)—was based only on the preferences of a specific group of academics, who did everything to defend their convictions against any substantial challenges from outside.

This group of academics was incorporated in the "Board of Education," the authority within the ministry of education that develops and licenses curricula and schoolbooks, during a chain of unlikely events that occurred after the landslide victory of the Justice and Development Party (JDP) in November 2002. This victory gave one party the power and legitimacy to start reforms in different areas without having to negotiate with competing parties. The JDP and its education minister, bereft of particular ideas for a new curriculum, then assigned the task to a professor, Ziya Selçuk, who previously had participated in discussions on new curricular approaches and had also made pioneering school experiments with constructivist and multiple intelligence curricula. Based on his organizational skills, a circle of academic friends, and the ability to express his educational ideas in the language of politics[4] (most importantly, of the JDP), Mr. Selçuk then used this "catalytic moment for policy change" (Steiner-Khamsi, 2006, p. 670).

However, the opportunities of this temporal window were hidden behind major obstacles that Mr. Selçuk would first have to overcome: He experienced what he saw as a passive resistance of bureaucrats in his own ministry, from the Higher Education Council ("YÖK") and from universities, which he could only bypass by securing a large budget from a European Commission program. Equipped with this budget—and thus freed from bureaucratic obligations—the new president of the Board of Education was able to handpick colleagues for the curriculum project, most of whom he had cooperated with for a long time. These curriculum developers were then introduced to the Board of Education as an independent "organizational milieu" (Nohl, 2014, p. 193); that is, as a group of academics who shared orientations both concerning the curricular approach and cooperation with the new government.

Up to this point, the making of a new curriculum was a process in which many actors were involved: the new government, the ministerial bureaucracy, academics, and more. Particularly in the curriculum's first steps, these actors followed diverse and sometimes even antagonist intentions. As we have seen, in the results of the 'passive resistance' by state institutions—that this resistance enabled Mr. Selçuk to independently form an organizational milieu of like-minded colleagues—such a complex change process may be seen "as a result of unintentional consequences of other processes and actions (some of which may have been 'intentional,' however, with respect to other goals)" (Altrichter, 2000, p. 2). In social science, the outcome of processes such as that of the new curriculum in Turkey is classified as "trans-intentional" (Altrichter, 2010, p. 150). If one also takes into account the practicing of the curriculum (see later), the classification of the curriculum as being beyond intentions holds true even for Ziya Selçuk himself.

Once Ziya Selçuk had formed a core team of like-minded colleagues, these collaborators built their curriculum commissions, one for each branch, thus expanding their organizational milieu within the Board of Education. Its members then authored the new curricula in strong cooperation and under the leadership of Ziya Selçuk. Although during the curriculum development process various suggestions from outside of this organizational milieu had been taken into account, these were limited to the *contents* of the curricula. In contrast, the *teaching approach* of the new curriculum, based on constructivism and the "multiple intelligence" theory, was fiercely endorsed by the organizational milieu and was never allowed to be questioned.

The fact that the new curriculum followed constructivism and the multiple intelligence approach was certainly not a matter of chance. These teaching approaches had previously been dispersed throughout the world (Altinyelken, 2011, pp. 138–141; Chen et al., 2009) which led to a certain "isomorphism" (Meyer et al., 1997, p. 152), although not to an "international education regime" (Parreira do Amaral, 2010). In fact, a growing "student-centeredness," an important prerequisite for these approaches, was identified by Bromley et al. (2011, p. 547) in a study on "533 secondary school social science textbooks from 74 countries." However, while the teaching approaches underlying the new Turkish primary school curriculum originated outside Turkey, they were certainly not borrowed for this very curriculum as a "conscious adoption" (Phillips & Ochs, 2004, p. 774); rather, during the theoretical inquiries and practical experiences within Turkey which preceded the making of the new curriculum, these approaches underwent a "process of recontextualization, 'indigenization' or local adaptation" in Turkish academia (Steiner-Khamsi & Quist, 2000, p. 275). Accordingly, when the education minister announced the curriculum to the public and underpinned that the "standards of the European Union"[5] had been taken into account, this is to be interpreted as an "externalization" which provides "legitimisation" (Schriewer, 2003, p. 276) rather than as the description of a feature of the curriculum making. However, whereas the general teaching approach for the new curriculum has certainly not been directly borrowed, the curriculum commissions occasionally made use of the assistance offered by international consultants from the European Commission for specific tasks (such as designing textbooks). Only in this limited sense "conscious borrowing" existed (Phillips & Ochs, 2004, p. 776).

7.3   Investigating a Curriculum

Different strands of research agree that formal rules adopted by organizations (such as the curriculum imposed on all Turkish primary schools by the ministry) may not be directly 'implemented' in the organizations' practices. As Westbury (2008) noted in a reserved way, "Leaders can champion their commitment to change; local authorities or teachers have the prerogative not to enact decisions or to enact them on their own terms" (p. 56). Whereas New Institutionalists here anticipate "loose coupling" (Bromley et al., 2011, p. 564) or even "decoupling" (Meyer et al., 1997, p. 155) between formal rules and organizational practices (see also Meyer & Rowan, 1977; Weick, 1976), and leave open by which factors practices are structured and in which way,[6] researchers who investigate "educational borrowing and lending" (Steiner-Khamsi, 2004) additionally analyze the adoption of formal rules by organizations as mechanisms of "re-contextualizing" (Steiner-Khamsi, 2012) (see also Dale, 1999). In this respect, they concur with scholars who view educational change as a problem of "complex multilevel systems" (Altrichter, 2010, p. 148) in which a curriculum, developed by the ministry, is always "recontextualized" in individual schools, or in other words, it is "reinterpreted and practically transformed" (Fend, 2009, p. 181).

As classroom instruction in individual schools is not necessarily tightly coupled to the formal rules of the curriculum defined by the ministry, curriculum inquiry needs to take into account the different social levels of making and practicing of a curriculum in a multilevel analysis (see Helsper et al., 2010; Nohl, 2013; Weiß & Nohl, 2012). To this end, our study did not stop at analyzing the making of the new Turkish curriculum, but also shed light on significant differences in instructional practices of a variety of schools (see later). Curriculum theory has further differentiated this distinction between the curriculum as a formal rule and as classroom practice, distinguishing between the "intended" curriculum (referring to its formal rules) and the "taught" and "learned" curricula, which are constituted in classroom practice (Cuban, 1992, pp. 222–223); the former by the organizational milieus of teachers and the latter by the social milieus of pupils and their parents.

As neither making a curriculum nor teaching and learning within its framework are practices which can be fully conceived of and explicated by the actors involved, curriculum inquiry needs methods for data gathering and interpretation which take into account aspects of practices that are trans-intentional, non-intentional, spontaneous, or habitual. Whereas for inquiring into curriculum making we have used expert interviews whose "narrative passages" (Meuser & Nagel, 2009, p. 32) expose the "operational knowledge" (p. 30) of the curriculum developers, instruction in schools has mainly been scrutinized on the basis of group discussions (Bohnsack, 2010), which served to reproduce the collective or "conjunctive" knowledge of teachers and parents (Mannheim, 1982, p. 265). Group discussions, therefore, are destined to reconstruct the collective knowledge and experience prevalent in organizational and social milieus. The data material—to which expert interviews with school principals and bureaucrats in province and district education administrations were added—was then interpreted with the Documentary Method (Bohnsack, 2014a; Mannheim, 1952), a methodology that gives special attention to the "tacit dimension" (Polanyi, 1966) of the data at hand, that is, to the "mutual implicit or intuitive understanding of the participants" (Bohnsack, 2010, p. 104). The Documentary Method does not stop at interpreting single cases (such as a single group discussion with teachers); rather, by comparing contrasting cases, typical collective "frameworks of orientation" (Bohnsack, 2010, p. 107) are identified which guide the practices of the actors under scrutiny. In this volume, we develop a "multi-dimensional typology" (Bohnsack, 2014a, p. 231) based on such comparisons, which depicts both the way the curriculum is put into practice and how these practices are socio-genetically based on dimensions such as the professional generation of teachers, the socioeconomic milieus of pupils and their parents, as well as the school's sociogeographic situatedness.

7.4 Organizational Milieus of Teachers and the Curriculum

The new curriculum was an important point of all the group discussions conducted with teachers, who explicitly positioned themselves vis-à-vis the new curriculum and, most importantly, concerning the topics stipulated by them. Because the curriculum reform was one of the first measures of the new government led by the JDP, the teachers identified the new curriculum with this controversially debated party. Accordingly, some groups of teachers who disapproved of the JDP also objected to the curriculum. Others identified themselves with the new curriculum and confirmed that they had wished for it for a long time. This finding is consistent with the assumptions of New Institutionalism (Meyer & Rowan, 1977; DiMaggio & Powell, 1983) to the extent that all teachers *discursively* took into account the new formal rules set by the ministry of education and, thereby, fostered the legitimacy of their actions. However, our interpretation of teachers' discourses on their everyday practices, both in dismissive and approving groups, reveals that these teachers' *practical orientations* were only loosely coupled to their explicit opinions of the new curriculum; that is, both groups of teachers—those who dismissed the new curriculum and those who approved of it—may bear commonalities in instructional practices. As we showed in chapter 4, these practical commonalities point to collective orientations of two different organizational milieus which are based on a set of similar "organizational routines" (Zucker, 1987, p. 456; Spillane et al., 2011, p. 586) and informal rules with which the formal rules of the organization (such as a curriculum) are put into practice. Ultimately, these "distinct constellations of pedagogical beliefs and practices" (Bidwell et al., 1997, p. 286) refer to specific profession-generational experiences.

The first organizational milieu is constituted by a generation of teachers who, based on long-standing professional experience, modify the new curriculum. All of these teachers drew from professional experience gained from 27 to 41 years to flexibly come to terms with the learning objectives and topics of the new curriculum. This commonality is not only based on the sheer length of their professional experience; rather, in the past, these teachers were professionally socialized in instructional practices that accorded the teaching staff significant freedom to design lessons on their own. The old, behavioristic curriculum only defined learning objectives and topics but did not provide detailed instruction guidelines (see Yildirim, 2003), in contrast to the new one. Hence, this organizational milieu is based on professional experience combined with a specific profession-generational affiliation.

The starting of one's career at a specific time (when the behavioristic curriculum of 1968—rather a syllabus of topics to be taught—was still valid) allowed for "a specific range of potential experience, predisposing" these teachers "for a certain characteristic mode of thought and experience, and a characteristic type of historically relevant action" (Mannheim, 1972, p. 106); that is, for a generation-typical habitus or orientation frame. Unlike *societal* generations, this *professional* generation is predominantly based on professional experience, although general social experience may reinforce a specific "tendency 'inherent in'" (p. 106) a certain professional generation. As such, this professional *generation of experience-based lesson designers* constitutes a specific organizational milieu with homologous orientations toward school instruction and classroom activities, within which teachers make sense of the formal rules of the new curriculum and put them into practice.

The contours of the first generationally bound organizational milieu became more evident when we compared the experienced teachers with newcomers who started service shortly before or after the introduction of the new curriculum. During group discussions with these young teachers, positive and negative opinions about the new curriculum were again explicitly articulated. However, beyond these explicit opinions, the experiences of a specific organizational milieu based on a generational location and the lack of professional experience were reconstructed. These young teachers made clear that they were theoretically acquainted with the teaching approach of the new curriculum. Evidently, they received their teacher training at a time during which the old curriculum was already heavily criticized for its behaviorist approach based on rote learning and teacher-centered education. Because the old curriculum was never a reference point for them, these teachers were dependent on the new curriculum and, in particular, on its detailed lesson plans and the teacher manual.

If we consider the curriculum and its practice in terms of change (Watzlawick et al., 1974), one may reasonably argue that the change from a behaviorist to a constructivist curriculum was transformative, as far as the formal rules imposed on primary schools were concerned. However, with regard to practicing the curriculum in the organizational milieu of novice teachers, they did not have to undergo such a transformation, as the new curriculum was the first in which they were trained. Likewise, the organizational milieu of 'experience-based lesson designers' did not transform, but adapted the new curriculum to its existing routines instead.

In the organizational milieu of the newcomers, however, we have identified a second point of reference. Whereas the experienced teachers developed their own maxims for what should be expected from a fourth or second grader, for example, the younger teachers worked toward curricular learning objectives and also pointed to the entrance tests for secondary education, in which pupils must score as successfully as possible. Since the

1990s, centralized exams regulated entrance to secondary education (grades 9 through 12) in Turkey. Whereas all graduates of the eighth class (then the final grade of primary school) are eligible for high school education, considerable differences in quality and prestige exist between these educational organizations, which vary from vocational and ordinary to exclusive 'Anatolian' and 'Science' high schools. Therefore, most pupils are determined to gain access to the best possible high school that they hope will provide them with the best opportunities, again, gaining highly competitive access to university education (see later). One reason the novice teachers referred to the entrance exams, organized as multiple-choice tests, is that their own biographical experiences were tightly connected to standardized tests: In their own educational and professional careers, this generation of teachers had to pass various standardized exams prior to entering university education. For this reason, they were well acquainted with the learning techniques that are important to succeed in multiple-choice tests. At the same time, they were socialized in this competitive culture and came to "see 'competition' as inevitable," as Ünal (2005, p. 9) critically wrote. The older teachers, in contrast, were never subjected to a standardized test, and experienced assessments only in the form of non-standardized exams internally organized in school.

In this sense, the teaching orientations dominant in the organizational milieu of the professional *generation of new curriculum and test preparation combiners* include two seemingly conflicting practices: closely following the guidelines of the new curricula and preparing pupils for entrance tests. However, the presence of these two different practices corresponds to two different needs of young teachers: The new curriculum helps them define daily aims for their teaching practice, and in turn test preparation provides them with long-term aims. Because young teachers lack work experience, both the new curriculum and the test preparation help them meet the complex and—from case to case—conflicting expectations of the educational sector, the school, parents and students, to which we attend in the following.

7.5 Between Formal Rules and Institutionalized Expectations: Curriculum and Standardized Tests

The informal rules and organizational routines embedded in these two organizational milieus of teachers[7] may be viewed as important "coupling mechanisms" (Spillane et al., 2011, p. 586) that regulate how instructional practice refers to the formal rules of the school organization. However, there are other factors that influence the way in which the curriculum is put into practice in schools and how far this practice is also influenced by the standardized exams for entrance to high schools. Among these factors is the degree to which the formal rules of the educational sector are institutionalized.

A formal rule obliges the members of an organization to follow a specific conduct by posing the threat of sanctions (up to the exclusion of the member, or for example, the suspension of the teacher). Therefore, organizations can be seen as collective actors responsible for their doings (Ortmann, 2004, p. 25). In contrast, institutions are based on explicit or implicit typifications of actions. As Berger and Luckmann (1991, p. 72) put it, an institution is a "reciprocal typification of habitualized actions by types of actors." Such reciprocal typifications—as "normative expectations" (Bohnsack, 2014b, p. 42)—only "restrict and enable" (Ortmann, 2004, p. 25) practices, without being attributed any responsibility. Nevertheless, as a formal rule always has to be put into practice somehow, institutions may interfere in this process. Moreover, formal rules themselves may be institutionalized; that is, beyond their explicit enforcement by the organization, formal rules may become reciprocally typified habitualized actions and, hence, tacit expectations. As we revealed in chapter 6, there are differential degrees and ways of institutionalization regarding the new curriculum, on one hand, and the standardized entrance exams, on the other.

One way to influence the way the formal rules of the *curriculum* were put into practice was to substantialize the curriculum by preparing schoolbooks and teacher manuals. For this purpose, the curriculum developers had to cooperate with the ministerial bureaucracy and experienced teachers who had been socialized in the old, behaviorist curriculum (see section 6.1). Hence during this "reform by the book" (Ball & Cohen, 1996), the curriculum originally intended by its developers had to be linked to the "historical" curriculum; that is, to the "the accumulated weight" (Cuban, 1992, p. 223) of previously institutionalized educational practices. This inevitably led to a mutated institutionalization of the new curriculum which, during this process, was adapted to the existing "grammar of schooling" (Tyack & Tobin, 1994); or in other words, adapted to the existing "beliefs about authority, habits of deference and resistance, and knowledge about how things work" (Cohen & Spillane, 1992, p. 31; see also Kliebard, 2002, pp. 81–84). The transformative character of the curriculum change, obvious on the level of formal rules, hence was mutated when the formal rules were institutionalized.[8]

As we have empirically revealed, this institutionalization itself could only be accomplished to a limited degree, as the ministry of education did not offer enough time and resources for training teachers in practically using the new curriculum. As Altinyelken (2013, p. 114) noted, "in-service training" was—according to her interviews with teachers—overwhelmingly "viewed as a general introduction to the new curriculum," which "was too theoretical and lacked practical guidance." Whereas the importance of intensive in-service training for fostering curriculum change is apparent (Wildy et al., 1996, p. 17), most teachers in Turkey were only informed about the new teaching approach in mass lectures—if at all—and thus had to rely on the written material. It is for this reason that the new curriculum underwent a process of *partial* and *mutated institutionalization*; therefore, under certain circumstances it could be easily predominated and even subdued by a second institution: the standardized entrance exams.

These *entrance exams,* which are centrally organized by the ministry of education, are the most important threshold for students who wish to be enrolled in the best possible high school. Far more than their performance in school, the test results determine whether or not students will have access to a prestigious secondary school. Given the massive differences in the prestige of high schools (see MEB, 2012, pp. 12–15), success in these exams has become a concern not only within the educational sector, but also in society at large. Those with the best test results are publicly praised by the media, and every year newspapers and websites publish the average test results certain schools' and educational districts' pupils have achieved. Thus, these standardized tests, rather than measuring the success of school education, become an institution on their own (see section 6.2). As people generally believe in their objectivity and started to perceive it as "natural" and "acceptable" that access to education is subject to standardized tests (Ünal, 2005, p. 8), one could even argue that these tests have become a phenomenon of enchantment.

Private instruction centers, which had emerged and expanded since the 1980s (Tansel & Bircan, 2008, p. 29), did their best to enhance the popularity of the standardized tests. Preparing students for high school and university entrance exams in highly expensive courses (p. 25) and thus "marketing hope" (Gök, 2010, p. 123), they used their students' success for advertisement and developed workbooks (so called "source books") that served not only their own students, but also those who could not afford enrolment in these private instruction centers and prepared at home. These workbooks condense learning contents to testable knowledge and leave aside many elements of the new curriculum, and most importantly, its student-centeredness—even though the exams comply with the curricular content of some disciplines (such as mathematics). With these activities, private instruction centers established what could be called "shadow education" (Stevenson & Baker, 1992). Whereas this term generally refers to a kind of private education which *complements* public school instruction (see also Bray, 2007; Bray et al., 2013), private instruction centers in the Turkish educational sector have institutionalized their own, *separate* set of teaching methods and materials. Participation in tutoring offered by private instruction centers, however, is not a phenomenon that is unique to Turkey. As Baker et al. (2001), based on TIMMS data, revealed for all participating countries, "more than a third of all seventh- and eighth-graders weekly participate" (p. 6) in some kind of tutoring, although this was usually intended to help children to stay in school rather than to be successful in high-stake tests such as is the case in Turkey.

The widespread (although, as we show, not total) institutionalization of the standardized entrance exams, however, does not originate only from their importance for students, their parents, and private instruction centers. As our group discussions with teachers, expert interviews with principals and local bureaucrats, and the websites of schools, provincial and district education directorates have indicated, an informal contest within the primary school system has emerged in which teachers, schools, districts, and provinces (each on their level) compete with one another, although the rewards for the winner are nothing but symbolic (see also Altinyelken, 2013, p. 121). This informal competition seems to point to an accountability system, which is based on the entrance exam results as the "database," on "the appraisal meeting [such as it is held among teachers in each school; the authors], the annual review, report writing," and "the regular publication of results" (for example, on websites) which serve to appraise and compare performativity (Ball, 2003, p. 220). Indeed, in this form of governing education, "comparison is deemed to be essential" (Ozga, 2008, p. 269). Such an (informal) accountability system helps institutionalize the standardized entrance exams within the school, among teachers and their principals, although these exams are not a part of the primary school organization's formal rules and even though the workbooks published by private instruction centers are officially forbidden for use in schools.

The factors discussed earlier lead to a comprehensive institutionalization of the entrance exams in Turkish primary schools and beyond, which itself promotes an image of the teacher as someone "who trains students to be successful in centralized exams" (Ünal, 2005, p. 10). This high degree of institutionalization heavily influenced school instruction, which, originally, should only be delivered according to the new curriculum. The competition between the new curriculum and standardized exams, both sets of expectations institutionalized to a different degree, can be viewed as a "struggle over the definition of the legitimate principles of division of the field" (Bourdieu, 1985, p. 734). However, this competition is certainly not the only—and not even the most direct—mechanism regulating instructional practice in the schools under scrutiny. As we subsequently discuss, in addition to (and connected with) the generationally embossed organizational milieus of teachers, the sociogeographical situation of the school and of the school's dominant social milieus (of pupils and their parents) are also influential factors of school instruction. To put it more precisely, the institutionalized expectations in the educational sector are mediated and rendered significant by factors connected to social heterogeneity and social inequality.

7.6   Schools and the Social Milieus of Pupils and Their Parents

With a teaching staff which nearly doubled between 1996 and 2012 (MoNE, 2007, pp. 3–5; 2012, p. 11), Turkey has—compared to other countries—extraordinarily young, and hence, inexperienced teachers (OECD, 2009). In addition to this general imbalance in numbers, experienced and inexperienced teachers are unequally distributed throughout the schools of the country. A formal rule of the ministry accords experienced teachers absolute primacy regarding workplace choice. At the same time, individual schools are not allowed to choose or reject teachers who have the status of a civil servant; in other words, all civil servant teachers are centrally assigned to their posts according to their applications and their seniority. For this reason, inexperienced, young teachers whom we have characterized as belonging to the *generation of new curriculum and test preparation combiners* usually work in the countryside or in urban areas with a majority of poor families and less well-integrated persons into the educational sector, whereas the older teachers of the *generation of experience-based lesson designers* have the chance to work in prestigious schools dominated by pupils from middle-class milieus (ERG, 2012, pp. 87–88).

This distribution is also reflected in the five schools where we carried out our field research. The group discussions with teachers and parents, as well as the expert interviews with principals, have been conducted in a purposeful selection of five schools. *Lale* school is situated in a central Anatolian village, has 148 pupils and an average of 18 children per class. *Sardunya* school is located in a central Anatolian town, has 446 pupils and an average of 21 children per class. *Zambak* school caters for 2000 children, 30 per class, and is situated in a middle-class district of the same province's capital. Also situated in a middle-class district, the Istanbulian school *Papatya* has 1248 pupils, with 35 pupils per class. *Karanfil* is an Istanbulian school located in a squatter neighborhood and catering for 4300 children, with 52 pupils per class.

This purposeful sampling enabled us to contrast teachers' organizational milieus in different school settings (from the small village to the overcrowded squatter neighborhood school) and to compare parents' rural, urban, middle- and lower-class social milieus (see chapter 5). The organizational milieu of the generation of experience-based lesson designers, however, was only identified in the schools of middle-class quarters and in the small Anatolian town school, whereas the organizational milieu of the generation of new curriculum and test preparation combiners completely dominated the school in the squatter neighborhood of Istanbul, and was altogether absent in the middle-class schools of our sample. The size of these educational organizations and their individual classes already indicates that this was not the only difference between these schools. Other aspects, to which we attend in the following, also influenced instructional practice, including the ways in which the curriculum is put into practice.

Given the circumstances of *Karanfil* school in the squatter neighborhood— big class size, use of one classroom by two classes in shifts, lack of educational equipment—its teachers, all belonging to the generation of curriculum and test preparation combiners, not only added standardized test preparation to curricular activities but also saw the two as contradictory. Teachers only filled in the official documents (such as class registers) according to the formal rules by copying from the teacher manual. Apart from this, the teachers decoupled this formal aspect of the curriculum from their instructional practices, which were centered on preparing children for the entrance exams. This "decoupling" (Weick, 1976, p. 5) of the official curriculum and instructional practice did not benefit teachers' "self-determination," as Weick (1976, p. 7) assumed, but was the result of organizational constraints. Decoupling enables teachers to use test-preparatory books that serve to render pupils more 'successful' and help the individual teacher excel in the annual ranking within the school (see earlier). Evidently, primary school instructional practices that are only loosely coupled to (or even decoupled from) the official curriculum were tightly coupled to the informal rankings based on the results of high school entrance tests. Weick (1976) already underpinned that "tight couplings in one place imply loose couplings elsewhere" (p. 10). This "trend toward test-based accountability systems" (Rowan, 2006a, p. 22) leads, as far as schools like Karanfil are concerned, "to a narrowing of the institutional focus of teachers and principals" (Linn, 2003, p. 4). Not only is the teaching approach mutated toward test preparation; moreover, "what does not get tested may get less attention or may not get taught at all" (Herman, 2004, p. 150).

Such a 'teaching to the test' (see also Cheng & Curtis, 2004) responded not only to the competition between the teachers of the squatter neighborhood school. The group discussions with the parents of this school's students revealed that they, too, exerted considerable pressure on the entire school to prepare their children for the entrance exams and to leave the curriculum aside. These parents, together with their children, are affiliated with a social milieu characterized by both poor financial means and the conviction that education is an important device for social climbing. Hence, with the term 'social milieu' we refer not only to the income of a respective social group, but also to an entity in which people share commonalities in the "stratification of experience" (Mannheim, 1972, p. 112) within society; that is, where they draw from social experience that is structurally similar or identical. The parents at Karanfil were convinced that educational success was pivotal for their social positioning. Because schools in Turkey are poorly financed by the ministry and depend heavily on (financial) assistance even from poor parents, the school willingly responded to their demand. Furthermore, parents at *Karanfil* school made clear that in addition to teachers using test-preparatory books, they preferred to buy the book themselves so that their children would also study at home.

Entirely different from parents in the squatter neighborhood, parents in the middle-class schools of our sample (*Zambak* and *Papatya*) did not see the curriculum as contradictory to the success of their children on entrance exams. They were confident that teachers closely followed the curriculum, only demanding that they provide a high-quality education that prepares children for a competitive labor market and society. Appreciating the good opportunities that the school (and its curriculum) provided for their children's personal development, these parents were confident that their children can become prepared for the standardized entrance exams to high school through home education or in private instruction centers. The teachers, the majority of which belong to the generation of experience-based lesson designers, also did not feel responsible for test preparation. In this sense, the middle-class social milieus and the specific organizational milieu that dominate *Papatya* and *Zambak* schools led to a tight-coupling of instruction to the new curriculum, whereas test preparation remained unimportant in the classroom. Nonetheless, the school administrations still prided themselves on the superb test results of their pupils.

As we have shown, in the three city schools of our sample—*Karanfil, Papatya,* and *Zambak*—success in the entrance exams for high schools was highly valued by the principals and the parents, although there were significant differences as to who was responsible for preparing the children. This indicates that in the social milieus dominating these schools the institutionalized expectations of the centralized entrance exams were highly valid. Irrespective of whether one belonged to a poor milieu or to a middle-class one, in the cities success in education and therefore high test scores and access to a reputable high school were widely pursued and viewed as an important means for social reproduction or even social advancement. In this sense, 'learning to the test' was highly popular in these city schools, even if not all schools 'taught to the test.'[9] In contrast, *Sardunya* and *Lale,* schools in rural areas of Turkey, do not feel pressure from superior authorities or from parents to focus their instruction on test preparation. These schools are dominated by social milieus in which education is certainly highly esteemed, but in which it is also an alien asset of children's life. Moreover, education is not without an alternative: Children of the dominant social milieu of this school are able to reproduce their parents' social position without excelling in education. Hence, neither the new curriculum nor the standardized high school entrance exams are important or highly valid institutions. The school administrations, putting no pressure on students or teachers regarding high-stake testing, are only concerned about their educational organizations working, that is, that the organizations are able to include all children and deliver education. Given these conditions, teachers of *Lale* and *Sardunya* schools (the latter with a combination of profession-generational affiliations) are free to follow their own teaching orientations in instruction. In other words, the older generation takes the new curriculum as a general frame within which one designs lessons that are experience-based and according to the limited opportunities of rural schools, whereas the younger generation combines the curriculum with test preparation.

7.7 Practical Capital Formations and the Curriculum

The manner in which organizational and social milieus as well as the school organizations influenced curricular practices is deeply linked to their respective endowment with resources, a point on which we shed light by drawing from Bourdieu's concept of "capital." Whereas "economic capital" is "immediately and directly convertible into money" (Bourdieu, 1986, p. 243), the other forms of capital are immaterial, but nevertheless effective and influential. "Social capital" refers to social relations; "cultural capital" encompasses acquired knowledge and skills; and "symbolic capital" consists of specific prestige. These forms of capital are convertible to a certain degree and under specific circumstances (Bourdieu, 1985, 1986). For our research we proposed to make a distinction between *endowment* with such *resources* and their *practical use* on a given market. For example, only if parents actually use knowledge and skills (as elements of cultural resources) to train their children to successfully pass the entrance test does this resource become *capital;* likewise, their economic resources can only become *capital* if they actually pay for training at private instruction centers. Hence, whether and how the endowment with economic, cultural, and other resources is capitalized on is a question of practice. In the following paragraphs we summarize how the practical capital formations of social and organizational milieus and of schools influenced instruction.

Concerning the practical formation of capital of the social milieu in the squatter neighborhood (*Karanfil* school), parents were rather ambitious for the educational success of their offspring, perceiving access to a prestigious high school as an important career step and as a precondition for social advancement. This quest for education is a response to social change in Turkey, which brought about the growing importance of higher educational qualifications for social positioning (see earlier). In Bourdieu's (1986) terms, this change implies that the original habitus generated by older generations in this social milieu (including their resource endowment) were no longer adapted to the field of the economy, including the labor market. As a matter of fact, the parents of *Karanfil* pupils usually had only graduated from primary education, if they had received any school education whatsoever. They needed education to adapt at least their children's habitus to the new labor market; conversely, being workers or jobless, these parents' economic resources were insufficient to finance their children's entrance test preparation at a private instruction center. They used—albeit small—donations to the school to influence teachers to prepare the pupils for the standardized entrance exams. Some of their economic resources were also capitalized on by purchasing test preparation material for their children.

In the middle-class milieus of *Zambak* and *Papatya* schools, parents had enough economic resources at their disposal to both make considerable donations to the school and to enroll their children in test-preparatory courses at private centers. Given their own long educational careers, they also had the cultural resources to practically assist their children with the accumulation of knowledge at home. Because test preparation and success were viewed as necessary but by no means sufficient components of education, the school was appreciated for additionally advancing their children's personal development.

The rural schools, *Sardunya* and *Lale*, catered for children from lower civil servant, worker, or farmer milieus. Although parents aspire their children to gain a better social position by successfully graduating from high school, they invest only very limited economic resources in school or private instruction centers. In contrast to the urban schools, neither the dominant social milieu of parents nor the school administration here view education as an issue of fierce competition. In any case, in these rural environments pupils do not have a choice between good or bad primary schools, not even between high schools of diverse quality, and thus must enroll in the only school available. Therefore, the expectations toward educational performance, as measured by standardized test scores, are low.

Dominated by differential social milieus and catering for their offspring, the schools of our sample are themselves endowed, in different ways, with various resources. Similar to all primary schools in Turkey—regardless of their geographical position and the socioeconomic conditions of the social milieus to which they cater—they are financed and equipped by the ministry of education in a nearly equal but also very limited manner; thus, they very much depend on financial donations and on other resources from pupils' parents and donors. Because of this, schools have varying levels of resources, and, such differences affect school practice.

The middle-class schools (*Zambak* and *Papatya*) are able to capitalize on the donations of wealthy parents by, for example, improving classroom equipment, but they also trust that their pupils are assisted by their parents (either directly or through enrolment in private tutoring) when preparing for standardized entrance tests for secondary education. Nevertheless, the success of these schools' pupils on the entrance tests improves the schools' prestige and their symbolic resources, which again enable them to capitalize on such resources to attract more pupils from middle-class families, resulting in a "creaming effect" (Smrekar, 2009, pp. 400–401). If they are not "cream-skimming the top of the students," these schools are at least "cropping off service to students" who seem to be disadvantaged (Lacireno-Paquet et al., 2002, p. 155). Moreover, the good prestige of these schools helps them attract donations from local businesses as well as attract experienced teachers who prefer to work at a school with convenient teaching conditions. Thus, symbolic resources are transformed into economic and cultural resources that, again, are useful in boosting the school's prestige.

Contrastingly, pupils attending the squatter neighborhood school, *Karanfil*, have parents with limited cultural and economic resources to assist them with test preparation. Because these parents' donations to the school are limited, classroom equipment is poor. The school, which is situated in a district with a constant influx of interior migrants, is overcrowded and pupils are taught in double shifts (morning and afternoon), making teachers' long- and medium-term classroom preparation impossible. Given these conditions, the pupils' poor scores on standardized tests only worsen the prestige of the school. The lack of symbolic resources results in the school not being able to attract donations from private businesses or add experienced teachers to its staff. Thus, the school becomes an educational organization at which only new, inexperienced teachers work. Such a poor endowment of teachers' cultural resources again deteriorates the symbolic resources of the school, which is furthermore confronted with a high turnover and general lack of teachers, some of whom are even untrained.

The two rural schools of the sample, *Sardunya* and *Lale*, similarly to *Karanfil* school, lack donations by the pupils' parents, not due to these parents' desperate financial situation, but because parents do not view primary education as valuable or as something that should be financed with private money. Furthermore, in contrast to *Karanfil* school, these rural schools suffer from migration in a reverse way; that is, the number of enrolled pupils is shrinking. On one hand, this leads to small class sizes, but on the other hand these schools, especially the village school, are not able to provide for a broadly differentiated teaching staff, resulting in that some branch teachers have to give lessons in branches other than their own. This already indicates that the organizational milieus of teachers are differentially endowed with cultural resources, on which they can also capitalize to a varying degree.

7.8   Conclusion

Modern education is not only a "replica, on a small scale of the conflicting purposes and tendencies which rage in society at large," as Karl Mannheim (1968, p. 138) suggested; our research demonstrates that education itself is a part of the social struggle. As "a site of struggle and negotiation" (Westbury, 2008, p. 53), schooling has its share in the conflict-prone dynamics of contemporary societies. Both curriculum making and practicing are manifestations of the struggles of divergent powers in society.

The conflicting tendencies prevalent in society come to prominence as soon as the curriculum becomes the focus of debate. Social change renders the old curriculum, established in another historical and social situation, obsolete. As the historical dynamics of society do not capture all people in the same way but lead to heterogeneity and inequality of social milieus (some of which become more dominant in society and politics than others), the quest for a new curriculum may be expressed by some milieus more than by others. There is certainly a range of ways to make a new curriculum, including more inclusive ones. But if a curriculum is then established by a specific group, which as a new organizational milieu, is able to work in behalf of the ministry of education, this curriculum most probably will respond to the (needs and expectations of) social milieus represented by this group in lieu of responding to others, first and foremost due to the common tacit knowledge that connects those attached to such milieu. Nevertheless, once it is formulated, the curriculum is made obligatory in the whole country. From then on, it serves to mainstream and homogenize the otherwise diverse social milieus (see Figure 7.1).

Our inquiries into curriculum *practice* then offer ample evidence for the curriculum being by no means able to easily and directly bring pupils from diverse social milieus onto one track. In fact, instruction itself, although stipulated to be serving the same learning goals throughout the country, becomes heterogeneous once the intended curriculum is put into practice in different schools; that is, once it is taught and learned.

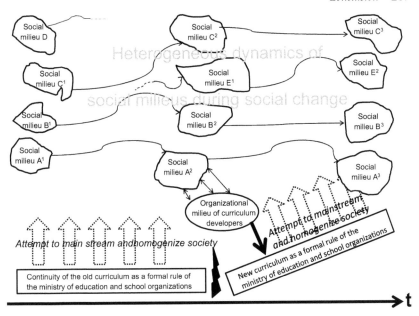

Figure 7.1 Curriculum making on the background of social change and dynamics.

One explanation for this is that social change not only captured social milieus in diverse ways, but it also had its *effects on the educational sector* itself. The significance of a curriculum changes through history, and other—sometimes even antagonistic—expectations may emerge in the educational sector over time. In other words, although the curriculum may be the only formal rule governing school instruction, other expectations (such as standardized exams regulating access to high school) may also have been informally—but in no way less influential—established as a "historical curriculum" (Cuban, 1992, p. 223). It is for this reason that the inquiry into education and social change should *distinguish* between *formal rules forced upon educational organizations* (which can easily be changed by the authorities) and *institutions*, that is, the *possibly tacit normative expectations prevalent in the educational sector.* On the background of social change, institutions may emerge, endure, and subsequently influence the ways new formal rules (such as a new curriculum) are put into practice (Figure 7.2).

However, neither formal rules nor institutions (or their combination) *directly* influence school instruction; they are always mediated by *organizational* or *social milieus* with their respective *resource endowments.* Hence, the second explanation for heterogeneity in instruction is the *influence of organizational and social milieus as well as of resource endowments.* Our empirical inquiries suggest that in organizational and social milieus, first of all, the significance that is given to formal rules and institutions of the educational sector is practically defined. There is ample evidence that there are organizational and social

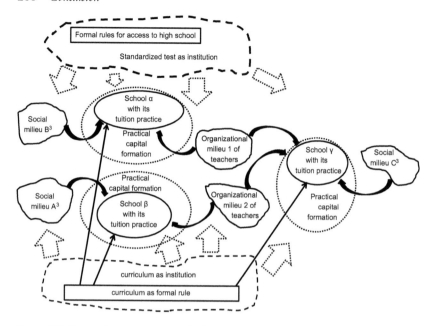

Figure 7.2 Curriculum practicing on the background of social heterogeneity and inequality. The straight arrows refer to organizational influence; the dotted arrows refer to institutional influence; the curved arrows refer to milieu influence.

milieus which are captured by an institution to a higher degree than others; that is, in these milieus the respective institutionalized expectations are rendered important, whereas other milieus do not identify with them. Likewise, formal rules, when put into practice, are given meaning by organizational and social milieus. In this sense the respective relation of formal rules or institutions and milieus is itself a result of social dynamics. This affirmation of an institution or a formal rule in/by a milieu is not a matter of choice and free will, but one that is tightly connected to the milieu's core collective orientations and experiences (that is, of its *collective habitus*). If and how the formal rule or the institution is given meaning is a matter of milieu-specific orientations that structure practice, and in such practices—such as in instruction and other learning practices—the resources of milieus and of the school organization itself are turned into capital. It is in this sense that practicing a curriculum is also dependent on resource endowment and the respective practical capital formation.

Therefore, the relation between education and social dynamics is manifested in a continuous struggle of homogenizing and heterogenizing forces that tacitly fight over the direction society should take. Whereas the formal rules of educational organizations (most importantly, the curriculum) and the institutions of the educational sector assume and strive for a homogeneity of instruction and of those involved in education (such as pupils and teachers), a broad range of social and organizational milieus heterogenize instruction practices. It is for this reason that social change is not only a result of education policy, but also of a process in which many different social forces—from organizations to institutions and milieus—are involved and that are, sometimes, even divergent.

Notes

1 With the term "societal sector" (Scott & Meyer, 1991), we refer to a network of social entities, mostly organizations, but also institutions and even milieus, the core operations of which have similar functions. Their interrelatedness is not based on geographical proximity but on functional congeniality.

2 In contrast to secular, that is, religion-free education, laicist education in Turkey implied that religion may be subordinated to secularist goals of education.

3 See http://arama.hurriyet.com.tr/arsivnews.aspx?id=248657 (retrieved November 18, 2014).

4 As Hopmann (1999) wrote, "on a programmatic level, on which the actual curriculum is written, it is necessary to reconcile the political with the school practical common sense. Curriculum work is successful here, when it can convey the feeling to politicians and the public that it meets their expectations" (p. 96).

5 Çelik's press communique on August 11, 2004, according to the press bulletin of the ministry issued on August 12, 2004 (see http://www.meb.gov.tr/haberler/haberayrinti. asp?ID=5821) (retrieved June 1, 2015).

6 In Steiner-Khamsi's (2012) words, "for neo-institutionalist theory loose coupling is the explanation (Latin: *explanans*) rather than the issue that begs for an explanation (*explanandum*)" (p. 272; italics original).

7 Additionally, we identify a third organizational milieu which is less stable in terms of collective experience and orientation because it consists of a mixture of both professional generations (see section 4.4).

8 For a comprehensive analysis of primary education in Turkey around 1990 (that is, before the new curriculum was developed), see Kaplan's (2006) ethnography of schools in a small Anatolian town.

9 An analysis of the PISA 2012 results shows that the aspiration to send one's children to a prestigious high school is not fully futile, even in the poor social milieus. Six percent of the pupils of the high-ranking "science high schools" and 9% of the pupils of the "Anatolian high schools" come from the lowest 20% of the population with regard to socioeconomic status. However, these prestigious high schools overwhelmingly serve pupils from the highest 20% of the population with regard to socioeconomic status, from which 51% of the "science" and 42% of the "Anatolian" high schools' pupils come (ERG, 2014, p. 31).

References

Altinyelken, H. K. (2011). Student-centred pedagogy in Turkey: Conceptualisations, interpretations and practices. *Journal of Education Policy, 26*, 137–160.

Altinyelken, H. K. (2013). Teachers' principled resistance to curriculum change: A compelling case from Turkey. In A. Verger, H. K. Altinyelken, & M. D. Konik (Eds.), *Global Education reforms and teachers* (pp. 109–127). Brussels: Education International.

Altrichter, H. (2000). Introduction. In H. Altrichter & J. Elliott (Eds.), *Images of change* (pp. 1–10). Buckingham: Open University Press.

Altrichter, H. (2010). Theory and evidence on governance: Conceptual and empirical strategies of research on governance in education. *European Educational Research Journal, 9*, 147–158.

Apple, M. (1993). The politics of official knowledge: Does a national curriculum make sense? *Teachers College Record, 95*, 221–241.

Baker, D. P., Akiba, M., LeTendre, G. K., & Wiseman, A. W. (2001). Worldwide shadow education: Outside-school learning, institutional quality of schooling, and cross-national mathematics achievement. *Educational Evaluation and Policy Analysis, 23*, 1–17.

Ball, D. L., & Cohen, D. K. (1996). Reform by the book: What is—or might be—the role of curriculum materials in teacher learning and instructional reform? *Educational Researcher, 25*, 6–8, 14.

Ball, S. J. (2003). The teacher's soul and the terrors of performativity. *Journal of Education Policy, 18*, 215–228.

Berger, P. L., & Luckmann, T. (1991). *The social construction of reality.* London: Penguin.

Bidwell, C. E., Frank, K. A., & Quiroz, P. A. (1997). Teacher types, workplace controls, and the organization of schools. *Sociology of Education, 70*, 285–307.

Bohnsack, R. (2010). Documentary method and group discussions. In R. Bohnsack, N. Pfaff, & W. Weller (Eds.), *Qualitative analysis and documentary method in international educational research* (pp. 99–124). Opladen: Barbra Budrich.

Bohnsack, R. (2014a). Documentary method. In U. Flick (Ed.), *Sage handbook of analyzing qualitative data* (pp. 217–223). Thousand Oaks, CA: Sage.

Bohnsack, R. (2014b). Habitus, Norm und Identität. In W. Helsper et al. (Eds.), *Schülerhabitus* (pp. 33–55). Wiesbaden: Springer.

Bourdieu, P. (1985). The social space and the genesis of groups. *Theory and Society, 14*, 723–744.

Bourdieu, P. (1986). The (three) forms of capital. In J. G. Richardson (Ed.), *Handbook for theory and research for the sociology of education* (pp. 241–258). New York: Greenwood.

Bourdieu, P., & Passeron, J.-C. (1990). *Reproduction in education, society and culture.* London: Sage.

Bray, M. (2007). *The shadow education system: Private tutoring and its implications for planners* (2nd ed.). Paris: UNESCO.

Bray, M., Mazawi, A. E., & Sultana, R. G. (Eds.). (2013). *Private tutoring across the Mediterranean.* Rotterdam: Sense.

Bromley, P., Meyer, J. W., & Ramirez, F. O. (2011). Student-centeredness in social science textbooks, 1970–2008: A cross-national study. *Social Forces, 90*, 547–570.

Buğra, A. (2002). Political Islam in Turkey in historical context: Strengths and weaknesses. In N. Balkan & S. Savran (Eds.), *The politics of permanent crisis* (pp. 107–144). New York: Nova Science.

Chen, J.-Q., Moran, S., & Gardner, H. (Eds.). (2009). *Multiple intelligences around the world.* San Francisco: Jossey-Bass.

Cheng, L., & Curtis, A. (2004). Washback or backwash: A review of the impact of testing on teaching and learning. In L. Cheng, Y. Watanabe, & A. Curtis (Eds.), *Washback in language testing* (pp. 3–17). Mahwah, NJ: Lawrence Erlbaum.

Cohen, D. K., & Spillane, J. (1992). Policy and practice: The relations between governance and instruction. In G. Grant (Ed.), *Review of research in education* (Vol. 18, pp. 3–49). Washington, DC: American Educational Research Association.

Cuban, L. (1992). Curriculum stability and change. In P. W. Jackson (Eds.), *Handbook of research on curriculum* (pp. 216–247). New York: Macmillan.

Dale, R. (1999). Specifying globalization effects on national policy: A focus on the mechanisms. *Journal of Education Policy, 14*, 1–17.

DiMaggio, P. J., & Powell, W. W. (1983). The iron cage revisited: Institutional isomorphism and collective rationality in organizational fields. *American Sociological Review, 48*, 147–160.

ERG (Eğitim Reformu Girişimi). (2012). *Eğitim İzleme Raporu 2011*. Istanbul: Author.

ERG (Eğitim Reformu Girişimi). (2014). *Türkiye Eğitim Sisteminde Eşitlik ve Akademik Başarı*. Istanbul: Author.

Fend, H. (2009). *Neue Theorie der Schule. Einführung in das Verstehen von Bildungssystemen*. Wiesbaden: VS.

Fortna, B. (2002). *The imperial classroom: Islam, the state, and education in the late Ottoman Empire*. Oxford: Oxford University Press.

Gardner, H. (1983). *Frames of mind: The theory of multiple intelligences*. New York: Basic Books.

Gök, F. (2010). Marketing hope: Private institutions preparing students for the university entrance examination in Turkey. In S. K. Amos (Ed.), *International educational governance* (pp. 123–134). Bingley: Emerald.

Günlü, R. (2008). Vocational education and labor market integration in Turkey. In A.-M. Nohl, A. Akkoyunlu-Wigley, & S. Wigley (Eds.), *Education in Turkey* (pp. 107–130). New York: Waxmann.

Helsper, W., Hummrich, M., & Kramer, R.-T. (2010). Qualitative Mehrebenenanalyse. In B. Friebertshäuser & A. Prengel (Eds.), *Handbuch Qualitative Forschungsmethoden in der Erziehungswissenschaft* (pp. 119–135). Weinheim: Beltz.

Herman, J. L. (2004). The effects of testing on instruction. In S. H. Fuhrman & R. F. Elmore (Eds.), *Re-designing accountability systems for education* (pp. 141–165). New York: Teachers College Press.

Hopmann, S. (1999). The curriculum as a standard of public education. *Studies in Philosophy and Education, 18*, 89–105.

İnal, K., Akkaymak, G., & Yıldırım, D. (2014). The constructivist curriculum reform in Turkey in 2004—In fact what is constructed? *Journal for Critical Education Policy Studies, 12*, 350–373.

Kaplan, S. (2006). *The pedagogical state: Education and the politics of national culture in post-1980 Turkey*. Stanford: Stanford University Press.

Kepenek, Y., & Yentürk, N. (2007). *Türkiye Ekonomisi*. Istanbul: Remzi.

Kliebard, H. M. (2002). *Changing course: American curriculum reform in the 20th century*. New York: Teachers College Press.

Lacireno-Paquet, N., Holyoke, T. T., Moser, M., & Henig, J. R. (2002). Creaming versus cropping: Charter school enrollment practices in response to market incentives. *Educational Evaluation and Policy Analysis, 24*, 145–158.

Linn, R. L. (2003). Accountability: Responsibility and reasonable expectations. *Educational Researcher, 32*, 3–13.

Mannheim, K. (1952). On the interpretation of Weltanschauung. In *Essays on the sociology of knowledge* (pp. 33–83). New York: Oxford University Press.

Mannheim, K. (1968). *Ideology and utopia*. London: Routledge.

Mannheim, K. (1972). The problem of generations. In P. Altbach & R. Laufer (Eds.), *The new pilgrims* (pp. 101–138). New York: McKay.

Mannheim, K. (1982). *Structures of thinking*. London: Routledge.

MEB (Milli Eğitim Bakanlığı). (2012). *İlköğretimden Ortaöğretime Ortaöğretimden Yükseköğretime Geçiş Analizi*. Ankara: Author.

Meuser, M., & Nagel, U. (2009). The expert interview and changes in knowledge production. In A. Bogner, B. Littig, & W. Menz (Eds.), *Interviewing experts* (pp. 17–42). London: Palgrave.

Meyer, J. W., Boli, J., Thomas, G. M., & Ramirez, F. O. (1997). World society and the nation-state. *American Journal of Sociology, 103,* 144–181.

Meyer, J. W., & Rowan, B. (1977). Institutionalized organizations: Formal structure as myth and ceremony. *American Journal of Sociology, 83,* 340–363.

MoNE (Ministry of National Education). (2007). *National education statistics: Formal education 2006–2007.* Ankara: Author.

MoNE (Ministry of National Education). (2012). *National education statistics: Formal education 2011–2012.* Ankara: Author.

Nohl, A.-M. (2013). *Relationale Typenbildung und Mehrebenenvergleich: Neue Wege der dokumentarischen Methode.* Wiesbaden: VS.

Nohl, A.-M. (2014). *Konzepte interkultureller Pädagogik* (3rd ed.). Bad Heilbrunn: Klinkhardt.

OECD. (2009). *Creating effective teaching and learning environments: First results from TALIS.* Paris: Author.

Okçabol, R. (2005). *Türkiye Eğitim Sistemi.* Ankara: Ütopya.

Ortmann, G. (2004). *Als Ob. Fiktionen und Organisationen.* Wiesbaden: VS.

Ozga, J. (2008). Governing knowledge: Research steering and research quality. *European Educational Research Journal, 7,* 261–272.

Parreira do Amaral, M. (2010). Regime theory and educational governance: The emergence of an international education regime. In K. Amos (Ed.), *International educational governance* (pp. 57–78). Bingley: Emerald.

Phillips, D., & Ochs, K. (2004). Researching policy borrowing: Some methodological challenges in comparative education. *British Educational Research Journal, 30,* 773–784.

Polanyi, M. (1966). *The tacit dimension.* New York: Doubleday.

Rowan, B. (2006a). The new institutionalism and the study of educational organizations: Changing ideas for changing times. In H.-D. Meyer & B. Rowan (Eds.), *The new institutionalism in education* (pp. 15–32). Albany: SUNY.

Schriewer, J. (2003). Globalisation in education: Process and discourse. *Policy Futures in Education, 1,* 271–283.

Scott, W. R., & Meyer, J. W. (1991). The organization of societal sectors: Propositions and early evidence. In W. W. Powell & P. J. DiMaggio (Eds.), *The new institutionalism in organizational analysis* (pp. 108–140). Chicago: University of Chicago Press.

Smrekar, C. (2009). The social context of magnet schools. In M. Berends, M. G. Springer, & Dale Ballou (Eds.), *Handbook of research on school choice* (pp. 393–407). New York: Routledge.

Somel, S. A. (2001). *The modernization of public education in the Ottoman Empire 1839–1908 —Islamization, autocracy and discipline.* Leiden: Brill.

Spillane, J. P., Parise, L. M., & Sherer, J. Z. (2011). Organizational routines as coupling mechanisms. *American Educational Research Journal, 48,* 586–619.

State Institute of Statistics. (n.d.). *2000 Census of Population—Social and economic characteristics of population.* Ankara: Author.

Steiner-Khamsi, G. (Ed.). (2004). *The global politics of educational borrowing and lending.* New York: Teachers College Press.

Steiner-Khamsi, G. (2006). The economics of policy borrowing and lending: A study of late adopters. *Oxford Review of Education, 32,* 665–678.

Steiner-Khamsi, G. (2012). Measuring and interpreting re-contextualization: A commentary. In A. Verger, M. Novelli, & H. K. Altinyelken (Eds.), *Global education policy and international development* (pp. 269–278). London: Bloomsbury.

Steiner-Khamsi, G., & Quist, H. O. (2000). The politics of educational borrowing: Reopening the case of Achimota in British Ghana. *Comparative Education Review, 44,* 272–299.

Stevenson, D. L., & Baker, D. P. (1992). Shadow education and allocation in formal schooling: Transition to university in Japan. *American Journal of Sociology, 97,* 1639–1657.

Tansel, A., & Bircan, F. (2008). *Private supplementary tutoring in Turkey—Recent evidence on its recent aspects* (Working Papers in Economics No. 08/02). Ankara: ERC.

Tyack, D., & Tobin, W. (1994). The "grammar" of schooling: Why has it been so hard to change? *American Educational Research Journal, 31,* 453–479.

Ünal, I. (2005). Öğretmen İmgesinde Neoliberal Dönüşüm. *Eğitim Bilim Toplum, 3,* 4–15.

Ünder, H. (2012). Constructivism and the curriculum reform of the AKP. In K. İnal & G. Akkaymak (Eds.), *Neoliberal transformation of education in Turkey* (pp. 33–45). New York: Palgrave.

Üstel, F. (2004). *"Makbul Vatandaş" ın Peşinde—II. Meşrutiyet'ten Bugüne Vatandaşlık Eğitimi.* Istanbul: İletişim.

Waks, L. J. (2007). The concept of fundamental educational change. *Educational Theory, 57,* 277–295.

Watzlawick, P., Weakland, J., & Fisch, R. (1974). *Change: Principles of problem formation and problem resolution.* New York: Norton.

Weick, K. E. (1976). Educational organizations as loosely coupled systems. *Administrative Science Quarterly, 21,* 1–19.

Weiß, A., & Nohl, A.-M. (2012). Overcoming methodological nationalism in migration research: Cases and contexts in multi-level comparisons. In A. Amelina, D. D. Nergiz, T. Faist, & N. Glick Schiller (Eds.), *Beyond methodological nationalism* (pp. 65–87). London: Routledge.

Westbury, I. (2008). Making curricula: Why do states make curricula, and how? In F. M. Connelly, M. Fang He, & J. Phillion (Eds.), *The Sage handbook of curriculum and instruction* (pp. 45–65). London: Sage.

Whitty, G. (1985). *Sociology and school knowledge: Curriculum, theory, research and politics.* London: Methuen.

Wildy, H., Wallace, J., & Parker, L. (1996). Decentralising curriculum reform: The link teacher model of in-service training. *School Organisation, 16,* 17–28.

Yildirim, A. (2003). Instructional planning in a centralized school system: Lessons of a study among primary school teachers in Turkey. *International Review of Education, 49,* 525–543.

Young, M. (2008). From constructivism to realism in the sociology of the curriculum. *Review of Research in Education, 32,* 1–28.

Zucker, L. G. (1987). Institutional theories of organization. *Annual Review of Sociology, 13,* 443–464.

Zürcher, J. E. (2005). *Turkey—a modern history* (3rd ed.). London: I. B. Tauris

Appendix

Overview of the Turkish School System

Table A.1 The Turkish school system and its pupil enrollment

Age	School level (school types and their share in pupil population of the respective level in brackets)	Number of students	Enrollment rate (percentage of pupils within the total population of this age group)	Education type	Education type
3–5	Kindergarten and nursery	701,762	17.5%		
6–13	Primary school (public primary school: 97.92%; private primary school: 2.08%)	10,870,570	97.37%		
14 15 16 17	Secondary school (science HS: 0.60%; social science HS: 0.06%; Anatolian HS: 11.67%; Anatolian teacher HS: 1.74%; arts and sports HS: 0.32%; general HS: 39.67%; vocational and technical HS: 41.67%; Imam and Preacher HS: 4.26%) (overall private HS: 2.89%)	3,245,322	58.56%	Appren-ticeship	Nonformal education
18 19 20 21 22 23 24	Tertiary education (university undergraduate and graduate programs, higher education schools (between one and five years, with additional one or two years for master's degree) –	2,292,000 –	21.06% (of age 18–21) –		

Figures for the year 2007/2008, compiled according to information by Ministry of National Education (2008, 2009, 2012) and Eğitim Reformu Girişimi (2008).

Overview of Expert Interviews

Table A.2 List of expert interviews

No.	Name/pseudonym used in the book	Interviewed as	Date of interview	Interviewer	Remarks
1.	Erkan Mumcu	Minister of Education 19.11.2002–17.03.2003	25.1.2013	Arnd-Michael Nohl / Nazlı Somel	Quotes authorized by interviewee.
2.	Prof. Dr. Ziya Selçuk	President of Board of Education 21.3.2003–8.5.2006	5.7.2012	Arnd-Michael Nohl	Quotes authorized by interviewee.
3.	Önder Kaplan	Member of a Curriculum Commission	27.4.2012	Nazlı Somel	The name of the interviewee has been changed.
4.	Prof. Dr. İrfan Kaya	Leader of a Curriculum Commission	3.12.2012	Nazlı Somel	The name of the interviewee has been changed.
5.	Prof. Dr. Ahmet Aydın	Leader of a Curriculum Commission	17.12.2012	Nazlı Somel	The name of the interviewee has been changed.
6.	Dr. Mahmut Küre	Member of Board of Education	16.8.2012	Arnd-Michael Nohl	The name of the interviewee has been changed.
7.	Nuray Pars	Representative of NGO specialized in education	27.11.2012	Nazlı Somel	The name of the interviewee has been changed.
8.	Prof. Dr. İrfan Erdoğan	President of Board of Education 12.5.2006–21.2.2008	11.1.2013	Nazlı Somel	Quotes authorized by interviewee.
9.	Fehimdar Çiftçi	School inspector	3.12.2012	Nazlı Somel	The name of the interviewee has been changed.
10.	İbrahim Arslan	Principal of Papatya school	29.5.2012	Nazlı Somel	The name of the interviewee has been changed.
11.	Mehmet Uzun	Principal of Zambak school	13.12.2011 14.12.2011	Nazlı Somel	The name of the interviewee has been changed.

No.	Name	Position	Date	Interviewer	Note
12.	Ahmet Sönmez	Principal of Karanfil school	25.5.2012	Nazlı Somel	The name of the interviewee has been changed.
13.	Ali Akbaba	Principal of Sardunya school	30.11.2011	Nazlı Somel	The name of the interviewee has been changed.
14.	Ata Vergin	Principal of Lale school	21.10.2011	Nazlı Somel	The name of the interviewee has been changed.
15.	Unnamed	Vice-principal of Zambak school	15.10.2011	Nazlı Somel	Interview not cited in the book.
16.	Unnamed	Vice-principals of Karanfil school (group discussion)	21.5.2012	Nazlı Somel	Interview not cited in the book.
17.	Unnamed	Vice-principal of Sardunya school	15.11.2011	Nazlı Somel	Interview not cited in the book.
18.	Unnamed	Vice-principal of Lale school	20.10.2011	Nazlı Somel	Interview not cited in the book.
19.	Unnamed	Former principal of Lale school	25.11.2011	Nazlı Somel	Interview not cited in the book.
20.	Unnamed	Former principal of Sardunya school	30.11.2011	Nazlı Somel	Interview not cited in the book.
21.	Unnamed	Former vice-principal of Zambak school	16.12.2011	Nazlı Somel	Interview not cited in the book.
22.	Unnamed	Director of National Education of Dalen province	6.12.2011	Nazlı Somel	Interview not cited in the book.
23.	Unnamed	Director of National Education of Safran district (Dalen)	14.10.2011	Nazlı Somel	Interview not cited in the book.
24.	Unnamed	Director of National Education of Enver district (Istanbul)	2.7.2012	Nazlı Somel	Interview not cited in the book.
25.	Unnamed	Director of National Education of Tahsin district (Istanbul)	29.6.2012	Nazlı Somel	Interview not cited in the book.
26.	Unnamed	Group discussion with branch director and school principals of Tahsin district (Istanbul)	3.7.2012	Nazlı Somel	Interview not cited in the book.

Rules of Transcription

The transcription of expert interviews and group discussions is verbatim and does not correspond to grammar rules. The English translation tries to reflect the colloquial style of the Turkish accounts. Punctuation marks are not used in a grammatical sense. The participants are referred to with a capital letter, followed by a lowercase indication for gender, for example, "Af" (female) or "Sm" (male). "Y" is used for the researcher. The transcription rules are listed in Table A.3.

Table A.3 Rules for transcription

Symbol in transcript	Explanation
(2)	seconds of a break
(.)	short break
Yes	emphasized
.	strongly dropping intonation
;	weakly dropping intonation
?	strongly rising intonation
,	weakly rising intonation
mayb–	interruption of a word
curriculu:::m	extension of a word, where the frequency of ":" corresponds to the length of extension
(well)	uncertainty in transcription, marked by brackets
( )	word(s) not understood, according to length
((sneezes))	nonverbal utterances
@no@	spoken while laughing
@(.)@	short laughter
@(3)@	laughter of 3 seconds
//mmh//	listener's signal (by interviewer, may be inserted into the text of interviewee)
L	overlapping of speech acts
⌐	end of overlapping of speech acts
°okay°	spoken very quietly

References

Eğitim Reformu Girişimi. (2008). *Eğitim İzleme Raporu 2007*. Istanbul: ERG.

Ministry of National Education. (2008). *National Education Statistics: Formal Education 2007–2008*. Ankara: MoNE.

Ministry of National Education. (2009). *National Education Statistics: Formal Education 2008–2009*. Ankara: MoNE.

Ministry of National Education. (2012). *National Education Statistics: Formal Education 2011–2012*. Ankara: MoNE.

Index